Praise for

PRACTICAL ETHICS *and*
PROFOUND EMPTINESS

"Khensur Jampa Tegchok was renowned in life as a Madhyamaka scholar with a profound understanding of emptiness. His teachings on Nagarjuna's *Precious Garland*, rendered into clear and entirely readable English by Bhikshu Steve Carlier and Bhikshuni Thubten Chodron, leave no room for doubt that Khensur-la had thoroughly unraveled the relationship between the conventionally functioning law of actions and their effects and the ultimate reality of the lack of inherent existence of self and all phenomena. This book is a must for any Dharma practitioner trying to do the same."

—JOAN NICELL, EDITOR OF *PURIFICATION IN TIBETAN BUDDHISM*

"Though written to a king and composed over eighteen centuries ago, this poetic text by Nagarjuna, the *Precious Garland*, offers advice like no other, for it guides us in leading a wise, compassionate, and ethical life even in tumultuous times like our own. A clear, readable, and urgent call to ethical action. This work offers amazing spot-on advice for our times, especially for our leaders and policy-makers."

—JAN WILLIS, AUTHOR OF *DREAMING ME*

PRACTICAL ETHICS *and* PROFOUND EMPTINESS

A Commentary on Nagarjuna's Precious Garland

KHENSUR JAMPA TEGCHOK

TRANSLATED BY BHIKSHU STEVE CARLIER
EDITED BY BHIKSHUNI THUBTEN CHODRON

Wisdom

Wisdom Publications
199 Elm Street
Somerville, MA 02144 USA
wisdompubs.org

Library of Congress Cataloging-in-Publication Data

Names: Jampa Tegchok, Geshe, 1930– author. | Thubten Chodron, 1950– editor.
Title: Practical ethics and profound emptiness: a commentary on Nagarjuna's Precious
    garland / Khensur Jampa Tegchok; translated by Bhikshu Steve Carlier; edited by
    Bhikshuni Thubten Chodron.
Description: Somerville, MA: Wisdom Publications, 2017. | Includes bibliographical
    references and index.
Identifiers: LCCN 2016031569 (print) | LCCN 2017001249 (ebook) | ISBN 9781614293248
    (pbk.: alk. paper) | ISBN 1614293244 (pbk.: alk. paper) | ISBN 9781614293354 () |
    ISBN 161429335X ()
Subjects: LCSH: Nāgārjuna, active 2nd century. Ratnāvalī. | Mādhyamika (Buddhism)—
    Early works to 1800.
Classification: LCC BQ2877 .J3613 2017 (print) | LCC BQ2877 (ebook) | DDC 294.3/85—dc23
LC record available at https://lccn.loc.gov/2016031569

ISBN 978-1-61429-324-8   ebook ISBN 978-1-61429-335-4

21 20 19 18 17
5 4 3 2 1

Cover design by Gopa&Ted2, Inc. Interior design by Gopa&Ted2, Inc., typeset by TLBG.
Set in Minion Pro 10.5 pt./14.125 pt. The image on the cover and on p. 1 is courtesy of
Himalayan Art Resources, www.himalayanart.org.

Wisdom Publications' books are printed on acid-free paper and
meet the guidelines for permanence and durability of the Production
Guidelines for Book Longevity of the Council on Library Resources.

🌾 This book was produced with environmental mindfulness.
For more information, please visit wisdompubs.org/wisdom-environment.

Printed in the United States of America.

Please visit fscus.org.

Contents

Editor's Preface   vii

Introduction   3

I. HIGHER REBIRTH AND HIGHEST GOOD   11

   1. Starting on the Path to Happiness and Liberation   13
   2. The Advantages of Ethical Living and a Fortunate Life   27
   3. The Path to Liberation and Full Awakening   45
   4. Refuting Inherent Existence and Establishing Emptiness   91

II. AN INTERWOVEN EXPLANATION OF THE CAUSES
   AND EFFECTS OF HIGHER REBIRTH AND HIGHEST GOOD   135

   5. Delving into the Profound   137
   6. Taming Attachment and Understanding the Qualities
      of Buddhahood   169

III. THE COLLECTIONS FOR AWAKENING   201

   7. Joyfully Taking Up the Boundless Work of a Bodhisattva   203
   8. Advice for Gathering Merit and Gaining Wisdom   225
   9. The Fruits of Merit and Wisdom   249

IV. ROYAL POLICY: INSTRUCTIONS ON THE PRACTICES
   OF A MONARCH   265

   10. Practical Advice for Leaders   267
   11. Spiritual Wisdom for Powerful People   289

V. PRACTICES OF A BODHISATTVA   327

   12. Abandoning Afflictions and Cultivating Goodness   329
   13. Excellent Qualities of the Ten Bodhisattva Grounds   351
   14. The Magnificent Qualities of a Buddha   371
   15. Closing Words of Advice   387

Glossary	395
Further Reading	403
Index	405
About the Author	423

Editor's Preface

DEAR READER, you are about to embark on a wondrous journey into the mind of one of India's greatest Buddhist thinkers and practitioners, Arya Nagarjuna. In *Precious Garland*, he gives teachings to a king, instructing him on both Madhyamaka philosophy regarding the nature of reality and practical matters such as how to govern the kingdom. It is evident by the way Nagarjuna addresses the king that they have a close relationship. The king is receptive to hear the teachings, and being fond of the king as well as compassionate toward his subjects, Nagarjuna teaches the king in a straightforward, no-holds-barred manner.

While Nagarjuna addresses the king directly, he explicitly says that the teachings are meant for everyone: people living then as well as many generations that will come afterward. The Dharma teachings themselves apply to everyone at all times and locales and of all cultures. In contrast, in a few places Nagarjuna gives advice that corresponds to the societal organization and customs of ancient India but needs to be adjusted to fit present cultural norms and values in the West.

If the teachings are meant for everyone, why, then, were they given to the king? Someone who has a lot of worldly power can influence a great number of people for better or for worse. In a kingdom where leaders do not change every few years due to popular election, a leader who admires and practices the Dharma can make good policies that will remain in place for decades. Viewed by the populace as being like a protective and wise parent, such a leader can encourage his or her subjects to live ethically and cultivate kindness. King Ashoka of ancient India (304–232 BCE) is an excellent example of this. Through his generosity and philanthropy, as well as his edicts and pillars containing wise advice, he instructed his subjects and brought peace to the land.

THE TREATISE AND ITS AUTHOR, COMMENTATOR, AND TEACHER

Precious Garland of Advice for a King, usually referred to as *Precious Garland*, is one of Nagarjuna's great treatises. Preceding the stages of the path literature (*lamrim*) popular in Tibet by twelve or thirteen centuries, *Precious Garland* is the basis for much of the material in other Indian treatises. Many of the points in *Precious Garland* are further elaborated in Shantideva's *Engaging in the Bodhisattvas' Deeds* (*Bodhicharyavatara*), Chandrakirti's *Supplement to the Middle Way* (*Madhyamakavatara*), and Asanga's *Compendium of Knowledge* (*Abhidharmasamucchaya*). *Precious Garland* is also a source text for the lamrim teachings.

The principal theme of *Precious Garland*—the method to attain higher rebirth as well as the highest good of liberation and full awakening—is reflected in the lamrim's division of practitioners into three capacities. The goal of a person of initial capacity is to avoid an unfortunate rebirth and to take a higher rebirth. Liberation—one aspect of highest good—is the aim of practitioners of middle capacity, and full awakening—the other aspect of highest good—is the goal of practitioners of advanced capacity.

Precious Garland explains that higher rebirth is a steppingstone to liberation and awakening, not an end in itself. Similarly, in the lamrim we are instructed in the practices in common with the initial capacity person in order to attain a series of fortunate rebirths, and on that basis to engage in the practices leading to liberation. But liberation from cyclic existence, too, is not an end in itself, and the lamrim encourages us to become someone of advanced capacity, who, motivated by the altruistic intention of bodhichitta, seeks to attain the full awakening of a buddha in order to most effectively benefit other sentient beings. Then, by engaging in the practices of an advanced capacity being, we will attain full awakening, buddhahood. In short, the meaning, purpose, and practices of the *Precious Garland* and the lamrim go hand in hand.

Precious Garland was authored by Nagarjuna, the most erudite and renowned scholar-practitioner of ancient India. Although the dates of his life are not known, some people place him circa 50–150 CE, others circa 150–250 CE. Born in South India, he was well learned in both the writings of the fundamental vehicle and the universal vehicle. His writings, especially the seminal *Treatise on the Middle Way*, unpacked the meaning of the Buddha's teachings in the perfection of wisdom sutras in a way that challenged the philosophical assertions of both Buddhists and non-Buddhists and sparked debates about the ultimate nature of reality that have continued to the present day. As the founder of what came to be known as Madhyamaka philosophy, Nagarjuna's thought spread into China, Tibet, Japan, and other Asian countries and is now a topic of discussion in universities and monasteries worldwide. His view of dependent arising and emptiness is regarded as the pinnacle of ontological and soteriological thought in Tibetan Buddhism. In China and Japan, Nagarjuna is a lineage master in both Chan (Zen) Buddhism and Pure Land Buddhism.

Which king to whom Nagaruna taught the *Precious Garland* is uncertain. Tibetans say it was King Udayibhadra. Some Western scholars say King Udayibhadra was also known as King Gautamiputra Shatakarni (ruled 80–104 or 106–30 CE) of the Shatavahana dynasty in present-day Andhra Pradesh, India. Some say he was the following king, Vashishtiputra Pulumayi (130–58 CE).

The Indian scholar Ajitamitra (perhaps of the eighth century) wrote the *Extensive Commentary on the Precious Garland*. The Tibetan scholar-practitioner Gyaltsap Darma Rinchen (1364–1432) wrote the commentary *Elucidation of the Essential Meaning of the Madhyamaka Precious Garland*. A close student of Je Tsongkhapa and a prolific writer, Gyaltsap also penned commentaries to Maitreya's *Sublime Continuum* (*Uttaratantra*) and Shantideva's *Engaging in the Bodhisattvas' Deeds*, among others.

Khensur Jampa Tegchok, the abbot and resident teacher at Nalanda Monastery in France from 1983 to 1993, gave this teaching there in 1989. Born in Tibet in 1930, Khensur Jampa Tegchok became a monk at the age of eight. He studied major Buddhist treatises at Sera Jé Monastic University in Lhasa for fourteen years before fleeing his homeland in 1959. A geshe lharampa, he was abbot of the Jé College of Sera Monastic University in India for six years. He was also a beloved teacher in the West, being the resident teacher at Nalanda Monastery in France, Land of Medicine Buddha in California, and teacher of the master's program at Istituto Lama Tzong Khapa in Italy. He passed away in 2014.

AN OVERVIEW OF THE *PRECIOUS GARLAND*

After offering homage to the Buddha, Dharma, and Sangha and promising to compose the book, Nagarjuna delineates the principal topics he will address in the *Precious Garland*: the causes and effects of higher rebirth and highest good. Higher rebirth refers not just to rebirth as a human or god but to a human or god rebirth in which we are able to learn and practice the Dharma. Highest good is liberation from cyclic existence and the full awakening of a buddha. The first and second chapters are dedicated specifically to explaining the causes for higher rebirth such as ethical conduct, generosity, and dedication of merit, and the causes for the highest good, the wisdom realizing emptiness. His discussions of selflessness, the emptiness of inherent existence, and freedom from the two extremes are incomparable in terms of stripping away all wrong views and false assumptions.

In chapter 3, he goes into more depth on the causes of full awakening: the two collections of merit and wisdom, which are the aspects of method and wisdom on the bodhisattva path. The practices of generosity, ethical conduct, fortitude, and so on, done with the altruistic intention of bodhichitta and viewed as both dependent and empty of inherent nature, contribute to the collection of merit. The practices of learning, contemplating, and meditating on the ultimate nature of persons and phenomena—their emptiness of inherent existence—fulfill the collection of wisdom. Both collections act as causes for a buddha's two bodies—the form body and the truth body. The form body, or *rupakaya*, of a buddha is of two types: the enjoyment body that teaches arya bodhisattvas and the emanation body that manifests in our world to teach and guide us. The truth body, or *dharmakaya*, is the omniscient mind of a buddha and its ultimate nature. The collection of merit is the principal cause of the form body; the collection of wisdom is the principal cause of the truth body. The verses describing how the king can fulfill the collection of merit by helping his subjects give us the vision of how a government based on compassion could operate.

Chapter 4 continues with Nagarjuna giving the king more specific advice on how to govern the kingdom in a way that accords with the Dharma. This ranges from the qualifications of ministers to the importance of establishing monasteries, and from the treatment of prisoners to the propagation of the teachings of the universal vehicle in the land. Here we learn how to be a skillful leader and at the same time a deeply spiritual, compassionate person who acts for the benefit of others. Nagarjuna teaches us how to be at peace with ourselves, due to living ethically and with kindness, and simultaneously how to be a successful leader who knows how to accurately appraise people's qualities and work with them effectively.

Chapter 5 gives more advice on the practices of bodhisattvas, those beings who aspire to become fully awakened buddhas. Here Nagarjuna speaks of faults to abandon and excellent qualities to cultivate. Learning about qualities that we have the ability and potential to cultivate inspires our mind to make our life meaningful by both benefiting the world and deepening our wisdom of the ultimate nature of reality.

In the concluding verses, Nagarjuna speaks of the importance of properly relying on a qualified spiritual mentor when practicing the path and again gives some practical advice on how to relate to others in our daily life so that our actions bring peace and harmony, rather than conflict and division. Since progressing on the path depends on our effort—no one else can practice the path for us—he then encourages us to do just that.

THINGS TO NOTE

Gyaltsap Je's commentary is organized according to an outline system employed in almost all Tibetan works. The full outline is not in the text itself, as that would add unnecessary length, but if you would like to refer to it when reading the book, it is online at http://thubtenchodron.org/2016/06/precious-garland-outline/.

One word may have different meanings in different contexts. Khensur Rinpoche usually notes this, but close reading of some passages is necessary. In general, repetitions have been removed, but in passages that are difficult to understand, Khensur Rinpoche explains the point more than once in different words to help us understand the point.

A glossary has been included to help you understand technical terms. Foreign words are italicized on their first usage only.

APPRECIATION

It has been my great privilege and joy to edit Khensur Jampa Tegchok's teaching on *Precious Garland* so that it will be available for all who will benefit from it for many generations in the future. I had the fortune to study with Khensur Rinpoche from 1982 to 1985 during the time he was teaching the monks of Nalanda Monastery and the nuns of Dorje Pamo Monastery in France. Many years later, he taught twice at Sravasti Abbey as a guest teacher. I had the fortune to edit two of his previous books, *Transforming*

Adversity into Joy and Courage and *Insight into Emptiness*, and before he passed away he encouraged me to edit and publish other teachings he gave.

In 2015, I worked on the manuscript of *Precious Garland* as a form of retreat, completely immersing myself in the text. The translation by Bhikshu Steve Carlier was so clear that I often felt like I was there in the hall while Khensur Rinpoche was teaching. The text came alive for me; editing is a very different process than reading or listening and forced me to think more deeply about the teachings. So it is with delight that I offer this text by the scholar-practitioner Nagarjuna, taught by Khensur Jampa Tegchok and following the commentary by Gyaltsap Je, to you. Please enjoy and let the teachings influence your mind and heart.

Appreciation goes first and foremost to the Buddha and Nagarjuna, as well as to the lineage of masters including Gyaltsap Je, His Holiness the Dalai Lama, and Khensur Jampa Tegchok that brings these teachings to us.

Precious Garland was composed in Sanskrit and translated into Tibetan by the Indian Master Jnanagarbha and the Tibetan Lotsawa Lui Gyaltsen. The Tibetan translation was edited and corrected by the Indian Master Kanakavarman and the Tibetan Lotsawa Patsap Nyima Drak. The verses of the root text predominantly accord with the translation by John Dunne and Sara McClintock, although in some verses Jeffrey Hopkins' translation was used. I changed some of the terminology of the translation of the verses to match the translation terminology of Bhikshu Steve Carlier, who did a wonderful job translating Khensur Rinpoche's teachings. I thank all of these translators for their wonderful work that enables those of us who are not Tibetan speakers to have access to these works. I would also like to thank Bhikshuni Sangye Khadro for correcting the manuscript, and the staff at Wisdom Publications, for their kind help. Special thanks go to the sangha community of Sravasti Abbey and all our benefactors for their support while working on this book. All mistakes are my own.

Bhikshuni Thubten Chodron
Sravasti Abbey

A Commentary on Nagarjuna's
Precious Garland of Advice to a King

Introduction

When we look at the Buddha's spiritual journey from an ordinary being to a fully awakened one, we see that in the beginning he generated bodhichitta, the aspiration to attain full awakening for the benefit of all sentient beings; in the middle he practiced the path to full awakening; and at the end he attained peerless awakening and gave abundant teachings in order to lead others to this most marvelous state. All the teachings he gave were given in accordance with the minds of the trainees, his disciples: to those who were primarily interested in being free from cyclic existence he taught the fundamental vehicle that leads to liberation, and to those who were primarily interested in attaining full awakening he taught the universal vehicle that leads to buddhahood.

The Context of Nagarjuna's Writings

The teachings of the universal vehicle fall into two groups: those that teach the perfection vehicle and those that teach the vajra vehicle. Of these, the *Precious Garland* contains teachings of the perfection vehicle. The most outstanding of the Buddha's teachings are the perfection of wisdom sutras that contain all the teachings of the perfection vehicle. These teachings are considered most marvelous because they clearly explain the profound meaning of the ultimate nature of reality, the emptiness of inherent existence of all phenomena. The realization of emptiness is crucial to attaining awakening because the wisdom directly realizing emptiness is the only antidote capable of completely eradicating the self-grasping ignorance that is the root of cyclic existence. The elimination of all the cognitive obscurations that prevent the attainment of full awakening also depends on direct perception of emptiness. In the *Questions of Rashtrapala Sutra* (*Rashtrapala-paripriccha Sutra*) the Buddha says that sentient beings wander in cyclic existence because they do not understand the three doors of liberation—emptiness, signlessness, and wishlessness. To be free of cyclic existence and all the duhkha (unsatisfactory circumstances) that it involves, we must realize the three doors of liberation, which comes down to realizing the emptiness of inherent existence. Given its immense importance, the Buddha taught many methods and logical reasons to help us understand emptiness.

Someone asked the Buddha, "After you pass away, who will explain the meaning of emptiness clearly and without error? Who will perfectly discriminate between definitive sutras that explicitly present ultimate truth in an unmistaken way and provisional sutras that do not deal with ultimate truth or whose words cannot be taken literally?" In reply the Buddha predicted that four hundred years after his passing, Nagarjuna would perform this important task.

To accomplish this, Nagarjuna composed six texts collectively known as the Collection of Middle Way Reasoning (*yuktikaya*), so called because they use reason to establish the meaning of emptiness. The six texts are *Treatise on the Middle Way* (*Mulamadhyamakakarika*), *Finely Woven* (*Vaidalyasutra*), *Refutation of Objections* (*Vigrahavyavartani*), *Seventy Stanzas on Emptiness* (*Shunyatasaptatikarika*), *Sixty Stanzas of Reasoning* (*Yuktishashtikakarika*), and *Precious Garland* (*Ratnavali*, or *Rajaparikatha-ratnamala*). Some people say that only five of Nagarjuna's texts are on reasoning, including *Precious Garland* in Nagarjuna's Collections of Advice instead. Nagarjuna also composed the *Compendium of Sutras* (*Sutrasamuccaya*), an anthology of quotations from many different sutras that demonstrate that his explanation of emptiness is just as the Buddha himself explained it and not a fabrication without a valid source in the sutras.

Among the texts that form the Collection of Middle Way Reasoning, *Treatise on the Middle Way, Finely Woven, Refutation of Objections,* and *Seventy Stanzas on Emptiness* were specifically written to explain emptiness of true existence, the object that one must realize to attain liberation, whereas *Sixty Stanzas of Reasoning* and the *Precious Garland* are mainly concerned with cultivating the mind that realizes that object. This mind is the wisdom realizing emptiness, and it is the root of liberation and full awakening.

Treatise on the Middle Way principally and directly addresses the thesis of the essentialists—those who propound true existence—while *Finely Woven* mainly addresses their reasons. Both of these texts point out the faults of asserting true existence. To counter the essentialists' assertion that all phenomena truly exist, *Treatise on the Middle Way* asserts that phenomena do not truly exist and cites the numerous faults that would follow if they did.

Finely Woven, on the other hand, refutes the reasons that the essentialists give to prove that things truly exist by showing that their reasons are not valid.

Here we see two different ways of proving that phenomena are not truly existent and are empty of true existence. One is to explicitly refute true existence, in which case non-true existence is implicitly proven. Another way is to explicitly prove non-true existence, in which case true existence is implicitly refuted. *Treatise on the Middle Way* and *Finely Woven* do the former. *Seventy Stanzas on Emptiness* and *Refutation of Objections* principally prove the non-true existence of persons and phenomena by mainly using the reason of tenability. That is, they say that phenomena must be non-truly existent because the functioning of agent and action, coming and going, causes and their results are all tenable within phenomena being empty of true existence. On the other hand, if phenomena were truly existent, they would not be able to function. Their functioning would be untenable because truly existent agents could not perform actions and truly existent causes could not bring results. Because of being non-truly existent, causes bring results and agents can perform actions.

Refutation of Objections is considered a supplement to the first chapter of *Treatise on the Middle Way*, and *Seventy Stanzas on Emptiness* is seen as a supplement to its seventh chapter. The first chapter of *Treatise on the Middle Way* examines the essentialists' argument that if things lacked inherent existence, the system of cause and effect would not work. Nagarjuna shows the contrary—that unless cause and effect were non-truly existent, they would be unable to function and incapable of change. *Refutation of Objections* elaborates and provides additional arguments for this.

Nagarjuna also deals with the essential assertion that it would be untenable for reasons to refute or prove statements if things do not inherently exist. *Refutation of Objections* demonstrates that reasons that prove and refute statements, as well as the acts of proving and refuting, work precisely because things do not truly exist.

In the seventh chapter of *Treatise on the Middle Way*, Nagarjuna explains that if arising, abiding, and ceasing existed inherently, they could not function. *Seventy Stanzas on Emptiness* further elaborates on this topic. There, Nagarjuna replies to the essentialist insistence that arising, abiding, and ceasing would not work if things lacked inherent existence. He demonstrates that, on the contrary, these three function only because they do not inherently exist; they are tenable only because they lack inherent existence.

In short, these four texts from the Collection of Middle Way Reasoning are the same in terms of explaining emptiness, but they differ in the way they do so. Some refute the object to be negated, inherent existence, and some refute the object the essentialists seek to establish, inherent existence. Both are right, since inherent existence is the object of negation according to the Prasangika view, and inherent existence is also the object to be proven according to the essentialists such as the Chittamatra and Svatantrika.[1]

As mentioned above, *Sixty Stanzas of Reasoning* and *Precious Garland* explain the subject or mind—the wisdom realizing emptiness—and why it is important as the root of liberation and full awakening. *Sixty Stanzas of Reasoning* discusses why the wisdom realizing emptiness is the main root of attaining liberation from cyclic existence and becoming an arhat.

If taken literally, Nagarjuna's texts that explain the wisdom realizing emptiness may give the impression that he believes that all phenomena neither exist nor do not exist, and that by meditating on that liberation is attained. However, he is actually saying that meditating on things being truly existent on the ultimate level and totally nonexistent on the conventional level cannot free us from cyclic existence. Instead, by understanding and meditating on the middle way view that phenomena are empty of inherent existence yet exist dependently, people gradually come to directly perceive emptiness and attain the path of seeing.[2] By further familiarizing themselves with emptiness, they will attain the path of meditation and finally the path of no more learning, nirvana.

---

1. According to the Geluk school of Tibetan Buddhism, the various strands of Buddhist philosophical thought in ancient India can be subsumed in four main tenet systems: the Vaibhashika, Sautrantika, Chittamatra, and Madhyamaka. The Madhyamaka has two main branches: Svatantrika and Prasangika, the latter considered the subtlest and most refined view of the ultimate nature of existence. Other Buddhist schools of philosophy, up to and including the Madhyamaka Svatantrika, in one way or another assert some kind of inherent essence, and thus those systems are considered essentialist. According to the Prasangikas, true existence, inherent existence, substantial existence, existence from its own side, existence by its own characteristics, and so forth are synonymous. However, this is not the case for the essentialist schools.

2. According to the different dispositions and interests of disciples, the Buddha taught three vehicles: the hearer and solitary realizer vehicles lead to arhatship, the state of liberation from cyclic existence. The bodhisattva vehicle leads to full awakening, buddhahood. Each of the three vehicles has five paths: the paths of accumulation, preparation, seeing, meditation, and no more learning. Upon realizing emptiness directly, a practitioner attains the path of seeing of his or her vehicle. The path of no more learning is the completion of that path.

Precious Garland emphasizes that the realization of emptiness is extremely important not only because it is the principal root of liberation but also because it is one of the principal roots of full awakening. Nagarjuna shows this when he refers to the so-called "three factors indicated on this occasion" that are essential to attain buddhahood—bodhichitta, wisdom realizing emptiness, and compassion (verse 175). Thus the *Precious Garland* is situated in the context of all of Nagarjuna's works on reasoning.

When attempting to understand the definitive meaning of emptiness as expressed by the Prasangika Madhyamikas, we must rely on Nagarjuna. Thus studying his Collection of Middle Way Reasoning is essential. Those with critical wisdom who wish to determine whether or not the meaning of emptiness that Nagarjuna explains in these six texts genuinely comes from the Buddha should read his *Compendium of Sutras* that conveniently gathers together all the principal sutra passages on the subject so that readers don't need to search through the sutras themselves.

If you wish to read further, look at *Four Hundred Stanzas on the Middle Way* (*Chatuhshataka*) by Nagarjuna's student Aryadeva. This text explains the Prasangika view of emptiness and the thought behind Nagarjuna's Collection of Middle Way Reasoning. You may also wish to consult the texts of Buddhapalita, Chandrakirti, and Shantideva. Of all the outstanding works that unpack Nagarjuna's meaning, Chandrakirti's *Supplement to the Middle Way* is paramount. A supplement to *Treatise on the Middle Way*, it principally explains the meaning expressed in that text and fills out the other practices to be done on the path to full awakening. This text clearly explains all of the difficult points of Nagarjuna's work. Chandrakirti explains the words of *Treatise on the Middle Way* in his commentary *Clear Words* (*Prasannapada*).

The above texts can still be quite difficult to understand, so it is useful to refer to Je Tsongkhapa's texts the *Ocean of Reasoning: The Great Commentary on the "Middle Way"* (*Tsashé Tikchen*), *Illumination of the Middle Way Thought* (*Gongpa Rabsal*), and *Great Treatise on the Stages of the Path* (*Lamrim Chenmo*), where he explains the meaning of the texts by Nagarjuna, Chandrakirti, Aryadeva, and Buddhapalita.

You may wonder, "Why make things so confusing by having to read all these books? Why can't we just refer to the words of the Buddha or study Nagarjuna directly?" The people who lived at the time of the Buddha were able to immediately understand the meaning of the Buddha's teachings because they had enormous merit, but those who lived after he passed away had less merit and couldn't properly understand his teachings by simply reading the sutras. Misconceptions about the meaning of the Buddha's teachings arose due to this, so great Indian sages wrote treatises to unpack and clarify the meaning of the sutras for the practitioners of that time who had the merit to correctly understand the view. Such people could realize emptiness by meditating on the six texts of the Collection of Middle Way Reasoning. But as time passed, people's merit again declined, and it became extremely difficult for most people to understand the previous texts. Therefore it is necessary from time to time for great scholars who correctly understand the meaning to compose texts to explain it and clarify the difficult points of prior works. To this end, in our study of the *Precious Garland*, we will refer to the commentary of Gyaltsap Je, one of Je Tsongkhapa's principal disciples.

MEANING OF THE TITLE

In Sanskrit the title is *Rajaparikatha-ratnamala*; in Tibetan, *rgyal po la gtam bya ba rin po che'i phreng ba. Raja* means "king," *parikatha* means "advice" or "instruction," *ratna* means "precious," and *mala* means "garland." The full title of the work in English is thus *Precious Garland of Advice to a King.* Some people say that the advice is for kings in general who lived in India at Nagarjuna's time. Others say this advice was given to a specific king who was one of Nagarjuna's benefactors. Some say the king was also the recipient of Nagarjuna's text *Friendly Letter* (*Suhrillekha*). His name was Dechö Sangpo in Tibetan.

Translator's Homage

Homage to All Buddhas and Bodhisattvas.

The Indian master Jnanagarbha and the Tibetan Lotsawa Lui Gyaltsen, who translated the text from Sanskrit into Tibetan, pay homage to all the buddhas and bodhisattvas. This indicates that this text belongs to the group of Buddhist teachings of the Sutra Pitaka, which chiefly explains the higher training of concentration. Buddhas and bodhisattvas are masters of concentration. When a text is on ethical conduct, it belongs to the Vinaya Pitaka and homage is made to the Omniscient One, the Buddha. Texts pertaining to wisdom are part of the Abhidharma Pitaka, and in those, homage is paid to Manjushri, the buddha of wisdom.

I. Higher Rebirth and Highest Good

1. Starting on the Path to Happiness and Liberation

PRAISE AND HOMAGE

At the beginning of a treatise, the author first pays homage to the Three Jewels. This humbles the mind and the author reminds himself that he will explain the Buddha's words; he is not going to make up something outside of the Buddhadharma. Here Nagarjuna pays homage to the Buddha, the Omniscient One.

After this, the author writes a promise to compose the text. Here Nagarjuna tells us his motivation for writing the *Precious Garland.* He also explains the subject matter, the immediate and ultimate aims in writing the treatise, and the connection between these three. He also explains why he will write this lengthy epistle of Dharma to the king: because the king is receptive to hearing the Dharma, will benefit from hearing it, and will put it into practice—in other words, because he is a suitable vessel. Although Nagarjuna has explicitly written *Precious Garland* for a king, he has implicitly written it for all of those in future generations who will benefit from reading and studying it.

> 1. I bow to the Omniscient One,
> [who is] utterly free of all faults
> and adorned with all good qualities,
> the sole friend of all sentient beings.

The Purpose of Praising and Paying Homage to the Buddha

Nagarjuna pays homage to the Buddha in order to fulfill his own and others' aims. It perfectly fulfills his immediate aim because offering praise to a special object with a mind of faith pacifies obstacles to composing the text. Nagarjuna will also attain his ultimate aim, because composing the text contributes to the accumulation of merit that will allow him to attain liberation. He perfectly fulfills the immediate aims of others because they will be able to use his text to learn and practice the instructions without difficulty. He fulfills their ultimate aims because liberation and full awakening are attained on the basis of such study and practice.

An alternative meaning is that attaining the Buddha's omniscient mind—the truth body or *dharmakaya*—fulfills one's own purpose because it is the most exalted and perfect state of mind. Attaining a Buddha's two form bodies—the enjoyment body and the emanation body—fulfills the aims of others because by appearing to sentient beings via these bodies, buddhas teach and lead them to liberation and awakening.

The Meaning of the Praise and Homage

The Buddha has fulfilled his own goal because he is utterly free of all faults and adorned with all good qualities. "Utterly free of all faults" indicates the Buddha's *excellent abandonment*. He has fulfilled his own aim of abandoning all that is to be abandoned in himself and is free of all defilements. This is an attribute of the Buddha's truth body, which is completely free from both the afflictive obscurations that prevent liberation and the cognitive obscurations that prevent full awakening.

The Buddha's quality of excellent abandonment covers the practice of the beings of three capacities—initial, intermediate, and advanced—as explained in the stages of the path, or *lamrim* teachings. The Buddha is free from all suffering of the lower realms and free from all suffering of cyclic existence in general. He is also free from self-grasping ignorance and self-centered thought. In short, he has abandoned all faults and defects of cyclic existence and of the personal peace of nirvana. All of these have been eradicated such that they can never return.

"Adorned with all good qualities" indicates that the Buddha possesses all *excellent realizations* and qualities of a fully awakened one's body, speech, and mind. He knows all objects of knowledge and is adorned with all good qualities, thereby attaining the truth body adorned with ten powers, the four kinds of fearlessness, and the eighteen unshared qualities that distinguish fully awakened buddhas from arhats. His truth body is beautified with the wisdom that directly understands all sixteen aspects of the four truths of the aryas[3] and perceives all phenomena with direct, unmistaken wisdom. Such excellent abandonment and realizations illustrate that the Buddha has fulfilled his own aim.

Nagarjuna also praises the Buddha because he fulfills the aim of others by having actualized the two form bodies of a fully awakened one. Motivated by love and compassion, he manifests physical bodies in order to lead sentient beings on the path. He appears to arya bodhisattvas as the enjoyment body in a pure land and appears to ordinary sentient beings as emanation bodies who guide and teach them. In this way, the Buddha protects sentient beings from duhkha—suffering and unsatisfactory experiences—and establishes them in temporal and ultimate goodness.

"The sole friend of all sentient beings" indicates that the Buddha fulfills all the aims of others. He helps others attain their goals without being biased by attachment to some and adverse toward others. He doesn't favor those that help or revere him or discriminate against those who have harmed or insulted him, but rather helps all beings equally. Out of compassion he engages in every method possible to free each and every sentient being from all of their duhkha forever. He also works to bring about their happiness in any way possible. Thus he indeed is the sole friend of all beings.

To say that the Buddha is the sole friend of all beings highlights the difference between the Buddha and non-Buddhist teachers who may harm sentient beings by giving incorrect instructions that lead disciples to engage in destructive actions. For example, such teachers may tell their disciples to kill or may kill others themselves; they may instruct disciples to adopt stringent, ascetic lifestyles or opulent, self-indulgent lifestyles. The Buddha, however, knows the disposition and aptitude of each disciple and teaches accordingly, without leading them on erroneous paths.

---

3.   Aryas are those who have realized emptiness directly and nonconceptually. They constitute the Sangha Jewel in which we take refuge.

PROMISE TO COMPOSE THE TREATISE
General Meaning of the Promise to Compose

To understand Nagarjuna's reason for composing this text, we need to know its subject matter, its immediate and ultimate purposes, and the connection between these. The subject matter is higher rebirth and the highest good together with their causes and effects. In other words, this text teaches us how to improve our mind in the present so that we will attain a higher rebirth—a fortunate rebirth in the human or celestial realm—in the future, which is the immediate purpose. On the basis of that higher rebirth, we can continue to improve our minds over a series of good rebirths, until we attain the ultimate goal, buddhahood, which is the highest good.

Nagarjuna writes on these subjects because studying and understanding the methods by which we can attain higher rebirth and the highest good gives us the knowledge we will need in order to practice and to attain liberation and awakening, which is the essential purpose.

Attaining liberation and awakening is based on understanding the causes of higher rebirth and the highest good. This understanding comes from studying the subject matter of the commentary. In this way, the subject matter, immediate purpose, and essential purpose of the text are related.

Contrariwise, without teachings that explain how to attain higher rebirth and the highest good, we would be unable to create their causes effectively, and we would be unable to attain their effects—liberation and awakening. Therefore, Nagarjuna's text is indeed precious.

> 2. O King, I will explain to you the completely virtuous Dharma
>   so that you may accomplish it—
>   for the Dharma will be accomplished [when it is explained]
>   to a vessel of the true Dharma.

Meaning of the Promise to Compose in Detail

By saying "O King," Nagarjuna addresses a person who has dominion over his realm. He wants to tell the king about the completely virtuous Dharma—Dharma practices that are virtuous in the beginning, middle, and end—so that the king may accomplish them and fulfill his own and others' aims.

Dharma is that which holds us back from falling into the lower realms or any other rebirth in cyclic existence. Nagarjuna will go on to explain the practices that are the causes for accomplishing our own and others' aims. Practicing the ten virtuous paths of action and so forth is the Dharma that is virtuous in the beginning, because it leads to rebirth as a human being or a celestial being. Cultivating the wisdom realizing emptiness is the Dharma that is virtuous in the middle, because it leads to awakening for those following the hearer, solitary realizer, or bodhisattva paths. Conjoining this wisdom with bodhichitta and the bodhisattva deeds is the Dharma that is virtuous in the end, for it brings buddhahood, our final objective.

Rebirth as a human or celestial being is considered higher rebirth because these beings enjoy more happiness and experience less pain than others in cyclic existence. The three types of awakening are called highest good because they are states in which all duhkha has been eradicated forever.

The Reason to Explain the Dharma to a Suitable Vessel

When those who are suitable vessels hear the Dharma, they will practice it and gain magnificent results. In the *Four Hundred Stanzas,* Aryadeva says that those who are suitable vessels possess three qualities: they are unbiased and open-minded, neither opinionated nor encumbered by preconceptions; they are intelligent and can discern what is correct and incorrect; and they are eager and interested in the Dharma, seeking out teachings and enthusiastically practicing them.

Given that the king is such a person, Nagarjuna knows that great benefit will come from teaching him the Dharma. The study of the Dharma—which includes reading and hearing it—is a treasure that can never be stolen from us. It is the lamp that clears away the darkness of confusion in our minds. It is our best friend that will never leave us. Studying the Dharma is the best path because it leads to liberation and awakening.

Nagarjuna gives a series of instructions on the causes to attain higher rebirth and the highest good in both meditation sessions and daily life. Applying this to the king's life, he advises how to treat citizens and travelers in the kingdom, to help monasteries, and to offer honor, respect, and service to the Three Jewels.

Overview of the Causes and Effects of Higher Rebirth and Highest Good

The actual explanation of the subject matter now begins. Nagarjuna identifies higher rebirth and highest good as the outcomes to work toward and gives a brief overview of the main and secondary causes for each one. He then goes into a more detailed explanation regarding their causes.

> 3. That [vessel] first [practices] the Dharma of higher rebirth;
>   afterward comes the highest good,
>   because, having obtained higher rebirth,
>   one proceeds in stages to the highest good.

The Order in Which Higher Rebirth and Highest Good Are Taught

Higher rebirth and highest good are taught in this order because it is very difficult to attain highest good without having first secured a higher rebirth. The purification, collection of merit, and study, contemplation, and meditation on the teachings that are needed in order to attain liberation or awakening require a series of higher rebirths to complete. If we practice the various types of virtuous activities to the best of our ability in this life, we will be able to secure a higher rebirth again in our next life.

The idea is to continue like this over a series of lives as we cultivate the qualities of sharp intelligence, enthusiasm, profound wisdom, great altruism, and so on. We do this by first learning and practicing the foundational topics—impermanence, refuge, and karma and its effects. As we mature in the Dharma, we learn and practice the more difficult topics such as emptiness. In this way we gradually come to attain the highest good. Thus, creating the causes for higher rebirth is our immediate concern. If we fall into lower realms, we will not only suffer, we will also have no opportunity to progress along the path to liberation and awakening.

Another reason that higher rebirth and highest good are presented in this order is to properly prepare the student for instruction in more advanced practices. If emptiness is taught to someone who is not a suitable vessel, he or she may mistake emptiness for total nonexistence and thereby disregard the law of cause and effect. Living as if our actions had no consequences creates destructive karma that is certain to result in rebirth in the lower realms.

We cannot attain the highest good by meditating on an incorrect understanding of emptiness, nor can we attain liberation or higher rebirth by ignoring the law of karma and its result and behaving however we wish. We must proceed by observing karma and its effects in such a way that our understanding of it doesn't harm our understanding of emptiness. Likewise, our meditation on emptiness should be done in a way that doesn't harm our understanding of karma and its effects. When we correctly understand these two, we will see that they do not contradict each other but complement each other. In this way we will progress on the path to the highest good.

The Order in Which Higher Rebirth and Highest Good Are Ascertained

In terms of ascertaining higher rebirth and highest good with reliable cognizers, the order is reversed: higher rebirth and its causes are more difficult to ascertain than highest good and its causes. Why is this? There are three types of phenomena: evident phenomena—such as a table and the sound of a bell—that can be realized by our senses; slightly obscure phenomena—such as subtle impermanence and emptiness—that must initially be realized through inference by power of the fact; and very obscure phenomena that are understood by relying on an authoritative scripture.

To understand liberation and awakening, and their causes, we must realize emptiness and understand the way in which the wisdom realizing emptiness overcomes ignorance. All phenomena exist dependently, but self-grasping ignorance apprehends them as existing independently. Because self-grasping apprehends phenomena contrary to the actual way they exist, it is a wrong consciousness. Through reasoning we can gain an inference realizing that all phenomena are empty of independent existence because they exist dependently. This correct understanding—the wisdom realizing emptiness—knows that phenomena exist in the exact opposite way than ignorance grasps them to exist. This wisdom is free from all false projections and fabrications, and in addition, it has valid support: it is accompanied by factors on the method side of the path such as love, compassion, and bodhichitta. As the wisdom realizing emptiness grows in strength, it eradicates increasingly subtle levels of afflictions until all self-grasping ignorance and afflictions have been completely eradicated so that they can never reappear. This is nirvana, liberation. In this way liberation—a slightly obscure phenomenon—can be ascertained through sound reasoning. Relying on scriptural authority to ascertain it is not necessary.

On the other hand, understanding higher rebirth and its causes involves understanding the law of karma and its effects—a very obscure phenomenon that is more difficult to realize. Higher rebirths are considered higher not only because the beings born in them experience less pain than those in the lower realms, but also because the causes for such rebirths—virtuous karma—are loftier than the causes for lower rebirths. Because the causes are higher, the effects are also higher. Our practice in previous lives of pure ethical conduct, accompanied by the six perfections and stainless prayers, led us to attain higher rebirth in this life.

As a human being, I am a higher rebirth. But simply knowing me does not mean that you understand higher rebirth. To understand that I am a higher rebirth requires a lot of thought. For example, you can see a book that is empty of inherent existence without realizing the emptiness of inherent existence. Similarly, there is a difference between knowing a person who is a higher rebirth and knowing that a person is higher rebirth. To know that a person is higher rebirth necessitates having studied the virtuous paths of action that are its causes. Realizing that higher rebirth arises from those causes comes only by depending on a reliable scriptural quotation to that effect. That, in turn, depends on ascertaining that the scriptural passage is reliable and can be accepted as authoritative. The three factors for discerning an authoritative scripture are mentioned on page 23.

In brief, realizing that liberation and full awakening are highest good is easier and is done first. Understanding that rebirth as a human or celestial being is higher rebirth is more difficult and is done later. This is due to the former being a slightly obscure phenomenon that can be realized through inference and the latter being an extremely obscure phenomenon that can only be understood in dependence on authoritative scripture.

The order of attainment is the other way around. First we practice the causes for higher rebirth and attain higher rebirth. Then we practice the causes of highest good and attain the highest good.

> 4. Here, [we] maintain that higher rebirth is happiness,
> and highest good is liberation.
> In brief, the method for attaining them
> is summarized as faith and wisdom.

Briefly Identifying the Causes and Effects of Higher Rebirth

"Higher rebirth is happiness" refers to the happiness that human beings and gods experience. Here happiness is an example of the characteristics of higher rebirth. Equanimity is also included since beings in the fourth concentration of the material realm and in the four immaterial absorptions do not experience feelings of happiness; they feel only equanimity.[4] Those who enjoy higher rebirth as humans or celestial beings experience more happiness and equanimity than do beings in lower realms.

Highest good is liberation—the cessation of ignorance, afflictions, and polluted karma. Karma literally means actions or work, specifically the actions of our body, speech, and mind. These may be destructive physical actions such as killing or destructive verbal actions such as lying. They may also be constructive actions, which include abstaining from destructive actions or acting in the opposite way. For example, abandoning killing is refraining from killing and saving life is doing the opposite of killing. The karmas that cause rebirth in cyclic existence are polluted because they are created under the influence of ignorance. Destructive actions are clearly underlain by self-grasping ignorance, but so are the constructive actions of ordinary beings. For example, under the influence of self-grasping we are generous and keep good ethical conduct. Even though constructive karmas bring happiness, when they are created under the influence of ignorance they are considered polluted and lead to rebirth in cyclic existence. Liberation is the eradication of ignorance, other afflictions, and the polluted karmas that lead to rebirth in cyclic existence.

Being born in cyclic existence is like being bound, hand and foot, snared in a very tight net, and thrown into a river in the dark of night. It is already hard enough to escape when one's hands and feet are bound, but it is even

---

4. The world of sentient beings consists of three realms: the desire, material, and immaterial realms. Desire realm beings are preoccupied with objects of the five senses—sight, sound, smell, taste, and touch. Within the desire realm are three lower realms, so-called because the beings born there experience a preponderance of suffering. These are beings temporarily born as hell beings, hungry ghosts, or animals. The three fortunate realms are those of human beings and two types of celestial beings; these beings experience much more happiness and joy. In the material and immaterial realms, beings enjoy the bliss and equanimity of deep meditative concentration. In the material realm they have bodies made of very refined material; in the immaterial realm, they have no gross bodies at all.

harder to do so when also snared in a net. If, bound in such a way, we were thrown into a river during the day, we'd still have some hope of escape—we could at least see the shore. If we were thrown into a river in the dark of night, escape would seem hopeless. Being bound hand and foot signifies being bound by our previous karma; being captured in a tight net represents grasping at true existence; darkness symbolizes ignorance. The river represents the four currents of sensual desire, craving for existence, ignorance, and wrong views. Liberation is freedom from all that.

Highest good is good in every way. The first two truths of an arya—true duhkha and its origins—have been abandoned in such a way that they can never return. This state of true cessation—the third truth—comes about by meditating on the wisdom realizing selflessness, which is the fourth truth, the true path.

In the second half of the verse Nagarjuna answers the question, "What are the causes of higher rebirth and highest good?" In brief, they are faith and wisdom. Although there are many causes for higher rebirth, faith is the fundamental one. Similarly, while there are many causes for the highest good, wisdom is principal.

"Faith" refers to belief or confidence in the law of karma and its results, the four truths of the aryas, the Three Jewels, and so forth. As we learn about these things and think about them, our confidence in them will increase and we will put the instructions into practice. "Wisdom" refers to the wisdom realizing the emptiness of inherent existence, the ultimate mode of existence of all persons and phenomena. As we cultivate this wisdom, our confusion will abate.

> 5. Due to having faith, one relies on the practices;
>   due to having wisdom, one truly understands;
>   of these two, wisdom is foremost,
>   but faith must come first.

Differences between the Principal and the Secondary Causes

Faith in the law of karma and its results begins with understanding the four principal aspects of karma: (1) happiness always comes from virtue, never nonvirtue, and suffering always comes from nonvirtue, never virtue; (2) a small action can bring large results in the same way that a tiny seed can grow into a huge tree; (3) if we don't create the cause, we won't experience the result; (4) karmic seeds do not get lost, and unless we impede or destroy them, they will eventually ripen into their effects. These four apply to both virtuous and nonvirtuous paths of actions. Due to having faith in the law of karma and its effects, we will engage in the practice of the ten virtuous paths of action, which are the cause of higher rebirth.

To generate this faith, we must rely on authoritative scriptures. But first we must investigate whether a scripture is reliable. We examine three factors: Does this scripture correctly present obvious phenomena— those knowable by our senses? Is its presentation of slightly obscure phenomena—such as emptiness—correct? Is its presentation of explicit and implied meanings free from contradiction and are its former and latter passages that discuss very obscure phenomena free from contradiction? If the answers to these questions are positive, there is reason to trust what this scripture says.

Furthermore, if a reliable person such as the Buddha taught the scripture, we can trust what is said in it. The Buddha is a reliable person because he has eliminated all defilements and cultivated all good qualities; he has no reason to deceive us and is motivated only by great compassion. In addition, we can verify other teachings he gave—such as on the disadvantages of cyclic existence and the problematic nature of the afflictions—so we can trust what he says about very obscure topics such as karma and its effects.

Of those two causes, faith and wisdom, the wisdom realizing emptiness is principal, because it is what actually liberates us from cyclic existence. It eradicates self-grasping ignorance so that it can never reappear in the future. While faith, compassion, and bodhichitta can limit our afflictions, they cannot eliminate them from the root.

People with sharp faculties are suitable vessels for realizing emptiness. They will hear teachings on emptiness, reflect on them deeply, and discuss them with others in order to gain a correct understanding. By then meditating on emptiness, the wisdom that leads to highest good will grow in them.

Faith in karma and its effects is a prerequisite to generating the wisdom realizing emptiness. Faith is the cause for ethical conduct, which leads to higher rebirth. Higher rebirth is the basis for generating the wisdom realizing emptiness, which, in turn, is the direct cause for the highest good of liberation and awakening. Thus, while faith in karma and its effects is a secondary cause, it is essential and cannot be overlooked.

In short, to attain highest good, we must directly realize the ultimate nature of phenomena by cultivating the wisdom realizing emptiness. To generate this wisdom, we must have a series of special higher rebirths that provide the freedom and fortune to learn about and cultivate this wisdom. The principal cause for such higher rebirths is abandoning nonvirtue and practicing virtue. Faith in the instructions on karma and its effects is essential for this.

> 6. One who does not neglect the practices
>   through partiality, anger, fear, or ignorance
>   is known as one with faith—
>   a superior vessel for the highest good.

A Person with Faith

A person with faith is someone who has confidence in the law of karma and its effects, and who, due to this confidence, does not forgo the practice of virtue by engaging in nonvirtuous actions motivated by four afflicted emotions. These four emotions, which are mentioned in the Vinaya (monastic discipline), are partiality or attachment, anger, fear, and ignorance. For example, people who forgo the virtuous action of abandoning killing may kill due to partiality or attachment to an animal's meat or skin, kill out of anger or hatred, kill due to fear of punishment by an authority that orders them to kill, or engage in animal sacrifice ignorantly thinking it will benefit the family. These are just a few examples; please think of other ways we forgo virtue due to partiality, anger, fear, or ignorance.

Someone who does not neglect or transgress virtuous practices due to these four emotions is a superior vessel for the highest good. He or she is the best kind of person to be led on the path to liberation by a spiritual mentor.

> 7. A wise [person] is one who,
>   having accurately analyzed
>   all actions of body, speech, and mind,
>   always acts for the benefit of self and others.

A Person with Wisdom

A wise person continuously examines his or her physical and verbal actions to see if they are virtuous, nonvirtuous, or neutral. Wanting to create virtue, she makes effort to abandon nonvirtuous and neutral actions and to engage in virtuous ones. She enthusiastically undertakes virtuous actions with bodhichitta, the intention to attain full awakening for the benefit of all sentient beings, and dedicates them for this purpose. In this way, she does what benefits herself and others. In short, a person who knows what to abandon and what to practice on the path and acts accordingly with a bodhichitta motivation is a wise person who is capable of engaging in the path to liberation and full awakening.

On the other hand, someone who lacks faith in karma and its results and is ignorant of what to practice and what to abandon does not possess wisdom. Such a person is not suitable to be led to liberation at this time. While in general all sentient beings can be led to awakening, they cannot actually attain awakening until they abandon wrong views about the law of karma and its effects.

In our world, somebody is considered wise or intelligent when he is able to learn quickly, excels at speaking or writing, or has knowledge about topics respected by society. However, that is not the meaning of a "wise person" in this context. From the Buddhist perspective a wise person has faith in karma and its effects and understands the points of the paths of the three beings—those of initial, intermediate, and advanced capability—and practices them correctly. Everything concerning the entire path to awakening is included in this simple idea.

2. The Advantages of Ethical Living and a Fortunate Life

Higher Rebirth and Its Causes

Having described a person with faith and a person with wisdom, Nagarjuna now goes into detail about the causal relationships leading to higher rebirth and highest good, beginning with the foundation, ethical conduct. To ensure we understand that these are the correct causes of higher rebirth, he explains that practices such as extreme asceticism do not bring higher rebirth; in fact, they bring the opposite. Those who practice such an erroneous path not only harm themselves by creating heavy destructive karma, but when they teach this wrong path to others, they ruin others' chance to attain higher rebirth and liberation as well. With compassion, Nagarjuna then explains the three results of karma so that we can consider the consequences of our choices before acting, restrain ourselves when necessary, and encourage ourselves to act in constructive ways.

> 8. Refraining from killing and from stealing,
>   not engaging in adultery;
>   restraining from lying,
>   divisive speech, harsh words, and idle talk;

> 9. abandoning covetousness, malice,
>   and nihilistic views—
>   these are the ten bright paths of action.
>   The ten gloomy ones are the opposite.

Refraining from the Ten Nonvirtuous Paths of Action

Developing ethical conduct involves ceasing thirteen activities and engaging in three practices. While we loosely refer to the first ten as destructive or nonvirtuous karma, more specifically they are paths of action, meaning they are paths to rebirth in cyclic existence. Of the ten, the seven of body and speech are also karma, or action, while the three mental ones are afflictions, not karma. Sentient beings take rebirth under the power of afflictions and karma by means of creating the ten constructive and ten destructive paths of action. For ease of speaking, now we'll call them the ten virtues and ten nonvirtues.

The ten nonvirtues are covered in Vasubandhu's *Treasury of Knowledge* (*Abhidharmakosha*) and are extensively explained in the lamrim texts. For one of these to become a complete nonvirtuous action three criteria must be present: (1) the preparation, which involves correct identification of the object, the intention to do the action, and the presence of an affliction such as attachment, anger, or confusion; (2) the action itself; and (3) the completion, accomplishing what we set out to do and rejoicing in it.

As I will only briefly explain the ten nonvirtues to abandon, please study the *Great Treatise on the Stages of the Path* by Tsongkhapa for a more detailed explanation.

1. *Restraint from killing* is to abandon taking the life of a human being or animal.

2. *Restraint from stealing* means not to take things that belong to others that haven't been freely given to us.

3. *Restraint from adultery* refers to abstaining from sexual relationship with others' partners, or if you are in a relationship, having sexual relationships with another person. These three are collectively called "turning our back on the three destructive physical actions."

4. *Restraint from lying* is to abandon false speech that changes others' minds so they believe the opposite of what is.

5. *Restraint from divisive speech* is to avoid speech that creates disharmony among people.

6. *Restraint from harsh speech* means to abandon speech that hurts others' feelings, such as calling them names, criticizing them, or ridiculing them.

7. *Restraint from idle talk* is to avoid speech about topics that have no meaning, speaking just to pass time, and speech that distracts or confuses others.

8. *Abandoning covetousness* refers to abandoning looking at the possessions of others and craving to possess them ourselves. Covetousness easily arises in shopping centers. For this reason, the Buddha advised us to walk with our eyes cast downward.

9. *Abandoning malice* is to give up planning how to harm the body or possessions of another sentient being out of anger or hatred.

10. *Abandoning nihilistic views* means to relinquish wrong views that deny the existence of the Three Jewels, the law of karma and its effects, the four truths of the aryas, and so on.

If we seek higher rebirth we should definitely abandon the ten paths of nonvirtue and engage in the ten paths of virtue.

> 10. In brief, Dharma consists of not taking intoxicants,
> maintaining a proper livelihood, abandoning harm,
> being respectfully generous,
> honoring the worthy, and [cultivating] love.

Refraining from Other Blameworthy Activities

The ten nonvirtues are not the only counterproductive actions to give up. Taking intoxicants, engaging in a wrong livelihood, and harming others are also activities to be relinquished. The reason for not taking intoxicants is that when we take them they impede our ability to think clearly and make wise decisions. We lose control of our speech and actions and easily engage in many destructive actions. Newspapers are full of stories of the harmful and regrettable things people say and do while intoxicated.

Nagarjuna also advises us to earn our living through a wholesome livelihood and abandon wrong livelihood. For lay practitioners this entails avoiding deceit in business—such as cheating or lying to customers, clients, employers, or employees—manufacturing goods that harm sentient beings or the environment, and killing others. It also includes employing guile to avoid repaying loans; for example, forcing others to repay more than you loaned them or not repaying the full amount you borrowed from others. Abuse of power is also considered wrong livelihood. For example, an official tells someone that a minor offense is a serious crime and asks the person to pay a large fine to avoid arrest. Not paying others fair wages could also be considered wrong livelihood.

A monastic lifestyle involves relying on the kindness of others to receive life's necessities such as food, shelter, clothing, and medicine. Monastics should abandon five wrong ways to gain these necessities from benefactors: hypocrisy, flattery, hinting, pretentious behavior, and misusing property to get more. All of these constitute wrong livelihood for monastics who are dependent on the kindness of others.

Hypocrisy is behaving impeccably in the presence of benefactors, relatives, or friends with the hope of receiving offerings, service, or respect from them. Normally we may lie around not doing much, but when we're with these people we sit up straight with our Dharma texts in front of us and our tantric implements close at hand to impress them so they will give us offerings and respect.

Flattery involves speaking sweet words to others with the hope of getting something in return. For example, we say, "I haven't seen you in so long. I came all this way to visit you because I was worried that perhaps you weren't well," or "You're so kind! You must be a bodhisattva!" Of course if you genuinely respect others it is good to praise them, and if you're genuinely concerned, it's fine to express that. But in this case, the motivation is to get something for yourself.

Hinting means with an ulterior motive to receive money or goods, saying things such as, "Last year you gave me some money. It was really useful; I did retreat and created a lot of virtue." Or we say, "That jacket you gave me last year was so warm," hinting that we'd like another one this year.

Pretentious behavior involves trying to get something by appearing to be what we are not; for example, saying, "I heard you are supporting your parents and that's wonderful. But what would you do if an arhat came to your house?" Or we tell them that when we go to visit another family, they treat us like an arhat.

Misusing your property to get more entails giving someone a small gift in the hope of receiving something big in turn. Another example is showing your benefactor your alms bowl, saying that the president, a movie star, or famous athlete gave it to you. In this way, you make the person think you're a special person who should receive fine offerings.

In addition to taking intoxicants and wrong livelihood, a third blameworthy activity to relinquish is harming others physically and verbally by beating or hitting them, destroying their possessions, humiliating them, or hurting their feelings in other ways.

Three Practices to Engage In

In addition to the thirteen actions to abandon, Nagarjuna recommends three activities to do: practice respectful generosity, honor the worthy, and cultivate love.

Respectful generosity is making offerings to those who are worthy—our preceptors, spiritual mentors, and sentient beings in general—with a respectful attitude and in a respectful manner. Rather than ask others to make offerings for us, it's better to give them ourselves, using both hands. In general, the Buddha spoke of four kinds of generosity: giving material possessions; giving fearlessness by protecting others from danger; giving love with the thought "May all beings be happy"; and giving the Dharma by giving teachings and sharing the Dharma with others.

Honoring the worthy entails showing respect to those who are superior to us in virtuous qualities. The worthy are our preceptors and spiritual mentors, as well as others who may not be our spiritual mentors but who have greater knowledge or more excellent qualities than we do.

Cultivating love indicates all four immeasurables: immeasurable love, compassion, joy, and equanimity. Contemplating these as much as possible will make our mind peaceful and improve our relationships with others.

Learning the causes for higher rebirth gives us a lot to contemplate. Examine your previous actions so that you can improve in the future. Also contemplate how to go about enacting these sixteen practices in your life.

> 11. Dharma does not come about
> merely through engaging in physical austerities;
> through that type of practice one neither ceases harming others
> nor does one benefit them.

Engaging in Imperfect Paths Harms Oneself and Others

Non-Buddhists have their own practices for attaining higher rebirth, many of which are very different from the sixteen Nagarjuna prescribed. Some non-Buddhists engage in ascetic practices that mortify the body, such as fasting for long periods of time, bathing in the Ganges, sitting in a fire, and jumping on top of a trident. Some of them walk around naked, and others stand on one leg for months. They believe these practices purify negativities and lead to liberation.

These practices are not causes of liberation; nor do they bring higher rebirth. The practice of asceticism does not forsake injuring others—which is essential for ethical conduct—nor does it help others.

Buddhists do fasting practices such as the Nyungné, the two-day fasting retreat of Avalokiteshvara, but our motivation, the actual practice, and the conclusion of the practice differ from those of non-Buddhists. Buddhists engage in a Nyungné with bodhichitta as their motivation. The fasting is not extreme, and we do prostrations, make offerings, meditate on compassion and emptiness, and cultivate serenity during the Nyungné. While Buddhist fire pujas may outwardly resemble non-Buddhist fire offerings, our motivation, the meditation we do during practice, and the conclusion of the practice are very different.

> 12. One who does not respect the great path of the true Dharma
>   with its manifest generosity, ethical conduct, and fortitude,
>   follows the mistaken path of inflicting hardship on the body
>   just as [a cow in a herd follows] the line of cattle.

> 13. Such a person with a body
>   entwined by the savage snakes of negative mental states
>   wanders for a very long time in the terrifying wilderness of cyclic
>   existence,
>   whose trees are limitless beings.

People Who Go on the Wrong Path

The sixteen practices can be summarized in three: generosity, ethical conduct, and fortitude. The four types of generosity were discussed above. Ethical conduct entails abandoning the ten nonvirtues and the three other blameworthy actions. Fortitude is of three kinds: the fortitude of not retaliating, of enduring hardship and suffering, and of practicing the Dharma.

People who have no respect for the true Dharma—as embodied in the three practices of generosity, ethical conduct, and fortitude—and engage in practices opposite to these such as self-mortification go on the wrong path. Many of them mistakenly believe that they have attained liberation because they have good concentration or can endure pain. Then when they experience suffering at the time of death, they lose faith completely and think there is no such thing as liberation or a path leading to liberation. Clinging to these wrong views, they fall into hellish rebirths.

In addition to doing these deviant practices themselves, non-Buddhists teach them to others and in doing so, they lead others astray. Their followers proceed after them, spending their entire lives adhering to wrong views and following a wrong path, thus wasting their time, putting latencies of wrong views on their mindstreams, and creating destructive karma.

For example, although there may be a broad and easy path to follow, the cow leading the herd goes off that path and follows a trail running along a precipice or through a thick jungle. The other cows follow and soon all of them find themselves on the edge of a cliff, or in a dangerous jungle where they encounter hornets, snakes, spiders, and the like. In the same way, non-Buddhist teachers follow a wrong path and ruin others by leading them on that path as well. Then all of them suffer.

The Disadvantages of Engaging in a Wrong Path

Some of these ascetics believe that acting like a dog in the present life will consume the karma to be reborn as a dog. Many such people came to the Buddha crawling on all fours, putting their mouths on the ground to eat and lap up water. Those who adhere to such wrong views and aberrant behavior not only fall into the lower realms but also are reborn in cyclic existence endlessly, experiencing the three types of duhkha and the six disadvantages of cyclic existence again and again.

Just as the cows wandering in the jungle become entwined with vicious snakes, these people are completely wrapped up in the savage snakes of attachment, anger, and ignorance. Entangled in the vines of wrong views— the view of personal identity, extreme view, and so forth—they wander among the trees of endless beings. Unable to free themselves, confused in the darkness of ignorance, they roam in the dreadful jungle of cyclic existence with no end in sight.

Nagarjuna counsels us: those of you who want to extract the essence from this life of freedom and fortune, who want to attain liberation and awakening, first seek an unmistaken path. If you adopt a wrong path and practice incorrectly, no matter how much effort you exert, no matter how courageous and brave you are, no matter how strong your practice may be, that path will not bring higher rebirth, let alone liberation and awakening. Therefore, it is crucial to examine a path and its teachers well and to choose wisely whom you will follow.

Even though many cows follow a path into the jungle, there is no safety in numbers and they are unable to help each other. Similarly, many people may follow a wrong path, but their efforts to attain higher rebirth and highest good are useless and they are unable to protect each other from the dangers of cyclic existence. For this reason, it is extremely important to pray to meet a qualified spiritual mentor who shows the unmistaken path to full awakening. Having found such a spiritual guide and unmistaken path, make sure you follow them by studying, contemplating, and meditating on the Dharma.

The Buddha was not motivated by anger, bias, or arrogance when he refuted others' wrong paths. Moved by compassion, he won their confidence through his impeccable actions and kind words, and when people were ready he taught the correct path using reasoning.

> 14. Due to killing one is born with a short life span;
>   due to violence one encounters much torment;
>   due to stealing one becomes impoverished;
>   due to adultery one has enemies.

Results Similar to Their Nonvirtuous Causes

When we follow a wrong path and engage in aberrant practices or are negligent or lazy when following the correct path, we create much destructive karma and will experience the results. Complete actions have three results: the ripening result, result similar to the cause, and environmental result. The ripening result is the rebirth we will take. Results similar to the cause are situations we experience that resemble those we caused others to experience. The environmental result influences where we are born and the type of environment in which we live.

This verse speaks of the results similar to nonvirtuous causes. Taking the lives of others will result in our life being cut short in future lives. Experiencing a short life in this lifetime is the result of killing done in past lives.

Harming and inflicting violence on others results in receiving much harm ourselves in future lives. Being beat up or maimed by others or experiencing great physical pain even though we haven't physically harmed others in this life is the result of inflicting violence on others in past lives.

The result of stealing and taking what has not been freely given to us is being poor and having few possessions. Experiencing poverty or having difficulties accessing and using our possessions in this life is the result of stealing in previous lives.

Adultery causes many relationship problems in future lives, so that your spouse becomes like an enemy. Alternatively, your spouse may run off with someone else, and in that sense as well you will have enemies.

> 15. By lying one becomes reviled;
>   through speaking divisively, one loses friends;
>   due to speaking harshly, one hears unpleasant sounds;
>   from engaging in idle talk, one's words will be disregarded.

Facing a lot of criticism and blame even though we haven't done anything to cause it in this life is the result similar to the cause of our having lied in a past life. Lying in this life will result in being criticized and reviled in future lives. Being separated from good friends and having longtime harmonious friendships crumble is the result of divisive speech. Hearing many unpleasant remarks, such as ridicule and scorn, is the result of harsh speech.

Sometimes other people think we're lying although what we say is true; other times we express an honest opinion or contribute a good idea, but others disregard it and don't respect what we say. These are results of idle talk.

> 16. Covetousness destroys one's desired objects;
>   malice is said to bestow fear;
>   wrong views lead to evil worldviews;
>   consuming intoxicants brings mental confusion.

Covetousness results in being unable to obtain what we desire and being hindered from accomplishing our plans and goals. Being easily frightened or very suspicious of others is the result of *malice* toward others. Inability to think clearly about the correct view, attraction to wrong views, and many deceitful thoughts are caused by holding *wrong views* in previous lives. *Consuming intoxicants* brings mental confusion and lack of clarity in both this and future lives.

The result similar to the cause is of two types: in terms of our experience and in terms of our behavior. The examples given above are results similar to the cause in terms of our experience. The result similar to the cause in terms of our behavior is the tendency to do those same actions again in the future. For example, as a result of killing in one life, someone has the wish to kill and enjoys killing in a future life. Someone may have a habit of lying or may repeatedly have extramarital affairs due to familiarity with those behaviors in previous lives.

When the three branches are complete, the action has the potential to bring all of the results over the span of several lifetimes. For example, taking life will bring the ripening result of rebirth in the lower realms. When later born as a human, that person will experience a short life (result similar to the cause in terms of the experience) and will be inclined toward violent behavior and killing in future lives (result similar to the cause in terms of behavior). The latter is the worst of the results of nonvirtue because it results in our repeatedly engaging in the same destructive action, thus creating more karma to experience all of the other results. This is much more serious than being born in the hell realms, because the pain of a hellish rebirth is finite— it stops when the action's karmic potential is exhausted. Remembering the disadvantages of the result similar to the cause in terms of our behavior is a good incentive for working to transform our destructive habits.

When we take and keep precepts, we make a determination to stop our habitual destructive tendencies, thus counteracting results similar to the cause in terms of our behavior. Purifying nonvirtuous paths of action by means of the four opponent powers also opposes this result, because one of the powers is the determination not to do the action again. The other three opponent powers are regret, taking refuge and generating bodhichitta, and engaging in remedial activities.

The environmental result manifests as our living in a certain place. For example, killing will cause us to live in a place filled with conflicts and war. In addition, the food, drink, and medicine there will not be potent. Lying will result in living in a place with a foul odor, surrounded by untrustworthy people where fear and corruption in society is rampant. Sometimes we meet people who have the opportunity to leave an unpleasant place and live elsewhere, yet they insist they must stay there. That is the environmental result of their past destructive actions.

Why do these three results come from one action? Each of the elements of a complete action principally brings one of these results. Our motivation principally brings the ripening result; the actual action mainly brings the result similar to the cause; and the conclusion of the action principally causes the environmental result.

> 17. Through not giving gifts one is poor;
>   wrong livelihood results in getting tricked;
>   arrogance leads to a lowly station;
>   jealousy brings about unattractive appearance.

> 18. From anger comes a bad complexion;
>   stupidity from not questioning the wise.
>   These are the effects when one is [reborn as] a human,
>   but prior to all of them is a bad rebirth.

Stinginess results in being poor in future lives, and financial difficulties in this life are the result of not being generous in previous lives. Being surrounded by people who try to deceive and trick us—for example, proposing bad investments or borrowing money they have no intention of returning—is the result of engaging in wrong livelihood in past lives. Being born in a low social position or in a group that faces prejudice is the result of being arrogant and condescending in past lives. When our body is feeble, lacks vitality, and has an unpleasant appearance, this is the result of being jealous of others' wealth and possessions in previous lives.

Having an unattractive face is caused by anger in past lives. Being of lesser intelligence comes from not following wise teachers or studying with unqualified teachers in previous lives. Perhaps we had the opportunity to learn the Dharma but weren't interested, got distracted, or didn't respect people with good qualities. As a result, in this life we don't meet wise spiritual mentors who properly explain to us what to practice and what to abandon on the path, and thus we remain confused and ignorant.

Ripening Results

The ripening result of an action is experienced first, then the results similar to the cause and environmental results. In the *Levels of Yogic Practice* (*Yogacharabhumi*) Asanga says that destructive actions done with a very strong motivation bring the ripening result of rebirth in a hell realm. Those done with a motivation of middling intensity result in rebirth as a hungry ghost (*preta*), and others done with a weak motivation cause rebirth as an animal. This is posited from the viewpoint of the intensity and duration of suffering because hell beings experience the strongest pain for a long time, hungry ghosts experience suffering of medium intensity, and animals have the least misery.

The *Sutra of the Ten Grounds* (*Dashabhumika Sutra*) explains the ripening result in a slightly different manner, saying that rebirth as an animal is the result of destructive actions done with a middling motivation and rebirth as a hungry ghost is the result of nonvirtue done with a weak motivation. This presentation is made from the perspective of the minds of sentient beings in those realms. Hungry ghosts have a clearer mind and are more intelligent than animals, so it is easier for them to improve their situation and enter the path to liberation than it is for animals. For that reason, they are said to have shorter and less intense suffering than animals. Both explanations are valid.

> 19. Such are widely known to be the ripening results
>   of these [actions] that are called the nonvirtues.
>   For all of the virtuous actions
>   there are the opposite effects.

To review, Nagarjuna first instructed us in the sixteen practices that will bring higher rebirth. A series of higher rebirths will give us the opportunity to generate the wisdom realizing emptiness, which is the actual antidote that brings liberation and awakening. He then explained that non-Buddhists do not follow this path, but with obscured minds, they follow incorrect paths that do not benefit and in fact harm themselves and others. With compassion, so that we won't waste our lives by mistakenly engaging in destructive actions, he explained their three results—ripening result, result similar to the cause, and environmental result.

The Result of Virtuous Karma

We create virtuous paths of action by either restraining from nonvirtuous paths of action or by acting in the opposite way; for example, saving life, protecting others' property, and speaking in ways that create harmony among people. Virtuous paths of action will bring results opposite to those of nonvirtuous paths of action. It is helpful to go through the paths of virtue one by one and contemplate the three results in terms of each.

> 20. Attachment, anger, confusion,
>   and the karma that arises from them are nonvirtuous.
>   Non-attachment, non-anger, non-confusion,
>   and the karmas that arise from them are virtuous.

Detailed Explanation of the Results of Virtue and Nonvirtue

Destructive or nonvirtuous karma refers to actions of body, speech, and mind done under the influence of attachment, anger, or confusion. Not only are attachment, anger, and confusion by nature nonvirtuous,[5] but also any actions of body, speech, and mind motivated by them are nonvirtuous.

It is not too difficult to understand that attachment creates destructive karma. When attachment arises to one's body, food, clothing, possessions, and so forth, people steal others' possessions, use their sexuality unwisely and unkindly, lie to get what they want, scream at others, talk behind their back, and so forth. This is quite apparent. It is also clear that when anger arises in our minds, it is easy for us to hurt others physically and verbally— hitting them, swearing at them, and threatening them—thus creating nonvirtuous karma.

In the Tibetan language, *confusion* (*gti mug*) and *ignorance* (*ma rig pa*) have the same meaning. There are two forms of ignorance/confusion: (1) ignorance of the ultimate nature of reality, which grasps phenomena as inherently existent, and (2) ignorance regarding karma and its effects. The

---

5. This pertains to the desire realm where attachment, anger, and confusion regarding karma and its effects are naturally nonvirtuous. In the material and immaterial realms, beings do not have anger, and their attachment and confusion are neutral, not nonvirtuous.

ignorance of the ultimate nature is not naturally negative—it is neutral—for it motivates both the nonvirtuous and virtuous karma of ordinary beings. However, the ignorance of karma and its effects is naturally negative because it is confused regarding virtue and nonvirtue; it believes that nonvirtue is virtue and virtue is nonvirtue. This confusion is present whenever we create nonvirtuous karma.

Propelling karma is the karma that propels us into the next life. All propelling karma—virtuous and nonvirtuous—is created under the influence of self-grasping ignorance and thus is polluted. However, virtuous propelling karma is not affected by ignorance of karma and its effects. For example, the self-grasping ignorance present when we make prostrations is neutral, while the strong faith that is also present is virtuous. This karma is polluted virtuous karma that will lead to rebirth as a human being or god.

On the other hand, nonvirtuous propelling karma is motivated by both ignorance of the ultimate nature and ignorance of karma and its effects. For instance, when someone has a false sense of entitlement he may lie to and cheat others, believing that as long as he doesn't get caught it is permissible to act in this way. Or someone may conduct an animal sacrifice, mistakenly thinking that it will please a god and the animal offered to the god will attain liberation. In both these situations, the destructive karma is motivated by both the ignorance of the ultimate nature and the ignorance of karma and its effects; it is polluted nonvirtuous karma.

The confusion spoken of in this verse is the ignorance or confusion regarding karma and its effects. Together with attachment and anger, these three poisons are negative by nature as are the actions produced by them. However, karmas created out of confusion are not necessarily destructive, because that confusion could be in regard to the ultimate nature of phenomena.

Non-attachment, non-anger, and non-confusion are not simply the absence of attachment, anger, and confusion, respectively. Rather, they relate to their object in the opposite way: non-attachment is an open, balanced attitude that doesn't crave or cling to the object or person; non-anger is loving-kindness; and non-confusion is intelligence that correctly understands karma and its effects. These three are virtuous by nature, and the karma they create is also virtuous.

21. From nonvirtue comes all suffering,
     likewise all unfortunate rebirths.
     From virtue comes all fortunate rebirths
     and the happiness within all births.

The ripening result of nonvirtuous karma is rebirth in the lower realms. The result similar to the cause of nonvirtuous karma is the pain and suffering in the mindstreams of humans and desire realm gods, as well as the pain and suffering in the mindstreams of those born in the lower realms. Although the karmic cause for a rebirth is either virtuous or nonvirtuous, the rebirth itself—the five mental and physical aggregates that are the ripening result of that karma—is neither virtuous nor nonvirtuous.

The ripening result of virtuous karma is higher rebirth. The happiness we enjoy in that life, as well as whatever little happiness sentient beings in the lower realms experience, are the causally concordant result in terms of our experience. Living virtuously creates the cause to experience happiness life after life.

The invariable propelling karma that leads to rebirth in the material and immaterial realms is a form of virtuous karma. It is called "invariable" because it is created by attaining certain levels of meditative concentration. Depending on the level attained, rebirth in the corresponding level of the material and immaterial realms occurs. The rebirth does not vary from the level of concentration attained by that human being.

22. Thus Dharma [of higher rebirth] is considered to be twofold:
     one should not engage in nonvirtue
     through mind, body, or speech,
     but one should always engage in virtue [through those three].

How to Practice and the Result of Practice

Every day reflect on lower rebirths and the pain experienced in them as well as the suffering experienced by humans and celestial beings of the desire realm. Reflect that all this misery arises for yourself and others due to ignorance, anger, and attachment, and the physical, verbal, and mental paths of karma motivated by them. Think about rebirth in the upper realms and the happiness experienced by beings there, as well as whatever happiness beings in the lower realms experience. All of the happiness and joy that you and others experience is due to non-attachment, non-anger, non-confusion, and the paths of action motivated by these. Then, strongly resolve to create virtue and abandon nonvirtue, and carry through on that resolve as best you can by abandoning the thirteen actions to abandon and practicing the three to adopt.

When attachment, anger, or confusion arises in your mind, try to notice it immediately and apply the antidotes. If you don't, the three poisons will increase until you won't even be able to see them as faults. When you are successful in taming your mind, your life will be meaningful, and you will accomplish your aims of higher rebirth and highest good.

> 23. Through this Dharma one is freed from
>   [rebirth as] a hell being, hungry ghost, or animal.
>   As a human or celestial being one obtains
>   all happiness, glory, and sovereignty.

> 24. And through the concentrations, immeasurables, and
>   immaterial [absorptions]
>   one experiences the pleasure of Brahma and so on.
>   Such, in summary, is the Dharma
>   for higher rebirth and its results.

As a result of practicing, you will not be born in the hell, hungry ghost, or animal realms. You will also experience the various kinds of happiness of humans and celestial beings. By meditating on the fourth material concentration and the four meditative absorptions of the immaterial realm, you will have the feeling of equanimity, which is said to surpass the bliss of the first three material concentrations. Abandoning the thirteen nonvirtuous actions and practicing the three virtuous actions is an excellent way of living that enables us to die without regret.

There are two kinds of desire: one is a positive aspiration and the other is attachment, an affliction. The desire to attain liberation and awakening doesn't disturb or agitate the mind. To the contrary, it makes the mind clear and peaceful. The desire to be born in the upper realms is considered a Dharma motivation, though higher rebirths themselves are ultimately to be abandoned because they are taken under the influence of ignorance and polluted karma. However, we need them in order to eventually attain liberation and awakening. In other words, the desire to have a higher rebirth, especially so that we can use it as a basis to attain highest good, is virtuous, even though it is motivated by ignorance and may be tinged with self-centeredness.

To create the virtuous propelling karma that brings about rebirth as a human being or god, we must have an aspiration to attain these. Ignorance is the initial or causal motivation for the virtuous karma that will ripen in a higher rebirth. The immediate motivation at the time of actually doing virtuous actions is not attachment. When we practice generosity, ethical conduct, and fortitude properly, our motivation is virtuous. Non-attachment is present when we give, non-harmfulness when we practice ethical conduct, and non-anger when we practice fortitude. Non-confusion is present during all three. These three are virtuous mental factors.

3. The Path to Liberation and Full Awakening

Cause and Effect of the Highest Good

To attain our noble spiritual goals of liberation and full awakening—the wisdom directly and nonconceptually realizing emptiness of inherent existence of all persons and phenomena is essential. This wisdom develops gradually, first by hearing and studying the teachings, then by contemplating and reflecting on them to ensure we understand them correctly, and finally by integrating them in our mind through meditation.

The way in which things presently appear to us is not the way in which they exist. They appear to have an inherent or true essence, to exist objectively from their own side. Our innate self-grasping ignorance, which keeps us wandering endlessly in cyclic existence, holds them to exist in the false way they appear. Our wisdom must question this false appearance in order to realize how phenomena actually exist.

People without sufficient merit are frightened to question the appearances of objects in daily life that they take for granted. Nagarjuna speaks of this first, then explains how we enter cyclic existence and how to cease it and attain nirvana. This is followed by an in-depth explanation of the ultimate nature of reality that is free of the two extreme views of absolutism and nihilism.

> 25. But the Victors said
> that the Dharma of the highest good
> is subtle, profound, and appearing;
> it is frightening to unlearned, childish beings.

The Qualities of the Highest Good

The practice or Dharma of the highest good refers to the methods or causes for attaining liberation and full awakening—principally the wisdom realizing selflessness. The object of the wisdom realizing selflessness is emptiness, the absence of inherent existence of persons and phenomena. Selflessness is subtle, in that the minds of ordinary beings and conventional consciousnesses cannot realize it directly. It is profound because it is difficult to fathom and understand completely. Its meaning is very deep because to realize emptiness or selflessness, we have to first realize the lack of a permanent, unitary, independent self. Going deeper, we must realize the lack of a self-sufficient, substantially existent person. Finally, refuting the assertions of the Svatantrikas and proponents of other philosophical schools, we must go very deep to realize the emptiness of inherent existence. Emptiness has the quality of appearing in that it appears to the minds of intelligent beings who possess great merit and special wisdom.

Unlearned, childish beings—people who are not versed in the meaning of emptiness, who lack great merit, and who haven't listened to many teachings—become afraid when they hear an explanation on the meaning of emptiness. As a result, emptiness cannot appear to their minds.

26. "I am not, I will not be.
    I have not, I will not have."
    Stated thus, [the teaching of selflessness] terrifies the childish.
    For the wise it puts an end to fear.

The Naive Fear Emptiness but the Wise Do Not

The naive become afraid when they hear about emptiness of an inherently existent person because they misunderstand it to mean that the conventionally existing self does not exist. When they hear that the person cannot be found when searched for in the basis of designation—the physical and mental aggregates that constitute the person—they think that the person does not exist at all. That idea terrifies them.

Similarly, when they hear that the mental and physical aggregates—what is possessed by the person and is considered mine—cannot be found in their bases of designation (the collection of their components), they mistakenly believe that the body and mind don't exist at all. Thinking that if the person and the aggregates do not exist now, they do not exist in future lives either, they become terrified that after death there is only nothingness, total nonexistence. In this way, they fall to the extreme of nihilism.

In brief, naive people think, "I do not exist in the present, so I will not exist in future. Since I don't have a body and mind now, then I will not have them in future lives either." Because they lack merit, wisdom, and intelligence, when they hear teachings on the meaning of emptiness, they think that everything becomes nonexistent. They erroneously believe that the person who meditates on selflessness, the person who realizes selflessness, and the person who attains liberation do not exist, and in this way they become afraid and shy away from emptiness. Nagarjuna says in *Treatise on the Middle Way* (24.11):

> By a misperception of emptiness a person of little intelligence is destroyed,
> Like a snake incorrectly seized or a spell incorrectly cast.

When those who lack proper study and a correct understanding meditate on emptiness, there is danger that they meditate incorrectly and come to the wrong conclusion. Falling to the extreme of nihilism and thinking that karma and its effects do not exist, their behavior becomes reckless and their destructive actions lead them to ruin. This is similar to a person who grasps a poisonous snake improperly—instead of being able to extract the medicine from the snake, he will be bitten by it.

However, for the wise—those who correctly understand the ultimate nature—meditating on emptiness liberates them, thus putting an end to their fear of the duhkha of cyclic existence. To meditate on the emptiness of the person, contemplate, "If a person exists from its own side, the way it appears, it must be findable either in its basis of designation—the mental and physical aggregates—or totally separate from them." Then investigate whether it is actually possible for a person to exist in either of these ways.

Under such investigation we do not find a person that exists from its own side: a person that exists totally independent of everything else. Understanding this, we conclude that the person is therefore empty of inherent existence and focus our minds on this emptiness. At this time we do not think, "I am meditating on emptiness." We just focus on the absence of an inherently existent person. When you go very deep into the meditation on emptiness, there is no appearance of any conventionalities such as the person or aggregates. There is only emptiness, like empty space.

During meditative equipoise on emptiness, the mind ceases to apprehend the person as truly existing. There is no appearance of the conventionally existing person at that time. A conventional reliable cognizer—that is, a mind that can apprehend the conventionally existing person—does not function during meditative equipoise on emptiness.

Upon arising from meditation on emptiness, we reflect that the person is not completely nonexistent; it does exist conventionally. It exists dependent on other factors. By meditating on emptiness repeatedly in this way, self-grasping ignorance is gradually worn down until it is completely dismantled.

To review, when people who are uneducated and naive regarding emptiness hear that I and mine do not exist objectively, from their own side, they misunderstand and think that a person who experiences pleasure doesn't exist and that the possessions and people that give them pleasure don't exist either. That thought causes fear. When one refutes inherent existence, even the followers of the lower Buddhist philosophical systems—the Vaibhashikas, Sautrantikas, Chittamatrins, and Svatantrikas—think that then the person who creates karma and the one who experiences its happy or painful results are nonexistent, and they, too, fall to the extreme of nihilism and become afraid at that prospect. None of these people actually meditate on the correct meaning of the emptiness of true existence.

On the other hand, the wise who understand the meaning of emptiness and the stages of the path do not become afraid because they know that while things don't inherently exist, they do exist dependently. Unlike those who believe emptiness means total nonexistence, they know that it means things exist nominally. This brings them great joy because they know they have now entered the path that will free them from the fears of cyclic existence and lead them to liberation.

> 27. All beings arise from I-grasping
>   such that they grasp mine;
>   this is what has been stated
>   by the one who speaks solely for the benefit of beings.

Fear Is Due to True-Grasping

Ordinary beings fear emptiness because they cannot differentiate between the conventionally existent I that is the object of the reliable cognizer apprehending I, and the inherently existent I that is the object of the I-grasping. The Tibetan word *'dzin* can be translated as either "apprehend" or "grasp," depending on the context. This double meaning illustrates two ways of cognizing a person. With the first, we apprehend a conventionally existent person. This occurs when without any special emotion we say, "I'm sitting" or "I'm thinking." That I exists, and the awareness that apprehends it is valid in that it correctly identifies a person. This is the person that creates karma, is reborn, and attains awakening. With the second, we reify the I, grasping it as inherently existent. The "object" of this cognizer, an inherently existent I, does not exist at all because nothing exists inherently. The I-grasping mind that grasps it is an erroneous awareness.

There are two types of self-grasping: the self-grasping of persons and the self-grasping of phenomena. According to the Prasangikas, they grasp their respective objects—the person and other phenomena—as truly or inherently existent. The difference between these two types of self-grasping is the basis of the grasping: the I or other phenomena, such as the aggregates. In general, the I or person is also considered a phenomenon, but when we talk of the two selves or the two selflessnesses, phenomena refers to all other phenomena except the person.

Don't get confused here: sometimes the word *self* refers to the person, the I, while other times it refers to inherent existence, the object of negation that doesn't exist at all. The latter is the meaning of "self" in "self-grasping," where the term applies to grasping any phenomenon as inherently existent, and "selflessness," which is the absence of inherent existence. For the Prasangikas, self-grasping has the same meaning as true-grasping (grasping true existence), grasping inherent existence, grasping phenomena to exist from their own side, and so forth. I-grasping is a type of self-grasping of persons: it grasps our own I or mine as inherently existent and is also known as the *view of a personal identity* (*satkayadrishti*).

The Buddha, the one who speaks solely for the benefit of beings, says that all beings arise from I-grasping. Chandrakirti explains the meaning of this in the introductory stanzas of his *Supplement*: ordinary beings first think "I," thus generating the view of a personal identity grasping I. They then generate the view of a personal identity grasping mine. The latter is generated by thinking "my body," "my eyes," and so forth and refers to the person who is the "owner" of these. Due to the innate[6] grasping at I and mine, sentient beings create polluted karma that causes rebirth in cyclic existence. In this way, the person arises due to the view of a personal identity.

I-grasping not only is the source of beings' rebirth in cyclic existence but also keeps them trapped in cyclic existence by making them fear emptiness, the realization of emptiness being the one thing that can liberate them. To benefit beings and free them from cyclic existence, the Buddha taught the meaning of emptiness.

DISPELLING CONFUSION ABOUT THE ULTIMATE NATURE OF REALITY

Nagarjuna now extensively explains the ultimate nature of reality so that we can cultivate the wisdom realizing the emptiness of inherent existence, which will destroy the true-grasping that binds us to cyclic existence. He begins by examining the I and mine—the person as she is and the person as the owner of the five aggregates. Although they falsely appear to exist with an inherent essence and we grasp this false appearance to be true, they do not exist in this way. Using the example of a reflection in a mirror helps us to understand this.

> 28. Ultimately, the notions "I exist"
>   and "What is mine exists" are false because
>   from the perspective of knowing [things] as they truly are,
>   there is neither [I nor mine].

Ultimately False, Conventionally Existent

Conventionally I and mine exist; ultimately they do not. The mind grasping I and mine as existing ultimately is an erroneous consciousness.

If I and mine existed inherently as they appear, they would be the object of an arya's wisdom of meditative equipoise. That wisdom directly and

---

6. There are two levels of grasping: innate and acquired. Innate grasping has existed begin-ninglessly in the mindstreams of ordinary beings and automatically goes from one life to the next. Acquired grasping is learned through contact with incorrect philosophies and psychological theories. Acquired grasping is easier to eliminate on the path; innate grasping is much more difficult to eradicate.

nonconceptually perceives ultimate reality; it knows phenomena as they actually are, and so it would certainly see them. However, aryas' wisdom of meditative equipoise does not perceive inherent existence. It perceives the opposite: the emptiness of inherent existence. Inherently existent I and mine—and any inherently existent phenomenon for that matter—are not perceived by this profound wisdom. Therefore, inherent existence cannot be the ultimate mode of existence. The wisdom of the aryas that knows things as they actually are perceives only the emptiness of inherent existence. Nothing else even appears to that mind.

There is no discrepancy between how emptiness appears to the aryas' wisdom knowing reality and how emptiness exists. Emptiness itself is empty of inherent existence and it appears as such. Since an inherently existent I and mine—the objects of grasping I and mine—don't appear to that wisdom, they don't exist at all.

Conventionally existent things, such as the I and mine apprehended by a valid mind, do not exist the way they appear. To our ordinary minds they appear to exist inherently whereas they do not. Although they do not appear to the aryas' wisdom of meditative equipoise, this does not negate their existence, because conventionally existent things are not in the purview of the aryas' wisdom of meditative equipoise. In other words, the wisdom knowing the ultimate nature is not capable of validating the existence of conventional objects; a conventional valid cognizer does that.

A valid mind apprehending I and mine is a conventional reliable cognizer. It is correct with respect to the conventional nature of things—it knows we can use a car to go somewhere. However, it is not correct with respect to the ultimate nature of things because its objects do not exist as they appear. They mistakenly appear inherently existent, whereas they are not. The conventional reliable cognizers of ordinary beings cannot perceive the ultimate nature of phenomena.

A reliable cognizer of the ultimate nature does not apprehend conventionally existent objects because they are not in its purview. It perceives only the emptiness of inherent existence. Because it does, it knows that inherently existent phenomena do not exist at all.

> 29. The aggregates arise from I-grasping;
> the I-grasping is ultimately unreal.

How then can there really be any arising
of that whose seed is unreal?

We have been wandering in cyclic existence since beginningless time. Under the control of the innate I-grasping mind, we generate afflictions, which create karma. Having created this karma that is polluted by ignorance, we take birth in cyclic existence by assuming the mental and physical aggregates of this life. In this way, our body and mind arise from innate I-grasping. Innate I-grasping is false and unreal in that things appear to it as if they existed from their own side, and it believes this is how they in fact exist. Yet ignorance is false and erroneous. If the cause is false, the result must also be false; and if the cause is erroneous, the result will not be good.

Think about it: How could ignorance produce buddhas and bodhisattvas? How could attachment, anger, and confusion produce holy beings who have eradicated those afflictions? It is impossible.

30. Seeing the way that the aggregates are unreal,
    one forsakes self-grasping.
    Having forsaken self-grasping,
    the [afflictive] aggregates do not arise again.

By Abandoning Ignorance, One Attains Liberation

The wisdom realizing emptiness ceases rebirth in cyclic existence. When we understand that the aggregates are not truly existent, we can see that the grasping at I and mine is false and erroneous. By repeatedly meditating on this, we can gradually eradicate the mind grasping them as truly existent. By abandoning this erroneous grasping, the afflictions based on it are gradually extinguished. Thus the karma motivated by self-grasping and afflictions is no longer created, rebirth in cyclic existence comes to an end, and liberation, the state free from true duhkha and its causes, is attained.

Since hearers and solitary realizers have attained liberation and become arhats, they have necessarily meditated on the emptiness of both the person and phenomena. Although the lower Buddhist philosophical systems say that simply realizing the selflessness that is the lack of a self-sufficient, substantially existent person is adequate to attain liberation, in fact it is necessary to realize the emptiness of inherent existence of both persons and the aggregates. Hearers and solitary realizers have done just that.

> 31. Depending upon a mirror,
>   the reflection of one's face is seen,
>   but it does not ultimately
>   exist at all.

> 32. Likewise, depending on the aggregates,
>   I-grasping exists,
>   but that [I] does not truly exist
>   just like the reflection of one's face.

Depending on a mirror, the reflected image of our face appears. That appearance of a face is false; there is in fact no face in the mirror. Similarly, dependent on grasping the aggregates as truly existent, grasping the I as truly existent arises. However, the truly existent I that is the conceived object of the I-grasping doesn't exist. Just as the appearance of a real face in the mirror is false and a baby's apprehension of it as real is erroneous, the appearance of a truly existent I is false, and grasping it as true is an erroneous consciousness.

When the reflection of a face appears in the mirror, a face appears from all parts of the reflection. It is not that some aspects or some parts of the reflected image appear to be a face and other aspects do not. Similarly, for ordinary beings, every aspect of the person and every aspect of the aggregates appear to be truly existent. It's not that some aspects or parts appear to truly exist and others do not.

Except for very young children, most people understand that a face appearing in a mirror is not real. However, that is not the case with the person and aggregates that appear to be truly existent. Most people assent to that appearance and believe things truly exist as they appear.

How to Meditate on the Emptiness of the I

One method to realize that the I does not truly exist—that it is empty of true existence—is to meditate on four essential points that examine the relationship of the I and the aggregates.

(1) Begin by identifying the object of negation (what is to be negated), the I as it appears to the innate I-grasping. One method to identify the way this false I appears is to think about especially bad or good situations you have experienced. At those times, the false I, the truly existent I, appears. You have to look at it skillfully and immediately, otherwise you won't be able to see the way it appears because it quickly becomes mixed with something else. The body does not appear to innate I-grasping, nor does the collection of the aggregates. However, the appearance of a truly existent I easily gets mixed with these.

The philosophical systems that assert a permanent, unitary, independent self and the systems that negate the self being the aggregates, the collection of the aggregates, or the shape of the aggregates all accept a coarse object of negation: the appearance of the color and shape of the body or the appearance of the collection of the aggregates. But this is not the appearance of the subtle object of negation, an inherently existent person.

The I appears to the innate I-grasping as if it had its own nature and yet was mixed in with the body and mind. It seems to be self-existent, able to stand alone as an objective entity. But this only happens for a very short moment before it appears mixed with something else. When we are either very upset and angry or very happy, the appearance of an inherently existent I is clearer, and it is easier to identify such an I as the object of negation.

To know only that inherent existence is the object to be negated is not sufficient to clearly recognize it as such. Although we may be able to explain what the object of negation is to others, our understanding is only on the level of words. We must understand it for ourselves more deeply through meditation. When you have ascertained the appearance of just the I itself appearing self-existent, without the appearance of the body or the collection of the aggregates, you have understood the first of the four essential points in the meditation on emptiness: ascertaining the object of negation.

(2) Now, while still holding the appearance of the inherently existent I, a corner of your mind decides, "If the I exists as it appears, then it must be one with the aggregates—identical to them—or different from the aggregates—totally separate from them. There is no other possibility." Only these two choices are possible if things existed inherently, because inherently existent things cannot depend on any other factors. Thus if the I existed inherently and independent of everything else, it would have to be either identical with the aggregates or totally unrelated to and separate from them. When your

mind is clear about this, you have understood the second essential point, ascertaining the pervasion.

(3) Next, while holding that appearance of an inherently existent I, a corner of your mind investigates whether the I exists inherently as it appears or not. Start with examining if the I is one and the same as the aggregates. Consider the various faults that would arise if they were identical. For example, if the I and the aggregates were identical, whatever you said about the I should pertain to the aggregates and vice versa. For example, the body arose from the combined sperm and egg of our parents, so the I should have also arisen from the combination of the sperm and the egg. But that isn't the case. If the I were identical with the body, then we would be our body and there would be no need for a consciousness from a previous life to join with the sperm and egg in order to create a person. Similarly, if the I were the consciousness, then when we said, "I'm walking," it would mean the consciousness is walking, which is ridiculous! If the I were one and the same as the consciousness, the word *I* itself would be superfluous and useless.

(4) On the other hand, if the person were different from the aggregates in the context of true existence, it would be totally unrelated to the aggregates. In that case if you took away each of the aggregates—form, feeling, and so forth—one by one, a person would still remain at the end. If the aggregates were on one side of the room, the person could be on the other. That, too, is not the case.

Thus we conclude that in the context of true existence, the person cannot be either one with or different from the aggregates, and we ascertain that the I does not exist independently in the way that it appears to the innate self-grasping mind. We then concentrate on the non-true existence of the I, the emptiness or lack of such an I.

When you meditate, don't think there is some kind of innate I-grasping over there and contemplate the I that appears to that. Rather, make this personal by thinking of your own I-grasping. How does the I appear to it? Does it actually exist in the way it appears?

In short, to realize that the I does not exist the way it appears, try to understand the way it appears to your innate self-grasping and then refute the I actually existing in that way. People who have received instructions on how to meditate on emptiness from their spiritual mentors first identify how the I appears to their mind. Then they observe how their minds grasp the I. In your practice, keep making this innate I-grasping arise and observe how the I appears and how the I-grasping holds it. When you do this repeatedly, you will gain some experience of the object of negation.

There are several reasons we can use to prove that things don't exist inherently as they appear: they are neither a truly existent unity nor a truly existent plurality; they are neither inherently identical nor different from their parts; they do not arise in any of the four extreme ways—from themselves, from another, from both, or without any cause; they do not exist in any of the seven ways Chandrakirti described in his *Supplement*; and they are dependent arisings.

Not Existing as It Appears

There are varying levels of subtlety to realizing that the face in the mirror does not exist as it appears. Ordinary people are able to realize with direct valid perception that although a reflection appears to be an actual face, it does not exist as it appears. This is the coarse level of false appearance. The reflection also appears to be truly existent; this is a subtler level of false appearance. The fact that ordinary people can realize that the reflection doesn't exist in the way it appears doesn't mean they have realized that it is not truly existent. If they had, they would have realized emptiness and become aryas. Rather, they have simply understood that it is not an actual face although it appears to be one.

The eye consciousness to which this reflection appears as a face is a mistaken consciousness. Although it is also mistaken with respect to the reflection appearing truly existent, principally it is mistaken with respect to the reflection appearing to be a face. That is because to realize that that consciousness is mistaken, we need to realize only that although the reflection appears to be a face, it is not actually a face.

Not every thought of I that we have during the day—such as "I am eating," "I am meditating"—is innate I-grasping. In the course of a day, when nothing special is happening, we have thoughts such as "I am going," "I am reading," or "I am thinking." These thoughts apprehend the conventionally existent I and are reliable minds. They are mistaken consciousnesses in that they have the appearance of inherent existence, but since they do not grasp that appearance to be true they are not erroneous. They correctly apprehend that we are walking, reading, or thinking. These consciousnesses are mistaken with respect to their appearing objects because the I appears truly existent to them. However, they are not erroneous because they know their apprehended object—the I—correctly. The Prasaṅgika system says that every consciousness in the continuum of a sentient being[7]—except for the aryas' wisdom of meditative equipoise—is a mistaken consciousness because it is mistaken with respect to its appearing object.

Those with meditative experience have explained this process sequentially. First there is a moment of valid mind to which a truly existent I appears. It thinks, for example, "I am walking," but it does not grasp the I as truly existent. The moment after that, the innate I-grasping arises, yet the continuity of that valid mind does not become the innate I-grasping. Rather, the next moment a distinct mind—the innate I-grasping—arises, grasping at the I as existing the way it appears.

The mind apprehending the conventionally existing I and the innate I-grasping are difficult to distinguish, because true existence appears to both of them. However, only the latter grasps true existence. For example, to the valid mind apprehending the table as existent, there is the appearance of the table being truly existent. However, that valid mind doesn't grasp the table as truly existent. If it did, it would be self-grasping, a wrong consciousness.

Those who have a great deal of experience meditating on emptiness and are close to realizing it say that recognizing the object of negation is difficult. But once this point is clear to you and you have correctly identified the I as it appears to the innate I-grasping, you are close to realizing emptiness.

New students should know that to arrive at this subtle point, meditators have observed the self-grasping of person and phenomena in their own minds for a long time. Because they have studied the great treatises and sutras, they know the different levels of subtlety of the self-grasping and can identify them clearly in their own experience.

Grasping inherent existence is an afflictive obscuration that must be eradicated to attain liberation. The appearance of inherent existence is a cognitive obscuration that is subtler and must be eliminated to attain buddhahood. Only a buddha has fully abandoned the appearance of inherent existence.

---

7. A sentient being is any being with a mind except for buddhas. The continuum of a sentient being is the psychophysical continuity of that sentient being that exists over time.

Abandoning All Conceptions Is Not the Realization of Emptiness

Some people do not know how to identify the object of negation correctly and assert that freedom from all conceptuality is liberation. They believe that both correct and incorrect conceptions must be abandoned, even at the initial stage of learning about emptiness. They say all conceptuality is the cause of cyclic existence, just as all shackles—be they gold or iron—bind us.

If this view were correct and all conceptuality were negative, we would have to give up bodhichitta and the entire method side of the path because to practice them we must use concepts. We would also have to stop learning and thinking about emptiness, and we could not use inference to realize emptiness, because those activities involve conceptual consciousness.

These people cannot be blamed for thinking like this. The Buddha said that the conceptual mind should be abandoned. But these people didn't understand that statement in light of the Buddha's skillfulness in teaching disciples according to their disposition and capacity. Nor did they understand that the Buddha gave both provisional and definitive teachings. While suitable for certain people at a particular time, the provisional teachings are not to be taken literally or applied to everyone. The definitive teachings, on the other hand, talk about profound emptiness. His statement about abandoning all conceptuality was a provisional teaching.

Along the same lines, some sutras say that when one thinks phenomena are neither existent nor nonexistent, one will be liberated. If we take that statement literally, we have a conundrum because then we can't validly establish anything. If we don't rely on Nagarjuna, who clearly indicated the difference between definitive and provisional sutras, we won't be able to discern which teachings were taught to people with a Chittamatra disposition, which were given to people with a Sautrantika disposition, and so on. By relying on Nagarjuna, we will be able to understand the Buddha's final intention and attain liberation.

> 33. Without depending on the mirror,
> the reflection of one's face is not seen.
> Likewise, without depending on the aggregates,
> there is no [notion of an] I.

Without a mirror, the reflection of our face doesn't appear. Similarly, without the aggregates, the innate I-grasping doesn't arise. To understand the way this occurs, we have to examine how the I that is designated in dependence upon the aggregates appears to that mind. This way we understand that the appearance of the I depends on the aggregates, although the aggregates do not appear to the innate I-grasping.

When the aggregates appear to us, they appear truly existent. The appearance of truly existent aggregates swiftly induces the self-grasping that grasps the aggregates as truly existent. Upon this basis, the notion of a truly existent I arises in our mind. Thus without the appearance of the aggregates, the I-grasping does not arise. The I appears to this innate I-grasping to be totally independent of everything else, as if it were an autonomous entity that set itself up and existed by itself. This is the object of negation. Remember, if it seems that the aggregates or the color and shape of the body appear to the innate I-grasping, then according to the Prasangikas we haven't yet arrived at the subtle object of negation.

The self-grasping of persons and self-grasping of phenomena arise in a certain order. First there is self-grasping of phenomena, when the mind grasps the aggregates to be truly existent. Based on that, self-grasping of persons arises, grasping the I as truly existent. However, when we seek to dismantle these misapprehensions of the I and aggregates, the order is reversed. First we meditate on the selflessness of the person—our own I—then we meditate on the selflessness of phenomena—our physical and mental aggregates as well as other phenomena.

The reason for this reversed sequence is twofold. First, when we contemplate how the I exists, it is relatively easy to see that it is dependent on its basis of designation, the aggregates. To identify a person, we have to perceive one or more of his or her aggregates. For instance, we know Tashi is there because we see his body, and we know Susan is nearby because we hear her voice. It's not difficult to see that the person depends on the aggregates and is designated in dependence on the aggregates. Being dependent, the person cannot be independent. However, seeing the aggregates as dependent is more difficult. It is not as obvious that they also depend on their basis of designation.

Second, self-grasping of the person—especially the view of a personal identity—is the primary cause of cyclic existence. Although all forms of self-grasping must be refuted in order to attain liberation, the worst in terms of provoking the afflictions and thus the creation of polluted karma is the self-grasping of the person. Thus negating it first is of great importance.

In short, although there is no difference in the object of negation or its subtlety with respect to the self-grasping of persons and the self-grasping of phenomena—it is inherent existence in both cases—we begin meditating on emptiness by negating the self of persons.

> 34. Having heard this kind of topic [emptiness],
>   the arya, Ananda, obtained the Dharma eye.
>   Then he himself repeatedly
>   taught this to the monastics.

The Causes of Liberation

The Buddha's personal attendant, Ananda, first realized emptiness by means of inference. By continuing to meditate on the meaning of emptiness, he got to the point where he realized it directly and nonconceptually; that is, he obtained the Dharma eye and simultaneously entered the path of seeing and became an arya. At that time, all doubt about emptiness vanished because he had realized it directly for himself. By continuing to meditate on emptiness, he attained the path of meditation and finally the path of no more learning, thus becoming an arhat. As an arhat, he was free from grasping at true existence and its seeds. He then taught emptiness to others, leading many people to become arhats.

In this verse, Nagarjuna refers to a sutra statement as a reason to prove that realizing emptiness is a cause of liberation. This point needs to be proven to the Svatantrika Madhyamikas and others who believe that simply realizing a coarse selflessness of person—the lack of a self-sufficient substantially existent I—will lead to liberation. By demonstrating that a sutra said that Ananda—who followed the hearer vehicle—attained arhatship by realizing the emptiness of inherent existence of both persons and phenomena, Nagarjuna causes proponents of the lower tenet systems to rethink their assertions and thus understand it is necessary to realize the emptiness of inherent existence of persons and phenomena. Through this, they will exert energy to study, contemplate, and meditate on emptiness.

CYCLIC EXISTENCE AND LIBERATION DO NOT INHERENTLY EXIST

To cease our wandering in cyclic existence, we must understand not only how we take one rebirth after another under the influence of ignorance, afflictions, and polluted karma, but also how to cease that process. Furthermore, it is important for us to know the nature of liberation—that it is the cessation of cyclic existence—so that we will strive to attain it.

35. As long as one grasps the aggregates,
     one will also grasp the I with regard to them.
     If one grasps the I, karma [will be created] again,
     and due to that [karma], one will again be reborn.

Identifying the Root of Cyclic Existence

The self-grasping of persons—specifically grasping at our own I—and the self-grasping of phenomena are both the root of cyclic existence. As mentioned above, the order of generating these two is first the self-grasping of phenomena—the aggregates that are the basis of designation of the person—then the self-grasping of persons. The order for realizing the two selflessnesses is reversed; we first realize the selflessness of persons and then the selflessness of phenomena.

The conceived object of the self-grasping of the aggregates is the true existence of the aggregates, and the conceived object of the I-grasping (self-grasping of persons) is the true existence of the I.[8] To realize the selflessness of persons, we do not have to first realize that the conceived object of the self-grasping of the aggregates is nonexistent. If that were the case, we would have realized that the aggregates are not truly existent, and therefore we would have realized the selflessness of phenomena before realizing the selflessness of persons.

On the surface Nagarjuna's lines seem easy to understand: as long as there is grasping at the aggregates, there will be grasping at the I. But we

---

8. The conceived object is the main object with which a conceptual consciousness is concerned. For conceptual consciousnesses, it is the same as the apprehended object. Self-grasping is erroneous with respect to its conceived object.

must look at the order in which the generation of the two self-graspings and the order in which the two realizations of the two selflessnesses occur. Only then will we have a clear and profound understanding of this difficult point.

Literally, it seems that as long as we have self-grasping of the aggregates, we will have self-grasping of the I. It seems that as long as we don't realize the nonexistence of the conceived object of the self-grasping of the aggregates, we cannot realize the nonexistence of the conceived object of the I-grasping. But it wouldn't be right to explain it this way because first we have to realize the selflessness of persons, which involves realizing the nonexistence of the conceived object of the self-grasping of the I.

Thus these lines do not mean we won't realize that the conceived object of the innate I-grasping is nonexistent as long as we do not realize the conceived object of grasping at the aggregates is not existent. That is, this does not mean that first we must realize the selflessness of phenomena and then the selflessness of persons, because the order in which they're realized is the other way around.

In *Ocean of Reasoning,* Je Tsongkhapa explains that these lines mean that as long as our acquired self-grasping of the aggregates that thinks the aggregates truly exist for this or that reason has not abated, we cannot realize the selflessness of the person. To realize the selflessness of the person, we must not be thinking of various reasons why the aggregates are truly existent.

There are two kinds of self-grasping of phenomena: innate and acquired. The innate naturally grasps its object as truly existent. Unlike acquired self-grasping, it doesn't think of various reasons why phenomena are truly existent. Acquired self-grasping of phenomena, which comes from learning incorrect philosophies, thinks the aggregates are truly existent because of this and that reason. The point is that as long as we think with various reasons that the aggregates are truly existent, there is no way to realize the selflessness of the person. It isn't necessary to abandon acquired self-grasping of the aggregates in order to realize the conceived object of the innate I-grasping is nonexistent. This isn't done until the path of seeing. But we cannot realize the selflessness of persons so long as we exaggerate the aggregates as truly existent because of this and that reason.

If one grasps the I, karma [will be created] again, and due to that [karma], one will again be reborn. This refers to the twelve links of dependent origination, which describes how we enter and leave cyclic existence. Each set of twelve links involves the causes and results of a new lifetime in cyclic existence. Self-grasping ignorance is the starting point for all that follows in one set of twelve links. Due to the ignorance grasping the I as truly existent, attachment arises for what we find attractive and gives us pleasure or anger arises for whatever we find disagreeable and disturbs our happiness. Motivated by these and other afflictive emotions, we do various actions—we create karmas—that leave seeds or potencies on our mindstream. When craving and clinging arise at the time of death, they activate these karmic seeds, which then propel a new rebirth. In that new rebirth, self-grasping again generates afflictions, which again create karmas, which again propel more rebirths in cyclic existence.

Without understanding this causal chain that produces our cyclic existence and without deeply understanding the duhkha of cyclic existence we experience as a result, we cannot develop the wish to cut the root of cyclic existence. For this reason it is essential to meditate on the topics in common with the beings of middle capacity as described in the lamrim texts.

36. With these three phases mutually causing each other,
     cyclic existence whirls around
     like the circle [formed by a whirling] torch,
     without beginning, middle, or end.

How We Transmigrate in Cyclic Existence

This verse explains how we circle in cyclic existence by way of the twelve links. Put succinctly, from ignorance (link 1), formative action or karma (link 2) is created. This leaves a karmic seed on the consciousness (link 3). At the time of death, this karma is nourished by craving (link 8) and clinging (link 9), which activate renewed existence (link 10), the karmic seed ripened by craving and clinging that is about to become the next life. This leads to a new birth (link 11) with the seven results that are duhkha by nature.

These twelve links form three phases: afflictions, karma, and birth, with "birth" referring to the resultant birth in cyclic existence. Three of the twelve links—ignorance, craving, and clinging—are afflictions. Two are karma—formative action and renewed existence. The remaining seven—consciousness, name and form, six sources, contact, feeling, birth, and aging and death—are grouped under birth. They are the results of afflictions and karma and are unsatisfactory or duhkha by nature.

When one set of the twelve links is enumerated, the twelve have an order. However, when we view cyclic existence from a global perspective the links are all intermingled, and we cannot say that one of the three phases is first, another in the middle, and the third at the end. For example, while experiencing a birth from one set of links, we generate ignorance and create karma that cause a second set. Then at the end of the present birth, craving and grasping, afflictions from a third set, arise. In this way, they have no beginning, middle, or end, and sentient beings are entwined in a net of perpetual afflictions, karma, and duhkha.

This is similar to time. Within one day we can say there is a definite order in which the hours occur: one o'clock, two o'clock, and so forth. But when we consider three days together, we can't say that one o'clock precedes two o'clock, because one o'clock on day two comes after two o'clock on day one.

If we think about this we may get overwhelmed, feeling that cyclic existence is endless. We should meditate on the twelve links so that we think: "Since beginningless time until the present, I have experienced all the different types of duhkha without end. I cannot count how many times I have already experienced the three types of duhkha, the six disadvantages of cyclic existence, and the eight sufferings of human beings. Unless I practice the Dharma, this will go on and on without respite."

Of the three types of duhkha, the duhkha of pain is physical and mental pain that all beings do not want. The duhkha of change is the fact that even pleasant feelings don't last; if we continue to do the activity that causes these feelings, it will eventually become painful. The duhkha of pervasive conditioning is the fact that our aggregates are under the influence of afflictions and karma. Contemplating this latter form of duhkha is especially effective for generating the determination to be free from cyclic existence. By contemplating its meaning in depth, we will clearly see the drawbacks of repeatedly taking polluted aggregates. These polluted aggregates are the basis not only for the misery of this life—birth, aging, sickness, death, and so forth—but also they are in the nature of duhkha because they are under the control of afflictions and karma. We experience the duhkha of pain and the duhkha of change without choice due to having these aggregates. They are also the basis for future suffering because motivated by attachment, we create many karmas when giving pleasure to these aggregates and protecting them from harm. In doing so, we perpetuate our cyclic existence.

Look at one day in your life and consider that before even one set of the twelve links is finished, you have created so many more karmas that will propel you into continued rebirth in cyclic existence. Ask yourself, "Is there something that can stop cyclic existence?" If there is no cause or method that can destroy the karmas that keep this cycle going, then it makes no sense to become distressed; we should resign ourselves to being tormented by cyclic existence without any hope of relief.

But if there is a method to become free, we must seek it and employ it. For example, if we have a serious heart problem, we never forget about it and constantly look for a cure. We need to determine to be free from cyclic existence and to attain liberation with the same intensity and earnestness. Je Tsongkhapa says, "When you have, day and night unceasingly, the mind aspiring for liberation, you have generated the determination to be free." This is a firm, clear, and unfabricated understanding that will motivate us to practice the path. No matter how well things are going for us, how many beautiful possessions we have, we will have no attachment to them. Instead, we will focus on freeing ourselves from cyclic existence and attaining liberation.

On the other hand, if we do not contemplate the defects of samsara and clearly understand its root, we are like a pig being chased by a dog. When the dog bites its backside, the pig knows it has a problem and squeals, but the rest of the time it lives at ease. Similarly, we have some sort of determination to be free only when things go wrong in our lives and we're unhappy, but the rest of the time, we don't bother with the Dharma.

There is a difference between the determination to be free and the aspiration to attain liberation. The determination to be free focuses on the duhkha of cyclic existence and wants to be free from it, while the aspiration for liberation focuses on liberation and seeks to attain it. For example, a drowning person wishes to be free of the ocean and to reach dry land.

The general order to meditate on this is to first reflect on the various types of duhkha in cyclic existence. Then recognize that ignorance, afflictions, and polluted karma are its causes and generate the wish to destroy them. Next, aspire to attain the liberation that is free from that cause. From this the aspiration to practice the three higher trainings—the path leading to liberation—will blossom.

Compassion will arise for sentient beings by contemplating that sentient beings are subject to the gross sufferings—birth, old age, sickness, death, hunger, and thirst—and wishing them to be free of that suffering. However, our compassion will be more profound if we contemplate that sentient beings wander in cyclic existence endlessly, continually taking one rebirth after another in the six realms of existence due to the twelve links. Even when born in fortunate lives, they are still under the control of afflictions and karma, and may soon be born in unfortunate realms.

While meditation on bodhichitta and the practice of the six perfections help to reduce our afflictions and accumulate merit, they cannot cut the root of cyclic existence. Only the wisdom directly and nonconceptually realizing emptiness can abolish self-grasping ignorance once and for all.

We may think that since bodhisattvas pledge to stay in cyclic existence as long as even one being is not liberated, they don't want to be free from cyclic existence and don't aspire for liberation. But, in fact, it would be very difficult for bodhisattvas if they did not generate the aspiration for liberation, because in order to benefit others most effectively they have to remove all defilements from their own minds and cultivate all the excellent qualities of a buddha. Actually, their aspiration reaches far beyond liberation, because they aspire to attain the non-abiding nirvana of a buddha that is free from not only cyclic existence but also the personal peace of one's own nirvana. Bodhisattvas don't yearn for personal liberation and peace for their own sake, like hearers and solitary realizers do, but seek only what is most beneficial for others.

To generate unfabricated bodhichitta that wishes to lead all sentient beings out of cyclic existence, we must first cultivate the determination to be free and the aspiration for liberation. Without a strong feeling of repulsion toward our own cyclic existence, we will not be able to generate strong compassion for others' horrific experiences in cyclic existence. Both the determination to be free and compassion are based on repulsion of cyclic existence and seek freedom from suffering, but the former seeks our own freedom while the latter seeks the freedom of all beings.

Meditation on the twelve links of dependent origination makes it clear that our cyclic existence and our liberation arise dependently. Each link depends on the preceding one; the cessation of each link depends on the cessation the previous one. Bondage in cyclic existence and liberation from it are both dependent phenomena and are thus empty of inherent existence.

37. But the [process of cyclic existence] is not attained from itself,
    from something else, or from both; nor is it attained in the three
      times.
    Therefore, [for one who knows this] the I-grasping ceases,
    and hence also karma and birth.

38. Seeing in this fashion the arising of effect from cause
    and also seeing its cessation,
    [the wise] think, "The world is ultimately
    neither existent nor nonexistent."

The Stages of Reversing Cyclic Existence

Just as one link follows another in the causal chain of cyclic existence, so do subsequent links cease when their prior link has ceased. This is an example of causal dependence and illustrates that whatever arises dependently cannot exist inherently. Even cyclic existence is empty of inherent existence. It is neither inherently existent nor totally nonexistent, but rather it exists dependently.

In the *Precious Garland*, Nagarjuna sets out many reasonings to prove emptiness. He elaborates on some more than others. In these two verses he speaks of what is called the diamond slivers reasoning that refutes inherently existent arising or production. This is expressed in the first verse of his *Treatise on the Middle Way*:

> Neither from itself nor from another, nor from both,
> Nor without a cause does anything anywhere ever arise.

If a thing existed inherently, it would have to arise inherently. There are only four options for how this could happen: it would have to arise (1) from itself, (2) from an inherently existent cause that was other than itself, (3) from both itself and an inherently existent other, or (4) without a cause. However, dependent things cannot arise in any of those ways. Thus they lack inherently existent arising and are empty of inherent existence.[9]

---

9. See Jeffrey Hopkins, *Meditation on Emptiness* (Boston: Wisdom Publications, 1983), 131–50, for more on this reasoning. See also rJe Tsong Khapa, *Ocean of Reasoning* (New York: Oxford University Press, 2006), 47–49.

Verse 37 also tells us that cyclic existence does not inherently arise and cease in the three times. Nagarjuna will discuss the unfindability of inherently existent things in the past, present, or future in verse 63.

Freedom from the causal process that perpetuates cyclic existence hinges on realizing that dependent arisings are not truly existent and meditating on this point repeatedly. How does this work? The deeper our understanding of dependent arising in its many facets, the more convinced we become that phenomena lack true existence. The wisdom realizing emptiness counteracts ignorance, the first of the twelve links. When that ignorance ceases, the karma motivated by it ceases. With the cessation of afflictions and polluted karma, birth in cyclic existence propelled by them ceases. The complete cessation of afflictions and polluted karma and the duhkha they cause is liberation.

Because the wisdom directly realizing emptiness needs to be focused and firm to overcome self-grasping, we must cultivate concentration. Stable concentration depends on training in the ethical conduct of abandoning the ten nonvirtues and keeping whatever precepts we have taken, such as the five lay precepts, monastic precepts, bodhisattva precepts, and the tantric precepts. In short, cultivating the three higher trainings is the key to reversing cyclic existence and attaining liberation.

> 39. Having listened to this Dharma
>   that puts an end to duhkha,
>   the undiscerning, afraid of the fearless state,
>   are terrified because they do not understand.

The Benefits of Realizing Emptiness

The benefit of realizing and meditating on emptiness is that we now have the means to cease our duhkha completely. When childish beings—those who lack proper discernment of reality—hear about this phenomenon called "emptiness," they develop aversion and fear toward it. They haven't eliminated their doubts about the ultimate mode of existence and thus are terrified of emptiness. In this way their own minds prevent them from going toward liberation. It's tragic that by fearing emptiness they will continue to wander in the fearful state of cyclic existence, when in the depths of their hearts they seek release from suffering.

The Nature of Liberation

Nagarjuna now begins an extensive explanation to discern the correct and incorrect views of the ultimate nature of reality. In doing so, he explains emptiness and the type of wisdom that realizes it. This wisdom is free of two extreme views—the view of absolutism that incorrectly holds the inherently existent appearances that we see every day as true reality, and the view of nihilism that incorrectly believes that if things don't exist inherently they don't exist at all. The middle way view that Nagarjuna champions avoids these two extremes, and someone who realizes it knows that while all phenomena are empty of inherent existence they still exist. How do they exist? They exist by depending on other factors, by being merely designated by name and thought. Thus there are two "truths"—ultimate truth, which is the emptiness of inherent existence, and conventional truth, which includes the diversity of phenomena that appear inherently existent although they are not. These two are not unrelated realities. They depend on each other. Emptiness is the ultimate nature of all conventional truths. Furthermore, emptiness exists conventionally. While it may sound strange to say that emptiness is the ultimate truth yet exists conventionally, we must remember that conventional existence is the only type of existence there is. Nothing exists ultimately or inherently. Emptiness is itself empty; it is not some absolute or independent existence unrelated to anything else.

> 40. You are not afraid [about the claim that]
>   all this will not exist in nirvana.
>   Why then are you afraid when told here
>   that the [three phases of samsara] do not exist?

Fear of the Extinction of True-Grasping Is Inappropriate

Not only non-Buddhists fear emptiness due to misunderstanding it, but so do some Buddhists. According to the Vaibhashikas and Sautrantikas, at the time arhats eliminate all afflictive obscurations they obtain nirvana with remainder. It is called "with remainder" because although arhats have eliminated all the afflictions and karma that cause rebirth, they still have a body born under the influence of afflictions and polluted karma. When they die and leave their body, they then obtain nirvana without remainder. The

Vaibhashikas and Sautrantikas believe that at the time of nirvana without remainder, the self and the aggregates—including the continuity of consciousness—totally cease.

Similarly, they assert that when the Buddha passed into parinirvana at the time of his death, the continuity of his consciousness and other aggregates ceased. These tenet systems do not posit the four Buddha bodies, especially the enjoyment body and the many emanation bodies. They accept only the supreme emanation body—the Buddha that first turns the Dharma wheel in a universe—not other kinds of emanation bodies. They believe that in his last life Siddhartha, as a bodhisattva on the path of preparation, was born as an ordinary being still under the control of afflictions and karma. He destroyed the four maras—ignorance, afflictions, death, and the "son of the gods"—under the bodhi tree and attained awakening at that time. Although he abandoned all duhkha, he still experienced pain since he had the same polluted body he had at birth. After he passed away and attained parinirvana at Kushinagar, the continuity of his consciousness ceased and, having attained nirvana without remainder, it became nonexistent.

Proponents of these schools do not understand or accept the secret, inconceivable assertions of the universal vehicle's explanation that the Buddha had actually attained full awakening eons ago but purposefully took birth to lead us on the path to liberation. By appearing to be an ordinary being who worked hard, overcame obstacles, and attained full awakening, his life became a teaching in itself to encourage us to practice.

Vaibhashikas and Sautrantikas also assert that all phenomena truly exist because if they didn't, they would not exist at all. Thus, they become afraid when Prasangikas negate the conceived object of true-grasping because they think that all existence whatsoever is negated. For them, that means that when arhats attain liberation, they become nonexistent.

Prasangikas say to them, "You believe that the aggregates are destroyed at the time of nirvana without remainder, and that doesn't frighten you. However, you are afraid when we explain that self-grasping ignorance, polluted karma, and birth are extinguished at nirvana." In other words, "Since you say that the person and aggregates, which are inherently existent, cease at the time of nirvana without remainder, why are you frightened when we Prasangikas say there are no inherently existent persons or aggregates at that time? As far as you are concerned, we are saying the same thing!"

41. In liberation there is neither self nor aggregates;
    if you are intent upon that kind of liberation,
    why aren't you pleased with [the teaching that] refutes self
    and aggregates here as well?

The Impossibility of Nirvana Being an Inherently Existent Non-Thing

Prasangikas explain to Vaibhashikas, "Why do you object when we say there are no inherently existent person or aggregates at the time of nirvana? Your own Vaibhashika system asserts that at the time liberation is attained the self and aggregates become completely nonexistent and extinguished. If there are no self and aggregates, there also aren't an inherently existent self or inherently existent aggregates." They reply, "We are not afraid because liberation that is completely free of suffering exists inherently."

The Prasangikas respond to their Vaibhashika debate partners, "If liberation existed inherently, it would have to be either an inherently existent person or an inherently existent phenomenon. There is no third option. But when arhats attain nirvana, the self-grasping of persons and the self-grasping of phenomena have been completely extinguished by the power of the antidote, the wisdom realizing emptiness. The objects of those two self-graspings—inherently existent persons and phenomena—have also been eliminated because the meditator has realized they are nonexistent. For that reason, nirvana cannot be inherently existent."

While Vaibhashikas may say this is not a problem because they assert a self of phenomena and nirvana is a self of phenomena, still their position would accrue all the faults of asserting inherent existence as the Prasangikas so adeptly explain.

Nirvana

Vaibhashikas and Sautrantikas assert that nirvana is the elimination of the afflictions and polluted aggregates, which exist inherently. Prasangikas disagree, "If the polluted aggregates and afflictions existed inherently before nirvana, then nirvana could never be attained because things that exist inherently can never change and can never be destroyed. This is because they would be independent of all other factors."

In addition, nirvana is not the elimination of inherently existent afflictions and aggregates. The realization of emptiness does not make something that was previously inherently existent now empty of inherent existence. Rather, all phenomena have always been empty. The realization of emptiness destroys the grasping at inherent existence; but inherent existence itself never existed.

Furthermore, the Vaibhashikas and Sautrantikas claim that at the time of nirvana without remainder, the aggregates no longer exist. Prasangikas disagree because if this were so, then at the time of final nirvana there would be no one who attained nirvana. That is, if the aggregates were destroyed there would be no basis of designation of the person. Contrarily, when the polluted aggregates exist and thus the person exists, there would be no nirvana, because according to the Vaibhashikas and Sautrantikas nirvana is the cessation of the aggregates. Either way, the tenets of these lower systems lead to many contradictions.

When Prasangikas say that the self and aggregates are eliminated in nirvana, it means that the self-grasping of person and the self-grasping of the aggregates are extinguished. Thus inherently existent afflictions, aggregates, and self—which never existed—are eliminated in the sense that they are no longer apprehended. Only emptiness is seen; there is no remainder of the appearance of inherent existence. In this way, Prasangikas lead us to see that nirvana and emptiness are not separate.

> 42. Nirvana is not even a non-thing,
> so how could it be a thing?
> Nirvana is said to be the cessation
> of the notions of things and non-things.

The Impossibility of Nirvana Being an Inherently Existent Thing

A "thing" is an impermanent and conditioned object that produces an effect; a "non-thing" is a permanent or unconditioned phenomenon. Nirvana cannot be an inherently existent thing because it is neither inherently existent nor a thing.[10]

---

10. See Tsongkhapa's refutation of nirvana as a thing or non-thing in Tsong Khapa, *Ocean of Reasoning*, 521–55. Also see Daniel Cozort's *Unique Tenets of the Middle Way Consequence School* (Ithaca, NY: Snow Lion Publications, 1998), 394–95.

Vaibhashikas, however, assert that nirvana is a thing. It is like a dam that halts the movement of water, they say, and functions to stop the continuation of afflictions and birth in cyclic existence. Yet if nirvana were a thing, it would age and cease, in which case it would not be unchanging, lasting peace.

Sautrantikas say that nirvana is the cessation of afflictions and samsaric rebirth and is inherently existent. If nirvana were inherently existent, it would have to be either a self of persons or a self of phenomena, but it is neither, because those two selves have never existed. Neither self-grasping of persons nor self-grasping of phenomena exists at liberation, and those two selves that the two graspings apprehend also do not exist. Wisdom realizes they are nonexistent.

Some people say nirvana is the mere destruction or disintegration of the afflictions. According to the Prasangikas, nirvana would then be impermanent. Prasangikas assert the destruction or death of something or someone to be a thing: it is a "having ceased" (Tib. *zhig pa*), which is an affirming negative that produces an effect. For example, although death is a negative it is a conditioned phenomenon, produced by birth. The destruction of afflictions and karma is similarly a thing produced by a cause, in this case the wisdom realizing emptiness. However, nirvana is permanent; it is a non-affirming negative, an absence that doesn't imply anything in its stead. It is not a thing.

Since nirvana is not an inherently existent thing, it cannot be an inherently existent non-thing either. This is because non-thing is posited in relation to thing, and inherently existent phenomena must be totally independent and unrelated to all other factors.

The Actual Meaning of Liberation

Nirvana is also posited from the viewpoint of the extinction of the apprehension of things and non-things as inherently existent.

According to the Madhyamikas, there are two kinds of purity: the natural purity—the emptiness of inherent existence—that has always been present, and the purity of adventitious stains that is brought about through the wisdom realizing emptiness. Ordinary beings have the natural purity since their minds by nature are empty of inherent existence. While ordinary beings have no stains of inherent existence and no inherently existent stains, they haven't yet extinguished their afflictions and karma, thus they do not have the purity of adventitious stains.

In nirvana there are neither inherent stains nor adventitious stains. There is simply emptiness. Thus true cessation, nirvana, liberation, and peace are all emptiness.

When we say that nirvana is the extinction of afflictions, it not only means that afflictions—things—have been extinguished, but also that there are no inherently existent afflictions—non-things[11]—in nirvana. This absence of inherently existent afflictions is emptiness, an ultimate truth.

According to most Prasangikas, true cessation is emptiness because the stains are extinguished within the sphere of reality, emptiness. Thus it is posited from the viewpoint of the emptiness of inherent stains.

> 43. In brief, a nihilistic view is the belief
>   that karma has no effects.
>   It is non-meritorious and leads to lower rebirth;
>   it is said to be a wrong view.

> 44. In brief, a realistic view is the belief
>   that karma has an effect.
>   It is meritorious, and it leads to higher rebirth;
>   it is said that it is a right view.

Distinguishing between Correct and Incorrect Views

These verses follow up on the Vaibhashikas' and Sautrantikas' objection that if nirvana is not inherently existent, it must be totally nonexistent. They accuse the Prasangikas of being nihilists because the Prasangikas assert that nothing exists inherently. To this Prasangikas respond, "We are not nihilists. The nihilistic extreme is stubbornly believing that the four truths of the aryas, the Three Jewels, the law of karma and its results, and so on are nonexistent. If a person adheres to this non-meritorious view, he will create much destructive karma and be reborn in the lower realms. To say that these same things do not inherently exist is not the extreme of nonexistence. There is a huge difference between not existing inherently and not existing in general.

---

11. Here "non-things" means nonexistents.

On the other hand, a realistic view believes that the four truths and so on, while not existing inherently, do exist conventionally. Since they exist conventionally, it is possible to forsake what is to be abandoned and practice what is to be adopted on the path. Thinking that karma and its results exist, for example, is meritorious and leads to higher rebirth. As the sutras explain, this is the worldly right view.

> 45. Through knowledge one subdues the [notions of] existence and
>   nonexistence,
>   and one thus transcends negativity and merit.
>   Hence, one is liberated from high and low rebirth;
>   this is what the holy one says.

Liberation Is the Extinction of True-Grasping

True-grasping is extinguished in both nirvanas with remainder and without remainder. These two types of nirvana can be posited in different ways. The general way acceptable to all Buddhist tenet systems was explained above. In addition, the Prasangika school has a unique way of positing these two.[12] When hearer or solitary realizer arhats are in nonconceptual meditative equipoise on emptiness, only emptiness appears; there is no appearance of true existence at all. This is called nirvana without remainder, "remainder" here referring to the appearance of true existence. "Subsequent attainment" is the time after those arhats have arisen from meditative equipoise on emptiness, when they go about their daily activities or do other types of meditation. Although true existence appears to them at this time, they do not grasp phenomena as truly existent. This is called nirvana with remainder, the "remainder" again being the appearance of true existence.

This verse explains that the liberation in the continua of hearer or solitary realizer arhats at the time of nirvana without remainder, when they are meditating single-pointedly on emptiness, is the extinction of true-grasping. In addition, at the time of the nirvana with remainder, when those arhats are not in meditative equipoise and going about their daily activities, the liberation in their continua is the extinction of true-grasping.

---

12. See Cozort, *Unique Tenets*, 253–55.

"Through knowledge" means that meditation done with the wisdom directly realizing emptiness will pacify the views of true existence and nonexistence. That is, one will abandon grasping phenomena to be truly existent and grasping them to be conventionally nonexistent. Even at the time of nirvana with remainder, when arhats are not meditating on emptiness and have the appearance of true existence, true-grasping is no longer present in their continua. Due to this, constructive and destructive karma motivated by true-grasping are also pacified. In other words, the results of birth, aging, sickness, and death that arise from them are also pacified and these practitioners are liberated from both high and low rebirths. "*This is what the holy one says*" indicates that Nagarjuna is quoting a statement the Buddha made in a sutra.

In short, through directly realizing and repeatedly meditating on emptiness, true-grasping is gradually extinguished and the virtuous and non-virtuous karmas motivated by it are also pacified. New karmas that cause rebirth in cyclic existence are no longer created and those previously created cannot ripen into new high or low rebirths in cyclic existence. In time all afflictive obscurations are extinguished, and practitioners attain liberation.

> 46. Seeing that production has a cause,
>   one transcends [the notion of] nonexistence.
>   Seeing that cessation has a cause,
>   one does not accept [the notion of] existence.

Freedom from the Extremes of Existence and Nonexistence Regarding Cause and Effect

Following the middle way, Prasangikas are free from the two extremes of nonexistence and existence. *Production has a cause* means that cyclic existence has causes. Prasangikas know with reliable cognizers that the arising of duhkha has its cause, self-grasping. In this way, they transcend the wrong view that there are no causes or effects of wandering in cyclic existence and are free from the extreme of nonexistence.

They also don't accept inherent existence because they see with reliable cognizers that the cessation of duhkha has a "cause," the true path. True cessation comes into being due to the power of meditating on the true path, the direct realization of emptiness. In this way Prasangikas also avoid the extreme of absolutism or existence.

Cessation does not have a cause in the same way that cyclic existence does, since cessation is permanent. So what does Nagarjuna mean when he says that seeing that cessation has a cause, one does not accept the extreme of inherent existence or absolutism? Cessation is said to have a nominal cause because it comes into being due to the power of meditating on the true path, the wisdom realizing emptiness. Emptiness exists because it can be realized by a reliable cognizer. Through directly realizing emptiness and continuing to meditate on it, we attain true cessation. This dependent sequence refutes the notion of independent existence, and thus Prasangikas reject the notion of inherent existence and do not fall into the extreme of absolutism.

> 47. A cause that occurs before [its effect] or simultaneously [with it]
>   is not really a cause at all,
>   because [such causes] are not accepted nominally,
>   and arising is not accepted ultimately.

Cause and Effect Do Not Inherently Exist

This verse presents another reasoning to refute inherent existence that is also touched upon in *Treatise on the Middle Way* (10.21–22).[13] It is impossible for an inherently existent cause to produce an inherently existent effect. If a cause existed inherently, it would have to exist before its effect, simultaneously with it, or subsequent to it. There is no other possibility, and none of these three are viable. A cause cannot exist simultaneously with its effect because the cause has to cease for its effect to arise. The cause existing after its effect is absurd. An inherently existent cause cannot exist before its effect because something that exists inherently is independent of everything else. As a self-enclosed thing it could not give rise to an effect. Thus inherently existent arising cannot exist.

If an inherently existent cause could produce an inherently existent effect, there should be a valid reason that proves that and a reliable cognizer that realizes that effect. But no such valid reason or reliable cognizer can be found.

---

13. See Tsong Khapa, *Ocean of Reasoning*, 417–18.

In the conventional way that effects arise from causes, a cause has to exist before its effect. Inherently existent causes and effects do not exist either conventionally (nominally) or ultimately.

> 48. When there is this, that arises,
>   just as when there is long, there is short.
>   When this is produced, that arises,
>   just as when a lamp's [flame] is produced, light arises.

We Do Not Contradict What Is Well Known in the World

Someone poses a question, "If an inherently existent cause doesn't give rise to an inherently existent effect, that contradicts what is well known in the world. Farmers know that if seeds are planted in the spring, a crop can be harvested in the autumn." This person doesn't differentiate between inherently existent and conventionally existent cause and effect, and thus thinks that when inherently existent cause and effect is refuted, the entire system of cause and effect is negated.

Nagarjuna replies that his assertion doesn't contradict common knowledge. He is not negating all existence, only a certain kind of impossible way of existing—inherent existence. To disprove inherent existence, he presents the reasoning of dependent arising.[14]

This verse speaks of two kinds of dependence: causal dependence and mutual dependence. "When there is this, that arises" and "when this is produced, that arises" both indicate causal dependence, the fact that effects arise dependent on their causes. First-link ignorance produces second-link formative actions, and so forth, forming the rest of the twelve links. This is similar to a lamp's flame giving rise to light.

If a cause and its effect existed inherently, they would be totally independent of each other. That would mean that the effect could arise without a cause, and that the cause wouldn't need to cease to produce an effect. The cause and its effect could exist simultaneously and eternally. These are unwanted consequences of asserting inherently existent causality.

"When there is long, there is short" indicates mutual dependence. Some-

---

14. See Tsongkhapa's "Praise to Dependent Arising." Several English translations are available.

thing is long in relation to another thing that is short. Long and short exist relative to each other, not independent of each other.

Usually we think that an effect depends on its cause, not the other way around. However, thinking more deeply, we see that for something to be a cause there must be the possibility of an effect arising from it. In this way, cause and effect are posited relative to each other. Being mutually reliant, they don't exist independently or under their own power. In the same way, past, present, and future are established in dependence on each other. Friend, enemy, and stranger are also mutually dependent. All these things exist by conceptual designation; they are fabricated by our minds and lack objective existence. In this way they are like illusions and do not exist objectively.

When we understand these two forms of dependence—causal dependence and mutual dependence—we can establish that things do not exist independently or from their own side. However, they do exist conventionally, nominally. The correct view is that phenomena are empty of inherent existence and exist by being merely designated.

49. When there is long, there is short;
    they do not inherently exist;
    and when a lamp's [flame] is not produced,
    the light also does not arise.

If the cause doesn't exist, the effect cannot arise. If ignorance is destroyed by wisdom realizing emptiness, formative actions cannot arise. By ceasing formative actions, consciousness ceases. Name and form, the six sources, and the remaining links also cease. This is just like when a candle's wax is consumed, the flame ceases. When the flame ceases, its light also stops.

Just as effects cannot exist without their causes, things that are mutually dependent cannot exist without each other. Without a teacher there is no student, and without a student there is no teacher. A valid object and a reliable cognizer depend on each other; without one, the other cannot be established.

The Svatantrikas and below say that inherently existent causes and effects are seen by reliable cognizers, because the fact that effects come from causes is well known in the world. Once again, they confuse existence and inherent existence, thinking they are the same. They also mistakenly believe emptiness and total nonexistence are the same. Thus they assert that if a cause exists, it inherently exists, and if it is empty of inherent existence, it must be totally nonexistent. As said before, if something existed inherently, it would exist from its own side, without depending on causes, conditions, or anything else. But nothing exists independently like this. Everything exists dependent on other factors. Functioning things depend on causes and conditions; all phenomena rely on their parts; all phenomena are also mutually dependent on other phenomena as well as on conceptual designation.

> 50. Seeing that an effect arises from a cause,
>   one does not claim that [causality] is nonexistent,
>   having accepted conventional [causality] in accord
>   with the way it arises for the world from conceptual fabrication.

> 51. [Ultimate causality is] refuted:
>   it would be absolutist to accept that it has not arisen from
>   conceptual fabrication
>   and that it is truly real, just as it is. [Its ultimate reality] is not
>   [accepted].
>   Thus not relying on the two [extremes], one is liberated.

Realizing Nonduality Brings Liberation

In these two verses, Nagarjuna shows the correct view free from the extremes of nihilism and absolutism. He is free of nihilism because he accepts that effects arise from their respective causes. Conventional reliable cognizers know that an effect arises from its cause. Nagarjuna demonstrates his acceptance of conventional existence and causality as merely designated by conception when he explains the causes for higher rebirth, the Buddha's thirty-two signs, and a bodhisattva's progression through the ten grounds to buddhahood.

Nagarjuna does not abide in the extreme of absolutism—also called the extreme of existence, permanence, or eternalism—because he refutes the ultimate existence and true existence of cause and effect and asserts that things do not exist inherently in the way they appear. Causes and their effects do not exist ultimately and cannot be found by ultimate analysis, but they do exist nominally, dependent on conceptual designation. We will attain liberation by meditating on this view of the middle way, free of absolutism and nihilism.

While Prasangikas say true existence and inherent existence are the same, Svatantrikas differentiate between them, negating true existence but asserting inherent existence conventionally. They accept dependent arising and do not say that phenomena exist in a totally independent fashion. Nevertheless, they still subscribe to the inherent existence of all objects, believing objects still have a degree of independent existence. They do not recognize the internal contradiction in their assertions. In fact, they believe that a thing's existing dependently proves that it exists inherently. However, Svatantrikas do use dependent arising as a reason to prove that something is not truly existent, saying that dependence and reliance of one thing on another indicates that things cannot be truly existent.

If you have already studied the Buddhist philosophical tenet systems in depth, these points will be clear to you. If you haven't, the points will not be so clear to you now; you will understand them better after you have done more study.

52. A form that is viewed from afar
      is seen clearly by those nearby.
      If a mirage were actually water,
      why would those nearby not see it?

53. As in the case of a mirage,
      those far away who [view] the world
      see it to be real just as it is,
      but being signless, it is not seen by those nearby.

An Example of Realizing and Not Realizing the Suchness (Emptiness) of Things

From a distant mountain, people who are lost in the desert see a place where sunlight and sand meet and believe water is there. Thirsty, they run toward it, only to find when they arrive that there is no water. If the mirage were actually water, water should have appeared more clearly as they approached.

Similarly, being far from the correct view, ordinary beings see the world as truly existent. If phenomena truly existed as they appear, those truly existent phenomena should become clearer the more we analyzed to see how they existed. However, this is not the case; aryas in meditative equipoise on emptiness see the absence of truly existent phenomena in sparkling clarity.

Just as the appearance of water vanishes when we go closer to a mirage, so too the appearance of true existence disappears the more we investigate whether truly existent phenomena actually exist. In fact, aryas' wisdom, which is very close to emptiness (suchness), sees the opposite, the non-true existence of phenomena. Aryas know that the appearance of true existence is false and that therefore true-grasping is an erroneous mind.

Just as the mirage is not water although it appears to be, all phenomena do not exist from their own side although they appear to. Just as the perception of a mirage and the thought "this is water" are false, perceiving and grasping all phenomena as existing from their own side are both false.

Except for aryas' wisdom of meditative equipoise on emptiness, true existence appears to all other consciousnesses of sentient beings. For example, a table appears truly existent to the eye consciousness of an ordinary being. This eye consciousness is a conventional reliable cognizer because it realizes the table: it knows a table is there even though the table appears in a false manner to it. This reliable eye consciousness is mistaken with respect to its appearing object because the table appears truly existent, but it is not erroneous with respect to its apprehended object because it is able to realize the table. However, if someone is very attached to the table and craves it intensely, his or her mental consciousness is mistaken with respect to its appearing object because the table appears truly existent to it, and it is erroneous with respect to its apprehended object because it grasps the table to truly exist.

> 54. A mirage seems to be water,
>   but it is not water, nor is it real.
>   Likewise, the aggregates seem to be a self,
>   but they are not a self, nor are they even real.

The Aggregates Do Not Exist Inherently

Just as a mirage appears to be water but is not, similarly the aggregates appear to be a person, although they are not. Just as a mirage is not real, so too the truly existent aggregates that appear are not real. The way the aggregates appear and the way they exist are discordant.

> 55. [Seeing] a mirage, one might think,
> "That is water," and then go up to it.
> If one still grasped [the water, thinking], "The water isn't here,"
> it would be quite foolish.

> 56. Likewise, it is confused to apprehend this mirage-like world
> as either [truly] existent or [totally] nonexistent.
> If confused,
> one will not obtain liberation.

Liberation Is Impossible without Abandoning the Two Extremes

A thirsty person sees water where a mirage is and runs there to drink it. After finding no water there, he would be foolish to think, "There used to be water here, and it disappeared before I could get here." There never was any water there. Had he known that, he would not have run after it to start with.

Similarly, the aggregates appear truly existent although they are not. Through analysis we find there are no truly existent aggregates. At that time, if we thought, "The aggregates used to be truly existent, and my analysis made them nonexistent," we would be quite foolish. Had we realized sooner that truly existent things have never existed, we would not have suffered so much chasing them.

A person who thinks that a thing doesn't exist at all if it doesn't truly exist is like a person who thinks that the "water" of a mirage has disappeared when they can't find it. They think things used to truly exist and their analysis made them become totally nonexistent. Those who apprehend the world—that is, the aggregates—as either nonexistent conventionally or as existent ultimately are unable to understand that things were never truly existent and can only exist conventionally, through mere designation.

Without relinquishing the two extremes of absolutism and nihilism, they will not be able to free themselves from cyclic existence.

> 57. The nihilist goes to a low rebirth;
> 　　the essentialist attains a higher rebirth;
> 　　but through knowing [reality] just as it is,
> 　　not relying on the two [extremes], one is liberated.

The Importance of Realizing Nonduality

Nihilists—also called "proponents of nonexistence"—are those who deny the existence of the Three Jewels, the law of karma and its effects, rebirth, and so on. Under the influence of these wrong views, they do whatever they like, thinking they won't experience any detrimental effects. In this way, they accumulate a great deal of destructive karma and will be born in the lower realms.

Essentialists—or "proponents of true existence"—accept the existence of the Three Jewels, causality, and so forth. Hence they put effort into creating virtuous karma and as a result they are reborn in a higher rebirth. Essentialists hold the worldly right view but have not yet gained the supramundane right view—the right view of the ultimate nature of existence, emptiness.

As long as we hold either a nihilistic or an essentialist view, we have no choice but to be born in cyclic existence because we will continue to create either virtuous or nonvirtuous propelling karma. Neither nihilism nor absolutism is a viable path to nirvana. By abandoning these two extremes, aryas know reality just as it is, realize the right supramundane view, and attain liberation.

Some people misunderstand the statement "not relying on the two, one is liberated." They don't understand that "the two" refers to the two extremes—existence and nonexistence—but rather they take the words literally and believe that all phenomena are neither existent nor nonexistent. However, this is not possible. If something is not existent, by implication it must be nonexistent. If it is not nonexistent, it must be existent. Existence and nonexistence are direct opposites and contradictory. Nothing can be both of them, and there is no third option. So there is no possibility of things being neither existent nor nonexistent. A path based on this wrong view is futile, and those who think like this are paralyzed by confusion.

It is possible that explaining the statement "not existent and not non-existent" in a literal manner could be of some temporary benefit for a few disciples, even though that position is untenable. While this may be so, we must use reasoning to understand scripture correctly, analyzing it from this angle and from that angle, comparing the reasons for and against the two positions to see which one has the most supportive reasons and which one has the most reasons disproving it. Follow the one that has the most support and the least harm. By using reasoning, we can see that if all those terms are taken literally, it is not possible to find phenomena that are neither existent nor nonexistent. If we insist that there is something like that, when someone asks us to give an example, what will we say?

When we want to prove a thesis, it's good to cite a scriptural quotation to support what we say. For example, a passage in the *Sutra Unraveling the Thought* (*Samdhinirmochana Sutra*) says that conventional truth and ultimate truth are neither the same nor different and that if you cling to the thought of same and different you are mistaken, because things are beyond this duality. Taking this statement literally, someone could misconstrue it to mean there is a third possibility in addition to the two truths being either the same or different. This would be like someone citing this verse 57 and saying that there is a third option in addition to things being either existent or nonexistent.

When the *Sutra Unraveling the Thought* says the two truths are not different, it means they are not different natures; they are one nature. They cannot exist separate from each other. When it says that they are not the same, it means that they do not have the same isolate—they are nominally different. It is in this sense that they are neither the same nor different. The two truths are the same nature and nominally different. All of the great Indian sages and scholars explained it like this. Similarly, the correct understanding of "neither existent nor nonexistent" is that phenomena are neither inherently existent nor totally nonexistent—they are empty of inherent existence and exist nominally.

58. Asserting neither existence nor nonexistence
    by knowing [reality] just as it is,
    [if you think such wise persons] are thereby nihilists,
    why wouldn't you also be essentialists?

Dispelling Confusion Regarding the Correct View

Non-Buddhists and proponents of the lower Buddhist tenet systems believe that the Prasangika's example of the mirage shows that nothing exists inherently, and that therefore things don't exist at all. They then accuse Nagarjuna of being a nihilist.

In response, Nagarjuna uses an identical reasoning, "If you say our assertion that phenomena aren't inherently existent makes us nihilists, then by asserting that everything exists inherently, wouldn't you fall to the extreme of absolutism and thereby become essentialists?" The proponents of lower Buddhist systems don't like this, because they consider their position to be the middle way.

Negating inherent existence doesn't make someone a nihilist, and asserting the conventional existence of the Three Jewels, the law of cause and effect, and so on doesn't make someone an essentialist. You can negate inherent existence while still establishing the existence of the Three Jewels and so forth. Phenomena exist conventionally, by being merely designated, and at the same time they lack inherent existence.

There is another way to read this verse. Here Nagarjuna replies to the non-Buddhists and proponents of lower systems' accusation that he is a nihilist by saying, "Why don't you also accuse me of being an essentialist who has fallen to the extreme of existence because I assert that phenomena exist?" The previous way to read this verse is deeper and clearer.

> 59. If the refutation of existence
>   were to entail nihilism by implication
>   then why isn't absolutism entailed
>   by the refutation of nonexistence?

As in the previous verses, here "existence" refers to inherent existence and "nonexistence" to total nonexistence. Apprehending the world as either inherently existent or as totally nonexistent is ignorant. However, Svatantrikas and below assert that when inherent existence is refuted, existence is refuted and total nonexistence is established. For this reason they say Prasangikas are nihilists. Nagarjuna replies that if by refuting inherent existence he falls to the extreme of nihilism, then by refuting total nonexistence why wouldn't you fall to the extreme of absolutism? In other words, if his refutation of inherent existence makes him a nihilist, their assertion that things exist should make them essentialists. This is the same argument as in the previous verse.

According to Nagarjuna's system, asserting that things don't exist inherently is not nihilism and saying that they exist conventionally is not absolutism. Even though all phenomena are not inherently existent, Prasangikas can still present the entire system of agent, action, and object, and of cause and effect. When they accuse us of being nihilists, non-Buddhists and proponents of the lower Buddhist systems have misunderstood emptiness and the actual meaning of the middle way.

You may have noticed that Nagarjuna makes the same point many times, approaching it from different perspectives each time. He does that so that we will understand the importance of differentiating between conventional existence and inherent existence, affirming the former and refuting the latter. Similarly, we must not confuse emptiness with total nonexistence and must affirm the former and negate the latter.

> 60. [Prasangikas] do not actually assert nihilism,
>   nor behave nihilistically;
>   and because they rely on awakening, they do not think as
>   nihilists,
>   so how can they be called nihilists?

Realizing Freedom from Elaborations Is Not Nihilism

Some of the verses in *Precious Garland* imply a dialogue between Prasangikas and proponents of other systems. Sometimes the other proponents are identified, sometimes it just says, "Somebody says . . ." The following exchange principally refutes the idea of some hearers who accept that karma and its effects exist inherently. They misunderstand Prasangikas' negation of inherent existence to mean that they deny karma and its effects altogether and thus think they are nihilists.

Those following the hearer vehicle say, "Although you don't say that you deny the existence of karma and its effects, through your physical behavior it seems that you do." To this, Prasangikas reply, "While we assert that phenomena, such as the law of karma and its effects, are not inherently existent, we never say that they are totally nonexistent. We stopped all faulty behavior, so our physical conduct and our speech are not like that of nihilists."

Altering their accusation a little, the followers of the hearer vehicle retort, "You don't speak or act like nihilists because you are worried about not receiving as many offerings and as much respect. To prevent that from happening, you make sure that your outer behavior doesn't accord with that of nihilists, but inside you still think there is no law of karma and its effects." To this, Prasangikas reply, "We have perfectly realized the path to awakening, and thus understand karma and its effects correctly. We don't deny their existence."

This is a subtle point, because everyone from the Svatantrikas downward says that if karma and its results—or anything else for that matter—does not inherently exist, it does not exist at all. The assertion that phenomena can lack inherent existence yet still exist is a unique feature of the Prasangikas.

> 61. Ask the worldly [philosophers, such as] the Samkhyas,
>   Vaisheshikas, and Jains,
>   who assert [the real existence] of the person and aggregates,
>   whether they maintain that
>   [the interdependent is] beyond existence and nonexistence.

> 62. Realize, therefore, that the nectar of the Buddha's teaching,
>   which is beyond all notions of existence and nonexistence,
>   and which is called the profound,
>   is [our] unique Dharma inheritance.

Only the Buddha Spoke of Freedom from the Two Extremes

To know if the assertion that phenomena lack inherent existence but exist conventionally is the unique quality of the Prasangikas, ask non-Buddhist philosophers and proponents of the lower Buddhist tenet systems if they have this quality. They will respond that they do not. Even our fellow Buddhists, let alone the non-Buddhists, cannot explain this point.

The Samkhya (followers of Kapila) was a prominent non-Buddhist school in ancient India, as was the Vaisheshika (followers of Kanada), the Naiyayikas who were associated with them, and the Jains (Nirgranthas, or Unclad Ones). Followers of these philosophical systems assert that persons and phenomena are substantially existent; they do not understand the profound phenomenon of the emptiness of inherent existence. If you discuss with them, you will find out for yourself that they don't talk about the unique Prasangika attribute of dependent arising free of the two extremes.

When you carefully examine and understand this profound Dharma free of absolutism and nihilism, you will see how precious and important it is. Then put in the effort to become learned in it, leaving far behind all ideas of a truly existent ultimate reality, a permanent, unitary, and independent self, and permanent tiniest particles that are the building blocks of all existents.

Nirvana, the nectar of immortality, is beyond birth, aging, sickness, and death; the Buddha's teachings on nirvana are unrivaled. The path for attaining it is the unpolluted arya path: the true path, which is the fourth of the four truths. The apprehended object of the true path—the emptiness of inherent existence—is profound and free of the extreme views of existence and nonexistence. This is our unique Buddhist heritage that the Buddha set forth with compassion.

4. Refuting Inherent Existence and Establishing Emptiness

OVERCOMING WRONG VIEWS ABOUT REALITY

Nagarjuna now leads us deeper into the nature of reality. He destroys our wrong views and true-grasping by refuting coming and going as existent from their own side and by refuting the inherent existence of momentary, impermanent things. He also introduces us to the refutation of things being either one or many.

> 63. The world does not go out of existence
>   nor come [into existence]:
>   it does not remain for even an instant;
>   it has a nature beyond the three times, so how could it be real?

Refuting that Coming and Going Exist from Their Own Side

This refutation of inherently existent coming and going is similar to that found in chapter 2 of Nagarjuna's *Treatise on the Middle Way*.[15] *The world* here refers particularly to the aggregates that are the basis of designation of the person, but it also includes outer phenomena such as the environment that are not associated with the person. The aggregates do not arise, remain, or disintegrate from their own side, independent of all other factors. In this way they have a nature beyond the three times of past, present, and future.

If the mind, for example, existed inherently, it could not come to this life from a previous one or go to a future life after death, because whatever exists inherently is unchanging. It could not interact with other factors, so it could not change, and coming and going from one life to the next involves

---

15. See Tsong Khapa, *Ocean of Reasoning*, 101–26.

change. An inherently existent mind would be frozen in time and remain unchanging throughout the past, present, or future.

If cause and effect existed inherently, they would exist independent of each other. In that case, an effect could exist at the time of its cause, and a cause would not have to cease in order to produce its effect. Furthermore, both a cause and its effect could exist in the past, present, and future simultaneously.

When the aggregates arise, they don't come unchanged from somewhere else; when they cease, they don't go somewhere else unchanged; and in the moment after they arise, they don't endure unchanged. Our body, for example, is not a permanent phenomenon that exists fully formed in the previous moment and comes into the next moment without changing. Rather, the body changes in each moment, never remaining the same. Things with such an impermanent nature depend on causes and conditions, therefore they do not exist independently or inherently. Thus the aggregates do not have a nature that exists autonomously in the past, present, or future. For that reason, they have a nature that transcends inherent existence in any of the three times.

If the body existed inherently, it would have to exist in the past, present, or future. If it existed in the future, it would have to stay in the future; a present body could not come about. Furthermore, an inherently existent future body would already have attained its entity, which means it would be a present object. Something that has attained its own entity—something that exists in the present—doesn't need to arise; it already exists, and in that case, it could not be a future object.

If the body were inherently a present object, it wouldn't have a past or future. Without a future, it could not come into existence, and without a past, it could not cease. If it were inherently a past body, it would be frozen in the past and could never have been a present body.

Conditioned things do not abide for an instant—they change even as they arise. Because they do not stay fixed, they are beyond abiding in any of the three times. Inherently existent things would have to exist as findable entities in the past, present, or future, which would preclude their momentary change. Since they don't exist in this way, how could they be real?

Treatise on the Middle Way speaks of the agent and the action of going. A person (the agent) walks from here to there (the action). A person also goes from one life to the next. However, neither the person nor the action of going is an inherently existent entity. There is no going and no one who goes over the part of the path that has already been traversed. That going and goer don't exist right now. Similarly, there is no goer or going on the part of the path yet to come in the future, because that hasn't happened yet. Neither an inherently existent action of going nor the goer who is the agent can exist in the future.

With respect to the part of the path that is presently being traversed, there is no inherently existent going or goer. The action of going involves lifting one foot up and putting it down, picking up the other and putting it down. Which one of these movements is the action of going? As soon as one foot moves in the smallest instant, that action of going has ceased and the next action of going is yet to come. So where is an inherently existent present moment in which going occurs? It is unfindable.

The present is posited in relation to the past and the future; the three times are mutually dependent on each other, so they don't exist independently or inherently. In short, the action of going can't inherently exist in the future because that action of going is yet to come. It can't exist in the past, because it has already ceased, and it can't exist in the present because the present cannot be pinpointed.

> 64. Ultimately, the world and nirvana do not come [into existence],
> nor do they go [out of existence], nor do they remain [existent].
> So what kind of distinction could there really be
> between the world and nirvana?

Here, *the world* refers to cyclic existence. Cyclic existence and nirvana do not inherently come into existence or inherently go out of existence. They also do not remain in an inherently existent manner. On the ultimate level, there is no difference between cyclic existence and nirvana in terms of their being empty of inherent existence.

Furthermore, cyclic existence and nirvana are posited in relation to each other. Being mutually dependent, they do not exist independently or inherently; in this way, too, they are equal in terms of being empty.

Some scriptures speak of "the equality of samsara and nirvana." If we misunderstand this phrase we may think, "Samsara (cyclic existence) and nirvana are exactly the same. Since samsara is already nirvana, there's no need to practice ethical conduct or restrain my desires." A person who acts with such a belief creates a lot of destructive karma because he or she ignores the law of karma and its effects. Furthermore, if such a person teaches this wrong view to others, he or she will lead them into the thick jungle of suffering like the first cow in a herd who takes a wrong path.

The proper way to understand the equality of samsara and nirvana is to know that both of them lack inherent existence and are established nominally in mutual dependence on each other. Since they both lack inherent existence and are not frozen entities, it is important to practice the path to overcome samsara and attain nirvana.

> 65. Since abiding does not [really] occur,
> ultimately there is neither arising nor cessation.
> How can [something] ultimately arise,
> or cease, or abide?

Refuting the Inherent Existence of Arising, Abiding, and Ceasing

Now Nagarjuna refutes the inherent existence of three attributes of impermanent things—their arising, abiding, and ceasing.[16] We usually think these three occur sequentially: first something arises or is produced, then it abides, and finally it ceases. In fact, these three occur simultaneously in one object. Arising is the new production of what didn't exist before. Abiding is the persistence of a previous continuum. Ceasing is a thing's not lasting for a second moment after it arises.

When we negate inherently existent arising, abiding, and ceasing, we can pick any one of the three, show that it doesn't exist inherently, and use that as the reason to prove that the others also do not exist inherently. For example, if arising existed from its own side, then the object that is arising—let's say a sprout—would do so without depending on any other factors, such as its cause. Not depending on anything else, the sprout would be permanent and unable to change, so its abiding and ceasing could not occur. An inherently existent sprout would be frozen in time and space, unable to function.

This verse focuses on abiding, saying that since a sprout can't abide inherently, it can't arise or cease either. If it inherently abides, it cannot arise;

---

16. See chapter 7 of *Treatise on the Middle Way* and Tsong Khapa, *Ocean of Reasoning*, 175–220.

it would always be there. If it inherently abides, it cannot cease because it cannot change moment to moment. The sprout would be unrelated to its cause or its effect. In short, arising, abiding, and ceasing are not inherently existent because abiding does not inherently exist.

66. If always changing,
how could things be non-momentary?
And if they did not change,
how could they be altered in fact?

67. [Something is] momentary
because it either ceases partially or entirely.
Neither of these two [possibilities] makes sense
because a difference is not perceived.

A Few Related Topics

Nagarjuna goes into a few side discussions in verses 66–68 where he examines the assertions of the Vaisheshikas, members of an orthodox Hindu school that follows the Vedas, and claims of the Vaishnavas, followers of the god Vishnu.

The Vaisheshikas say, "The arguments above regarding not existing in the three times apply to those who say that functioning things arise and disintegrate. We don't have that fault, because we accept that the tiniest particles composing all matter are inherently permanent. They are neither produced nor destroyed."

Nagarjuna replies, "Do all things change or not? If they do, then the tiniest particles are not permanent; they are momentary, produced, and perish. If things don't change, then how could they become different than they were? How could the natural changes from child to adolescent to adult to senior citizen occur? It would absurdly follow that they could not because our bodies would be permanent."

Acknowledging this fault, the Vaisheshikas change their assertion, "The tiniest particles are inherently existent and inherently momentary." Nagarjuna replies, "Do they completely change or only partially change? If a particle has one part that changes and another part that does not, then when we look at a plant, for example, we should see one part that continues on unchanged and another part that changes, either growing or dying. However, we don't see that at all.

"On the other hand, if the tiniest particles change completely in every way, then how could they exist inherently? Inherently existent things cannot change."

Here we see two faults of the Vaisheshikas' position: one follows from asserting that the tiniest particles are permanent, the other from asserting that they are inherently existent yet still change.

> 68. If [a real thing] is momentary, then since it would cease to exist
>   entirely [at each moment], how could anything be old?
>   And if a real thing is non-momentary,
>   then since it would persist [without change], how could anything
>   be old?

The Vaishnavas declare that their assertions don't have the faults mentioned above because they assert that the person is permanent and old, *old* meaning primordial, without beginning or end. Nagarjuna replies that an inherently existent person that is impermanent and momentary would completely cease in each moment, and a totally new person would arise in the next moment. In that case, how could the body grow old?

On the other hand, if an inherently existent person were non-momentary and permanent, it could not change and would remain as it was before. In that case, how can it be considered old? To be old, the person must have arisen, changed, and declined, and only an impermanent person that doesn't endure beyond its first moment does that. Therefore, the person can't be permanent. Furthermore, if the person were permanent, someone couldn't be unhappy in the morning and happy in the afternoon. Ten-year-old Tashi would be the exact same person as eighty-year-old Tashi. We can directly perceive that people's moods change and that Tashi ages, thus contradicting the Vaishnavas' assertion.

The Vaishnavas and other non-Buddhists don't assert a permanent person for no reason; they have thought a lot about this and give reasons for their claim. Whether those reasons are good and will hold up when challenged is another matter. If the person is transitory, they say, how can the person who creates karma be the one who experiences the result? If the person who creates the karma changes moment to moment, an entirely different person would experience the result. In that case a person could experience the results of actions he did not do, and he would avoid experiencing the actions that he did do. Since that is unacceptable, the only way the Vaishnavas can understand the law of karma and its effects is to posit a permanent person. They cannot explain how a momentary person could experience the results of her karma.

Buddhists say that the person is impermanent, and the result of karma is experienced by the continuum of that person. This reasoning pacifies the above concerns, and we see that karma and its effects work very well when the person is impermanent. In fact, if the person were permanent, it would be difficult to explain how an action could produce its result in the future when a permanent person is frozen in time. The person being impermanent or permanent is one of the fundamental differences between Buddhists and non-Buddhists.

> 69. Just as one conceives of a moment as having a last [part],[17]
>   so too one should conceive of it as having a beginning and
>   middle.
>   Since a moment has a threefold [temporal] nature,
>   the world does not remain for [even] a moment.

The Momentary Must Have Parts

The momentary refers to impermanent phenomena, things that do not remain in the next moment. These impermanent phenomena are the things we see around us—people, the environment, our thoughts and perceptions. Although change is the very nature of momentary phenomena, we still grasp them as inherently existent. Nagarjuna now refutes this wrong view.

Some people say that a moment is the time when something has arisen and not yet ceased. They accept that a moment does not endure for a second instant, but they assert that while it lasts it is an inherently abiding moment.

---

17. The reason *last part* is used instead of *end* is because in the technical language of debate, *end* refers to the moment a thing has ceased, whereas it is still present during its last part. Following its last part is its end, at which time it is no longer present. The end of one moment occurs simultaneously with the beginning of the next moment. For example, at the time of the last moment (or last part of a moment) of a seed, the seed is present. In the next moment, it has ended, and the sprout exists. At the end of the seed, the seed no longer exists and the sprout is present. The seed and its sprout cannot exist at the same time because a cause must cease for its result to arise.

Nagarjuna asks, "Since a moment has a last part, it must also have a middle part and a beginning part. A moment is always changing because it has these three parts; thus it cannot inherently abide and cannot inherently exist."

A moment depends on its three parts. Being dependent in this way, it cannot inherently exist because an inherently existent thing cannot depend on anything else, including parts.

When we apply this reasoning to the world—the environment and its inhabitants—we see that the world cannot abide for even a moment. To say this in the form of a syllogism: the subject, the world with its environment and inhabiting sentient beings, doesn't abide inherently for a moment, because a moment has parts—its beginning, middle, and last part.

> 70. As with a moment, one should also consider
> the [tripartite nature of its] beginning, middle, and last [part].
> There is no beginning, middle, or last [that arises]
> either from itself or something else.

Refuting the Inherent Existence of That Which Has Parts

Somebody now says, "Although one moment has a beginning, middle, and last part, the beginning abides inherently as do the middle and the last part."

Nagarjuna counters this by explaining that the beginning, middle, and last part do not abide inherently. Just as one moment has three parts, each part also has a beginning, middle, and last part. Each of those parts also has beginning, middle, and last parts. Because it is dependent on other factors—in this case its parts—time does not inherently abide.

Just as a moment of time can be mentally broken down into parts, all phenomena—whether they are large objects such as the universe, or miniscule ones such as subatomic particles—are made of parts. Anything that has parts—whether these parts are directional, material, or temporal parts—cannot exist inherently because it depends on its parts.

The people asking questions in these debates are rational individuals; if we state something that isn't reasonable, they won't accept it. But if we point something out with correct reasoning, they are able to see that what they believe is incorrect and change their minds. They are not closed-minded or stubborn. When Buddhists debate together, we clarify points using both reasoning and scriptural quotations. But when discussing with non-Buddhists, we must depend solely on reasoning because they do not accept our scriptures as reliable sources of knowledge.

71. No [material thing] is a unitary whole, because it has many
        directional parts,
    and there is no [material thing] that does not have directional
        parts.
    Further, without there being one, there cannot be many;
    without the existent, there cannot be the nonexistent.

The Reasoning of Not Being One and Many

Now someone says that things exist inherently, and Nagarjuna asks them, "Does a thing inherently exist as one, meaning one sole thing?" If he says yes, Nagarjuna responds, "Take a material object, such as this page, for example. It is not an inherently existing one (thing) because it has many directional parts—its front, back, right, and left; its north, south, east, and west parts."

There is nothing that cannot be physically or mentally broken down into its various parts. If something has directional parts, it cannot be an inherently existent one; it would not inherently be one thing. Something that is an inherently existent one cannot be analyzed into directions and parts; it would be just one thing and have no parts whatsoever.

The person sees that is correct, so he changes his approach and says, "There are inherently existent many—*many* meaning more than one." To this Nagarjuna counters, "Since there is no inherently existent one, there cannot be inherently existent many or several, because inherently existent many is a collection of inherently existent ones." To have many, first there needs to be one, and there is no inherently existent one. In short, things are not truly existent, because they do not inherently exist either as one or many.

If you can see that material things do not inherently exist because of not being one or many, you will be able to use that same reason to understand that phenomena without form, such as consciousness, are also not inherently existent. Is there inherently one moment of consciousness? No, there isn't, because each moment has a beginning, middle, and last part. If there is not one inherently existent moment of consciousness, there cannot be many inherently existent moments of consciousness, because in order to have many, there must be a collection of inherently existent ones.

The line *without the existent, there cannot be the nonexistent* refutes the claim that a thing's emptiness is truly existent. Here *existent* refers to that which is conventionally existent—for example, a table—and *nonexistent* refers to the emptiness of true existence[18]—in this case the table's emptiness. The table is the basis of its emptiness of true existence. Since the basis—the table—lacks true existence, an attribute or property of that basis—in this case the emptiness of true existence of the table—cannot be truly existent.

An object and its emptiness are posited in dependence on each other. If there is not a table, we cannot talk about the emptiness of true existence of the table. The fact that an object and its emptiness are mutually dependent means neither of them is an independent entity. Thus neither of them inherently exists.

> 72. The existent becomes nonexistent
>   because it either ceases naturally or is counteracted [by
>   something else].
>   But since the existent is impossible,
>   how could there be [its] cessation or counteragent?

> 73. Therefore, ultimately the world is not lessened
>   by [someone] attaining nirvana.
>   When asked whether there is any end to the world,
>   the Victor remained silent.

On the gross level, a thing can be destroyed in two ways: it either ceases naturally because its causes have been exhausted, or it is counteracted by something else. A peach rotting and a person growing old are examples of things ceasing naturally. No outside force is exerted to make them deteriorate. To be *counteracted* means to be destroyed by a separate agent, such as

---

18. Existence and nonexistence have different meanings according to the context. The former may refer to conventional existence or inherent existence; the latter may refer to total nonexistence or to emptiness.

a clay pot smashed by a hammer. If things were inherently existent, neither of those two ways of becoming nonexistent could occur because an inherently existent object cannot be affected by other conditions; it would be a permanent, self-enclosed entity that remains unchanged forever. However, since inherently existent things do not exist to begin with, they cannot be destroyed in either of the two ways.

In verse 73, *world* refers to samsara or cyclic existence. When someone attains nirvana, an inherently existent samsara does not disappear or become nonexistent. If it did, then before someone attained nirvana, an inherently existent samsara would have existed. However, cyclic existence arises dependently, as illustrated by the twelve links of dependent origination. Samsara has never been inherently existent.

Furthermore, an inherently existent samsara would be permanent and could not cease. In that case, when someone attains liberation her inherently existent samsara could not disappear. However, when someone attains nirvana, her samsara becomes nonexistent. The samsara that ceases at liberation is conventionally existent samsara. Samsara does not become nonexistent by natural means, however. A counterforce—the wisdom realizing emptiness—must be applied to cut its continuum.

Although many of these points are aimed mainly at refuting the ideas of non-Buddhists, we should use them in our own meditation to uncover how we think of the world as inherently existent. Perhaps we hold concepts about permanent subatomic particles, a permanent person, or an inherently existent person with an unchanging personality. We ordinary beings grasp inherent existence, so the arguments refuting this are very helpful to us. We should investigate whether material objects, minds and mental factors, and so on have parts or not. If they do, why does that preclude their being inherently existent one or many and thus their being inherently existent? Whether you analyze gross objects or tiny ones, the arguments work equally on both.

You may wonder, "The person is momentary and disintegrates moment by moment. How can someone who creates destructive or constructive karma ever experience the result?" This question resembles that of the non-Buddhists refuted above, and it is helpful to use the same reasoning to refute your own misconceptions. Reflect that if a person is momentary, there isn't the fault of an effect being experienced without its cause having first been created. Also reflect that if a person is impermanent, there is not the fault of the result being experienced by a person who didn't create the cause. Both of these faults would occur, however, if a person were unchanging. Contemplate the continuum of the person—one moment of the person gives rise to another. The later moments are dependent on the former ones but are not exactly the same as them. Such a continuum enables a cause to bear its result later on. However, this isn't possible if the person is permanent and static.

The line *When asked whether there is any end to the world, the Victor remained silent* introduces the following verse, which deals with the Buddha declining to respond to particular questions.

> 74. Because he did not teach the profound Dharma
>   to beings who were not [suitable] vessels,
>   the wise understand that the Omniscient One
>   is indeed omniscient.

The Reason for Not Saying Whether the World Has an End

When the Buddha was asked if the self and world had an end or not, he didn't reply. Here, *self* refers to the person, and *world* refers to the aggregates, both the internal aggregates that are the basis of designation of a person and external forms and so forth in the surrounding environment. Because the Buddha did not reply, the people who asked the question thought he was not omniscient.

These people believed the person was permanent, unitary, and independent, whereas the Buddha stated that such a self could not exist. According to the Buddha, there is no person who can be the basis for the attributes of permanent, unitary, and independent, nor can there be any aggregates that a permanent, unitary, independent person depends on. However, the people asking this question assumed the existence of such a self and world. For this reason, it was inappropriate for the Buddha to answer one way or the other, because both would be incorrect according to their way of thinking. If he said, "Yes, there is an end to the aggregates," they would have thought that there is no continuity of the mind or of the person after death. If he answered, "No, there is no end to the aggregates," they would have thought that an inherently existent person continued on to the next life. Both are incorrect.

If he said the self has an end, they would have thought a permanent, unitary, independent person has an end, and thus such a person exists now. However, no permanent, unitary, independent person exists at all. If he said that it does not end, that would only reinforce their wrong conception that a permanent person exists. Either way their view of the person would become firmer. If he told them such a person didn't exist at all, they would either get angry or think that no person whatsoever exists. Although well meaning, these people were not suitable vessels for learning selflessness because they would misunderstand selflessness to mean nonexistence, and that would not help them at all.

For example, let's say someone has made up his mind to steal a car. He then asks you, "Should I steal it today or tomorrow?" Neither response is right. There is also no use telling him not to steal because he won't listen to you. His mind is completely set on stealing the car. Whatever answer you give won't suit the situation.

The very fact that the Buddha did not answer the question is the answer to their question. Because the Buddha is omniscient, he knows their disposition and the best way to guide them. The wise understood why the Buddha did what he did and, to them, the Buddha's silence confirmed that he was indeed omniscient.

In general, there are four ways to reply to different types of questions. (1) Some questions can be answered straightforwardly. If someone asks, "Is sound permanent or impermanent?" we can clearly say that it is impermanent. (2) Some answers require qualifications. If someone asks, "Are all sentient beings who die born under the control of afflictions and karma?" we would say that sentient beings who have abandoned afflictions and karma won't be born under their influence, while those who haven't abandoned afflictions and karma will.

(3) To respond to some questions, we need more information. If somebody asks, "Is a person on the path of accumulation superior?" we have to answer with a question, "Compared to whom?" This is because such a person is superior in relation to those who haven't entered the path but not in relation to the buddhas and arya bodhisattvas.

(4) Some questions are better left unanswered. An example is the question above, "Does a permanent, unitary, independent person have an end or not?" There are fourteen such questions that the Buddha didn't answer because he knew that whatever answer he gave would not help the person. For this reason, he remained silent.

75. Thus the all-seeing perfect buddhas have said
     the Dharma of the highest good
     is profound, inapprehensible,
     and also without any foundation.

How the Buddha Taught the Profound Meaning of Emptiness

The *Dharma of the highest good* is nirvana, the emptiness of a mind free of afflictions and the polluted karma that causes rebirth. It is *profound* because it is difficult to realize. It is *inapprehensible* in that it cannot be established, apprehended, or grasped as either of the two extremes of absolutism and nihilism. This profound emptiness is without a *foundation* of inherent existence, meaning there is no line of reasoning that can establish it as inherently existent.

The Buddha taught that by realizing and meditating on emptiness, we can attain the results of the three vehicles. In short, the profound—emptiness—isn't established as either of the two extremes and cannot be apprehended in either of the two extreme ways. Emptiness also does not have a foundation, or reason, for being inherently existent.

76. But persons who delight in foundations,
     not having transcended [notions of] existence and nonexistence,
     are terrified by this foundationless Dharma,
     and being unskilled, they are ruined.

77. Terrified of that fearless state,
     ruined, they lead others to ruin.
     See to it, O King, that no matter what,
     you are not led to ruin by those already ruined.

The Fault of Fearing Emptiness

Emptiness is *foundationless* in that true existence does not exist at all. True-grasping is a mind apprehending signs—*signs* meaning true existence. The foundation of the true-grasping mind—that is, its conceived object—is a truly existent object. Since truly existent objects do not exist, true-grasping has no foundation or basis.

Some people become terrified when they hear there is no truly existent self. Their fear is due to their strong grasping at the self to be truly existent and to the build-up of the imprints of this grasping in their mindstreams since beginningless time. They have very few imprints for understanding selflessness.

While no one except a buddha is completely free of the imprints of true-grasping, there is a difference in the strength of the imprints among those who have them. People also differ in the strength of imprints they have for understanding selflessness and the extent of their collection of merit. Understanding this, we see how important it is for us to listen to teachings on emptiness and to study, contemplate, and meditate on it as much as we can, because doing so will have a powerful effect on our ability to understand and realize emptiness in this and future lives.

Being *unskilled* and lacking wisdom, some people grasp phenomena as truly existent and think that if phenomena don't truly exist, they don't exist at all. They become terrified when they hear about emptiness, believing that nothing exists or that karma and its effects don't exist. Their response is in stark contrast to those who have the imprints and merit to understand emptiness and whose hearts are joyful when learning, contemplating, and meditating on emptiness.

People may go astray in many different ways. Some are not interested to learn about emptiness. They never listen to teachings or contemplate emptiness and thus ignorance lives happily in them. As a result, they will continue to cycle in samsara endlessly.

Other people abandon emptiness, saying it is nonsense and folly. These people are *ruined* in that they don't make an effort to learn and contemplate the correct view of emptiness and like the people who are uninterested in emptiness, they, too, will continue to cycle in samsara without end.

Still other people reject emptiness and fall to the nihilist extreme, abandoning karma and its effects. Thinking there are no future lives and that their actions have no ethical consequences, they engage in many destructive actions and fall to the lower realms.

Still others misunderstand emptiness and think there is no existence and no nonexistence. They, too, are led astray and reborn in the lower realms.

What is even more tragic than one individual ruining himself due to wrong views is that person teaching his misconceptions to others. Ruined himself, he leads others to ruin by encouraging their wrong views and condoning their destructive actions.

Usually we think that people who slaughter animals for a living create great negativity. However, compared to giving up emptiness, that is not so bad. When someone fears emptiness and abandons it, she dims the lamp that dispels the darkness of ignorance in the mindstreams of all sentient beings. She abandons the unique cause for attaining the truth body of a buddha—the dharmakaya—and will not be able to attain any of the four buddha bodies. While a butcher kills a limited number of sentient beings, someone who abandons emptiness—and especially someone who teaches wrong views to others—interferes with countless sentient beings being able to attain peerless awakening. We should definitely be alert and vigilant so that we don't become such a person.

Nagarjuna addresses the king directly here, but what he says applies to all of us. He advises us to exert ourselves to understand that empty means dependent arising, and dependent arising means empty. In this way, we will be able to posit emptiness and dependent arising without contradiction.

When people deny dependent arising, they also repudiate cause and effect, the existence of the Three Jewels, and so forth. To avoid that, we need to understand how to posit dependent arising correctly. In addition, everything that is dependently arisen is empty of inherent existence. To understand that, we must learn how to posit emptiness correctly. If we accept true existence, there is no way to posit either dependent arising or emptiness. It is essential to know how to posit the two truths—conventional truth and ultimate truth—as being complementary—they are one nature but nominally different.

Saying things are empty of inherent existence negates only a particular type of existence—existence from its own side, objective existence, and so forth. It does not negate all existence. Phenomena exist, but they exist as mere name, mere designation, and mere convention. To say that a phenomenon exists by mere designation does not mean that someone has to be actively designating it at that very moment. For example, if you see a blue object with your visual consciousness, before you have the conception of a blue object, that blue object still exists by being merely designated by conception.

When you think deeply and understand that all phenomena—anything included in the two truths—cannot exist inherently, you may wonder, "How do they exist?" If you are already familiar with the notion that phenomena exist by mere name, mere convention, and mere designation by conception, that doubt won't arise. If it does, it is quickly resolved. Otherwise you might easily think phenomena don't exist at all, even though you may not feel comfortable with that idea. For this reason, with great compassion Nagarjuna explained to us that although phenomena don't inherently exist, they do exist.

SELFLESSNESS OF PERSONS AND SELFLESSNESS OF PHENOMENA

Nagarjuna continues his argument to help dismantle our true-grasping, the source of our wandering in cyclic existence with all the misery that entails. After exhorting the king—and us, the readers, too—he explains that both persons and all other phenomena lack a self—that is, they lack an inherently existent essence.

> 78. King, so that you might not be ruined,
> I will explain in accord with the scriptures
> this correct, transcendent approach
> that does not rely on the two [extremes].

Exhorting the King

Nagarjuna and the king have a particularly close relationship. The king is Nagarjuna's benefactor, and out of compassion Nagarjuna wants to advise him to learn profound emptiness. Indirectly Nagarjuna shares this advice with all of us. He teaches us the transcendent approach that does not rely on the two extremes of absolutism and nihilism so that we can avoid mistakes that would lead to our being endlessly lost in cyclic existence. Using reasoning and scriptural quotation, he perfectly explains to us this path of the middle way exactly as it is explained in the sutras of definitive meaning.

> 79. Beyond both negativity and merit,
> it is the profound meaning derived [from the scriptures];
> other [philosophers, such as] the *tirthikas*, and even some of our
> own
> have not tasted it for they fear the foundationless.

To go beyond both the non-meritorious and meritorious karma that produce rebirth in cyclic existence, we must meditate on profound emptiness.
Doing so will lead us to the highest good. The non-Buddhist tirthikas and
even some of our own Buddhist followers—adherents of the Svatantrika
and lower philosophical tenet systems—have not been able to fully understand emptiness as it is explained in the Buddha's definitive sutras. They
lack experience of emptiness due to their fear that phenomena lack any
inherently existent foundation.

To avoid being paralyzed in that fear, it's important to understand that
emptiness and dependent arising support each other. Because things are
empty, they arise dependently; because they arise dependent on other factors, they are empty. Since everything is empty of inherent existence, there
is no other way for phenomena to exist except as dependent arisings. Even
though you may not understand the full import of this statement, just having a general belief that it is true brings enormous benefit. As long as you
follow the Buddha's definitive teachings, never feel discouraged or think,
"I don't know anything."

> 80. The person is not earth, not water,
>   not fire, not wind, not space,
>   not consciousness, not all of them [together].
>   What person is there other than these?

The Selflessness of Persons and Phenomena

This verse has great meaning. Its key point is that the person and other phenomena such as the aggregates don't have the slightest existence from their own
side and are posited merely through the force of nominal convention. In other
words, phenomena do not exist inherently, but they do exist conventionally.

In his *Sixty Stanzas of Reasoning* (verse 37), Nagarjuna says:

> Since the buddhas have stated that the world is conditioned by
>   ignorance,
> why isn't it reasonable to assert that this world is [a result of]
>   conceptualization?[19]

---

19. The word *conceptualization* or *conceptuality* has many different meanings according

The world is conditioned by ignorance in that our environment and the sentient beings in it arise due to self-grasping ignorance, the chief afflictive obscuration that prevents liberation. The Buddha explained that from self-grasping ignorance arise all the afflictions, and from them comes the polluted karma that keeps us bound to the five polluted aggregates that a person appropriates anew in each lifetime.

The world does not exist in the way it appears to ignorance, nor does it exist in the way we ignorantly apprehend it. When we realize that the conceived object of self-grasping ignorance does not exist in the way that self-grasping apprehends it, we realize that the person and aggregates—or whatever object we analyze—do not inherently exist. However, the mere person and the mere phenomena that are the focal objects of both self-grasping and reliable cognizers exist conventionally, as mere name, by mere concept or designation. To have a full understanding of emptiness and dependent arising, after realizing emptiness we must realize their nominal existence.

Refuting the false mode of existence—inherent existence—of an object does not negate the general existence of the object. When we refute a truly existent object, we are implicitly positing a conventional object that exists as mere name and convention, due to the force of concept. This is the essential meaning of the Madhyamaka texts. While they also explain branch topics, the essence of all these texts is the compatibility of emptiness and dependent arising: all persons and phenomena are empty of inherent existence but exist dependently, nominally, as mere designations. Because it is difficult to understand, this important point is repeated often.

In general, understanding that phenomena exist as mere designations does not arise automatically from understanding emptiness. It comes only after having contemplated many reasons that lead to an inferential reliable cognizer of emptiness. Later, when you have a direct perception of emptiness and become an arya, because of having repeatedly contemplated existence by mere name and concept in the past, automatically

---

to the context. In this verse, it refers to true-grasping. However, when it is said that everything exists by mere concept, it simply means conceiving an object and giving it a name. In yet another context, conceptualization refers to distorted ways of thinking and false projections, and in still another way, it can refer to discursive thoughts that interrupt concentration. Virtuous conceptuality also exists, for example, when we engage in hearing and reflecting on the Dharma.

upon arising from meditative equipoise on emptiness you will see phenomena as illusion-like in the time of subsequent attainment—the time you meditate on other topics or engage in daily-life activities.

The ease with which you will be able to realize that all phenomena exist by mere name after realizing emptiness depends on the extent to which you have understood this topic beforehand. For example, a bodhisattva on the path of preparation, whose understanding of emptiness is still conceptual, spends time reflecting, "Although phenomena don't truly exist, they exist dependent on name and concept, on conceptual designation." After she gains direct, nonconceptual realization of emptiness on the path of seeing, when she arises from meditative equipoise on emptiness she will be able to establish phenomena as conventionally existent without much trouble. She will easily realize that although phenomena appear to be inherently existent they are not, and thus conventionally, phenomena exist falsely like illusions. This is because she previously contemplated that phenomena exist conventionally, by mere designation. For this reason, it is extremely important that we understand that things exist by mere name.

This is a subtle point. Let alone the Vaibhashikas, Sautrantikas, and Chittamatrin masters not being able to understand it, even great Svatantrika masters like Bhavaviveka could not see that phenomena can be empty of inherent existence and still exist conventionally as mere name, mere convention. So, of course, we will not be able to understand this point without thinking about it a lot.

In the *Four Hundred Stanzas on the Middle Way* (verse 178), Aryadeva says:

> Apart from conceptuality, desire and so forth have no existence.
> Who with intelligence would hold that [there are] real things
> [imputed by] conceptuality?

This and the preceding quotation are difficult to understand. Learned scholars and geshes must discuss a lot to figure out their meaning. The essential point turns out to be something we are already familiar with: because everything is merely designated by conception, it is not appropriate for the intelligent to apprehend phenomena as existing from their own side. They should know them as merely designated by conception on the conventional level.

Chandrakirti explains the meaning of this stanza in his commentary to the *Four Hundred*: if something exists by mere conceptual designation, it exists; if it does not exist by mere conceptual designation, it does not exist. Having said this, it is important to note that whatever is merely designated by conception does not necessarily exist. For example, a rabbit's horn and a turtle's mustache are merely designated by conception, but neither exists. However, all phenomena—all existents—are merely designated by conception. There is no other way for them to exist.

The way in which things are merely designated by conception is similar to a snake being merely designated by conception on a rope. Under certain conditions, such as being in a dimly lit place, we can't see well. When we see a thin, striped thing coiled in the corner, a snake appears to us. We think, "Oh no, there's a snake!" and are terrified. However, when we shine light on that place, we see it is only a rope and we are relieved. What happened? Based on the striped coiled object we imagined a snake; we designated "snake" in dependence on this and attributed all the qualities we associate with a snake to the rope. However, no part of the rope is a snake, nor is the rope as a whole a snake. There is no snake there; the snake was merely fabricated by thought; a snake was merely designated in dependence on the rope.

In the same way, all phenomena exist by being merely fabricated by thought. When the physical and mental aggregates appear, we conceive a person and designate "I." In fact there is nothing within the aggregates that is the I. One aggregate is not the person; the collection of the five aggregates is not the person. No part of an aggregate is the person, and the continuity of the aggregates is not the person. Furthermore, if we search outside of the aggregates, we cannot identify anything as I or me. Nowhere is an I or me to be found. The I is merely designated by conception, fabricated by thought. Nothing can be posited or identified as being the I.

Although both the snake and the I are the same in terms of being merely designated by conception and not being findable within its basis of designation (the rope and the aggregates respectively), there is a difference between them. The snake designated on the rope does not exist at all—it cannot perform the function of a snake—while the I designated in dependence on the aggregates does exist. There is a person who walks and smiles.

How do we know the I exists even though it cannot be found in the aggregates or separate from them? It fulfills the three criteria for conventional existence. First, the person is commonly known in the world. We all know that a person exists, goes here and there, performs actions, and experiences their results. Second, the existence of the I isn't contradicted by a conventional reliable cognizer. Other people whose senses are unimpaired look over there and see a person and it functions like a person. Third, the existence of the I isn't contradicted by probing awareness analyzing the ultimate nature. While probing awareness analyzing the ultimate can negate the existence of an inherently existent person, it cannot negate the existence of a conventionally existent person because the latter is outside of its purview.

On the other hand, the existence of the snake can be disproved. First, it isn't commonly accepted in the world for a rope to be a snake. Second, people with unimpaired senses in a brightly lit room do not see a snake there; they see a rope. Third, a probing awareness cannot establish a snake there.

In short, the verse from the *Sixty Stanzas of Reasoning* explains that although phenomena are not truly existent, true-grasping ignorance motivates the creation of karma, and due to this, the environment and the beings in it come into being. Although they come into being due to true-grasping, they are not truly existent; they exist by mere conceptual designation.

The stanza from the *Four Hundred* explains that true duhkha and true origins exist by being merely fabricated by thought. Apart from being merely designated by conceptuality, true duhkha and true origins cannot be found. Therefore, the wise do not grasp them as inherently existent, nor do the wise deny that they are merely conceptually designated. All phenomena exist by being merely designated or fabricated by conception; the example of a snake being designated on a coiled, striped rope illustrates this.

As we know, identifying the object of negation is the first step in realizing emptiness according to the Prasangika view. One sutra states that all the attractive and unattractive things in the world are posited by conception. Anything more than what is merely designated by conception is the object of negation.

The above verses by Nagarjuna and Aryadeva highlight two key points for understanding emptiness according to the Prasangikas' view: the reasons why phenomena do not exist inherently and the faults of believing them to exist in that way, and the meaning of mere designation by conception and why phenomena exist in this way.

Verse 80 explains that the basis of designation of the person is the six constituents: earth, water, fire, air, space, and consciousness. Although it is usually said that the five aggregates are the basis of designation of the person, saying the six constituents are the person's basis of designation is also correct. Five of the constituents—earth, water, fire, air, and space—comprise the first aggregate, the body. The body's solidity is the earth element, its cohesiveness is the water element, its heat is the fire element, and its motility is the air element. The space inside bodily cavities—for example, in the stomach and intestines—is the space element. The consciousness constituent comprises the four mental aggregates.

When meditating on emptiness, we do not look for an inherently existent person. Rather, we search to see if the person inherently exists. If a person existed inherently, it would have to have certain characteristics. We then investigate to see if the person is like that or not. We examine whether the person who comes and goes, who reads and eats, who experiences happiness and pain, and so forth exists in the constituents individually or in the collection of constituents, or if it exists separately from them.

Although an inherently existent person is an object of negation in the meditation on emptiness, and the first step in meditating on emptiness is to identify the object of negation, we can't realize an inherently existent person with a reliable cognizer because it doesn't exist. Rather, we think of what such a person would be like if it did exist and hold a conceptual appearance of an inherently existent person in our mind. An inherently existent person would be totally independent of causes and conditions, parts, or any other factors, including name and conceptuality. Then we investigate whether the person actually exists like that or not. The person isn't any one of these constituents and it is not the collection of all of them. Separate from these six things that constitute the basis of designation of the person, we cannot find a person. What person is there other than these? These few lines have tremendous meaning; understanding them requires deep contemplation.

> 81. Just as the person is not real
>   due to being a composite of six constituents,
>   so each constituent also is not real
>   due to being a composite.

Anything that exists inherently should be findable either in its basis of designation or separate from it. As established in the previous verse, the person is not any of the six constituents and cannot be found in the collection of constituents. The person also cannot be found separate from the constituents.

However, this does not mean the person is totally nonexistent, because it depends on the composite of six constituents. It also depends on being merely designated by conception in dependence on the collection of the six constituents. Something that exists by being merely designated by conception cannot exist inherently, because inherently existent things would have their own independent essence. We can state this in the form of a syllogism as follows: consider a person; it does not inherently exist because it is merely designated in dependence on the collection of the six constituents that are its basis of designation.

Having refuted the inherent existence of the person, lest we then think that its constituent parts exist inherently, Nagarjuna refutes that as well. Using the same reason—being merely designated in dependence on the collection of its parts—Nagarjuna shows that each of the six constituents doesn't exist inherently. Just as the person exists by being merely designated in dependence on its basis of designation, the six constituents, so too does each constituent exist by being merely designated by conception in dependence on the collection of its parts.

For example, the earth element doesn't inherently exist, because it arises depending on the collection of its parts. The earth element cannot be found in any of its parts individually, in the collection of its parts as a whole, or in the continuity of its parts. Nor is it separate from its basis of designation. What other earth element could there be? We investigate the other constituents in a similar way. None of them can be found independent of their basis of designation and the mind that conceives and designates them.

This reasoning—of not being identical with or totally separate from its parts—can be used for any phenomenon. Once we understand it clearly in relation to one object, we can apply it to any phenomenon. Similarly, the reasoning we use to show that the person is merely designated by conception can be used for all phenomena.

82. The aggregates are not the self, nor do they exist in the [self];
    nor is the [self] in the [aggregates]; but without them, the [self]
        cannot exist.
    And the self and aggregates are not mixed like fire and fuel.
    Therefore, how could the self exist?

The Selflessness of Person

This verse explores the relationship of the self and its basis of designation, the aggregates. If the person existed inherently, it should exist in one of the five ways mentioned in this verse. Nagarjuna also discusses this in chapter 22 of *Treatise on the Middle Way*, where he examines the existence of the Tathagata.[20]

Before we examine these five, it's important to understand that there are two selves: a self that exists and a self that is negated. The self that exists is the person who creates karma and experiences the pleasurable, painful, and neutral results. This is the mere I that exists by being merely designated by conception. This self is the focal object of self-grasping as well as the focal object of a conventional reliable cognizer apprehending I.

The self that is negated is the conceived object and the apprehended object of self-grasping. It doesn't exist. Here *self* means inherent existence, true existence, existence from its own side, and objective existence of both persons and phenomena. This is the self that is negated by reasoning, the self that is refuted when we realize selflessness.

If the person existed inherently, it would have to exist in one of these five ways in relation to the aggregates that are its basis of designation. We'll examine each point to see if the self exists inherently.

(1) *The aggregates are not the self.* The person and the aggregates are the same entity or nature, but they are not inherently one entity. If they were inherently the same entity, they would have to be identical: the I and the aggregates would be inseparably one, exactly the same in every way.

Generally speaking, when something is the same entity or same nature as another thing, the two things don't have to be inseparably one without any difference at all. But if we talk about two things being inherently one entity, they have to be inseparably one and totally identical. If the aggregates and the person were inherently one entity, several faults would ensue. First, just as there are five aggregates, there would have to be five selves, or just as there is one self, there would have to be one aggregate. Both of these are impossible.

Someone might say, "There are many persons because there is the person of the past life, the person of the present life, the person of the future life,

---

20. See Tsong Khapa, *Ocean of Reasoning,* 439–52.

the person experiencing happiness, the person experiencing suffering, and so on." That is true; however, here we are speaking about the person that exists at any given instant of time. Are there five persons at that moment just as there are five aggregates? Is there one person who is just the body, another person who is the feelings, and so on? Of course not. Similarly, we can't say that since there is one person, there is only one aggregate.

In addition, if the self and the aggregates were inherently one, asserting a self would be useless because it would be identical to the aggregates. If the self were the body, for example, every time we used the word *I* we could substitute the word *body*. Thus instead of saying, "I got a job," we would say, "the body got a job." The body would also think and do everything else that the I does.

If the self and the aggregates were inherently one, we wouldn't be able to remember events from the past. In addition, karma we created in the past would get lost, and we could experience the results of karma we didn't create. Why would these unwanted results come about if the person and the aggregates were inherently one? Just as the aggregates arise and cease inherently, the person would arise and cease inherently.[21] Something that arises and ceases inherently is not part of a continuum. When it ceases, it is gone forever. In that case, each moment of a person would be a separate person that was unrelated to the previous and subsequent moments of the person. If the person of each moment of our continuum were inherently separate from all the other moments, we could not remember what we did in the past, because an entirely different person existed in the past. In addition, any karmic seed the person of one moment created would not be passed on in the continuum of that person. If that were the case, either the result of the karma a person created in this life would not be experienced by the continuum of that person in the next life, or if it were, then the person in the next life would experience results of actions created by a totally different person. In that case, that person could experience the results of karma created by anyone in the universe because everyone else would equally be a totally separate person.

Furthermore, if the I were one with the body, since the person of this life came from the previous life, the body of our previous life would also exist in this life. Or since the body of this life came from the sperm and

---

21. See Tsong Khapa, *Ocean of Reasoning*, 369–91.

egg of our parents, we'd have to say the I came from the sperm and egg of our parents. So many foolish consequences would arise if the I and the aggregates were identical.

Additionally, (2) *the aggregates are not in the self* and (3) *the self is not in the aggregates*. In general, the aggregates and the person have the relationship of "basis and dependent" or "support and supported." The I is the dependent, the supported, and the aggregates are the basis or the support. However, they are not inherently basis and dependent. The aggregates are not in the I—that is to say, the aggregates don't depend on the I. For example, if there is a bowl of yogurt, the bowl is the basis and the yogurt fills it and depends on it. In this case, the I would be like the bowl and the aggregates like the yogurt. There would be a person and the aggregates would fill it up and depend on it. But the relationship between the I and the aggregates isn't like this. Thus the aggregates are not in the I. Alternatively, the I is not in the aggregates—it does not inherently depend on the aggregates. Here the aggregates would be like a house and the person would be a separate entity living in it and depending on it. Again, this is not the relationship between the I and the aggregates.

These two kinds of dependence could occur only if the I and the aggregates were inherently different. In general, the I and the aggregates are different. They have different names and meanings. While things that are different conventionally don't have to be totally unrelated, things that are inherently different must be totally separate with no relationship to each other at all. For example, cause and effect are different and they are different entities but they are related in that one produces the other. The wood that forms the table and the table are different, but they are related because they are one nature.

In both of these examples, if the two things were inherently existent, they would have to be totally unrelated, which is not the case at all. It is the same with the person and the aggregates: they are different but related. The person is designated in dependence on the aggregates.

If the aggregates and the person were inherently different and unrelated, the aggregates would not be the basis of designation of the self. They would be distinct like flowers in a vase. The flowers depend on the vase but are different from it. But the person and the aggregates aren't separate like this, even though they are basis and dependent. They are one entity; we don't observe them separate from each other in the way that we observe the flowers and the vase as two different things.

The verse goes on to say (4) *without them, the self cannot exist.* Without the aggregates, there wouldn't be a person. It is impossible to identify a person without the presence of the aggregates. The person cannot exist on its own, independent of the aggregates.

If the I and the aggregates were inherently different, they would be totally different and unrelated. In that case, if the aggregates were eliminated one by one, the person could still remain there. In addition, the aggregates could be in one place and the person in another.

Lastly, (5) *the self and aggregates are not mixed like fire and fuel.* Some people believe the person and the aggregates have an inexpressible relationship that is neither one nor different. They believe the person and aggregates are mixed in an ineffable, inexpressible fashion like wood and the fire burning it. When wood is burning, the fire is inseparable from it. In fact, the fuel becomes the fire. However, the self and the aggregates aren't mixed in that way, and one does not become the other. This option is not acceptable because in an inherently existent world, things must be either completely identical or totally unrelated.

These five possible relationships can be condensed into two: the person and aggregates are either inherently one or inherently different. To say they are mixed like fire and fuel is similar to saying they are inherently one. Thinking they are inherently basis and dependent is thinking they are inherently different.

In place of the fifth point above, in *Treatise on the Middle Way* Nagarjuna says that the person does not inherently possess the aggregates. Generally speaking, the person does possess the aggregates—we say, "This is my body, this is my mind." But the person doesn't inherently possess them. There are two ways to inherently possess something: either (1) the person possesses the aggregates the way we own a house—a case of them being different entities, or (2) the person possesses the aggregates in the way Joe possesses his ear—they are one nature. The relationship of possession is not inherent, however. If it were, then in the first case the faults of the person and the aggregates being inherently different would accrue, and in the second case the faults of their being inherently one would obtain.

If the self does not exist in any of these five ways in relation to the aggregates, how could it inherently exist? So many undesirable consequences arise when we examine if the self and aggregates have some sort of inherently existent relationship. The only viable conclusion to reach after this analysis is that an inherently existent person does not exist.

In the *Supplement*, Chandrakirti adds two more points: (6) the self is not the collection of the aggregates, and (7) the self is not the arrangement of the aggregates. Together with the above five, this forms the well-known sevenfold analysis. The two latter points can be subsumed into the self and aggregates not being inherently one or inherently different.

Because the five or seven points can be condensed into the self and aggregates not being inherently one or inherently different, the lamrim and thought-training literature speak of four essential points to use when meditating on the emptiness of the person: (1) identifying the object to be refuted, the inherently existent person, (2) ascertaining the pervasion that if the person existed inherently it would be either inherently one or inherently different from the aggregates (there is no other option), (3) determining that they cannot be inherently identical, and (4) determining that they cannot be inherently different or separate. From this analysis, we then conclude that the person does not inherently exist and thus is empty of inherent existence.

When we go into the proof of non-true existence more elaborately, five principal reasonings can be used for analysis: (1) the reasoning of being free of one and different, which analyzes the entity of phenomena; (2) the diamond splinters reasoning that analyzes the cause; (3) the reasoning that refutes production from the existent and nonexistent, which analyzes the effect; (4) the reasoning that refutes production from the four extremes, which analyzes both cause and effect; and (5) dependent arising, the monarch of reasonings.[22] All of these are precious tools for us to use to discover the nature of reality.

> 83. The [other] three elements are not earth, nor are they in earth;
>   nor is the [earth] in them, but without them, the [earth element]
>   cannot exist.
>   Such is also the case for each [of the other elements].
>   Therefore, as with the self, the elements are unreal.

---

22. See Hopkins, *Meditation on Emptiness*, 131–93.

Refuting Inherently Existent Phenomena

In the previous section, Nagarjuna examined the person and instructed us how to meditate on the selflessness of persons. In this section, he focuses on the selflessness of phenomena, which include impermanent things such as the five aggregates and permanent phenomena such as space. Here, too, the analysis centers on determining if things are inherently identical or inherently different.

Nagarjuna begins with investigating impermanent things—the five aggregates—using the fivefold reasoning found in the previous verse, without the option of possession. First among the aggregates is form. While the definition of *form* is vague—it is "whatever is suitable to be form"—it principally refers to material objects, which may be gross or subtle. The definition of gross form is "that which is composed of a group of the eight atomic substances."[23] Examples are the body, the table, a leaf, the planet Neptune, and so on. The eight atomic substances are the four tiny particles—the elements of earth, water, fire, and wind—and the four elemental derivatives—visual form, smell, taste, and tangibles. While *atom* is not a perfect translation for a tiny particle as conceived in this ancient system of physics, we will use it for convenience. First we examine the four elements that are the bases of the form aggregate to see if they exist inherently, then we do the same for the form derivatives. Having done that, we can conclude that the form aggregate, the four elements, and the elemental derivatives do not exist inherently.

The four elements are parts of a collection that is the basis of designation of a larger material object. These elements do not inherently exist because they exist in relation to and reliant on each other. Just as the person and the aggregates—as the designated object and as its basis of designation— are mutually reliant on each other, so too are the four elements mutually reliant on each other. For this reason, the mode of analysis to see if they inherently exist is the same: we examine if they are inherently identical or inherently separate.

This examination leads us to four conclusions: first, *the other three elements are not earth*. Air, water, and fire are not inherently one with the

---

23. These definitions are from the *Collected Topics* (dura), one of the first texts studied at monastic universities.

earth element. If they were, they would have to be inseparably one, and then earth would be the defining characteristic of all the other elements. In that case earth would be hot and burning (the defining characteristic of fire), light and moving (wind), and wet and cohesive (water). Clearly the earth doesn't have those characteristics. In this way, the claim that earth is one with the other three elements is refuted through direct perception.

Conventionally, the four elements that compose the form aggregate are mutually the basis of each other. However, they are not inherently one or different. The earth element, for example, has all of the other elements complete with it, but it is not inherently one with them. It possesses the other three elements, but not inherently.

The line *nor are they in earth; nor is the earth in them* expresses the next two conclusions. The other three elements are not inherently dependent on earth, and earth is not inherently dependent on them; such a relationship would have to be the case if they were inherently different. Fourth, without them, the earth element cannot exist; that is, the earth element cannot stand alone on its own without the other three elements. They exist in mutual dependence on each other.

This same reasoning is used to show that water, fire, and wind do not exist inherently. For example, water is not inherently one with the other three elements, nor is it inherently the basis of the other three. The other three elements aren't inherently based on or dependent on water. Also, the water element cannot exist by itself without the other elements. Therefore, as with the self, the elements are unreal; they do not inherently exist.

To review, Nagarjuna first showed that there was no inherently, existent person. Then he analyzed the components of the body, the four elements. In the same way, these elements, which are part of the basis of designation of the person, do not exist inherently because they do not exist in any of the four ways. Thus, like the person, the four elements are not real, and the mind that grasps them as inherently existent is erroneous.

84. Earth, water, fire, and wind
    are each not inherently existent,
    since each one does not exist without the [other] three,
    and the other three do not exist without each one.

85. If each one does not exist without [the other] three,
    and [the other] three do not exist without each one,
    then individually they do not essentially exist,
    so how could they arise as a compound?

Mutual Reliance Precludes Inherent Existence

Individually, earth, water, fire, and wind are not inherently existent since each one does not exist without the other three. If we removed three of the four elements, the fourth one would no longer be present. Similarly, if one element were removed, the other three would not be there. For example, in a collection of elements, if the fire element were missing, the other three elements would also not be present. Since they are dependent and reliant in this way, the four elements cannot exist inherently by themselves. Even conventionally they have to exist as a group.

All four elements exist within the collection of elements and derivatives that makes up a given material object. In this composite, the components rely on each other. While they exist in a mutually reliant manner, the four elements are not mixed with each other in the sense of being indistinguishable from the others. Instead, each still retains its own properties and characteristics.

Inherent existence is the same as independent existence; independent existence and dependent existence are contradictory. Therefore, anything that arises dependently cannot exist independently and thus is not inherently existent.

86. If each [element] existed on its own,
    why wouldn't fire occur without fuel?
    Likewise, why wouldn't there be water, wind, and earth
    without coherence, motility, and hardness?

Someone says, "Each of the four elements exists inherently, and when they come together, they form an inherently existent composite." This cannot be. Since each element does not inherently exist, a form that is a composite of them cannot inherently exist.

In the context of inherent existence, two or more things cannot rely on each other; they must be totally unrelated, independent, and separate. If each element existed inherently, there could be fire without firewood because fire would be completely different and not reliant in any way on the other three elements. In that case, fire would not need to depend on fuel.

> 87. If you claim that [only] fire is well known [to depend on fuel],
> then according to you, how could the other three be
> independent?
> It does not make sense for those three to be incompatible
> with what is interdependently arisen.

Dispelling Further Arguments through the Reasoning of Dependent Arising

In these debates with philosophers from other traditions, we see that after Nagarjuna responds to their claim, they listen and change their assertion. If the new assertion is also incorrect, Nagarjuna refutes it as well. In response to Nagarjuna's previous refutation, now someone says, "Everyone knows you can't have fire without fuel. But the other three elements are different. If one is not there, the other three can be, so they exist inherently."

Nagarjuna meets this head on, saying, "If you claim that only fire is well known to depend on fuel, how could the other three be independent?" Fire needs fuel to exist and fuel is composed of the other three elements, so fire cannot exist without relying on the other three. Following this logic, none of the other three elements can be posited without relying on fire.

If this were not the case, then without earth (hardness) being in a composite of elements, water (cohesion), fire (ripening), and wind (motility) could still be present. The property of cohesion could exist inherently and independently, without there being anything to adhere together. Motility could exist by itself without anything that moves. Fire could exist by itself without anything to heat.

Nagarjuna goes on, "It does not make sense for those three to be incompatible with what is interdependently arisen." In other words, each of the other three elements arises dependent and related to the others, so they are not inherently existent. If each of them existed inherently, it would not rely on causes and conditions and would not be mutually dependent on the others. If the wind element, for example, did not exist in reliance upon causes and conditions, it would either always exist everywhere or it would exist nowhere. It could arise without a cause and cease without its cause having ceased. Causes and conditions could have no effect on it at all.

The four elements in any collection cannot be separated. They cannot exist on their own, totally apart from the others. Each one exists dependent on the others and vice versa. Something that is reliant cannot exist independently or inherently.

The four elements are the basis for a gross material object, and the gross object arises dependent on those elements. The above argument refutes the inherent existence of the elements that are the basis for a material object. After refuting this, it is easy to prove that the derivatives and the material object itself do not exist inherently.

> 88. [If] those [elements] each exist on their own,
>   how could they exist mutually?
>   And [if they] do not each exist on their own,
>   how could they exist mutually?

Now someone says, "Although the elements rely on each other, the entity of each one exists inherently." Nagarjuna responds by giving an unwanted consequence, "If what you say is true, then the elements can't be mutually reliant because inherent existence and mutual reliance are contradictory." Since the lower systems cannot accept that the four elements are not mutually reliant, they must give up their assertion that they inherently exist.

Furthermore, if things exist with their own inherent essence, they cannot arise from causes because inherently existent things cannot be affected by any other factors. Svatantrikas and below think that dependent things such as cause and effect both rely on other factors and exist inherently. They are not able to understand how to use dependent arising as a reason to prove emptiness, whereas Prasangikas use dependent arising and mutual reliance as reasons to prove that phenomena lack existence from their own side. Because things depend on other factors, they cannot exist under their own power, with their own inherent essence.

On the other hand, if the elements did not each exist on their own, they would be mixed and could not be distinguished individually. In that case, they could not be mutually reliant. They must be conventionally distinct—but not inherently different—in order to depend on each other.

89. If each does not exist on its own,
    but whenever there is one, the remaining [three are present],
    then [if] not mixed, they cannot be present in one locus,
    and [if] mixed, they cannot each exist on their own.

Someone says, "When one element is present in a place, the remaining three come with it. All of them exist from their own side because when there is one element, the defining characteristics of each element come together with it." Nagarjuna asks, "If the remaining three elements are also present wherever there is one element, are their natures mixed or unmixed?" If they are not mixed, they cannot be present in one locus, because the four cannot abide together unmixed on one object. If their natures are mixed, they cannot each exist on their own. In this case, the nature of each element can't exist inherently because it's been mixed with the natures of the others. In short, it is not correct to think that although the four elements do not inherently exist individually on their own, they exist inherently as mutually reliant.

90. How can elements that do not exist on their own have inherent
    characteristics?
    [When mixed, one element] cannot predominate
    [since it] does not exist on its own.
    [Hence, their] characteristics are stated conventionally.

We define or identify the four elements depending on their individual, specific characteristics. Abhidharma literature states the defining characteristics of each element. Earth is hard and solid; fire is hot and burning; water is wet and moistening; wind is light and moving. These characteristics do not exist inherently because the elements don't exist individually on their own.

Someone asks, "If the characteristics of the four elements are mixed, we couldn't distinguish one from the other, and since they exist inherently we should be able to. When elements join to form a collection and their natures are mixed, their specific characteristics still exist inherently because there are differences in the extent to which they dominate the mixture. We can distinguish each element according to its preponderance in the mixture."

Nagarjuna answers, "We aren't contradicting Abhidharma; we agree that each element has its own specific defining characteristics. However, when the four elements exist together, although there is a difference in the degree of preponderance of each one's specific characteristics, none of them exist inherently. The characteristics of hard, hot, wet, and moving depend on each other."

This person has confused having specific characteristics with existing by its own characteristics. Existing by its own characteristics is synonymous with inherent existence. Each element has its own specific characteristics conventionally, but these characteristics do not exist inherently; they exist by relying on each other. In brief, specific characteristics do not exist by their own characteristics or inherently.

In his *Supplement*, Chandrakirti uses the reason that material objects have parts to prove that the form aggregate does not inherently exist. These parts are the tiny particles of the four elements that come together to form a collection. These tiny particles, in turn, have parts, and are therefore dependent arisings and lack inherent existence. By first proving that the individual elements lack inherent existence, it is easy to show that a collection of them gathered together also lacks inherent existence. Anything that depends on parts does not exist independently and therefore does not exist inherently.

The reasoning in *Precious Garland* is slightly different. Here Nagarjuna emphasizes the fact that the elements rely on each other. We usually speak about impermanent things being dependent on their causes and conditions, but here dependence is illustrated by analyzing the tiny particles and showing that the eight particles that make up a collection rely on each other.

> 91. This approach also applies to colors,
>   odors, tastes, and tactile [objects].
>   Such is also the case with the eye [faculty], consciousness, and
>   [visible] forms;
>   ignorance, karma, and birth,

> 92. Agent, object, and action, number,
>   conjunction, cause and effect, and time,
>   long and short, and so on—
>   designation and designated as well.

Refuting the Inherent Existence of Elemental Derivatives and Applying This to Other Phenomena

To prove the non-inherent existence of the elemental derivatives, Nagarjuna instructs us to use the same reasoning that proved the four elements are not inherently existent. Just as the four elements exist in reliance upon each other, so too do colors, odors, tastes, and tactile objects. Where one is, the others are also; when one is missing, the other three also are not present. Thus, because they exist dependent on one another, the derivatives do not inherently exist.

Nagarjuna now extends the analysis to many different kinds of phenomena. The eye faculty, consciousness, and visible forms compose a set of three dependent factors, as do the sense faculty, consciousness, and object of each of the other senses. The eye sense faculty helps to connect the object (a visible form) to the consciousness (the visual consciousness that perceives that form). These three are also mutually dependent in that the sense faculty and its object cannot be causes unless there is an effect—the visual consciousness that perceives that form.

Ignorance, karma, and birth are another set of causally related factors. Ignorance refers to the first of the twelve links and other afflictions. Karma denotes the virtuous, nonvirtuous, and neutral actions created under its influence. Birth refers to the fortunate and unfortunate births in cyclic existence that result from the various karmas. These, too, are mutually related in that something cannot be a cause without there being an effect or the possibility of an effect.

Agent, object, and action form a set of dependently related factors present whenever any activity occurs. *Number* means one and many, all the different numbers. *Conjunction* refers to the meeting of two or more phenomena. It also refers to an object, such as a person born in cyclic existence, possessing the attributes of impermanence, unsatisfactory nature, emptiness, and selflessness. *Cause and effect* are another related set. Something is an effect because it arises from a cause; something is a cause because it has the potential to produce an effect. *Time* refers to the past, present, and future as well as to different lengths of time such as months, years, and so forth. *Short and long* are distinguished in relation to each other; *and so on* refers to various other shapes such as round and square and other sets of dependent phenomena. *Designation and designated* refers to phenomena and their definitions. For example, "thing" is a designation, and "that which is able to perform a function"—the definition of "thing"—is the designated. Just as the elements and their derivatives are not inherently existent, all of these phenomena similarly lack inherent existence because they exist dependent on other factors that are not themselves.

As well has the sense of "like that." Initially the non-inherent existence of the person was explained. Just like that, the non-inherent existence of the four elements was established; and like that the emptiness of the elemental derivatives and all these other phenomena is established. The mind to which these things appear inherently existent and that grasps them as inherently existent is mistaken. The person appears to be inherently existent to the self-grasping of the person, and self-grasping apprehends the person as inherently existent. Similarly, all the other minds to which inherent existence appears or that grasp inherent existence are mistaken. Their objects are false; they don't exist as they appear.

> 93. The Sage has stated that earth,
>   water, fire, and wind,
>   short and long, thick and thin, virtue and so on
>   cease in the awareness [of the ultimate].

The Meaning of All Phenomena Being Empty of Inherent Existence

Phenomena from earth and water, up to virtue and so on—all other phenomena—can be the subject of a syllogism proving non-inherent existence. For example, "Consider earth: it does not inherently exist, because it is not seen by the aryas' wisdom of meditative equipoise. The reason is indicated because the Sage—the Buddha—stated that the elements cease in the awareness of the ultimate." In other words, if they were inherently existent, they would be seen by the aryas' meditative equipoise on emptiness. However, for that awareness they have ceased, in that they do not appear to that mind.

The aryas' meditative equipoise on emptiness is a nonconceptual wisdom that directly and nonconceptually perceives the emptiness of inherent existence. This is a nondualistic mind in that there is no appearance of subject and object. To this mind, only emptiness appears; conventional objects do not appear to it, and there is no appearance of inherent existence whatsoever. This mind is mixed with the object emptiness inseparably, like water mixed with water.

This wisdom knows the ultimate nature of all phenomena and perceives phenomena as they really are. If earth and so forth existed inherently, this wisdom should perceive them in this way. However, to the aryas' meditative equipoise on emptiness these things do not appear. Thus the Buddha stated that they cease in the awareness of the ultimate.

In general, if things exist they don't have to be seen by the aryas' wisdom of meditative equipoise that sees reality. This is because things exist conventionally and this wisdom perceives only their ultimate nature. But if their ultimate mode of existence were inherent existence, then that wisdom should perceive inherent existence. However, it perceives the opposite; it perceives the emptiness of inherent existence. Thus all these things lack inherent existence.

> 94. Earth, water, fire, and wind
>   cannot find any place [to exist]
>   in that indemonstrable, limitless,
>   fully sovereign awareness.

> 95. Short and long, subtle and coarse,
>   virtue and nonvirtue,
>   and also name and form,
>   all cease in this [awareness].

For the aryas' nonconceptual wisdom of meditative equipoise that is free of true-grasping, true existence does not exist. This wisdom awareness is *indemonstrable*—it cannot be shown to another person in the same way we can show someone an apple. Aryas cannot point to something and say, "This is emptiness" or "This is the wisdom realizing it nondualistically," so that others immediately understand. We must experience this wisdom awareness ourselves. It is *sovereign* in that it perceives the actual mode of existence of all limitless phenomena.

From the perspective of this ultimate wisdom, earth, water, fire, and wind cannot find any place to exist. There is no footing for them to stand on because these objects, which appear inherently existent to our ordinary

consciousnesses, do not appear to this mind. This wisdom sees only emptiness; it does not in the slightest perceive conventionalities that are empty.
Similarly, all these bases that possess the attribute of emptiness—*short and
long, virtue and nonvirtue, name and form* (this last pair being the fourth
of the twelve links)—have ceased from the perspective of this wisdom. Just
their reality—their emptiness or suchness—is seen.

A sutra says, "Not seeing is the best seeing." Do not misunderstand this to
advocate blank-minded meditation. Rather, it means that not seeing inherent existence is the most exalted kind of seeing. That mind does not see
inherent existence or the conventionalities that appear to be inherently existent. *Best seeing* refers to seeing the emptiness of inherent existence of conventional phenomena—their actual mode of existence, their reality—that is
seen directly and nonconceptually only by the aryas' meditative equipoise on
emptiness. For this reason, that awareness is considered supreme and holy.

The "not seeing" of aryas' meditative equipoise on emptiness is far superior to the inferential realization of emptiness of ordinary beings. While an
inferential realization of emptiness has a powerful impact on a meditator,
it is still a conceptual consciousness. It realizes emptiness with the dualistic appearance of subject and object. True existence and conventional
phenomena still appear to it. Inferential consciousness does not perceive
emptiness intimately, like water poured into water; it knows emptiness via
a conceptual appearance. Aryas, in contrast, see emptiness free of dualistic
appearance, free of conventional appearance, free of the appearance of subject and object, free of conceptual appearance, and free of the appearance
of true existence. They know emptiness directly, just as it is.

Although the aryas' wisdom of meditative equipoise does not see conventional phenomena, that does not make them nonexistent. Rather, conventionalities are not in the purview of the wisdom realizing the ultimate
nature. It is similar to a reliable visual consciousness not seeing a sound.
That doesn't mean the sound is nonexistent; it is simply that sound is not
in the scope of what a visual consciousness can perceive.

> 96. All that previously appeared to awareness,
>   due to not knowing that [reality],
>   later will likewise cease in awareness
>   because one has come to know that [reality].

Here Nagarjuna addresses someone with a doubt: "Do all conventional objects cease in the perspective of the aryas' meditative equipoise on emptiness because this wisdom destroys conventionalities? Does wisdom make things empty that were not previously empty of inherent existence?"

If conventionalities existed inherently and aryas' wisdom did not see them, then that wisdom would destroy things that previously existed. That is, if conventionalities existed inherently they would exist as they appear, and this appearance would be their ultimate nature. Since aryas' wisdom of meditative equipoise perceives the ultimate nature of phenomena, it should perceive inherently existent conventionalities. In that case, if inherently existent conventionalities were not seen by this wisdom of aryas, that wisdom would have destroyed them.

However, this is not the case. The appearance of conventionalities as inherently existent is false, so the fact that they are not seen by aryas' wisdom realizing the ultimate nature doesn't destroy something that previously existed. Rather, aryas' wisdom of meditative equipoise sees the absence of something—inherent existence—that never existed. This wisdom is not nihilistic.

Emptiness exists primordially. Things, by their very nature, have always lacked inherent existence. The emptiness of inherent existence is not newly created by aryas' wisdom of meditative equipoise. Rather, that wisdom realizes what has been there all along.

For example, when someone's sight is obscured by vitreous floaters, an eye disease that makes one see falling hairs, he cannot see forms clearly. Although from the outset the form itself was clear, this person could not see it due to the obscurations caused by the disease. However, when the eye disease is cured, and his eyes are free of that defect, he can clearly see what was there all along. Similarly, when ordinary beings' minds are covered by afflictive obscurations, they cannot see the emptiness of inherent existence that has always been the ultimate nature of phenomena. By practicing the path, they remove obscurations and purify their wisdom so they can then directly perceive the emptiness of true existence that has always been there. In short, the arya's meditative equipoise on emptiness neither destroys something that previously existed nor makes something empty that previously existed inherently. It simply sees what has been there all along, the emptiness of inherent existence.

97. It is maintained that all beings and [their] qualities
    are fuel for the fire of awareness.
    Having been incinerated by brilliant true analysis,
    they are [all] pacified.

When fire burns fuel, the fuel ceases to exist. When the aryas' wisdom of meditative equipoise sees emptiness, all the conventional phenomena that appear inherently existent cease in the sense that they do not appear to that wisdom. The aryas' wisdom does not see them as nonexistent—they just do not exist for that wisdom. Just as sunlight eliminates darkness, the aryas' wisdom of meditative equipoise directly sees reality and pacifies all elaborations of dualistic appearance. This wisdom sees the ultimate mode of existence of conventional phenomena without seeing those objects themselves. However, when aryas come out of their meditative equipoise on emptiness, conventionalities reappear and are ascertained by their conventional reliable cognizers.

98. The reality is later ascertained
    of what was formerly imputed by ignorance.
    When a thing is not found,
    how can there be a non-thing?

Ignorance—specifically true-grasping ignorance—means not knowing. This distorted mind is not only blind to the ultimate nature of reality but also superimposes true existence on what is not truly existent. After we study, reflect, and meditate on emptiness and determine through reasoning that phenomena are empty, we ascertain reality and understand that the actual mode of existence of phenomena is their emptiness. It is clear to us that the true existence imputed by ignorance does not exist at all.

Someone says, "Although things don't truly exist, that non-true existence itself truly exists." To this Nagarjuna responds, "When we analyze things to see if they truly exist, we don't find any truly existent things. How, then, could a non-thing—the emptiness of true existence of things—be truly existent?" That "non-finding" of truly existent things is not truly existent, because the things themselves are not truly existent. Emptiness exists in relation to conditioned phenomena that are the bases of emptiness. Since those bases don't truly exist, what is based on them—their emptiness—cannot truly exist.

99. Since it is merely the absence of form,
   space is merely a designation.
   How can there be form without the elements?
   Therefore, the mere designation also does not exist.

Refuting the Inherent Existence of Unconditioned Space

In the previous verses, Nagarjuna established the non-inherent existence of conditioned things such as the person, aggregates, elements, and their derivatives. This verse examines unconditioned phenomena to see if they exist inherently.

As an unconditioned phenomenon, space is merely designated on the absence of obstructing form. It is a non-affirming negative that is the mere negation of obstructing form. Because obstructing form—which is its object of negation—does not exist inherently and is a mere name, space too must be a mere designation. Since it is posited in relation to form and form lacks inherent existence, space must also lack inherent existence.

Nagarjuna asks, "How can there be form without the elements?" Form or material objects depend on and cannot exist without their parts, the elements. Since the elements lack inherent existence, so do the material objects that are composed of them and that are designated in dependence on them. Since the bases for designations don't exist inherently, the designated objects also lack inherent existence. *Therefore, the mere designation also does not exist.* Since the elements lack inherent existence, so do the forms designated in dependence on them. And since form is empty of inherent existence, so is space, which is designated in dependence on the absence of form.

Saying that objects are mere names does not mean that they are words or sounds. If a tree were a sound, it couldn't grow leaves. Being "mere names" means that objects exist by being merely conceptually fabricated or designated.

100. One should consider feelings, discriminations,
   volitional factors, and consciousnesses
   in the manner [that one considered] the elements and self.
   Hence, the six constituents are selfless.

Applying the Same Analysis to the Remaining Aggregates

Nagarjuna has explained why the person, as well as form, which is the first of the five aggregates that are the basis of designation of the person, does not inherently exist. He analyzes whether the person was inherently identical or different from the aggregates, and analyzes the parts and attributes of gross material objects—the elements and elemental derivatives. To understand that the four mental aggregates—feelings, discriminations, volitional factors, and consciousnesses—also do not exist inherently, he applies a similar analysis. We should meditate on each of the four mental aggregates individually to determine if it exists inherently or not. This way we can conclude that the six constituents are selfless—they do not exist inherently, truly, from their own side, objectively, substantially, by their own characteristics, and so forth. While the lower tenet systems have different meanings for these terms, Prasangikas say they all come to the same point and thus negate them all.

In short, nothing that is totally independent of causes and conditions, or any other factors, can be found under ultimate analysis, which searches for the ultimate mode of existence. Everything relies on something else that is not the thing itself. Because of this, nothing exists inherently. That doesn't mean that things don't exist at all. They exist, but not independently. They exist by being merely designated by conceptuality, and everything still performs its own function in this interdependent world.

This completes the commentary to part I of the *Precious Garland* by Nagarjuna, entitled "Higher Rebirth and Highest Good."

II. An Interwoven Explanation of the Causes and Effects of Higher Rebirth and Highest Good

5. Delving into the Profound

In part I, Nagarjuna explained higher rebirth and then highest good. Now he interweaves these two topics, first discussing the causes and effects of highest good, followed by the causes and effects of higher rebirth. Then he once more returns to the causes and effects of highest good.

CAUSES AND EFFECTS OF THE HIGHEST GOOD

Having stimulated us to reflect on emptiness, Nagarjuna continues on that theme. If phenomena don't exist inherently, how do they exist? They exist like illusions, falsely, deceptively. While they are not illusions, they are similar to them in that they appear to exist one way but actually exist in another. Things appear to exist inherently but in fact are empty of inherent existence and exist dependently. As such, they exist by being merely designated by name, merely fabricated by conception.

> 101. When one splits apart the plantain tree along with all its parts,
>   [one finds] no [core] at all,
>   so too, when one "splits apart" the person with its six
>   constituents,
>   [one finds] no [essence] at all.

An Example

When the bark of most trees is removed, we find hardwood underneath. But this is not the case with a plantain tree. If we search for a core of hardwood by peeling off its bark layer by layer, nothing is found.[24] Similarly,

---

24. Although plantain plants are commonly called "trees" and can grow up to twenty to twenty-five feet in height, they are not actually trees. What appears to be a tree trunk at the base of the plant is actually a pseudostem made of layers of leaf sheaths.

when we use ultimate analysis and search the basis of designation to find a person, we don't find one. Whether we search in the aggregates, the constituents, the elements, or the elemental derivatives, we cannot identify a person. Although the person depends on these, it is not any of them individually. Nor is it the collection of them as a whole. The person is also not found separate from these components. The same holds true for all phenomena: they cannot be found in their basis of designation as either inherently one or inherently separate from their parts. Furthermore, they are not the collection of parts.

> 102. Hence, the Victors have said
>   that all things are selfless;
>   it has been demonstrated to you
>   that the six constituents are selfless.

> 103. In this way, neither self nor non-self
>   are ultimately perceived just as they are.
>   Therefore, the Great Sage refuted
>   both views of self and non-self.

Self and Selflessness Do Not Inherently Exist

The Buddha is called the *Great Sage* because his body, speech, and mind are not stained by even the subtlest faults. He has rejected the views of self and of non-self as inherently existent, and he leads others to abandon these erroneous views. Here *self* refers to the person and *non-self* refers to emptiness or selflessness. Neither the person nor its emptiness exists from its own side.

In verse 98, someone said that refuting the inherent existence of things proves that emptiness exists inherently. This is incorrect and is refuted again here. Both things and non-things (their emptiness) lack inherent existence; both self and selflessness do not exist from their own side.

Someone argues, "For you to say all phenomena are selfless contradicts what the Buddha himself stated, because he taught the existence of a self to some people." It is true: he said that the person is self-sufficient, substantially existent to a group of disciples who formed a Vaibhashika subschool called the Sammitiya. But when he spoke to people similar to Sautrantika adherents in disposition, he taught the lack of a self-sufficient, substantially existent person but said the person inherently exists. Although it seems the Buddha contradicted himself when speaking to these diverse groups of followers, this was not the case because none of these statements represented his final view. Rather, he taught what was suitable according to the dispositions of these different audiences, and in this way, he skillfully and gradually led them to understand the most profound view.

In fact, the Buddha's intention was that there is no self. He rejected both an inherently existent person and the inherent existence of the selflessness of that person. *Neither self nor non-self are ultimately perceived just as they are* indicates that when we analyze both the person and its selflessness, we don't find even an atom of inherent existence. For this reason the Great Sage refuted both views of an inherently existent self and non-self. In other words, the person is selfless and that selflessness itself is also empty, or selfless. This is one way of explaining this verse according to the Buddha's own thought.

We can also read this verse as saying that a conventionally existent self comes from the previous life and goes on to the subsequent life. This person creates karma and experiences its happy and painful results. Such a self exists, but not inherently. The Great Sage refuted the view that grasps the inherent existence of both a conventionally existent self and its selflessness. Both a person (self) and its emptiness (its selflessness) exist, but neither exists inherently.

In short, as a skillful teacher who addressed the specific needs of each audience, the Buddha taught the existence of a self to some followers and refuted the existence of such a self to others. His definitive meaning is that both the person and the emptiness of the person do not exist inherently. The view that there is a self was a provisional teaching, a method to lead certain people to the definitive meaning over time.

Someone protests, "Claiming that all phenomena are selfless contradicts the sutra passage that says, 'The self is your protector.'" The self that is mentioned in this passage is not an inherently existent self; it is the conventionally existing self. Nagarjuna does not dispute that a person exists conventionally.

104. As for what one sees, hears, and so on,
 the Sage did not call them either true or false.

If from one position its opposite arises,
both do not exist in fact.

105. Hence, this world is ultimately
beyond truth and falsity.
Therefore, [the Buddha] does not accept
that it really exists or does not.

Absence of Inherent Existence of Existents and Non-Existents

What one sees, hears, and so on refers to the six objects of the six consciousnesses—the five sense consciousnesses and the mental consciousness. The Buddha said that these objects are not *true* or real, meaning they are not truly existent. He also said that they are not *false* or unreal.

This might puzzle us. Generally speaking, objects of the senses are said to be false because they do not exist as they appear. They are obscured truths (conventional truths). Ultimate truth—emptiness—on the other hand, exists the way it appears and is said to be true. Ultimate truth is empty and appears empty.

In saying that objects of the six consciousnesses are neither true nor false, the Buddha negates the two extremes. Here, *true* means truly existent; *false* means totally nonexistent. Sights, sounds, and so forth are not truly existent, but neither are they totally nonexistent. Saying they are not true refutes the extreme of absolutism, and saying they are not false eliminates the extreme of nihilism. *Both do not exist in fact* indicates that both the true existence and total nonexistence of conventionally existent things do not exist.

If from one position its opposite arises, both do not exist in fact. Someone says, "When true existence is negated on an object, it must be non-truly existent, because non-true existence and true existence are directly contradictory. In that case, non-true existence must be truly existent." As discussed above, emptiness is posited in relation to objects that are empty—the person, aggregates, and so on. Being dependent on these objects, emptiness is also empty of true existence. Both non-true existence (emptiness) and true existence do not truly exist. This is a difficult but important point.

Ultimately the world transcends being truly existent and totally nonexistent. For this reason, the Sage doesn't say it really exists or does not exist.

106. How could the Omniscient One say
that what [he knows to be]
utterly nonexistent
is finite or infinite, both or neither?

The Buddha's Reason for Not Making a Statement Regarding the Four Extremes

As noted in verses 73 and 74, during the Buddha's lifetime people posed questions to him regarding the self and the world based on their assumption that phenomena existed inherently. Given their wrong conceptions, the Buddha remained silent. To answer would have reinforced their misconception that phenomena existed inherently. They would have thought that an inherently existent world didn't have an end or that an inherently existent person had an end; such beliefs would harm them.

Within the context of inherent existence, he could not give a truthful answer. Asked if the self had an end, didn't have an end, both, or neither, he could not make an accurate statement because an inherently existent person does not exist at all. Such questions are like asking if a turtle's moustache is soft, coarse, both, or neither, when no turtles have moustaches!

Most of these questions take the form of a tetralemma. For example, someone asked the Buddha if the world (1) has an end, (2) doesn't have an end, (3) both has an end and doesn't have an end, or (4) neither has an end nor doesn't have an end. While the fourth option seems to be a reworking of the third, it refers to another inherently existent option.

If cyclic existence had a beginning, there must have been a time in the past when it did not exist and then later it came into existence. In that case, what brought cyclic existence into being? The only options are there was either no cause or a discordant cause, such as an external creator. Both of these are untenable. Firstly, a functioning thing such as cyclic existence must be produced by a cause. In addition, it could not have a discordant cause—a cause that doesn't have the capacity to produce cyclic existence, such as an external creator. Such an assertion creates many questions: Why did the creator create? If the creator is permanent, how can he or she create anything, because creation entails change? What was the cause of the creator?

While cyclic existence has no beginning, it does have an end. If we hold a seed in our hand and think about its causes, the causes of its causes, and so on, we cannot reach an initial cause that was the beginning. However, if we burn the seed so that it is completely destroyed, it has an end and its continuity and potency cease. Similarly, while the ignorance that causes cyclic existence is beginningless, it can be eradicated by the wisdom realizing emptiness. In that way, the continuity of cyclic existence ceases.

> 107. There have been innumerable past buddhas;
>   likewise, future buddhas and present buddhas are innumerable.
>   And the extent of the three times' sentient beings
>   is considered to be zillions of times more [than those buddhas].

> 108. The world's cessation, occurring in the three times,
>   does not cause its increase.
>   Why then did the Omniscient One [maintain that]
>   its beginning and end are indeterminate?

Dispelling an Objection That Not Teaching an End to Cyclic Existence Is Wrong

These two verses express a question someone asked the Buddha: "It's wrong for the Buddha not to answer the question about cyclic existence having an end, because it does have one. There is a time that the continuity of each sentient being's samsaric lives will cease, because there are numberless buddhas throughout the past, present, and future." This person says that even though there are zillions of times more sentient beings than buddhas, the number of sentient beings is always decreasing because each of these buddhas leads zillions of sentient beings to liberation and awakening by showing them the path.

This person continues, "Furthermore, no new sentient beings are coming into existence, so their number will only decrease as more sentient beings are constantly attaining liberation and awakening. Thus there will be an end to cyclic existence. Why, then, didn't the Omniscient One make a statement to that effect?"

Saying that sentient beings are innumerable or countless means that the number is so great, we are unable to count or grasp how many there are. This is not the same as infinite. It's true that the number of sentient beings is continuously decreasing. Although he did not say there is an end to cyclic existence, the Buddha did not refute this fact. He did not respond because the person asking the question was under the assumption that sentient beings inherently exist. If the Buddha had replied, it would have only strengthened that person's belief in an inherently existent person. For example, the person could have thought that if samsara has an end, the continuum of an inherently existent person ends at that time and the person becomes totally nonexistent.

Suppose the Buddha replied, "What kind of sentient being are you referring to? If it is a conventionally existent sentient being who exists by mere name, then yes, there is an end to this person's samsara. A sentient being that exists by mere conceptual designation wanders in cyclic existence under the control of afflictions and karma. When this being encounters the Buddhadharma, and studies, contemplates, and meditates on the path, he or she can abandon samsara and attain liberation. But if you are talking about a sentient being that exists inherently, I can't say that there is an end to cyclic existence because an inherently existent sentient being doesn't exist to start with."

There is no beginning to sentient beings or to cyclic existence, but each being's cyclic existence has an end, no matter what realm he or she is currently born in. Each and every sentient being has the buddha nature—both the naturally abiding buddha nature and the transforming buddha nature—as an inseparable part of his mind. The adventitious stains that cause cyclic existence do not abide in the nature of the mind and there exists an antidote to remove them, the wisdom realizing emptiness. Since this is the case, even someone currently in a hell realm can become a buddha after her buddha nature and the seeds of constructive karma on her mindstreams are awakened.

While that hell being may not attain liberation in her present body, she will become a buddha in the future when she has a favorable rebirth that allows her to learn and practice the path. In a future life, the continuity of that hell being will one day be a bodhisattva at the end of the tenth ground, who in the next moment becomes a buddha. So in general there is a time when each sentient being will attain full awakening.

If countless buddhas have helped and are currently helping sentient beings attain awakening, why haven't we become buddhas yet? All the conditions necessary for practice need to be present in order for us to become buddhas, but we haven't attained those yet. We must live at a time and place where a wheel-turning buddha has come, meet with fully qualified

Mahayana and Vajrayana spiritual mentors, and have interest and enthusiasm for the Dharma. We know from the stages of the path literature that it is extremely difficult to create the causes for all the optimum conditions to attain awakening. And even if we attain them, do we make use of them?

While all sentient beings have the potential to attain awakening, most sentient beings are not receptive to the Dharma and do not study, contemplate, and meditate on the path. Without creating these causes, there is no way for them to attain resultant buddhahood. All the buddhas and bodhisattvas in the world can neither convince nor force a person to practice the Dharma. For this reason it is difficult to think of a time when all sentient beings will be awakened.

No matter how far back we go in time, buddhas have been present, but that does not mean that some beings have always been buddhas. Everyone who is now a buddha must have become a buddha gradually through amassing the collections of wisdom and merit. Every buddha was formerly a sentient being; there is no one who has always been a buddha.

The virtue sentient beings create is related to the buddhas' awakening activity and is due to the blessings and inspiration of the buddhas. Since virtue has existed in the mindstreams of sentient beings since beginningless time and its cause is the buddhas' awakening activity, there must be countless buddhas stretching back in beginningless time. The buddhas' awakening activities manifest chiefly by giving teachings. Through hearing the buddhas' teachings, sentient beings learn to discern virtue and nonvirtue. By then practicing virtue and abandoning nonvirtue, they gradually actualize the stages of the path to awakening. They could not do this without the buddhas' awakening activities. In general, if no buddhas arose in the universe, there would not be any bodhisattvas, hearers, or solitary realizers, and thus no new buddhas. Nevertheless, this does not mean that there are buddhas who were never sentient beings prior to attaining awakening.

Some people say that the first buddha is the all-pure dharmakaya. However, each sentient being has to attain the dharmakaya through training in the path. To say there was a first buddha, we would have to posit another buddha prior to him who was his teacher and guided him on the path so he could attain full awakening. And that buddha would have received teachings from a previous buddha, and so on.

In a historical sense, we can talk about the first buddha in our particular world system. One thousand buddhas will appear as supreme emanation bodies in the present fortunate eon; three have already appeared and the current one is Shakyamuni Buddha. However, before these buddhas, there were also buddhas who appeared in the form of emanation bodies in other world systems and in other times.

> 109. Such is the profound Dharma
>   that is obscure to ordinary beings;
>   that the world is like an illusion
>   is the ambrosia of the buddhas' teaching.

The Profound Is Hidden for Those Who Are Unsuitable Vessels

Samsara and nirvana lack true existence; this is the profound Dharma that is obscure to ordinary beings. The world and the sentient beings in it are like magical illusions; they are false in that they appear truly existent but do not exist in that way in the least.

Those sentient beings whose self-grasping ignorance is strong and who are extremely attached to things existing as they appear cannot understand this profound teaching. While they ask the Buddha questions such as "Is the self permanent, impermanent, both, or neither?" underlying their question is the assumption that the self truly exists. If the Buddha tried to explain emptiness to them, they would reject it and criticize the Buddhadharma, and thus create unbearable destructive karma. For this reason the Buddha did not share this ambrosia of immortality—the teaching that leads to the deathless state of nirvana—with them.

> 110. An elephant created through magical illusion
>   might seem to arise and cease,
>   but ultimately there is not
>   any arising or ceasing at all.

> 111. So too, the world, like a magical illusion,
>   might seem to arise and cease,
>   but ultimately there is not
>   any arising or ceasing at all.

An Example

In ancient India, magicians could make sticks and stones appear as real horses and elephants through the use of special substances and mantras. Some of the animals may even look like they are being born or dying.

The audience, magician, and latecomers to the show relate to the magical display in different ways. These three examples are profound, and we must take our time to contemplate them. The audience is under the influence of the spell of the mantra and the special substance, so they see real horses and elephants with their eyes, and they mentally believe there are actual horses and elephants there. Similarly, phenomena appear truly existent to ordinary sentient beings. Under the influence of ignorance, they apprehend and conceive of truly existent people being born and dying, although there are no truly existent people or things at all. Never doubting the accuracy of those appearances, ordinary beings do not see things as illusory but believe they exist the way they appear.

The magician is affected by the spell and magical substance, so real horses and elephants appear to him. However, unlike the audience he knows they are illusions and does not grasp them as real. In other words, his visual consciousness sees horses and elephants, but his mental consciousness knows they are only an appearance and doesn't think they are real. Similarly, things appear truly existent to ordinary beings who have realized emptiness conceptually and to aryas in post-meditation time. However, they are not deceived by the false appearances because they have realized that things do not truly exist in the way they appear to. They know they are empty and do not grasp them as truly existent.

Latecomers to the show are not affected by the special substance and mantra, so horses and elephants neither appear to them nor do they apprehend horses and elephants. Similarly, to aryas' meditative equipoise on emptiness, truly existent phenomena neither appear nor are they apprehended.

Spectators are terrified when a magical elephant charges at them; the magician sees the elephant but knows it is not real and thus is not afraid. Latecomers see only sticks and stones and wonder what all the fuss is about. Similarly, sentient beings react with attachment and aversion to the false appearances they believe are true. In post-meditation, aryas and those who have realized emptiness inferentially see the appearance of truly existent things but, knowing they are false, remain calm and do not respond with attachment, aversion, fear, or any other disturbing emotion. Aryas in meditative equipoise on emptiness perceive only the ultimate nature—emptiness.

> 112. An illusory elephant does not come from anywhere,
>   nor go anywhere;
>   since it is merely [a manifestation of] mental confusion,
>   it does not ultimately exist.

> 113. So too the world, like a magical illusion,
>   does not come from anywhere nor go anywhere;
>   since it is merely [a manifestation of] mental confusion,
>   it does not ultimately exist.

In fact, illusory horses and elephants don't come from anywhere and don't go anywhere even though actual horses and elephants appear to parade around to spectators. Just as the audience is befuddled by the magical substance and mantra and believes that real horses and elephants are there, in the same way, ordinary beings are confused and deceived by ignorance. A truly existent world and truly existent people appear to them, and they believe them to be real when in fact they do not exist at all.

How would understanding that things are like illusions influence our lives and our interactions with the world? Words that we previously considered offensive or insulting would no longer elicit an angry response from us. The prospect of inheriting wealth or meeting the ideal person would no longer spark selfish desire and yearning. We would stop comparing ourselves to others in a way that makes jealousy or arrogance surge in us. Seeing all these things as like illusions and similarly seeing ourselves as like an illusion, we would remain balanced and able to interact with others without being obscured by attachment or aversion.

> 114. The nature of the world transcends all three times.
>   Except for [being designated in] conventional terms,
>   how could it be ultimately
>   either existent or nonexistent?

Everything Is Only Designated by Name

Since they do not truly arise and cease in the past, present, or future, objects and people are mere conceptual designations. They are not found in their bases of designation or separate from their bases of designation. Like illusions, they appear and they do things, but they are neither ultimately existent nor totally nonexistent. They exist by mere name; they are mere appearances. Like illusions, there is nothing really there that we can point to and say, "This is the world" or "This is the person."

> 115. For this reason and no other,
>   the Buddha said that [the world] was indeterminate
>   with regard to four aspects—
>   having or not having an end, both, or neither.

Therefore the Buddha Didn't Make a Statement Regarding the Four Extremes

The four alternatives—the world has a truly existent end, doesn't have an end, both, or neither—were propounded by different philosophical systems in ancient India, and today some people have similar ideas. Since the world transcends these four extremes, the Buddha did not make any statement about them.

Members of the Charvaka School—also called the Lokayatas or "Hedonists"—accept that the world has an end. They assert that a truly existent person exists in this life but at the time of death completely ceases to exist, like the flame of a candle whose wax has been consumed. There is no continuity of the person into the next life. Giving the reason that they can't see past and future lives, the Charvakas deny their existence.

Samkhyas (Enumerators) propound that the person does not have an end because it is permanent and does not cease. They propose that a permanent person exists and goes from the past life to this life and from this life to future lives, endlessly.

The Jains (Nirgranthas) say the person both has an end and doesn't have an end. The person is life and is the same size as the body. Its nature is permanent, but since it changes states it is also impermanent. This is similar to thinking that, overall, I am exactly the same person as yesterday, yet a few things about me are different.

A Buddhist sect called the Vatsiputriya states that the person neither has an end nor doesn't have an end. The person is such that no specific existential state of having an end or not having one can be determined. The person is a self-sufficient substance but its properties cannot be explicitly determined.

All of these philosophies are based on the notion that a person exists from its own side. Their proponents must assert a truly existent person because otherwise they do not know how to posit the process of karma bringing its results. For them a person that exists as a mere designation could not possibly create karma and go on to a future life where it experiences the result of its karma. Since they stubbornly hold on to wrong views, none of these people could benefit from the Buddha explaining selflessness to them. However, he could not answer their questions by going along with their assumption that the world and the person truly exist.

> 116. The impurity of the body is obvious—
> it is an object of direct perception:
> although one can see it constantly,
> it does not remain in one's mind.

> 117. If that is the case, then how could this
> extremely subtle, profound, and unlocated holy Dharma,
> which is not directly perceptible,
> easily enter into one's mind?

Why It Is Difficult to Realize the Profound

We will look at verse 117 first. The Dharma of highest good is difficult for those who aren't suitable vessels to understand, because to do so, they must realize the nonexistence of the conceived object of true-grasping. Due to their strong true-grasping, ordinary people have a hard time understanding that nothing exists in the way true-grasping holds it to exist.

Sentient beings can't directly see things such as subtle impermanence or gross and subtle selflessness with their sense faculties. These must be realized by depending on a sign that has the three criteria—the property of the subject, the subsequent pervasion, and the reverse pervasion. In other words, a syllogism with a perfect reason must be employed and properly understood in order to have a correct conceptual understanding of subtle impermanence and of emptiness. After realizing impermanence and selflessness inferentially, we must meditate on them single-pointedly to realize them directly. These topics require deep contemplation and perfect reasoning; there is no easy way for ordinary people to understand them. Even hearing the words "syllogism" and "three criteria" is intimidating to some people, so how can this holy Dharma easily enter their minds?

In comparison to the difficulty of comprehending these subtle topics, it is easier to understand the unclean nature of the body spoken of in verse 116. Everything that comes out of the body—from our eyes, ears, nostrils, mouth, skin pores, excretory orifices, and reproductive orifices—is unclean. As soon as we see these substances, we want to wash them away. That our body is unclean is easy to realize; these filthy substances are coarse objects that can be known with direct sensory perception—we see, smell, and touch them. It is not necessary to make a perfect syllogism as is necessary to initially understand subtle impermanence and emptiness.

Yet ordinary beings in general don't realize that the body is unclean and instead perversely conceive of it as clean. This misconception and three others—conceiving feelings as pleasant, the mind as permanent, and phenomena as self-existent—make up a group called the four distorted conceptions. Because of these we constantly engage in various destructive actions. Even if we have some understanding of the filthy nature of the body, it doesn't remain in our mind; we quickly forget and return to seeing the body as pure and a source of pleasure.

It is no wonder that it is difficult for us to realize profound emptiness when we consider that even though it is relatively easy to realize the body is unclean, this awareness doesn't stay in our minds for long.

118. Hence, having attained awakening,
    the Sage realized that since this Dharma was so profound,
    people would not understand it;
    so he refrained from teaching the Dharma.

Why the Buddha Didn't Teach the Profound to Unsuitable Vessels

Just after he attained awakening, the Buddha said, "I have found the nectar of the deathless, a Dharma that is profound, peaceful, free of elaborations, clear light, and unconditioned. Since whomever I teach this to will not be able to understand it, for a while I will stay in the forest and be silent." For forty-nine days, he didn't manifest turning the wheel of Dharma of the four truths of the aryas for ordinary trainees.

The Dharma he spoke of was emptiness. Emptiness is profound because it is not obvious and must initially be realized by employing reasoning. It is peaceful because by meditating on it, the afflictions in our mindstream are pacified. It is free of elaborations because it is free of the appearance of true existence. It is clear light, because the nature of the mind, for example, is not stained by true existence. It is unconditioned in that it is not unstable and does not arise and cease due to fluctuating conditions.

119. If this Dharma is misunderstood,
    it will ruin the unwise,
    for they will sink deeply
    into the filth of nihilistic views.

120. And from misunderstanding this,
    fools who presume themselves pundits,
    ruined by their denial of it,
    plummet straight down to Avici hell.

The Disadvantages of Misconceiving the Profound

Someone says, "If the profound is easy, there's not much purpose in the Buddha explaining it. If it is difficult to understand, he should explain it repeatedly with many reasons."

Again the question arises about who should be taught emptiness, and the disadvantages that ensue from teaching it to inappropriate vessels. Emptiness should not be taught to the unwise—those who are not intelligent in the way of Dharma—because they would not understand it; they would think that if things don't inherently exist, they do not exist at all. They then will think the Three Jewels don't exist and lose their refuge; they will believe that the law of karma and its effects doesn't exist and will not live in accord with precepts. Misunderstanding the causes for the truth body and enjoyment body of a buddha, they will give up their practice. Such a reaction to the teaching of emptiness confirms their inability to think properly about emptiness. It destroys their chances of having a higher rebirth and attaining the highest good of liberation and awakening. They will be ruined by committing a grave error and as a result will experience great suffering, and they will live in the filth of the lower realms as a result of holding such wrong views.

Emptiness should also not be taught to arrogant people who have an inflated sense of their intelligence—or as Nagarjuna refers to them, "fools who presume themselves pundits." These people arrogantly consider themselves highly educated and intelligent, yet they, too, misunderstand the meaning of emptiness. Some think that emptiness means total nonexistence, while others think that the emptiness of inherent existence isn't the ultimate nature of all phenomena. In this way they, too, abandon emptiness. Practicing emptiness incorrectly they cannot attain a perfect result. Both are ruined by their denial of emptiness and consequently plummet straight to the hell of unceasing torment. Because their minds cannot properly understand the meaning of emptiness, explaining it to them does not help them, and in fact, it harms them.

If you find that you do not appreciate the meaning of emptiness and are unsure if it is the ultimate truth, or if you are going in the direction of thinking that nothing exists at all, it is better to leave emptiness aside for the time being with a sense of equanimity. Do not push yourself to understand it, but focus instead on other Dharma topics and practices that you find help you to tame your mind.

This advice is specifically for those who think they are going down the path to nihilism. However, when we think about emptiness it is quite natural to sometimes wonder, "What is this 'not inherently existent' all about? If things are not inherently existent, do refuge and karma all become nonexistent?" It is normal to ask yourself such things. But once you are in the process of making up your mind that things do not exist at all, you should just leave contemplating emptiness aside for a while. Meditate on bodhichitta or study other topics instead.

Someone asks, "It is said that except for aryas' wisdom of meditative equipoise directly realizing emptiness, all consciousnesses of sentient beings are mistaken in that they have the appearance of true existence. In that case, are all the reliable consciousnesses of sentient beings mistaken?"

According to the Prasangikas, a reliable consciousness can be mistaken. A mistaken consciousness is posited according to whether the mind is mistaken with respect to its appearing object, the object that appears to it. It is not posited in relation to its conceived or apprehended objects, the object it apprehends or conceives. A mistaken consciousness does not necessarily misapprehend its conceived object. For example, a visual consciousness sees a pen. The pen appears truly existent to that mind, but that mind does not apprehend or grasp the pen as truly existent. This visual consciousness is mistaken with respect to its appearing object, a pen that appears truly existent, but is not erroneous with respect to its apprehended object, a pen. It is a reliable cognizer knowing the pen. An erroneous visual consciousness would be, for example, one seeing the green color of the pen as black due to lack of light in the room.

The pen appears truly existent to a conceptual consciousness thinking about the pen and is mistaken in that regard. However, that mind doesn't grasp it as truly existent and is a reliable cognizer of the pen. Nevertheless, a mental consciousness that is attached to the pen and thinks "That is *my pen!*" is both mistaken regarding its appearing object and erroneous regarding its conceived object, because the pen appears truly existent to it and it grasps the pen as truly existent.

Bodhichitta, compassion, love, and the inferential realization of emptiness are all mistaken consciousnesses in that their objects appear truly existent. However, they are not erroneous consciousnesses such as thinking a scarecrow is a person or thinking that phenomena truly exist. They are reliable cognizers. Don't think you shouldn't meditate on love, compassion, and bodhichitta simply because one element of that mind is mistaken!

121. Through eating poor food,
    one will come to ruin;
    but by eating the right food,
    one attains vigor, health, strength, and pleasure.

122. Likewise, through poor understanding,
    one will come to ruin.
    But through the right understanding,
    one attains happiness and unexcelled awakening.

Just as we *come to ruin* and become severely ill if we eat spoiled food, misunderstanding emptiness brings dire results, such as rebirth in the hell realms. By eating nourishing food in proper amounts, we experience long life, good health, freedom from illness, strength, and physical and mental comfort.

An intelligent and conscientious person who is skilled at subduing snakes can apply a certain substance to a snake, cast a spell on it, and then be able to handle the snake. However, a person who doesn't do this correctly is in great danger if he tries to handle a venomous snake—he will be bitten and fatally poisoned.

Similarly, if we don't hear teachings on emptiness and instead follow our own ideas, or if we misunderstand the teachings we have heard, we will *come to ruin* spiritually, which is far more serious than eating bad food or getting bitten by a snake. However, if we meditate on emptiness properly, we will go from happiness to happiness—we will have a series of good rebirths with all the conditions necessary to learn and practice the Dharma, and we will finally reach the state of peerless awakening.

> 123. Therefore, do not deny this Dharma,
> and abandon nihilistic views.
> In order to obtain all aims,
> strive for perfect understanding.

The view of existence is absolutism; the view of nonexistence is nihilism. Having abandoned these two extreme views and seeing the importance of the correct view to fully accomplish the welfare of yourself and others, exert yourself in the middle way that is free of extremes. Learning how to think about emptiness properly, apply yourself to realize emptiness and to know the ultimate mode of existence. Do your best to make your life meaningful.

CAUSES AND EFFECTS OF HIGHER REBIRTH

In the first chapter Nagarjuna outlined the general causes for higher rebirth; now he again turns to the topic of higher rebirth and goes into more depth about it. Since we may not attain highest good in this life, it is important to create the causes for higher rebirth so that we will have an uninterrupted series of higher rebirths during which we can practice the Dharma and eventually attain liberation and awakening. To do this, we should act in accord with the Buddha's teachings. For a king, that means to abandon following bad political treatises and to enact Dharma policies. Nagarjuna also discusses many practical actions to implement in daily life in order to create virtue, including the four ways of attracting others in order to introduce them to the Dharma; the four good practices to adopt—truth, generosity, peace, and wisdom; choosing companions wisely; remembering impermanence and death; and forsaking the causes of rebirth in the lower realms.

124. When this Dharma is not understood,
    I-grasping continues.
    Due to that, one engages in constructive and destructive karma,
    and from that comes fortunate and unfortunate rebirths.

Circling in Samsara Because of Not Realizing Emptiness

When we do not understand this Dharma of emptiness, I-grasping—the view of a personal identity—will continue to arise spontaneously. Due to this, attachment will automatically arise toward objects that our inappropriate attention exaggerates as being attractive and the source of happiness. Similarly, anger will persistently arise toward experiences and objects that our inappropriate attention exaggerates as being unpleasant or threatening to our well-being. Due to attachment, anger, and other afflictions that stem from I-grasping, we will create destructive karma.

When these disturbing emotions aren't manifest in our minds we can create constructive karma, but this, too, originates with I-grasping and results in rebirth in samsara—albeit a higher rebirth as a human or celestial being. In either case, as long as we are under the influence of ignorance, we will continue to take rebirth in cyclic existence. In this way, wandering in cyclic existence is caused by not realizing emptiness.

If we allow ignorance and afflictions free rein in our minds, we are not even able to help ourselves, let alone others. A sutra explains that sentient beings wander in cyclic existence because they do not understand the three doors of liberation—emptiness, signlessness, and wishlessness. These three come down to the two, the selflessness of persons and of phenomena, and those two come down to one, the door of emptiness.

125. Therefore, as long as you have not understood
     this Dharma that destroys the I-grasping,
     devote yourself to the Dharma
     of generosity, ethical conduct, and fortitude.

Exert Yourself to Have Higher Rebirths Until You Realize Selflessness

Until you can eradicate the view of a personal identity by generating the wisdom realizing emptiness, train in the practices of generosity, ethical conduct, and fortitude. These three practices include the sixteen causes of higher rebirth that Nagarjuna spoke about earlier. In that way, you will be able to have a series of fortunate rebirths during which you can accumulate merit and wisdom and eventually attain liberation or awakening.

126. King, if you undertake deeds that begin with Dharma,
     have Dharma in the middle and Dharma at the end,
     you will not be harmed
     in this world or the next.

127. Through Dharma you attain fame and pleasure,
     you have no fear now or at death;
     and in the next world, you will have great joy—
     so always devote yourself to the Dharma.

The Advantages of Training in the Cause

Before acting with your body, speech, or mind, cultivate a virtuous motivation. In all your actions have Dharma in your mind by maintaining that positive motivation, and when completing an action, have Dharma at the end by dedicating the merit for the awakening of yourself and all others. By doing so, you will not experience harm in this life or future lives.

You will also gain five benefits: (1) by acting with integrity and kindness, you will have a good reputation; (2) due to not acting in destructive ways, you won't be overwhelmed with remorse and regret and will have a happy mind; (3) by practicing nonviolence, in this life you will be free of fear and neither human beings nor spirits will have reason to harm you; (4) at the time of death you will die peacefully, free from fear of an unfortunate rebirth; and (5) in this life and in future lives your happiness will continue to expand. Therefore, always maintain a virtuous attitude before, during, and at the completion of all actions. If you practice like this, you will begin to experience these results in this life.

> 128. Dharma is the highest policy;
> Dharma pleases the world;
> and if the world is pleased,
> you will not be deceived here or hereafter.

General Training in the Holy Way

Between the two, the way of Dharma and the way of the world, choose the way of Dharma because it is holy—it originates from a positive mental state and brings benefit to ourselves and others. On an individual level, practicing Dharma leads us to a higher rebirth, while on a broader level, it enables the king or anyone in a leadership position to be successful. For people in positions of leadership or authority, Dharma is the highest policy, because leaders set the tone for a group's behavior by acting as an example. They can give citizens, followers, employees, and friends Dharma advice, which helps them to solve their problems nonviolently. This enables the members of the group to avoid backbiting, harsh speech, lying, and gossip, which fracture their harmony and prevent the group from attaining its goals. Also, by acting according to the Dharma, leaders are honest, fair, and impartially care for the welfare of everyone concerned. In this way, the people of the world will be happy and the people in the kingdom, country, workplace, monastery, or family will abide harmoniously. By engaging our body, speech, and mind in virtuous actions, we will not have enemies in this life or fall to an unfortunate rebirth in the next.

> 129. But a policy that proceeds without Dharma
> will not please the world.
> And if the world is not pleased,
> you will not be happy here or hereafter.

> 130. A useless [political] theory
> is one that intends to deceive others.

It is harsh and a path to bad rebirths—
how could the unwise make such a theory useful?

131. Since it will just [deceive] oneself
for many thousands of rebirths,
how could one intent on deceiving others
be a true statesman at all?

Abandon Following Bad Political Treatises and Their Harmful Policies

Some treatises on the formation of government policy are pernicious. Advocating violent and malicious policies that disturb harmony and create ill will in society, such theories permit or encourage cheating or lying to the populace, taking advantage of the poor or infirm, and discriminating against certain groups. For example, in the king's time some treatises encourage animal sacrifice—they state that killing animals and offering their blood and flesh to the gods will bring happiness and that both the animals and those performing the sacrifice will have fortunate rebirths. Another treatise says that when brahmins are destitute, it is suitable for them to steal others' possessions, while other treatises say that women are just like a highway that everyone has the right to travel on—that they are available for anyone who wants to have sex with them. In modern times, this could apply to political treatises advocating fascist, totalitarian, or racist policies.

Misguided people who formulate such treatises say that these various behaviors are good policy, even though in fact they harm others. Some directly harm people's lives, others their possessions, bodies, or minds. None are appropriate methods for the wise to gain what they desire. When you enact these policies you deceive yourself, because although you desire happiness, for many thousands of rebirths you will suffer through one rebirth after the other in the lower realms. If you involve others in such nonvirtue, although you say you're working for their benefit, you deceive them because they also will be reborn in the lower realms. How could someone intent on deceiving others be a true statesman?

It is simple, really—those actions are nonvirtuous. Whatever way you look at it—whether you consider the ripening result, the environmental result, the causally concordant results similar to the experience or to the behavior, or even the results in this life—only suffering comes from these actions. Harming others brings harm and trouble upon yourself. When you understand the gravity of the ten paths of nonvirtue you have followed, you have reason to feel sorrow and regret. That being the case, turn away from such policies and from the treatises that teach them.

Non-harm and nonviolence are basic tenets of Buddhism. They are guidelines we promise to follow when we take refuge in the Dharma. Regarding somebody who generates ill will and harms others, the Buddha said, "I am not their guide, and they are not my followers."

The buddhas' and bodhisattvas' heartfelt wish, which is echoed in a verse we often recite, is "May sentient beings be happy, may they be free of suffering." This is the reason they worked so hard to become buddhas and bodhisattvas, and it is what they spend all their time trying to bring about. If we harm a single sentient being, we contradict the heartfelt wish of all the buddhas and bodhisattvas and interfere with their work. If we are malicious or harm sentient beings, even if we make vast prayers and incredible offerings to the buddhas and bodhisattvas in the ten directions, they will not be happy in the least. On the other hand, establishing policies that encourage tolerance and compassionate action makes society more peaceful and encourages citizens to reach out to benefit each other. It creates the causes for well-being now and in the future, and it pleases holy beings.

> 132. If you wish to make your foes unhappy,
>   do away with your faults and enhance your good qualities.
>   That way you will gain great benefit,
>   and your enemies will also be displeased.

Dharma Policies Are Best

In situations when someone is doing great harm and you have the ability to stop them, if you generate a virtuous motivation and intercede, this will benefit you and will displease the enemy. Even though the enemy will be unhappy, you will actually benefit him by preventing him from creating destructive karma.

We become better people when we make effort to abandon our faults and enhance our good qualities. In addition to benefiting ourselves, our actions will benefit others, which pleases them. They will admire us and we will have more ability to influence them in a virtuous direction. That will make our enemies unhappy, because other people will be more attracted to us and will follow our ways rather than theirs.

> 133. Be generous, speak gently, be beneficent;
>   act with the same intention that you wish from others;
>   through these [actions], bring together the world,
>   and also sustain the Dharma.

Training in the Four Means of Attracting Others

The four means of attracting others are ways to care for others by influencing them to go in a good direction and ripening their mindstreams. To guide the minds of others to the Dharma, attract them by (1) being *generous* and giving them material support. In addition, practice the generosity of fearlessness by protecting them from danger and the generosity of love by offering emotional support and counseling. By making others happy in these ways, they will be friendly and attracted to you, which gives you the opportunity to (2) *speak* in a pleasant way to them about the Dharma by instructing them in the causes for higher rebirth and highest good. Then, (3) be *beneficent* by encouraging others to practice the Dharma and implement the teachings you have given them, and (4) *act* in a way that accords with what you have instructed them to do. In other words, practice what you preach and tame your own body, speech, and mind.

With kindness as your motivation, guide others to the Dharma. Because you embody the four ways of attracting others, on the worldly level sentient beings will practice the sixteen factors leading to higher rebirth and on the ultimate level they will create the causes for liberation and awakening. In this way, ripen the mindstreams of others.

> 134. A single truth [uttered] by kings
>   makes [their subjects] have firm trust in them.
>   Likewise, one falsehood on their part
>   is the best way to lose that trust.

> 135. [To speak] the truth is [to speak in a manner] that is not
>   deceptive;

it is not what is in fact distorted by an intention.
[A statement] is true by being of benefit to others;
the other [kind of statement] is false since it is not beneficial.

Training in Truth

While Nagarjuna is directly addressing the king as a leader, his advice also applies to us because we are in leadership roles in smaller groups such as at our work place, in our family, in sports teams, and among our group of friends. A mind that wishes to deceive others leads us to speak falsely, to trick others into believing what is not true. Speaking truthfully stems from a mind that respects others and wants to benefit them. Among the four nonvirtues of speech, lying is the heaviest and most destructive.

Speaking the truth causes others to trust the leader and have confidence in her decisions. This enables her to be able to enact policies that will benefit them and they will follow those policies. However, if a leader tells even one lie, the followers will be skeptical and mistrustful of her words, motives, and behavior. Even when she tells the truth in the future they won't believe her. Thus it's essential to speak truthfully, especially when you are in a position of authority or leadership. Politicians and businesspeople who lie, engage in fear mongering, misappropriate funds, and so on destroy the fabric of trust that a healthy society depends on.

We may think that small lies are unimportant or even beneficial if they help us get our way or accomplish a project. I knew a young boy who thought telling the truth was foolish because when he told the truth to his teacher, the teacher would scold him for playing rather than studying, whereas when he told a few little lies the teacher would praise him and give him a sweet. Lying definitely harms us as well as others—it destroys trust in relationships. Once damaged, trust is hard to restore. Nagarjuna is pointing out to the king as well as to us, his readers, that we lie all too often. If you have a habit of telling lies, even little ones, give it up.

When you speak only the truth, engage in a path of truth, and always act on the basis of truth, then even if temporarily things may not go very well for you, in the long term you will get a true result. From truth comes truth. Travelling a true path, you will reach a true result. Even if you have other faults people will trust you, and trust is the basis of all good relationships.

To speak the truth is to speak in a manner that is not deceptive—in other words, do not try to make someone believe something that is counter to the facts. In addition to being factual, truthful speech has another important element: it must not harm another person or be spoken with the intention to harm someone. Our intention must be to benefit others in the long term. To tell a hunter where to find deer harms not only the deer but also the hunter—for he creates destructive karma by killing. A true statement must benefit others, and it must be told with a motivation to benefit. Saying what is factually accurate with the intention that others suffer is not truthful speech.

> 136. A single, shining act of generosity
>   hides the flaws of a king;
>   likewise, an instance of greed
>   will contradict all of his good qualities.

Training in Generosity

Just as speaking the truth engenders trust in others that allows them to overlook some of your small faults, being generous diminishes the significance of your faults. On the other hand, being stingy even once will cause people to overlook your good qualities; they will only remember your self-centeredness and unwillingness to share.

In the *Precious Garland*, Nagarjuna repeatedly encourages us to be generous. Chandrakirti also praises generosity in the *Supplement*, saying that so much human misery is due to not having the requisites for life—food, clothing, shelter, and medicine. Conversely, when people have what they need, much suffering is eliminated. Thus, for those of us who aspire to be bodhisattvas who benefit the world, it is good to start with practicing generosity to those in need.

Generosity causes the giver to have much happiness while in cyclic existence—even the temporal happiness of those who are extremely selfish comes from their being generous in previous lives. If they realized the important role that the karmic seeds of generosity play in their lives, they would become more generous in this life.

If you have a habit of frequently giving to a lot of people, there is the likelihood that emanations of buddhas and bodhisattvas are among those who receive your gifts. Having received your offering, they make dedication prayers for your benefit. By the combined power of your generosity and the bodhisattvas' prayers and dedications, the imprint—a potential for liberation—is placed on your mindstream. Milarepa said that a person giving a little food or other requisites to a great meditator could augur their simultaneous awakening. This occurs because the donor actively provides the conditions for the meditator to gain realizations of the path and the meditator makes special dedication prayers for the donor's benefit.

> 137. It is profound to be tranquil;
>   and for its profundity, tranquility is highly respected.
>   From respect come glory and authority.
>   Therefore, devote yourself to tranquility.

Training in Tranquility

Tranquility or peacefulness is the result of being conscientious of your physical, verbal, and mental actions and pacifying disturbing or superfluous actions of body, speech, and mind. To become more tranquil inside yourself, practice "binding the doors of the senses." Physically this means being careful where you go and not letting your senses wander. We all know that just looking here and there and going to places where people indulge in sense pleasures can easily incite our afflictions. Keep yourself balanced by eating and sleeping an appropriate amount, not indulging in more than you need, and not being harshly ascetic.

Verbally, peace entails being mindful of your speech—specifically, abandoning the four verbal nonvirtues and practicing their opposites. Avoid talking casually or recklessly for no particular purpose. While you may not have a harmful intention, talking about all sorts of unworthy topics when a lot of people are around can make others restless or resentful, or incite their craving. This occurs because those around you take what you say seriously.

Similarly, take care not to use your speech to create disharmony or to further dissension among those who are not in harmony. Sometimes you may be unconsciously jealous and thus make small remarks that make people suspicious or disrespectful of each other. These comments can later blow up into a huge argument with each party defending itself and attacking the other.

If you say only what is necessary and to the point, people will pay attention when you speak and will *respect* your words. If you speak kindly, without swearing or ridiculing others, they will listen to you. This is the meaning of having authority.

Mentally, don't let the mind wander or dwell on memories and daydreams. Don't spend hours planning the future or worrying about events that may never happen; instead focus the mind on what is meaningful.

If you behave in this way, you will have a calm and dignified demeanor and people will naturally respect you. They will want to emulate your peacefulness and will help accomplish your various worthwhile projects.

> 138. By being wise, your mind will not waver.
>   Not dependent on the opinions of others,
>   you will be steadfast, kind, and not deceived.
>   Therefore, devote yourself to wisdom.

Training in Good Wisdom

If you have clear wisdom that can discriminate between good and bad, between what to practice and what to avoid, you won't be adversely affected by what others say and will be immune to misleading advice. Rather than trying to please confused people or succumbing to people who pressure you, you will be able to think for yourself, make wise choices, and carry them out with confidence.

Sharp wisdom is very important in both Dharma and practical matters. Wisdom enables you to think clearly and logically and to understand what is and isn't beneficial. You will be able to get the information you need and listen to others' ideas with an open mind, but you will also have the strength and clarity to make decisions by yourself. You won't be deceived by bad companions or be wishy-washy, changing your mind according to whomever you talk to, and you will be able to bear responsibility gracefully. Since there are many disadvantages to lacking wisdom and many advantages to having it, willingly work to develop it.

> 139. Truth, generosity, tranquility, and wisdom—
>   a king who has these four excellent qualities

will be praised by celestial beings and humans
just like these four excellent Dharmas.

Honesty builds trust and cooperation. Generosity enables people to connect in a lovely way and fulfills their needs. Tranquility gained by restraining the senses and regulating your physical, verbal, and mental activities
brings a dignified demeanor that others naturally respect. Wisdom that
can discriminate between what is to be practiced and what is to be abandoned enables us to make wise decisions with confidence without being
influenced by misleading companions.

Anyone who cultivates these four qualities will be praised by humans
and celestial beings. These qualities are especially important for monarchs
and leaders who make policies that affect many people—cultivating them
will make leaders effective and their actions more beneficial. They will be
able to encourage people in the Dharma path without using Dharma jargon
and will easily be able to accomplish projects on a practical level.

140. Wisdom and Dharma always increase
    in [a king] who consults with those who are
    restrained in speech and pure,
    and possess undefiled wisdom and compassion.

A Special Friend

To continually improve your wisdom and virtue, rely on special friends and
advisors. Nagarjuna outlines four qualities of such friends. First they are
honest and their speech is restrained. A monarch does not need someone
who flatters him and says he is a good leader when he is in fact harming
others. A monarch has no use for those who sing his praises and tell him that
people love him dearly when in fact he is unpopular. Rather a leader needs
those who, with a good motivation, speak to him directly and frankly, saying what is helpful. He needs friends who care about him and tell him when
people are unhappy with the leadership. These companions will tell a leader
when he is making a mistake and will counsel him in how to fix the situation.

Second, such friends are content and have few desires. They are pure—
meaning they are not always looking out to get something more or better
for themselves—but consider what is good policy and what benefits others.

Third, they possess wisdom and intelligence regarding both the Dharma and worldly affairs, which enable them to give sound advice. Fourth, they deeply wish to benefit others and are not easily angered. Such compassionate friends give unbiased advice. Although it is difficult to find companions who are completely free of anger, at least they should not be irritable and complain constantly.

When you develop friendships with such people, automatically you will come to have the same qualities as them. Keeping the company of those who are honest, good-hearted, contented, and wise makes a big difference not only to you but also to other people who are influenced by your actions. Spending a lot of time with people who encourage you to lie, cheat, drink, gamble, and do other ignoble things will influence you to do the same. In addition, clear-thinking, ethical people will see the type of people you associate with, project those same demeaning qualities onto you, and lose their respect for you. Their bad behavior will gradually rub off on you, and without you even realizing it, your values and behavior will degenerate.

Lamrim teachings tell us that it is difficult to distinguish misleading friends—it is not as if they have horns on their heads. Rather, we identify them by noticing the detrimental effect they have on us over a long period of time. If you find that your mind becomes harsher, more uncontrolled, and deluded, and that your destructive actions increase and your good qualities decrease, that's a clear indication that you're associating with misleading friends. In that case, distance yourself from them and cultivate friendships with wise and ethical people. Of course, by that time it may be too late—they may already have exercised strong influence over you and you, too, may be blind to the negative consequences of your friendship.

At present, with all our heart, we want our practice to be excellent. We sincerely want to relinquish all that is adverse to higher rebirth and highest good and to adopt everything that is in accord with them. Since we are ordinary beings, that wish is still not stable in us, and we don't have much control over our thoughts and actions. For this reason it is especially important that we keep our distance from misleading companions and associate with good friends.

Because many unpleasant and unfortunate things result from being with misleading friends, great masters have composed prayers to never, even for a second, come under the influence of misleading friends in all future lives. We should pray like this too.

141. Those who speak beneficially are rare.
    Even more rare are those who listen.
    And more rare yet than these are those
    who quickly implement something beneficial.

142. Having realized that though unpleasant
    it is helpful, quickly put it into practice,
    just as a prudent person, in order to become healthy,
    takes medication, even though it is noxious.

Parents who want to benefit their children in the long term and prevent them from cultivating bad traits must sometimes say things that the children don't like to hear. Similarly, friends with the four qualities—who are people who want to benefit us—may give us good advice that challenges our afflictions. Even if it piques our pride, we should trust them and follow it. If, simply because it is unpleasant to hear, we turn our back on those who care about us and give us good advice, we are the ones who lose. That would be like refusing to take medicine when we are very ill simply because it is foul-tasting.

It is rare for someone to speak words that are beneficial in the short term as well as in the long term. It is even more rare for someone to listen to such advice thoughtfully and with an open mind. It is rarer still for someone to consider the meaning of the advice and implement it with willingness to undergo immediate discomfort in order to accomplish a long-term beneficial purpose.

143. You should always reflect upon
    the impermanence of life, health, and political power,
    that way you will with true effort
    strive uniquely [to practice] Dharma.

Continually Meditate on Death and Impermanence

Nagarjuna tells the monarch, "Right now your power and fame are intact, the kingdom is safe, and the populace praises you—yet all this is ephemeral, like clouds in the sky. Someday it will all disappear and become nonexistent. You, too, will die, although you don't know when. For this reason, engage in Dharma practice with great diligence."

Your situation may be similar: in this moment, there is no threat to your life or well-being. You are healthy, your affairs are in good order, and you live in a relatively peaceful place, free of famine and epidemic diseases. Nevertheless, remember that all of this is subject to change and disintegration. Life is fragile like a water bubble; in a moment, you could have a stroke, heart attack, or accident. Keeping this in mind, put all your effort into practicing the Dharma—it is the only thing that will benefit you at the time of death—and do not complacently assume that your pleasant situation will continue as it is. Do not be smug and unconcerned but make your life meaningful through purifying destructive karma, creating virtuous karma, listening to teachings, and practicing the six perfections.

6. Taming Attachment and Understanding the Qualities of Buddhahood

The causal practices for higher rebirth and highest good have been explained above in detail. Now follows an explanation of the causes of lower rebirth, which are to be avoided. These include attachment to intoxicants, gambling, sexual lust, and hunting. When we tame our attachment to these, much of our harmful behavior will automatically stop, we will have more time for Dharma study and practice, and we will have more mental space to cultivate love, compassion, and bodhichitta.

> 144. Seeing that you will definitely die,
>   and that, when dead, you suffer from your negativity,
>   do not engage in any negativity
>   even for the sake of temporary pleasures.

> 145. In some cases, the dire [result of negativity] is not observed;
>   in other instances, the dire [result] is observed.
>   If there is comfort in one,
>   why do you have no fear of the other?

We are definitely going to die. If we have engaged in destructive actions, after death we will find ourselves in an unfortunate rebirth as the ripening result of these actions. Once that destructive karma is expended and that lower rebirth is finished, some virtuous karma may ripen that will lead to our birth as a human or celestial being. But even in an upper rebirth, more suffering will ensue. The different types of problems human beings experience—from extreme poverty, terrorism, discrimination, and excruciating illness to minor annoyances, relationship problems, and drought—are results similar to the cause in terms of our experience and the environmental results of our destructive actions. Seeing all these disadvantages of destructive actions, we should definitely give them up.

As a leader, the monarch has a lot of power. He should take care not to misuse this power by killing or compelling others to kill. In fact, considering the karmic results that would befall him in future lives, he should never even think about killing. Government leaders and people with economic power have the opportunity to create great virtuous karma by benefiting society. However, should their afflictions overwhelm them, they also have the ability to create significant destructive karma by harming large numbers of people as well.

Engaging in destructive actions may seem to bring some immediate benefit. For example, if you steal money through extortion, misuse funds that have been entrusted to you, overcharge customers, or avoid paying taxes and fees, you can buy food, clothes, medicine, a house, maybe even some luxury goods, or you can go on a wonderful vacation. But ultimately you will have to experience the karmic results of that action. In addition, the pleasure that you experienced as the immediate consequence of the action isn't true happiness—it is the duhkha of change, which will eventually bring you problems and disappointment.

Furthermore, that fleeting happiness isn't actually caused by stealing. It is the result of virtuous karma created in past lives; depriving others of their property is only a secondary condition for experiencing that happiness now. So even though happiness seems to come from destructive actions, don't be fooled—you will eventually have to experience their painful results. While you may do destructive actions and think that there is nothing to fear because no one saw you and no one knows you did them, you will still have to undergo their suffering results in future lives. Therefore, have a strong determination to abandon destructive actions.

Sometimes we don't experience the horrid results of our destructive actions until future lives and other times we experience them in this life. If we feel comfort and security when the results aren't seen in this life, shouldn't we be afraid of those actions when we see people experiencing the results of similar actions? Instead of thinking that our good situation in this life nullifies or excuses our destructive actions, seeing others experience the results of their harmful actions now, we should refrain from committing those destructive actions ourselves.

Implicitly, Nagarjuna advises us to do virtuous actions such as prostrations, circumambulations, and meditation. Even though to do so may entail some temporary discomfort or hardship, ultimately such actions are of enormous benefit. When we remember that creating virtue brings the bliss of awakening we will be encouraged to work for what is beneficial in the long term.

> 146. From intoxicants come the world's disdain,
> your own failure, and the loss of your wealth.
> Confused, you do what you should not.
> Therefore, always refrain from intoxicants.

Give Up Attachment to Intoxicants

People who drink and drug a lot are disdained even by ordinary people, let alone by the wise. People who are frequently intoxicated are not reliable and can't be trusted to accomplish their work or to do anything properly. Colleagues and family members talk derisively about them.

Drinking and drugging also consume a lot of time—you have to buy the alcohol or drugs, prepare and take them, and then after the immediate high wears off, spend time recovering your senses. It is also financially detrimental—not only do you spend money on liquor and drugs, but you don't show up at work or you make bad business decisions while intoxicated. As a result your family suffers from the lack of funds as well as from the lack of your emotional presence in their lives. Children suffer from shame when the community knows that their parent has a substance-abuse problem. In addition to children losing respect for their intoxicated parents, the parents' example also sets the stage for the children to self-medicate through drinking or taking drugs.

In addition, getting intoxicated makes you confused physically and mentally. Eventually your body and health deteriorate; you may neglect your appearance, becoming disheveled and dirty. Being intoxicated makes you lose the ability to discriminate between what is good to do and what isn't, and as a result you get involved in activities that make you look foolish. People who are usually discreet lose control of their speech and say all sorts of things that they later regret. They fight with strangers or quarrel with family members, destroying relationships with people they cherish. Unable to restrain their emotions, some people commit violent crimes and are arrested when intoxicated. While their life may have been going quite well before this, now the course of their life is changed because they must serve time in prison, pay fines, or spend a lot of time and money in the court system.

While there are many more disadvantages, these are the easiest ones to see. Thus as an act of kindness and respect for yourself as well as the people who care about you, abandon drinking and drugging.

> 147. Gambling causes attachment, unpleasantness,
>   and anger, deception, trickery, and an occasion for wildness,
>   lying, pointless chatter, and harsh speech.
>   Therefore, always refrain from gambling.

Give Up Gambling

Gambling also has many disadvantages, though nine are specifically pointed out here. You become greedy for others' wealth; worry about whether you will win or lose makes your mind uneasy and unpleasant. You will be overcome by unhappiness and anger when you lose, and will resort to deception and trickery in order to win. When you gamble, your mind and behavior become excited and wild. Your speech becomes uncontrolled, you lie to others and get involved in pointless chatter and harsh speech. Seeing the faults of gambling, give it up.

> 148. Most attachment to women
>   comes from the belief that women's bodies are pure.
>   But in actuality there is no purity
>   in a woman's body at all.

General Refutation of the Cleanliness of the Body of an Attractive Person

When the text says *women*, we should understand this to mean "women, for example."[25] In fact, male and female bodies are equally unclean. Nagarjuna

---

25. Nagarjuna is speaking to a heterosexual king and has in mind a future audience of monks who are assumed to be heterosexual. Thus he refers to the unclean nature of the female body, the object of their attachment. Nowadays society recognizes multiple gender identities and sexual orientations. The main point is to focus on the body of

points this out at the end of the section when he reminds the king that his own body is impure. In *Engaging in the Bodhisattvas' Deeds*, Shantideva also discusses the filthy nature of the body at length. There, too, you should understand that he was teaching an antidote to sexual desire to an audience of monks.

For yogis who practice mother tantra, it is obligatory to prostrate to and circumambulate women. Women are considered extremely precious and equal companions in Dharma practice—one gender is not higher than the other. Also, from the viewpoint of the subtle body—the formation of the channels, winds, and drops—men and women are the same.

According to the Vinaya—the monastic code of discipline—the Buddha established full ordination for both men and women, as well as novice and lay ordination for both men and women.

Because of the distinct physical difference between men and women, when a couple has a child, the mother undergoes more hardships on behalf of the child and extends more compassion to the child. A mother keeps the child in her womb for nine months, and after giving birth, she is usually the one who looks after the child more, always making sure the child is safe, healthy, and happy. For this reason, we emphasize recognizing others as having been our mothers in past lives and recalling the great kindness of our mothers.

In *Engaging in the Bodhisattvas' Deeds*, Shantideva also discusses the filthy nature of the body at length. There, too, you should understand he was teaching an antidote to sexual desire to an audience of monks.

Attachment to the body arises dependent on conceiving the body of the person you find attractive to be clean and pure, when in fact it is filled with filth. When you feel attachment arising, contemplate the unclean nature of the body as described in the verses below. This will counteract your incorrect conceptions about the body and make your view more realistic. Whether male or female, from head to toe there is not one bit of the body that is clean. We can see this is true because we have to continually clean our body. If the body were clean, we wouldn't need to constantly wash it.

What follows is a clear explanation of reasons not to be attached to a woman's body. Attachment to a man's body is to be dealt with in exactly the same way, with exactly the same reasons.

---

whomever you are sexually attracted to, remembering at the same time that your own body is just as foul.

149. Her mouth is a vessel of impurity,
    with putrid saliva and gunk between her teeth.
    Her nose is a pot of snot, phlegm, and mucus,
    and her eyes contain eye-slime and tears.

150. Her torso is a container of excrement,
    holding urine, the lungs, liver, and such.
    The confused do not see that a woman is such;
    thus, they lust after her body.

Attachment Is Inappropriate Because
the Body Is Unclean in Nature

The mouth is not clean—it is filled with saliva that has a sour, rancid taste. There is scum and leftover food around the teeth. We are all the same, aren't we? Our mouth is a container full of unclean substances.

In the nose are snot, phlegm, and mucus. The eyes have their own special kind of dirt that congeals around the edges of the eyelids and in the corners of the eyes. If you put your finger in your ear and wiggle it, you'll see all the dirt and earwax that is in there. The torso is full of filth as well—urine, bile, and organs that, when seen, we find disgusting. There's no need to mention the filth that comes out of the anus. In short, filth leaks from all bodily orifices. The body is like a bag filled to the brim with filth and tied up at the top—a full garbage bag that is soft and smooth to the touch, but when it is pierced, disgusting substances ooze out.

Meditation on the body being unclean is one of the principal meditations involved in the establishment of mindfulness of the body. Together with establishing mindfulness of feelings being duhkha in nature, the mind being impermanent, and phenomena being selfless, mindfulness of the body is part of the four establishments of mindfulness, a practice done by those on the hearer, solitary realizer, and bodhisattva paths.

151. Like unknowing persons, who have become
    attached to an ornamented vessel filled with filth,
    ignorant and confused worldly beings
    are attached to women.

152. If the world is greatly attached
     to the putrid objects that are bodies
     that should cause non-attachment,
     how then can it be led to non-attachment?

One Attached to Sexually Attractive Bodies Cannot Be Free of Attachment

Someone may become attached to a beautiful vessel studded with jewels, not knowing that it is filled with excrement. Similarly, out of ignorance people become attached to the bodies of others, even though inside they are completely foul.

We are greatly attached to the putrid body that should evoke non-attachment in us. As long as we are attached to such a bag of fetid crud, how can we be free of attachment? When we consider the undesirable consequences of attachment—how it keeps us bound in cyclic existence and causes us problems in this life as well—our inability to free ourselves from it is frightening.

153. Just as filth-loving pigs are greatly attached
     to heaps of feces and urine,
     so too are desirous people greatly attached
     to heaps of feces and urine, like filth-loving pigs.

154. Foolish persons imagine
     that this city [of bugs] that is the body,
     with cavities that are sources of filth,
     is something conducive to pleasure.

Foolish People Superimpose Beauty and Cleanliness on the Body

The foolish impute beauty on the body and are attached to it, although in fact it is feculent. Similarly, pigs perceive human excrement, urine, and vomit as delicious and are attached to them. Flies see the phlegm we spit on the ground as wonderful food. While we see these substances as foul, we superimpose cleanliness and beauty on the body that is their source.

This unclean body is verminous, like a great metropolis bustling with thousands of different parasites, worms, and microbes that happily reside inside it. Why be attached to one of the holes in it, deceiving ourselves that it is attractive and desirable?

> 155. When you yourself see the impurities
>   of excrement, urine, and such,
>   how can the body, being composed of them,
>   be something pleasant for you?

> 156. It is produced by a seed of impure essence,
>   an admixture of ovum and semen.
>   How can the lustful be attached to it
>   when they know its nature is impure?

> 157. One who lies with this filthy mass,
>   covered with skin moistened by those fluids,
>   is doing nothing more than
>   lying on top of a woman's bladder.

Refuting Attachment to the Body of a Sexually Attractive Person

The body is produced from causes—the ovum and semen of our parents—which are unclean and filthy in nature. How can we think that this body that grows from these causes is pure? Attachment perversely superimposes cleanliness and beauty upon the body that is unclean and repulsive, even though when we examine the body, it is clear that it is composed of filth. When people have sex together, one sack filled with filth is connecting to another sack filled with filth, with a thin bit of skin separating them.

> 158. Whether it be beautiful or ugly,
>   whether it be young or old,
>   the body of a woman is filthy,
>   so to what special quality could you be attached?

Whether someone's body is beautiful or ugly, young or old, what about it is worthy of attachment? Because the inside of the body is camouflaged by a layer of skin, some bodies appear beautiful to the naive. But inside, all bodies are composed of the same filthy substances. Since this is the case, how can you discriminate and lust after some and not others? Look at each organ or part of the body and examine if there is something worthy of attachment there. Seen in this way, it doesn't make sense to talk about beautiful and ugly bodies when all are equally dirty and lacking in beauty.

True-grasping mistakenly apprehends an object such as the body as truly existent, and attachment arises based on that. The object mistakenly appears beautiful and clean to the mind of attachment, and that mind incorrectly apprehends it to be beautiful and pure. Attachment to the body is a wrong consciousness. There is nothing in the body to be attached to, and nothing about it to justify seeing it as attractive. Rather, see the body as it really is—unclean and ugly—and give up attachment to it.

> 159. It is not right to yearn for a pile of excrement,
> even if it has a nice color or is very fresh or nicely shaped;
> likewise, one should not yearn
> for a woman's body.

> 160. While the nature of this rotting corpse,
> with its putrid core covered with skin,
> looks extremely terrible,
> why [do the lustful] not see it?

> 161. "The skin is not impure;
> it is just like a soft cloth."
> Like a leather bag filled with a turd,
> how could it be clean?

Does is make sense to be attached to a nicely colored, beautifully shaped, fresh heap of excrement? The shape and color of the body are actually no different from this. In addition, the body's nature is like a rotting corpse—given the passage of time, the person you now find attractive will die and the body will then in fact become a rotting, wet, messy, and putrid corpse.

When unclean organs and tissue are covered with skin, we project beauty and cleanliness on the body. In fact, it is like a bag of skin filled with a turd. If our minds were able to see that the body is unbearably disgusting, we would never lust after another person. Whatever way we look at it, attachment to the body is always inappropriate. How is it that we do not see this?

> 162. While a vase filled with excrement might glitter,
>   it is still objectionable.
>   The body, whose nature is unclean, is filled with filth;
>   why isn't it objectionable?

> 163. If you object to excrement,
>   why not object to this body
>   that takes pure perfume, garlands, food, and drink
>   and turns them into filth?

Rather than lusting after that which is not worthy of lust, we should see the body as foul. A beautiful jeweled vase full of feces is nothing to praise. Similarly, the body is nothing to extol and marvel at but rather is deserving of antipathy. If we found the excrement or entrails now stored in the body outside on the floor, we would be repulsed and immediately turn away in disgust.

We eat and drink all kinds of things that start out as appetizing, but the next morning they are feces and urine. Our very own body causes this transformation. No matter how clean and delicious food and drink may look at first, from the moment our body takes possession of them, it transforms them into nauseating substances. Therefore, the body is disgusting and not worthy of attachment.

> 164. A pile of excrement is objectionable,
>   whether it comes from you or someone else.
>   Why not then object to these filthy bodies,
>   whether [they are] your own or someone else's?

> 165. Your own body is just as filthy
>   as the body of a woman.
>   So doesn't it make sense to be unattached
>   to both the external and the internal?

Your Own Body Is Also Unclean

The filthy substances inside your own body and the bodies of others are equally disgusting. Rather than think your own body is pure simply because it's yours, see that all bodies are equally foul. None of them are worthy of attachment.

If we came across some vomit from a person's stomach, would it matter whose vomit it was? Not at all—we would want to get rid of that disgusting mess as soon as possible. Vomit is vomit, and ours is just as repulsive as the vomit of the person we love and the person we dislike. Since our body and the bodies of others are equally unclean, shouldn't we regard our body as a sack of filth?

> 166. Even though you daily rinse off
>   the discharge from your "nine wounds,"
>   if you still do not realize that the body is impure,
>   then what is the point of explaining this to you?

People wear jewelry and apply cosmetics and fragrances to their bodies to inflame others' desire. The seeming attractiveness they bestow is artificial and not in the least characteristic of the body itself. It is not at all appropriate to be taken in by a lovely smell and beautiful colors, thus allowing lust to fill the mind.

Nagarjuna says to the king, "The dirty nature of our body is visible to direct perception. Every day you see that this body constantly drips filth from its nine orifices, and you have to clean your body daily. Knowing this from your own experience, why don't you realize that the body is impure? If you can't see something as visibly obvious as this, what is the use of explaining it to you?"

Someone says, "It doesn't make much difference whether we know or don't know that the body is unclean." This is not true, because by apprehending that which is unclean as clean, we create a lot of destructive karma. Stop for a moment and consider everything that is involved when you sexually desire someone. You do so many things to get the object of your desire; many of these activities are motivated by attachment, anger, jealousy, arrogance, and confusion, and thus you create destructive karmas.

Previously we discussed the four distorted conceptions that apprehend as clean, pleasant, permanent, and self what is actually filthy, unsatisfactory in nature, impermanent, and lacking true existence, respectively. Due to these wrong conceptions, afflictions arise and we engage in various destructive actions. Practicing the four establishments of mindfulness that are antidotes to the four distorted conceptions will increase our mental clarity and wisdom.

Each establishment of mindfulness correlates with subduing a different distorted conception. Mindfulness of the body overcomes thinking what is filthy is clean; mindfulness of feelings frees us from thinking what is unpleasant is happiness; mindfulness of the mind overcomes grasping what is impermanent as permanent; and mindfulness of phenomena counteracts believing what lacks a self to have one. The antidotes to these four misconceptions involve understanding the four aspects of the truth of duhkha—impermanence, unsatisfactoriness, emptiness, and selflessness. These are among the first topics the Buddha taught in his first discourse on the four truths of the aryas, which indicates how important it is to realize them.

In brief, the mind that apprehends the body as unclean is a valid mind, and the mind that apprehends it as clean is not. Even a buddha sees what is clean as clean and what is unclean as unclean. Although things do not exist from their own side, conventionally we can still differentiate clean and unclean. Someone may say, "Feces and other filth are not dirty in themselves. That is just a conception that you made up." If that is so, would that person eat feces and drink urine, blood, and lymph for dinner? On a conventional level, people from all cultures consider excrement, urine, and other discharges from the body unclean.

Another person may say, "But flies consider our feces clean and eat it, and pigs will eat our vomit, so not all sentient beings consider bodily excretions foul. It is just due to our mental fabrications that we see these substances as filthy." As human beings, we posit things as clean and unclean in relation to how they are seen in the human realm. Similarly, we posit what is edible in relation to ourselves. Although termites think a piece of wood is delicious, we human beings do not consider it food.

That person may then say, "But high tantric yogis can eat feces and urine." When a skilled practitioner who has realized emptiness actually transforms filthy substances into inner offering, they become clean nectar. This situation is very different from that of ordinary beings.

167. Some compose romantic poetry
    about this filthy body—
    O, what shamelessness! What idiocy!
    How worthy of people's contempt!

168. In this [world], sentient beings,
    obscured by the darkness of unknowing,
    quarrel about what they lust for,
    like dogs fighting over filth.

Romantic Poetry Is Laughable

Some people compose romantic poetry, praising the body of the person they are attracted to as being like the sun, the moon, or a lotus. They admiringly say it is fragrant, beautiful to behold, blissful, and smooth to the touch. These poems superimpose qualities on the body and their purpose clearly isn't to be liberated from cyclic existence. If we think that these poems accurately portray the nature of the body, we are really foolish. The wise consider such poems laughable.

Obscured by the darkness of not knowing that the actual nature of the body is foul, most living beings are attached to their own and others' bodies. Filled with jealousy and lust, they fight to gain the pleasure they seek from others' bodies. In India, many stray dogs gather in the street and fight over the most disgusting-looking tidbits of refuse. Just like that, human beings fight over our own disgusting, unclean bodies and the bodies of others.

169. If you scratch an itch, it feels good,
    but it feels even better not to have an itch at all.
    So too, one is happy in obtaining worldly desires,
    but there is greater happiness in having no desires at all.

Refuting the Attachment Is the Cause of Happiness

Eczema is a skin disease that makes your skin itch terribly. While scratching it provides some small pleasure, people who are free of eczema altogether are happier. Similarly, those who drink and use drugs derive some modicum of pleasure from them, but people who don't take these are happier. They have more comfort in their body, more peace of mind, and are not troubled by the nagging desire to get high.

Ordinary people think their attachment and desire for others' attractive bodies is happiness and consider sexual intercourse to be the greatest pleasure. While they may experience some slight happiness from it, it is not ultimate happiness. If it were genuinely fulfilling, people would not have to have it again and again. In fact, there is even more happiness in not having sexual desire—those who are completely free of attachment, such as the arhats, have the most happiness.

> 170. When you analyze things in this fashion,
> even if you are not yet freed from desires,
> you will cease lusting after women
> through the gradual decrease of your desire.

The Result of Meditating on the Unclean Nature of the Body

By meditating on the foul nature of the body, you will know the body for what it is—foul. After your meditation sessions, it may still appear beautiful to you due to the power of your attachment to it. But as you repeatedly engage in this practice, your attachment will gradually lessen, and your wisdom will increase. Over time your lust will diminish, bringing you more peace and relaxation.

The more you are able to subdue romantic attachment and sexual lust, the easier it will be to practice the three higher trainings. If you don't meditate on the foulness of the body, you will continue on as before and will experience many obstacles in your practice of the three higher trainings.

Similarly, we should think about the body's impure nature to counteract attachment to our own body. The purpose of this meditation is not to hate our bodies—to do so is neither realistic nor useful. We must take care of this body because it is the basis of our precious human life, which enables us to practice Dharma and progress on the path. We can keep our body healthy without considering it, or others' bodies, as pure or worthy of attachment.

Total freedom from attachment comes only with meditation on emptiness. Meditating on impermanence, the foul nature of the body, and duhkha are preliminaries that are definitely necessary for meditation on emptiness to be successful.

> 171. Hunting is the terrible cause
> of a short life, fear, and suffering,
> as well as rebirth in the hells.
> Therefore, always firmly refrain from killing.

Give Up Killing

Since another cause for lower rebirth is killing, you should give up fishing, hunting, and any other means of trapping and killing animals, whether for food or sport. The ripening result from killing is rebirth in the lower realms. Should you finally manage to find freedom from the lower realms and be born as a human being, you will have to experience the results similar to the cause in terms of your experience: you will have a short life, will encounter terrifying situations, and will be fearful, sometimes for no reason. The result similar to the cause in terms of your habitual behavior is being attracted to killing and then actually killing others again. To avoid these dreadful consequences, make a firm decision to refrain from killing.

Although we may not go hunting or fishing, Nagarjuna still encourages us to treat animals and our natural environment with care. Some rulers are cruel not only to citizens but also to the animals in the forests and seas, killing them and destroying their habitat. Nagarjuna speaks adamantly against such behavior. In modern times, he would encourage us to care for other species and our global environment so that all beings living on the planet would be safe.

> 172. Like a snake all smeared with filth,
> poison dripping from its fangs,
> despicable indeed is the one
> on account of whom others feel terror.

Give Up Making Others Afraid

If we saw a poisonous snake whose body was smeared with filth and whose fangs and tongue were dripping with poison, we would become afraid and flee. This is how our prey feels when we hunt and trap them, and how other human beings feel when we intimidate, menace, or brutalize them either physically or verbally. Terrorizing others like this is a despicable act, one we should definitely give up. It is especially contemptible when someone relishes doing it.

Some people confuse fear and respect. People acquiescing to our coercion because they're afraid of us is not the same as their respecting us because they truly admire our good qualities and abilities. People who fear us do not support us, while those whose respect we have earned are true friends.

> 173. When a great rain cloud appears,
>   farmers experience much joy;
>   excellent in this way is the one
>   on account of whom beings feel joy.

Make Others Happy

When clouds appear and rain falls, farmers are extremely delighted because this is just what their crops need. Here Nagarjuna counsels the king to put effort into doing what benefits others and makes them happy. Then the people in the kingdom will remember his kindness and feel happy when they see him.

We should not only abandon actions that cause others fear but also act in ways that bring them happiness. Of course, that doesn't mean doing nonvirtuous actions that some confused people may feel happy about. Rather, motivated by kindness, we should focus on doing virtuous actions that bring joy to others' hearts. Acting like this will bring us happiness too—we will have no regrets when we die and will gain self-confidence, knowing that our virtuous actions have a positive impact on the lives of others.

> 174a. Therefore, refrain from what is not Dharma.
>   Heedfully practice the Dharma.

Here Nagarjuna sums up how to practice Dharma and abandon what is contrary to Dharma. He has pointed out behavior that damages ourselves and others and provided many reasons to abandon destructive actions and adopt constructive ones. He doesn't simply tell us what to do and not do—he provides explanations for everything he says. If we think about these reasons, his advice will make sense to us and will be easy to follow.

Nagarjuna directly addresses the king, but indirectly he speaks to all of us who are his followers. He gave so much advice to the king because in those days, there were no democratically elected governments, and kings wielded power. By positively influencing a person who has worldly power, Nagarjuna will benefit the entire society. When the king becomes disciplined, subdued, and benevolent, he will make Dharma-based laws and codes of conduct for his people. Then when the populace follows these laws, they will find happiness. The kingdom will be harmonious and the citizens will create virtuous karma.

PRACTICE THE CAUSES OF THE THIRTY-TWO SIGNS OF A BUDDHA

Since this is an interwoven explanation, Nagarjuna now returns to the topic of the causes and effects of highest good. Specifically, he describes the causes of the thirty-two signs of a special human being that appear on a buddha's body.[26] The principal causes of these signs are the general causes for full awakening—the collections of merit and wisdom, and the integration of the method and wisdom aspects of the path. In addition, each of the thirty-two signs has its own specific cause, which is an activity we can practice now.

174b. If you and the world
        wish to attain unexcelled awakening,

175. its roots are bodhichitta
        that is as firm as the king of mountains,
        compassion that is as vast as space,
        and wisdom that relies not on duality.

---

26. The thirty-two signs were commonly known in Indian culture and their presence was used to confirm someone's spiritual attainments. Nevertheless, as verse 198 explains, the thirty-two signs of a buddha are unique due to his or her great collection of merit.

The Three Principal Causes of Awakening

Here, *you* refers to the king and *the world* refers to all the sentient beings wandering in cyclic existence. To attain the peerless awakening of a buddha, everyone must cultivate the three principal causes: (1) conventional *bodhichitta*, the primary mind with two aspirations—to work for the benefit of all sentient beings and to attain full awakening in order to do so most effectively, (2) *compassion*—the cause of bodhichitta—that extends impartially to each and every sentient being as far as the limits of space, and (3) *wisdom that relies not on duality*—wisdom not entangled with the two extremes of absolutism and nihilism.

In the homage in his *Supplement*, Chandrakirti mentions these "three factors indicated on this occasion"—bodhichitta, compassion, and wisdom free from the two extremes—and then extensively explains them. He draws on the *Precious Garland* as the source for the homage, which is quoted frequently in Tibetan Buddhist literature.

Generating bodhichitta depends on first generating great compassion, the wish for all sentient beings to be free from all duhkha and its causes. Generating compassion, in turn, depends on two factors: meditating on sentient beings' duhkha such that you feel it is unbearable, and cultivating affectionate love for sentient beings, primarily by remembering their kindness to you in the past, present, and future. There are two principal ways to generate compassion and bodhichitta: the seven-point cause-and-effect instruction and equalizing and exchanging self with others. We won't go into these now—you can learn them from the lamrim teachings.[27] Generating the wisdom free from the two extremes depends on meditating on emptiness as explained in the first chapter of *Precious Garland* as well as in other Madhyamaka texts. Together, these three are said to be the cause for a bodhisattva.

You may wonder, "How can bodhichitta be a cause of a bodhisattva, since someone becomes a bodhisattva and enters the universal vehicle path of accumulation at the same time she generates uncontrived bodhichitta in her mindstream?"

Here we must differentiate "bodhichitta like sugarcane bark" and actual

---

27. Khensur Jampa Tegchok's book *Transforming Adversity into Joy and Courage* contains clear and practical instructions on how to cultivate bodhichitta, compassion, and wisdom.

bodhichitta. The two have a similar referent—full awakening. They also have a similar aspect—the aspiration to attain full awakening. Both of them want to benefit all sentient beings. They differ in that bodhichitta like sugarcane bark is contrived; it doesn't arise spontaneously in your mind. You must cultivate it with effort by reviewing the steps of either of the two methods for generating bodhichitta. On the other hand, actual bodhichitta is uncontrived and effortless. It is a natural response to seeing or thinking about a sentient being. Bodhichitta like sugarcane bark is like chewing a piece of sugarcane bark. It is sweet, but its sweetness is nothing compared to biting into the actual sugarcane. Similarly, contrived bodhichitta is wonderful, but it can't be compared to the magnificence of actual bodhichitta.

Before generating actual bodhichitta, the contrived bodhichitta in your mindstream is bodhichitta like sugarcane bark. You already have great compassion and are just about to generate uncontrived bodhichitta. This bodhichitta like sugarcane bark is the cause of a bodhisattva.

In the *Supplement*, Chandrakirti says that hearers and solitary realizers are born or produced from the buddhas, meaning that they arise from the speech of the buddhas. By the Buddha coming into this world and turning the wheel of Dharma of the four truths of the aryas and dependent origination, those wishing to attain hearers' awakening listen to the teachings and those wishing to attain solitary realizers' awakening practice the teachings. They thereby enter their respective vehicles according to their aspiration. By practicing the methods the Buddha teaches to those disciples, they will complete their paths and attain arhatship.

Buddhas, in turn, arise from bodhisattvas, because before attaining full awakening they were bodhisattvas who practiced the universal vehicle. They entered that path by completing the three principal causes: bodhichitta, great compassion, and wisdom free from the two extremes. We could also say that a buddha arises in dependence on the bodhisattvas who care for and teach her the Dharma while she is still on the path.

Without a doubt the wisdom free of the two extremes is an essential cause for full awakening, because it is the agent that actually uproots the afflictions, their seeds, and their imprints so that they can never return again. You may wonder, "Why is that wisdom said to be a cause of a bodhisattva when hearers and solitary realizers also cultivate and gain that same wisdom? Furthermore, has a new bodhisattva necessarily realized emptiness?"

Not all new bodhisattvas have realized emptiness. There are two kinds of bodhisattvas—sharp faculty bodhisattvas and modest faculty bodhisattvas. Modest faculty bodhisattvas are followers by faith—they practice what the Buddha taught principally due to faith in him. These individuals first generate bodhichitta and afterward generate the wisdom realizing emptiness. Since they gain the wisdom realizing emptiness after having become bodhisattvas, wisdom is not a cause for modest faculty bodhisattvas.

In contrast, sharp faculty bodhisattvas first generate the wisdom realizing emptiness and afterward generate bodhichitta. So the "three factors explained on this occasion" are the causes of only sharp faculty bodhisattvas.

Someone may then ask, "How can new bodhisattvas have wisdom that does not rely on duality if 'nonduality' means the lack of appearance of subject and object in aryas' meditative equipoise on emptiness?" Here *duality* doesn't refer to the appearance of subject and object—rather "the two" that it is free from are absolutism and nihilism. Thus the wisdom that is a cause for sharp faculty bodhisattvas is an inferential realization of emptiness that is free from the two extremes. Sharp faculty bodhisattvas attain this before entering the bodhisattva path.

These bodhisattvas are called "sharp faculty" because before making the commitment to attain full awakening for the benefit of all sentient beings, they want to make sure that it is possible to do so. To gain certainty about this entails understanding that it is possible to eliminate all defilements, their seeds, and their imprints from the mindstream forever. This, in turn, depends on understanding that the conceived object of true-grasping does not exist at all. The wisdom that realizes its nonexistence can eliminate true-grasping. When the trunk of true-grasping is uprooted, all the afflictions, which are its branches, also die, and rebirth in cyclic existence ends. This wisdom also has the power to eliminate the cognitive obscurations that prevent full awakening. Thus by gaining a conceptual or inferential realization of emptiness by generating nondual wisdom, that person gains confidence that attaining full awakening is possible. He or she then cultivates bodhichitta and enters the universal vehicle path of accumulation.

Some hearers and solitary realizers have sharp faculties and some have modest faculties. They cultivate the same wisdom as bodhisattvas; however, because they aspire for hearers' or solitary realizers' awakening and do not generate bodhichitta, they enter their own vehicles when they have a stable determination to be free from cyclic existence and a firm determination to attain arhatship.

All the causes for full awakening can be subsumed into method and wisdom and also into the collections of merit and wisdom. Great compassion and bodhichitta are included in method and through practicing the first three perfections—generosity, ethical conduct, fortitude—with that motivation, bodhisattvas build up their collection of merit. Wisdom free of the two extremes and the aryas' meditative equipoise on emptiness build up their collection of wisdom.

Alternatively, we can describe the path to full awakening in terms of the practice of the two truths, conventional and ultimate. In that case, compassion and conventional bodhichitta are included in the practice of conventional truth. The wisdom realizing emptiness and ultimate bodhichitta are included in the practice of ultimate truth.

Someone asks, "Why are there three causes of bodhisattvas, when one of them—great compassion—is a cause of bodhichitta, which, in turn, is a cause for a bodhisattva?" We could say there are only two causes of a bodhisattva, but great compassion is so important that it is mentioned separately. Compassion is important in the beginning of our practice, because with it we enter the bodhisattva path. In the middle, it stimulates us to engage in the bodhisattva deeds and fulfill the collection of merit. And in the end, when we have become a buddha, great compassion makes us effortlessly turn the wheel of Dharma by teaching the Dharma to sentient beings according to their dispositions and interests. Thus at all stages of our practice, meditating on great compassion is crucial. Even if we have developed bodhichitta, if we don't continue to meditate on compassion, there is danger of losing our bodhichitta on the initial level of the bodhisattva path and falling to the extreme of personal peace.

To summarize, if you and other beings wandering in cyclic existence want to attain the state of peerless awakening, then as ordinary beings you must emphasize these three practices, enter the bodhisattva path, and continue to practice them well until you have completed the collections of merit and wisdom and become a fully awakened buddha.

> 176. Great King, listen now to the way
> that your body will be adorned
> with the thirty-two distinct signs
> that indicate a great being.

Asking the King to Listen

Nagarjuna tells the king, "Respected king, if you wish to attain a body that is adorned with the thirty-two signs and the eighty marks of a great being, pay attention to what follows, for I will explain their causes."

Bodhichitta is the uncontrived wish to attain peerless awakening—the state of a buddha—in order to benefit all beings. In this context, *buddha* refers to the four buddha bodies—the two truth bodies and the two form bodies. The two truth bodies are the nature truth body and the wisdom truth body. The two form bodies—the enjoyment body and the emanation body—are adorned with thirty-two signs and eighty marks indicative of a great person. Bodhisattvas at the last moment of the bodhisattva path will attain buddhahood in the next moment, at which time they will simultaneously attain the four buddha bodies.

Sentient beings cannot see the truth bodies, as they are formless. Only aryas can see an enjoyment body in a pure land. Ordinary beings with great merit are able to see the signs and marks of a supreme emanation body; many people who lived at the time of the Buddha saw his supreme emanation body with its signs and marks.

A bodhisattva on the tenth ground has a mental body—a body in the nature of mind—that is adorned with the thirty-two signs, although they are not exactly the same as those of a buddha. When this bodhisattva becomes a buddha, his or her mental body becomes the enjoyment body of the new buddha, and from it manifest many emanation bodies that appear throughout the universe to work for the welfare of sentient beings and lead them on the path to buddhahood. His mind becomes the wisdom truth body—the omniscient mind of a buddha. The emptiness of that mind and the true cessation of that buddha are the nature truth body. The naturally abiding buddha nature—the tathagata essence (*tathagatagarbha*) of that sentient being—becomes the nature body of that buddha when all stains have been abandoned.

To attain these four bodies we must cultivate their cause—the unified practice of the two collections—also called the unified practice of method and wisdom. Bodhichitta and the wisdom realizing emptiness need to be conjoined in the sense that they mutually support each other. Neither the truth bodies nor the form bodies can be attained if either collection is missing, even though the collection of wisdom is the principal cause for the truth bodies and the collection of merit is the chief cause for the form bodies.

The thirty-two signs may not mean much to us initially, but the more we understand the qualities of a buddha and the causes required to become one, the more we will appreciate the significance of these thirty-two physical signs. Unique to a fully awakened buddha, these signs arise on a buddha's body as the result of that bodhisattva having practiced virtue for a myriad of eons. While universal monarchs who rule the world, solitary realizer arhats, and high-level bodhisattvas have these signs as well, they are incomparable to those of the buddhas. In fact, due to the difference in the quality of merit created and the time over which the merit was created, the thirty-two signs on each of these beings also varies.

The *Ornament for Clear Realization* (*Abhisamayalamkara*) by Maitreya also speaks of the causes of the thirty-two signs, and in some instances their causes differ from the ones described in *Precious Garland.* There is no contradiction, because each of the thirty-two signs requires numberless causes. There are so many causes for each sign that we cannot actually point out one and say, "This, and only this, is the cause of this sign." So despite the seeming difference in the two texts, the main point is still the same—these signs illustrate in a visible manner the inner qualities of buddhas and indicate the great collections of causal merit they accumulated from doing limitless virtuous deeds for eons.

Nagarjuna now describes the unique cause of each sign, one by one. Since we aspire to become buddhas, it is good to know their causes so we can begin to create them. As you read each cause, reflect on how it relates to its result similar to the cause. Contemplate how you can create that cause and generate its corresponding virtuous mental state—beginning now.

> 177. Due to honoring *caityas* and those
>   who are worthy, aryas and also elders,
>   your glorious hands and feet will be wheel-marked,
>   showing that you shall turn the wheel.

Explanation of the Causes of the Thirty-Two Signs of a Buddha

(1) *Caityas* or stupas are monuments that symbolize the Buddha and often house the relics of great masters. Here *caitya* also refers to the Buddha

himself, to something blessed or empowered by the Buddha, and to the arya sangha, our preceptors, and Dharma teachers. *Chorten*, the Tibetan word for *caitya*, literally means "basis of offering," indicating that the Buddha is the basis to whom gods and human beings make offerings. They honor and revere him in this way because he is completely free of all faults and possesses all excellent qualities.

Those who are worthy include our parents, the ill, and so forth. *Elders* refers to our seniors. We should help, honor, serve, and benefit these people in every way. As a result, we will possess the sign that is a thousand-spoked wheel on the palms of our hands and soles of our feet. These wheels look as if they were engraved on our skin.

The wheel represents ability and power—a universal monarch turns the wheel of political power, and a transcendental buddha turns the wheel of Dharma. These wheels and the abilities that they represent arise as a result of having made offerings to buddhas and having honored those worthy of respect for many eons.

> 178. King, always be steadfast
>   in your commitments concerning the Dharma.
>   That way, you shall become
>   a bodhisattva who has level and even feet.

The soles of our feet are arched. In contrast, the Buddha's feet are level, not concave but full and flat like the underside of a tortoise. If you want to become a buddha who has this sign, carefully guard the precepts and commitments you have accepted without letting them deteriorate, and keep whatever you have learned firmly in mind. This sign also comes as a result of practicing wisdom and method evenly and inseparably while on the bodhisattva path.

> 179. Through generosity and gentle speech,
>   and by acting beneficently and consistently,
>   you will have hands and feet
>   with digits joined by glorious webs.

We have gaps in between our fingers and the toes, whereas a buddha has flesh joining them, like the webbed feet of a swan. This flesh is of the nature of light, so there is no obstruction to putting on a ring, for example. This sign results from practicing the four ways of gathering followers to ripen their mindstreams, as discussed in verse 133.

> 180. Through abundantly giving the best food and drink,
> your glorious hands and feet will be soft,
> and you will have a large body
> with seven broadly curved parts.

Generously offering great amounts of food and drink to those who are hungry and thirsty is the cause for two signs: (4) our feet and hands will be very soft, like the skin of a baby, and (5) the seven broadly curved parts—two hands, two feet, two shoulders, and the nape of the neck—will be full, rather than concave as they typically are for ordinary people.

> 181. Through renouncing violence and freeing those to be killed,
> your body will be beautiful, straight, and tall.
> You will have a long life,
> your digits will be long, and your heels broad.

If we restrain from harming others with malice and save the lives of humans, animals, and insects who are about to be killed, (6) we will have a tall and beautiful body. Such a body will attract others and give us the opportunity to share the Dharma with them. By abandoning crooked or deceptive dealings with others, our body will be straight. These actions also create the cause for (7) our fingers and toes to be long and (8) our heels to be broad.

> 182. Through enhancing the practices that you have undertaken,
> you will be glorious, you will have a good complexion;
> your ankles will not be prominent,
> and you will be marked with body hairs that curl upward.

> 183. By both learning and imparting with respect
> the sciences, crafts, and other fields of knowledge,
> you will have the calves of an antelope
> and have a sharp mind and great wisdom.

Keeping our precepts well and spreading the Dharma to others are causes for having (9) good color and ankles that do not jut out, as well as (10) body hairs that lie in an upward direction and curl clockwise. For example, the hair on our arms will lie in the direction of the shoulder rather than the wrist.

(11) As a result of both having received instruction and having taught the arts, sciences, various crafts, and so forth with respect, when we become a buddha our calves will be beautiful, like those of a special type of antelope, and we will have sharp intelligence.

> 184. Through the avowed practice of quickly giving
> your wealth at the request of others,
> your arms will be broad and facile,
> and you will be a leader of the world.

> 185. Through seeing to the reconciliation
> of friends who have had a falling out,
> you will be a holy person
> with secret organ retracted into the abdomen.

(12) When we are committed to generosity and help others immediately whenever they request material aid, we will have long and facile arms. When the Buddha stands up straight his arms are long like an elephant's trunk and come down to just below the knees. This differs from our arms, which only reach below our knees when we slouch.

(13) The Buddha's sex organ retracts inside, like that of a horse. This is a result of reconciling those who are not in harmony.

> 186. By giving pleasant and excellent dwellings
> adorned with carpets,
> your skin will have a gentle hue
> like refined, untarnished gold.

> 187. Through giving unexcelled authority
> and properly following your guru,
> your resplendent body hairs will grow one by one,
> and your face will be adorned with the forehead curl.

Through continually offering good dwellings to the sangha, with carpets and cushions for them to sit on, (14) our skin will have a hue like refined gold, and (15) our skin will be soft and fine.

By repeatedly empowering those who ask for help when we are in a position of power or authority and by correctly following our spiritual mentors when studying and practicing the Dharma, (16) each hair on our body will grow separately from its own pore and curl clockwise, and (17) we will attain the hair curl in the center of the forehead. This curl can be stretched out very far, although usually it stays in its place curled up.

> 188. By listening properly, speaking in a pleasing manner,
>   and acting in accord with the well spoken,
>   your shoulders will be well rounded
>   and you will have a leonine upper body.

Due to not speaking harsh words but speaking in a pleasant way with a happy mind, and by correctly responding in accord with a questioner's disposition when answering Dharma questions, (18) our shoulders will be well rounded and different from those of others and (19) our chest or upper part of the body will be broad and powerful like that of a lion.

> 189. Through serving and healing the sick
>   you will have a broad back,
>   you will be imperturbable,
>   and all tastes will be supreme.

Providing medicine and caring for people who are ill or injured is a wonderful, virtuous act. When doing this, we should not act as if we were a great lord helping the riffraff, but rather we should help with respect and consideration. For example, before giving food to someone in need, we should wash it and then offer it respectfully, with both hands. (20) As a result we will have broad shoulders and a broad chest, and (21) we will always experience excellent tastes. Food that tastes awful to us is delicious "food of a hundred tastes" to the Buddha.

> 190. By focusing on deeds that accord with Dharma,
>   you will have a crown protuberance on your head,

and your body will also have
the symmetry of a banyan tree.

Focusing on deeds that accord with Dharma here means to shoulder the main burden of any work that you do with others. Whether or not you are the leader, for the benefit of many be enthusiastic about the work, take responsibility, and do not hang back or slack off. This brings two signs: (22) the crown protrusion (*ushnisha*) and (23) a symmetrical body—where the distance from the crown of the head to the soles of the feet is the same as the distance between the fingertips when the arms are outstretched.

> 191. Having spoken truthful and gentle words
>   for a long period of time,
>   you will have a broad tongue, king,
>   and your speech will be Brahma's voice.

> 192. Through always and continually
>   uttering words that are true,
>   you will have a lion's jaw;
>   glorious, you will be undefeatable.

As a result of speaking truthfully and gently to others over the course of many eons, we will have (24) a long tongue, such that if we stick it out it will reach around to our ears and up to our hairline, and (25) a voice that is exceedingly pleasant to listen to. It is said that Brahma's voice has sixty special qualities that make it both pleasant and powerful.

(26) As a result of speaking truthfully to others over a very long period of time, our jaw will be firm and awe-inspiring like that of a lion.

> 193. Through behaving with respect
>   and serving in the appropriate manner,
>   your teeth will be very white and lustrous;
>   they will also be even, not jagged.

> 194. Having become accustomed
>   to words that are true and not divisive,

you will have glorious teeth, forty in number,
set closely together and excellent.

As a result of being respectful to others, serving and honoring them as
much as we can over a long period of time, our teeth will be (27) dazzling
white and (28) even—all being the same height, without irregular shapes
and sizes.

By habitually and continuously speaking truthfully to others and avoiding divisive speech over a long period of time, (29) we will have forty
teeth—twenty upper and twenty lower—not thirty-two teeth like ordinary people have, and (30) our teeth will be well arranged, without gaps
in between them.

195. From gazing on sentient beings with love,
 without attachment, aversion, or confusion,
 your eyes will be sparkling blue
 with eyelashes like a cow.

Through continually viewing sentient beings with love for eons, and never
letting our mind go under the control of attachment, anger, and ignorance,
(31) we will have sapphire blue eyes; the white and black parts of the eye
will be distinct, and our eyes will not be bloodshot. (32) In addition, our
eyelashes will be straight and well defined, like those of a cow.

As qualities of the Buddha's form body, these thirty-two signs and eighty
marks are the ripening result of meditating on emptiness with unpolluted
wisdom for many eons. Because each of the Buddha's signs is unlike physical attributes possessed by any other being, their corresponding causes
must also be unique.

These signs indicate that the person possessing them is a truly great
being, one who has abandoned all faults and realized all excellent qualities.
Sentient beings do not possess these signs because they have not yet created the cause by collecting merit and wisdom over many eons. Although
the signs of the Buddha are likened to various things, this simply indicates
the nearest analogy in our human experience. In fact, there is a world of
difference between the jaw of a lion and the Buddha's jaw, for example.

To have pure refuge, we need pure faith, and such faith comes from
pondering the qualities of the Buddha—in particular the qualities of the

Buddha's body, speech, mind, and awakening activities. To do this, we reflect on the thirty-two signs and eighty marks of the Buddha's body as well as their individual causes. To meditate on the qualities of the Buddha's speech, we consider the speech having sixty special attributes or the speech with five branches, together with their causes. Contemplating the qualities of the Buddha's mind involves considering the twenty-one types of unpolluted wisdom and reflecting on twenty-seven awakening activities of the truth body.

Lamrim literature usually doesn't describe the qualities of the Buddha in this much detail. Rather, to develop the faith that leads us to take refuge it recommends meditating on the four qualities of the Buddha's mind: the Buddha is free from all fears of cyclic existence and personal peace, so he can help others overcome their fear; he is skilled in method and wisdom, so he has effective means to help sentient beings; the Buddha has impartial compassion for all beings without holding some dear and others distant; and he fulfills the aim of all beings whether or not they help or honor him.

> 196. Thus you should recognize
>   that these are, in brief,
>   the thirty-two signs that indicate
>   a great lion-like person.

We generate respect by reflecting on the causes of the signs and marks, for it is indeed arduous to create the causes for all of them. Contemplating that the Buddha completed this great collection of merit solely for the purpose of benefiting sentient beings will inspire our faith in him.

Earlier, Nagarjuna discussed the filthy nature of the human body—a body caused by self-grasping ignorance. Here, he speaks of the special signs and marks of a buddha's body, caused by engaging in unpolluted virtuous actions for eons. There is a stark difference between these two types of bodies. It is our choice which one we want to create the causes for.

> 197. The eighty marks have love
>   as their concordant cause.
>   But concerned that this treatise will be too long,
>   I will not explain them to you.

Why the Causes for the Eighty Marks Are Not Explained Elaborately Here

The eighty marks of a buddha include such things as having fingernails that are the color of copper. The cause shared by all eighty marks is meditating on love—wishing all sentient beings to have happiness and its causes. Generating love for all sentient beings brings many other benefits as well. Each mark also has its own specific causes, but Nagarjuna does not explain them here since they are elaborated in other texts, and he does not want to make this text too long.

Mark has the sense here of "making known." When we see these marks we know that the person who possesses them is a great being with a beautiful, good, and pure body. When sentient beings see people with such magnificent bodies, they are very happy and are attracted to them. This facilitates those holy beings' ability to gather a circle of followers and teach them the Dharma.

> 198. Although all wheel-turning monarchs
>   have these [signs and marks],
>   their purity, beauty, and luster
>   cannot compare with a buddha's.

Differences between the Signs and Marks of a Buddha and Those of a Universal Monarch

Wheel-turning monarchs who rule over a world system and solitary realizers have signs and marks but they are only similar to the Buddha's in appearance. One difference is that the Buddha's signs and marks are pure, because he has totally eradicated the afflictive obscurations and the cognitive obscurations, whereas wheel-turning kings and the solitary realizers have not. Another difference is that the Buddha's signs and marks are extremely beautiful and pleasing to see; when others observe them, they feel inspired. Those of the others are not like that.

In addition, the Buddha's signs and marks are very clear, like a full, radiant moon. This is because they have arisen through the power of having obtained all excellent qualities and abandoned all obscurations. The causes of the Buddha's signs and marks and the length of time necessary to create them are also unique. In short, the signs and marks of wheel-turning kings and solitary realizers are incomparable with those of the Buddha.

> 199. Each of the signs and marks
>   of a wheel-turning monarch
>   are said to come from one cause—
>   clear faith in the King of Sages.

> 200. But even were such virtue to be uniquely amassed over a billion eons,
>   it would not be sufficient to produce even a single pore of a buddha.
>   The brilliance of the sun has some slight similarity to a firefly. Likewise,
>   the signs of the Buddha are slightly similar to those of a wheel-turning monarch.

To obtain one of the signs of a wheel-turning king, one must have tremendous faith in the Buddha. If this is the case for just one sign, the causes for all of the signs and marks must be enormous. But if we were to collect the causes for attaining all of the signs and marks of a wheel-turning king for a billion eons, we still would not gain even one body hair of a buddha— whose hairs are numberless.

A firefly's light glows in the dark. While it is similar to the light of the sun in that both are lights, it is insignificant compared to sunlight. Similarly, there is a vast difference between the signs and marks of a wheel-turning monarch and a solitary realizer and those of the Buddha.

In short, the signs and marks of the Buddha are far superior from the viewpoint of their purity, beauty, and clarity. They can only arise through collecting merit and wisdom over three countless great eons, and by abandoning everything to be abandoned and perfecting everything to be perfected. Otherwise, it is impossible to acquire them.

This completes the commentary on part II of the *Precious Garland*, "An Interwoven Explanation of the Causes and Effects of Higher Rebirth and Highest Good."

III. The Collections for Awakening

7. Joyfully Taking Up the Boundless Work of a Bodhisattva

Nagarjuna stated three main causes necessary to attain the state of peerless awakening: bodhichitta, wisdom free from the two extremes, and compassion. These three causes are precious; Chandrakirti praises them in his salutation for the *Supplement* by saying:

> The hearers and middling buddhas (solitary realizers) arise
>> from the excellent sages; the excellent sages are born from the
>> bodhisattvas;
> the compassionate mind and the nondual awareness, as well the
>> awakening mind—these are the causes of the bodhisattva.

These lines are taught and debated extensively and emphasize the importance of practicing these three causes in order to fulfill the collections of merit and wisdom that lead to the attainment of the truth body and form body of a buddha. It is to the topic of the collections of merit and wisdom that Nagarjuna now turns.

FULFILLING THE IMMEASURABLE COLLECTIONS OF MERIT AND WISDOM

201. Great King, listen to the way
in which the signs of a buddha arise
from an inconceivable amount of merit
according to the great scriptures of the universal vehicle.

Exhorting the King to Listen

In the previous chapter, we learned the specific verbal and physical actions that are needed to attain the thirty-two signs of a buddha but not how much virtue is needed or for how long that virtue must be cultivated. Relying on the scriptures of the universal vehicle, Nagarjuna will now explain the limitlessness of the collection of merit.

> 202. A single pore of a buddha is made
>   from ten times the following amount of merit—
>   the total merit from which all solitary realizers have risen,
>   the total merit that produced all learners and those beyond
>   learning
>
> 203. and the total merit of the entire universe,
>   which like the universe is measureless.
>   Each pore of a buddha likewise
>   arises from that much merit.

The Collection of Merit Is Immeasurable

Think of the inconceivably huge quantity of merit there would be if we added together all the merit needed to produce each and every solitary realizer and hearer, along with all the meritorious karma needed for every rebirth as a human being and celestial being. Multiply this by ten and that is the merit needed to receive just one of a buddha's numberless pores!

> 204. A single mark of a buddha
>   is obtained through one hundred times
>   the amount of merit needed
>   to produce all of a buddha's pores.
>
> 205. King, that amount of merit
>   completes one auspicious mark.
>   Likewise, from that amount of merit
>   arises each of them up to eighty.

If we compile all the merit required to attain all the pores of a buddha and multiply that by one hundred, that is the merit required for each of the eighty marks of a buddha.

> 206. A single sign of a great person
> comes from one hundred times
> the mass of merit
> needed to produce all eighty marks.

> 207. Through a thousand times
> the vast merit that causes thirty of the signs,
> arises like the full moon
> the swirl of hair between the brows.

The merit required for all eighty marks multiplied by one hundred is the quantity of merit necessary to attain one of the Buddha's signs.

The merit needed for thirty of the signs multiplied by one thousand is the amount of merit necessary for the forehead curl, which is said to be like a full moon.

> 208. For a hundred thousand times the merit required for the
> forehead swirl is produced
> the protector's crown protrusion, the top of which is
> imperceptible.
> You should realize that a single Dharma-conch of the One Who
> Possesses the Ten Powers
> arises from the amount of merit that produces the crown
> protrusion multiplied a million ten million times.[28]

One hundred thousand times the merit required for the forehead curl is needed to produce the crown protrusion.

The merit required for the crown protrusion multiplied by ten zillion is the amount of merit needed to attain the "Dharma-conch"—a name for

---

28. Dunne and McClintock, *Precious Garland*, 117: ". . . this verse does not appear in the Chinese version, and Gyaltsab Je does not comment on it. Nevertheless, it appears in all the versions in the canon."

the Buddha's speech that possesses sixty qualities. So much more merit is needed to attain the Buddha's speech because it is more important to sentient beings than either his mind or body. Through his speech the Buddha performs the supreme activity of teaching the Dharma to trainees and leading us on the path to liberation and awakening.

> 209. Thus, even though the merit is incalculable,
>   it is merely said to have a limit,
>   just as one expresses all the regions of the universe
>   by subsuming them in the ten [directions].

The Collection of Merit Is Incalculable but Is Taught to Trainees as if Measurable

Although the merit required to attain a buddha's body is immeasurable, Nagarjuna explains it to us trainees as if it were measurable. Although it is difficult to know exactly the qualities of each sign and how many causes are needed for it, we can be content to understand that in general the merit needed is inconceivable. Some trainees will want to know the cause of each sign in more detail and the amount of merit necessary to attain it, and the above explanation satisfies them. They will be pleased and want to engage in the path. But in truth we cannot grasp the full function of each sign, mark, and quality of the Buddha or the merit necessary to attain it.

The meanings of *buddha* and *arya buddha* differ, so some clarification may be helpful. The eighth chapter of Maitreya's text the *Ornament for Clear Realization* extensively explains this topic. *Buddha* is an ultimate quality that has arisen from its cause—the fulfillment of the two collections. Buddha includes the four buddha bodies, and each of the four is buddha. In general, a buddha's hands, arms, the thirty-two signs, and so forth are buddha, because they are a buddha's physical qualities. Similarly, the twenty-one unpolluted wisdoms in the continuum of an arya buddha are buddha. They are the ripening result of having meditated for many eons on the unpolluted path.

Arya buddha refers to a person who is fully awakened such as an enjoyment body or emanation body. Not everything that is buddha is an arya buddha. For example, the nature truth body of an arya buddha is buddha but not an arya buddha because it isn't a person. Likewise a buddha's physical characteristics, compassion, and wisdom are buddhas, but are not arya buddhas because they are not persons. Shakyamuni Buddha, on the other hand, is both buddha and an arya buddha.

> 210. If the causes of a buddha's form body
> are immeasurable, like the universe,
> how then could the causes
> of the truth body be measureable?

The Collection of Wisdom Is Immeasurable

Just as the universe is boundless, the collection of merit that is the principal cause of a buddha's form body is boundless. Just as the causes of the form body are immeasurable, so too is the collection of wisdom, which is the principal cause of a buddha's truth body. *Immeasurable* refers to a quantity so large that ordinary people cannot grasp, realize, or measure it—it is beyond thought.

> 211. If in all cases a vast effect arises from a small cause,
> then one should cease to believe
> that a measurable effect comes
> from the immeasurable causes of a buddha.

The Result of the Two Collections Is Immeasurable

An enormous tree, so huge that many thousands of people can sit in its shade, grows from a tiny seed. By extension, unfathomable results can come from a great cause. The collections of merit and wisdom are each immeasurable, and their results are immeasurable. As ordinary beings our minds cannot fathom them. However, the Buddha's omniscient mind can grasp this.

The qualities of the Buddha are inconceivable. So are the qualities of the Dharma, because practicing and realizing the Dharma enabled him to attain buddhahood and because the Dharma is the most valuable thing he teaches sentient beings. Because the Buddha is the ultimate Sangha member, the qualities of the Sangha are also inconceivable. Whenever, even for a moment, we generate faith in the Three Jewels and their inconceivable qualities, we create a cause to experience an inconceivable ripening result.

212. In brief, King, the buddhas' form body
     arises from the collection of merit,
     and their truth body is born
     from their collection of wisdom.

213. Thus, these two collections
     cause the attainment of buddhahood.
     Hence, in short, always devote yourself
     to merit and wisdom.

The Results of the Collections

While inconceivable, the virtuous actions required to become a buddha can be subsumed in two, the collections of merit and wisdom. Although the collection of wisdom is the principal cause for the truth body and the collection of merit is the principal cause of the form body, a unified practice of the two collections yields the union of the truth body and the form body.

Practices on the method side of the path—including the determination to be free from cyclic existence and bodhichitta—are called the collection of merit. Practices on the wisdom side, such as meditating on the two kinds of selflessness and the two truths, are called the collection of wisdom. Of the six perfections, generosity, ethical conduct, and fortitude are included in the collection of merit, and concentration and wisdom in the collection of wisdom. Joyous effort, a mind that takes delight in virtue, applies to both, depending on whether the action is method or wisdom.

Because hearers and solitary realizers lack bodhichitta and aspire for arhatship, their accumulations of merit and wisdom are not called the collections of merit and wisdom. To be the collection of merit or wisdom, practices must be motivated by bodhichitta and bear the result of buddhahood. For those who aspire to become a buddha, relying on the two collections is essential. Nagarjuna emphasized this in the dedication in his *Sixty Stanzas of Reasoning* (verse 60):

> Due to this virtue, may all beings complete the collections of
> merit and wisdom.

May they attain the two buddha bodies resulting from merit and
wisdom.

We should always devote ourselves to creating merit and wisdom because
the two buddha bodies arise dependent on this. Gyaltsap Je's commentary
to the *Precious Garland* explains this in more depth, beginning with the
syllogism: the subjects, the person and aggregates, do not exist inherently,
because they are dependent arisings. The reliable cognizer realizing the thesis (the person and aggregates do not exist inherently) is generated depending on a reason (dependent arising). This reason fulfills three criteria: (1)
the presence of the reason in the subject (the person and aggregates are
dependent arisings), (2) the pervasion (if it arises dependently, it doesn't
exist inherently), and (3) the counterpervasion (if it exists inherently, it is
not a dependent arising).

This syllogism combines the person and the aggregates as the subject.
However, when we initially establish emptiness, we do so first on the basis
of the person and later the aggregates. Only after realizing emptiness can
these two together be the subject of a syllogism. So this syllogism is not
meant for initial meditators—it presupposes that the meditator has already
realized emptiness.

Both of the collections, as well as the two truths, and method and wisdom are contained within this syllogism. Dependent arising is the reason,
and to fulfill the first criterion we must understand that it applies to the
subject—that the person and aggregates are dependent arisings. Dependent arising is a huge, limitless category that includes so many things: the
causal dependence of an effect depending on its cause; the dependence of
parts and wholes—for example, a car depending on its parts; and dependent designation—all phenomena depending on conceptual designation.
Within causal dependence, there are the twelve links of dependent arising
that describe how we take rebirth in cyclic existence and how to stop this
cycle. In short, dependent arising includes everything on the method side
of the practice. It corresponds with the collection of merit, conventional
truths, and the vast bodhisattva practices. All of these are limitless. Thus
when we contemplate the reason of the syllogism, dependent arising, there
is so much to ponder.

In the syllogism, the thesis that we want to understand is that the person and the aggregates do not exist inherently. The predicate (do not exist

inherently) has to do with emptiness, selflessness, and nirvana, which are the wisdom side of the path. This corresponds to the collection of wisdom, ultimate truths, the practices of the profound nature of reality. This, too, is a huge and limitless topic.

This syllogism is comprehensive because the reason and the predicate together contain the conventional and ultimate truths, which are the basis; the collections of merit and wisdom (method and wisdom), which are the path; and the truth body and form body of a buddha, which are the results. So when we meditate on the presence of the reason in the subject and on the thesis, we are meditating on the two truths, engaging in the practices of method and wisdom, accumulating the two collections, and creating the causes to attain the two buddha bodies.

We generate two important reliable cognizers by contemplating this syllogism. First, by pondering the method side of the path, we understand dependent arising in a comprehensive way and generate a reliable cognizer of the presence of the reason in the subject. Also, by contemplating dependent arising, we realize the pervasion—that whatever arises dependently is empty of inherent existence. Second, contemplating this enables us to establish the thesis—that the person and aggregates do not exist inherently and are empty. Meditation on the thesis becomes the collection of wisdom. These two reliable cognizers—one understanding that the person and aggregates are dependent arisings, and the other understanding that the person and aggregates are empty of inherent existence—contribute to fulfilling the two collections, which, in turn, give rise to the truth body and form body of a buddha.

Initially we have to understand the two truths and know that they are not incompatible. Without understanding conventional truths properly— the functioning of cause and effect; the relationship of agent, object, and action; and so forth—it is not possible to understand emptiness correctly.

Emptiness and dependent arising are not discordant; to the contrary, they are mutually supportive. Conventionalities exist—they arise and function, yet they are empty of inherent existence. The fact that things lack inherent existence doesn't interfere with their functioning on the conventional level. Conventional truths appear inherently existent to an ignorant mind, but in fact they are empty of inherent existence. In short, phenomena are dependent arisings because they are empty, and they are empty because they exist by depending and relying on other factors.

Nagarjuna expressed this in his seminal verses in *Treatise on the Middle Way* (24.18–19):

> That which is dependent arising is explained to be emptiness.
> That, being a dependent arising, is itself the middle way.

> There does not exist anything that is not dependently arisen.
> Therefore, there does not exist anything that is not empty.

Someone who lacks this integrated understanding of the two truths and is unable to posit that they are mutually supportive will have difficulty practicing method and wisdom in a unified manner on the path. They could end up with wrong philosophical ideas—for example, thinking that because the form body appears to sentient beings' minds, which have the elaboration of true existence, it does not exist in the continuum of a buddha, who has gone beyond elaborations. They will not be able to engage in the two collections properly and thus will not be able to attain the resultant two bodies of a buddha.

Practicing method and wisdom in an integrated manner means that our meditation on emptiness is supported by the motivation of bodhichitta, and our practice of the six perfections of generosity, ethical conduct, fortitude, and so on is supported by wisdom. This wisdom, for instance, contemplates the dependent nature of the giver, recipient, gift, and action of giving and understands that because they are dependent, they lack inherent existence.

ABANDON DISCOURAGEMENT

While both collections of merit and wisdom are immeasurable, there is no reason to feel discouraged or inadequate while practicing them. With bodhichitta it is possible to create unfathomable merit and wisdom. In other words, just as the resultant two buddha bodies are inconceivable, so are their causes, the two collections. When we are motivated by a genuine altruistic intention that works for the welfare of an inconceivable number of sentient beings, it is possible to create those vast causes without stress.

We need not fear suffering while collecting the requisite merit and wisdom. Bodhichitta gives us the courage to do difficult deeds that we were previously unable to do and to endure hardship without suffering. Due to arya bodhisattvas' great merit, they do not experience physical pain while doing the bodhisattva deeds such as giving away their bodies, and due to their great wisdom they do not experience mental pain or fear.

214. You should not be discouraged about
       accumulating the merit for obtaining awakening,
       since there are reasons to be reassured
       set forth by both reasoning and scripture.

Some people become discouraged when they learn that buddhahood is unfathomable and the collection of merit necessary to attain it is also inestimable. Thinking it is impossible for them to ever reach that state, they become discouraged and hesitate to even try to create the causes.

Such discouragement is a form of laziness; it makes us feel tired, procrastinate, and give up before we even begin. Instead of allowing our minds to go in that direction, we should generate the aspiration to attain awakening and decide to engage in the causes for awakening as much as possible.

Both reasoning and scripture prove that it is possible for us to attain awakening. Obscure phenomena can be realized through reasoning, and the Buddha taught those reasonings. Very obscure phenomena can be realized by relying on scriptural authority, and the Buddha taught us the criteria for evaluating if a scriptural passage is definitive or not. So it is possible to understand these things.

He also taught many methods for easily accumulating the two collections, and by engaging in these, we will not need to experience the physical and mental sufferings that would otherwise face us. Feeling discouraged and thinking "I'm just not able to do this" makes our cyclic existence endless, whereas striving in the practices to collect wisdom and merit, we will be able to free ourselves forever from the mass of duhkha that is cyclic existence.

Furthermore, there are many quick methods to help us collect merit and wisdom. In the perfection vehicle, bodhichitta enables us to accumulate wisdom exponentially. The tantra vehicle, and especially the highest yoga tantra, teaches effective methods to quickly generate and then unify serenity and insight. When we rely on these we can swiftly accumulate the inestimable two collections and attain the state of awakening.

215. In all directions, space, earth,
     water, fire, and wind are immeasurable;
     so too it is acknowledged the duhkha
     of sentient beings is immeasurable.

216. Through a bodhisattva's love and compassion
     those countless sentient beings
     are led out of their duhkha
     and definitely brought to buddhahood.

The Merit from Generating the Aspiration for Awakening Is Boundless

Space is immeasurable, stretching everywhere in the ten directions—above, below, in the four cardinal directions and four intermediate directions. Earth, water, fire, and wind also exist in all directions and are immeasurable. Similarly, the number of sentient beings experiencing intolerable duhkha is countless. Motivated by immeasurable love and compassion, bodhisattvas gradually lead all these sentient beings from their immeasurable temporal and long-term duhkha to a state of peerless awakening.

If it were impossible for sentient beings like us to attain awakening, buddhas and bodhisattvas wouldn't even try to lead us to that state. However, they do—in fact, their ultimate purpose is to benefit us especially by leading us to awakening—so it must be possible for us to attain it. Now, while we have a precious human life, it is possible for us to meet beings who are buddhas and bodhisattvas to guide us. Our situation is anything but discouraging—we have fortune and opportunities that are hard to come by!

217. Since sentient beings are immeasurable,
     from the point that this commitment is made,
     those who remain resolute
     whether they are asleep or awake,

218. or even careless, will still constantly amass merit that,
     like beings, is immeasurable.
     And since this merit is immeasurable,
     it is said that attaining immeasurable buddhahood is not hard.

Attaining Awakening Is Not Difficult

The same path as the buddhas and bodhisattvas practiced to reach their goal is open for us to practice. We progress on this path gradually, so don't think you must become a tenth ground bodhisattva overnight! On the basis of practicing the meditations to generate bodhichitta, the heartfelt aspiration to become a buddha in order to benefit sentient beings will arise in us. Initially this aspiration is weak—we have it occasionally and it doesn't last a long time. This is the stage of aspiring bodhichitta.

By continuing to do these meditations and generating this aspiration repeatedly, our bodhichitta will become sufficiently stable so that we are comfortable saying that we will not relinquish it. This is the stage of aspiring bodhichitta with a promise.

Continuing to habituate ourselves to bodhichitta and the bodhisattva deeds, we will reach a point where our bodhichitta will be uncontrived and spontaneous. At that time we will generate actual engaging bodhichitta, enter the bodhisattva path, and possess the actual bodhisattva precepts. From this time onward, whether we are sleeping, eating, or even distracted, we will continually accumulate merit equal to the number of sentient beings, and we will progress through the bodhisattva paths and grounds to peerless awakening. Since all this began with our first aspiration for awakening that was weak and unstable, we should never deprecate even our feeble efforts to generate bodhichitta.

In short, although right now we don't have actual aspiring or engaging bodhichitta, we are familiarizing ourselves with the meditations to generate them, and this will lead to our one day having spontaneous bodhichitta. Even now, we can generate fabricated bodhichitta and take the bodhisattva precepts, although our bodhichitta and bodhisattva precepts are similitudes of the actual ones. Nevertheless, we see that compared to the self-centered thought that constantly plagued our mind before, there is improvement and our bodhichitta has become stronger.

When we gain actual engaging bodhichitta, all our actions will be supported by this altruistic intention. This means, for example, that we generate bodhichitta before meditating on emptiness. Even though bodhichitta won't be manifest in our mind during the time we are meditating on emptiness, our meditation will be supported by and conjoined with bodhichitta. Similarly, any other virtuous activity done with bodhichitta will be supported by that excellent motivation. Although the initial motivation is not manifest, its power has not vanished or weakened.

Someone wonders, "Can buddhas really benefit sentient beings?" Yes, they can, but they can't help everyone immediately. Only when sentient beings are receptive to the buddhas' awakening activity are they able to receive the buddhas' help. Their receptivity at any particular moment depends on them—their disposition, interests, and aspirations. When sentient beings lack interest in the Dharma and have heavy, destructive karmic imprints, it is difficult for them to receive the buddhas' help. We must make ourselves receptive vessels in order for the buddha's awakening activity to affect us.

Consider whether you have benefited from the Buddha and bodhisattvas. If you hadn't met the Dharma, what would your life be like now? What would you be doing and what kind of karma would you be creating? As you reflect on this you see that you have definitely benefited from their awakening activities. When you become a bodhisattva and then a buddha, you will be able to benefit others in the same way.

Someone now asks, "Since there are already numberless buddhas, isn't it useless for me to attain buddhahood? Why don't I just take the easy path of ridding myself from all duhkha and become an arhat instead?" If you seek to free only yourself from samsara, when you attain nirvana your mind will still be obscured by cognitive obscurations. Becoming an arhat does not fulfill your potential. Furthermore, you have strong karmic links with some sentient beings that other buddhas don't have due to the relationships you developed in cyclic existence. Therefore, you will have a special ability to guide them once you become a buddha.

It is said that we accumulate great merit simply by going for refuge, such that if this merit were to transform into form, the universe would be too small to contain it. We create many times more merit when we generate bodhichitta and engage in the bodhisattva practices. There are many ways to create extraordinary amounts of merit on the bodhisattva path, so there is no reason to become discouraged. For example, if you tell someone living in India who wants to go to America that he will need at least seventy dollars a day just to live, he might get very discouraged. But when you tell him that when he's there, he'll be able to earn well over that amount every day, his discouragement will vanish and his enthusiasm will increase.

219. Remaining for an immeasurable time
    and wishing to obtain immeasurable awakening
    for the sake of immeasurable beings,
    the bodhisattvas perform immeasurable virtue,

220. so how could they not obtain before long awakening,
    even though it is immeasurable,
    through the collection of
    these four that are immeasurable?

The Ease of Attaining Awakening Due to the Four Immeasurable Factors

When it comes to attaining full awakening, everything is incalculable. Four immeasurable factors are involved: immeasurable time, sentient beings, qualities of the awakened state, and virtues. For the sake of countless sentient beings who have been wandering in cyclic existence for a limitless length of time, we aspire for awakening, which has unfathomable qualities. As a result of having that aspiration in our minds even for a short time, we gain inestimable virtue. When we generate the aspiration for awakening for the sake of all sentient beings, all four immeasurable factors are included.

Immeasurable time can be understood in two ways: bodhisattvas strive on the path for an immeasurable length of time in order to benefit sentient beings who have remained in cyclic existence for an immeasurable length of time. Depending on your perspective, you may become either discouraged or encouraged by this. One person may think, "Creating the collection of merit is not only difficult, but it also takes a long time." Another person may think, "If bodhisattvas can practice that long, so can I!" Seeing that your attitude depends on your perspective, make your perspective a positive one.

Even though it takes immeasurable merit to attain awakening, when we generate the mind that has these four immeasurables, why wouldn't we be able to attain full awakening quickly? Nagarjuna challenges his followers to explain why they wouldn't be able to attain awakening since they have access to such an incomparable method to do so.

In short, discouragement is out of place on the bodhisattva path. Nagarjuna gives three reasons why attaining awakening is not burdensome: we create immeasurable merit from generating bodhichitta; that merit is the cause to attain buddhahood; and the four immeasurable factors make it easy to attain awakening. Meditating on bodhichitta with the four immeasurable factors, you amass limitless merit and create all the causes needed for awakening. With such a method, you will be able to attain awakening comparatively quickly.

The Two Collections Counteract Physical and Mental Suffering

Some people fear that they may suffer while they engage in the bodhisattva practice. Nagarjuna now explains why this is not the case. Since our collections of merit and wisdom can prevent this, we need not be afraid.

> 221. What is called immeasurable merit
>   and also that called immeasurable wisdom
>   quickly eradicate the suffering
>   of both the body and mind.

When he encourages us to accumulate merit and wisdom, Nagarjuna implicitly discourages us from procrastination, discouragement, and nonvirtuous actions that cause rebirth in cyclic existence. If we're going to put anything off, it should be destructive actions—there's no hurry to do them right now.

> 222. Hunger, thirst, and other such physical suffering
>   occur in unfortunate rebirths due to one's misdeeds.
>   [Bodhisattvas] do not engage in misdeeds;
>   due to merit, they have no such suffering in other rebirths.

Merit Eliminates Physical Suffering

All physical suffering experienced in the lower realms and as human beings is due to our misdeeds. If we continue with such misdeeds, we will go from one life to the next experiencing only suffering. Even though we might experience a certain amount of suffering while amassing the two collections, we should not be discouraged. When doing a hundred thousand prostrations, for example, it doesn't make sense to feel dispirited by thinking about the difficulties and effort involved. We should focus on the fact that purifying negativities and collecting merit prevents future suffering—it stops nonvirtue from ripening and creates virtue that leads to the ultimate peace of nirvana as well as worldly happiness as a byproduct. Rather than feeling discouraged, feel invigorated.

> 223. From confusion comes the mental suffering
>   of attachment, anger, fear, lust, and such.
>   [Bodhisattvas] quickly eliminate this
>   by realizing that [all things] are foundationless.

Wisdom Eliminates Mental Suffering

Fear of mental suffering can also inhibit us from the worthy endeavor of engaging in the collections of merit and wisdom.

Confusion in this verse refers to both ignorance regarding the ultimate mode of existence and ignorance of karma and its effects. Ignorance of the ultimate nature involves grasping phenomena as being truly existent or as not existing even conventionally—extremes of absolutism and nihilism respectively. Due to this ignorance, attachment, anger, fear, lust, and other afflictions arise, which in turn motivate destructive karma, which causes us to undergo physical and mental suffering. In addition, just having these emotions manifest in our mind makes us unhappy right now. The mind of attachment is dissatisfied, the mind of anger is burning, the mind of fear is anxious and agitated, and the mind of lust is restless. These are not pleasant mental states at all.

There are many kinds of attachment, such as attachment to the body, possessions, praise, and reputation. Anger is a broad category that ranges from irritation to rage; it wants to destroy whatever it believes impedes our happiness or causes us unhappiness. Fear refers to anxiety regarding the four elements, such as fear of natural disasters and worry about falling ill. Fear could also arise regarding our financial security or possible harm caused by people who misuse their power. Lust refers to sexual lust or lust hoping to get other people's possessions. There are also many other kinds of disturbing emotions—arrogance, jealousy, and lack of integrity, to name a few.

We continually experience many disturbing mental states, all of them rooted in true-grasping ignorance. Bodhisattvas eliminate all this mental suffering by realizing that all phenomena are empty and foundationless—that is, ignorance is without a basis, and its conceived object is nonexistent. Knowing this, we should enthusiastically engage in the collection of wisdom to the best of our ability. The more we do so, the less mental suffering we will experience on the path, culminating in the cessation of all mental suffering when we attain liberation.

The collection of wisdom also eliminates physical suffering, and the collection of merit also eliminates mental suffering, but principally it is said that the latter eliminates physical suffering, and the former eliminates mental suffering.

> 224. If bodhisattvas are not greatly harmed
>   by mental and physical pain,
>   then even though in an endless universe they lead the world,
>   why would they be discouraged?

> 225. Even brief suffering is difficult to bear—
>   what need then to mention suffering for long?
>   But even if limitless in duration,
>   what could harm one who has no suffering and is happy?

There's No Reason to Be Discouraged About Accumulating the Two Collections

Because they cherish others more than themselves and cultivate the wisdom realizing emptiness, bodhisattvas do not experience physical or mental pain when they practice the path. The aspiration to lead innumerable sentient beings to the highest good does not make them discouraged or fatigued. On the contrary, it gives them great satisfaction and joy because they are doing what matters most to them—acting for the welfare of other beings.

In general, everyone finds suffering difficult to bear for even a moment, so it's natural to think that experiencing misery for a long time would be unbearable. Arya bodhisattvas take on many different kinds of bodies to benefit sentient beings, and they do that for an immeasurably long period of time. But because they are not reborn under the control of afflictions and karma and pray to take those bodies, they do not experience the suffering of birth, aging, sickness, and death. While their manifestations look the same

as we do and appear to undergo the same suffering as we do, arya bodhisattvas do not experience pain or distress because they have eradicated certain
degrees of afflictions and purified a great deal of karma.

> 226. [Bodhisattvas] have no physical suffering—
> how could they have mental suffering?
> But through compassion, they feel pain for the world;
> for that reason, they remain for a long time.

The Power of Great Compassion

Although from their own side arya bodhisattvas do not experience physical or mental suffering while they deliberately take rebirth in cyclic
existence, they do feel unhappiness when they see sentient beings experiencing birth, aging, sickness, death, and all the problems in between.
This mental pain is not the personal distress, despair, or depression
that we feel when we see others suffer. Bodhisattvas know that others'
suffering occurs only because its causes exist, and they also know those
causes can be eradicated. Bodhisattvas with stable bodhichitta would
happily go to the lowest hell realm for as long as necessary to save a
single sentient being from suffering and lead her to awakening. Due to
such great compassion, they experience only joy no matter what situation they are in.

Bodhisattvas' strong compassion also prevents them from attaining
the personal peace of arhatship. They stay in cyclic existence a long time,
taking birth after birth for the sake of benefiting sentient beings. According to the perfection vehicle, as recounted in the *Jataka Tales*, prior to
attaining full awakening Shakyamuni took many births purely to benefit others. He manifested many different forms to engage with sentient
beings, eliminate their suffering, and bring about their happiness. Most
bodhisattvas do likewise.

In general, the perfection vehicle speaks about amassing the two collections over three countless great eons in order to attain buddhahood.
For this reason, bodhisattvas take many lives in cyclic existence. According to the tantra vehicle, bodhisattvas can accumulate merit and wisdom
quickly by special tantric techniques, so they are not obliged to become

buddhas in Akanishta[29] or in one of the many pure lands where tantric practitioners can become awakened. Those bodhisattvas who attain the stage of actual clear light will definitely attain awakening in their present human life, while those who attain example clear light will attain it in the intermediate stage if not in this life. Alternatively, they may transfer their consciousness to a pure land at the time of death and attain awakening there.

> 227. Thus, do not be discouraged
>   by thinking that buddhahood is so distant.
>   Always be assiduous in this practice
>   to eliminate faults and obtain good qualities.

For the above reasons, don't be despondent or lackadaisical, thinking that it is a huge burden to collect so much merit and practice for such a long time to attain full awakening. Rather, practice the Dharma with enthusiasm to eliminate all your defilements and attain all the excellent qualities of awakening. Generating bodhichitta or understanding emptiness even for an instant can amass inconceivably huge quantities of merit and wisdom. Remembering this makes the mind extremely happy and eager to study and practice.

For example, to accumulate great merit when performing a Tara puja, make offerings of water, flowers, incense, food, and so forth in conjunction with the four immeasurable factors. Think that each offering arises from the enormous merit that you and others have created. Make offerings by imagining that what you offer expands in quantity and quality to fill all of space. Offer an inestimable number of magnificent offerings to incalculable assemblies of Tara and her entourage of deities. Request them to inspire you to receive the attainments of long life, merit, and wisdom. Thinking in this way amasses immense merit in a very short time.

To amass immeasurable wisdom, contemplate that the merit field of buddhas and bodhisattvas of the ten directions—the recipients of your offerings—appear but do not inherently exist. Similarly, the offerings themselves and you as the one making the offerings also appear but do

---

29. According to the perfection vehicle, this Akanishta is a pure abode where bodhisattvas first attain full awakening.

not inherently exist. Imagine that these recipients who appear and yet are empty accept the offerings and experience the wisdom of great bliss. This kind of contemplation can be done for any offerings you make, and by doing so, in a very short time you will accumulate inestimable merit and wisdom.

THE ENTITIES OF THE TWO COLLECTIONS

Nagarjuna now reveals the nature or entity of the two collections and discusses the three poisons that are the discordant factors interfering with our ability to create the two collections.

> 228. Recognizing that they are flawed,
>   abandon attachment, anger, and confusion.
>   Realizing that they are good qualities,
>   devote yourself respectfully to non-attachment, non-anger, and
>   non-confusion.

Advice to Abandon What Is Discordant with Merit and to Collect Merit

Understanding the defects of attachment, anger, and confusion, forsake them completely. These three poisons are called the three roots of non-virtue, whereas *non-attachment, non-anger, and non-confusion* are called the three roots of virtue. Non-attachment isn't simply the absence of attachment, it is the opposite—a balanced mind that isn't drawn into clinging and craving. Non-anger is love, and non-confusion is wisdom. Knowing the benefits of these three—that they are the source of all good qualities—put effort into practicing them. If you do, you will experience the benefits immediately in this life as well as in future lives, up to awakening.

> 229. Through attachment you go to the realm of hungry ghosts.
>   Due to anger, you are pitched into hell.
>   Out of confusion, you are reborn as an animal.
>   Through their opposites, you become a human or celestial being.

The Results of the Three Poisons and of Their Opposites

Following the three poisonous attitudes of attachment, anger, and confusion brings great harm to ourselves and others, while practicing the three roots of virtue brings benefit.

There are different ways to describe the ripening result of karma. That there are differences do not make one right and the other wrong—rather, each is posited from a different perspective, and each perspective is reasonable. According to the standard presentation of karma, engaging in the ten nonvirtues in a heavy way brings rebirth in the hell realms, while engaging in them in a middling way brings rebirth as a hungry ghost, and engaging in them in a mild way brings rebirth as an animal.

In another presentation, the ripening rebirth has to do with the affliction that motivated its causal action. From this perspective, attachment brings rebirth as a hungry ghost. For example, someone whose strong miserliness and attachment prevents him from making offerings to the Three Jewels or from being generous to sentient beings takes rebirth as a hungry ghost who cannot get what he needs. Similarly, if a person has deep-seated hatred or rage and, motivated by this strong emotion, physically assaults and severely injures someone, it is likely that he will take rebirth in the hell realms. There, this person will experience much fear and pain.

Actions motivated by confusion bring rebirth in the animal realm, as ignorance is their prominent characteristic. Animals lack intelligence regarding anything beyond staying alive and being comfortable.

However, it is not always the case that we are born as hungry ghosts through attachment and as animals through ignorance. In general, ignorance regarding karma and its results can cause rebirth in any of the three lower realms. Motivated by ignorance of suchness, people can also create polluted virtue that leads to a higher rebirth.

Conversely, by engaging in actions motivated by non-attachment, compassion, and wisdom, we create the causes for higher rebirths where these same mental states are more evident than in the lower realms.

> 230. Eliminating faults and acquiring good qualities
>   is the Dharma for one seeking higher rebirth.
>   The elimination of all grasping by means of wisdom
>   is the Dharma for one seeking the highest good.

The Actual Two Collections

Eliminating faults means to abandon the three roots of nonvirtue—attachment, anger, and confusion. *Acquiring good qualities* means to practice the three virtues: non-attachment, non-anger, and non-confusion. Together, they are the principal cause for attaining higher rebirths. If they are done in conjunction with bodhichitta, they become the collection of merit. When practices to create merit are conjoined with the wisdom realizing emptiness, they also become the collection of wisdom.

In addition to practicing wisdom when acting to benefit sentient beings, it is essential to cultivate wisdom in meditation in order to eliminate all grasping, cease cyclic existence, and bring about the highest good. To bring liberation, this wisdom must be supported by the determination to be free from cyclic existence. To attain full awakening, it must be conjoined with bodhichitta. Bodhichitta gives the practitioner the internal strength to apply wisdom to purify all defilements from the mind and to create the immeasurable merit necessary to attain a buddha's form body.

8. Advice for Gathering Merit and Gaining Wisdom

BRANCHES OF THE COLLECTION OF MERIT

Having described the general characteristics of the collections of merit and wisdom, Nagarjuna now describes branches of the collection of merit—specific deeds that bring enormous goodness in the world and create great merit that propels us along the path. This is followed by an explanation of the branches of the collection of wisdom—practices to do to increase our knowledge, understanding, and realization of the Dharma. This is presented in two cycles, first a brief explanation of the branches of the collection of merit and wisdom, followed by an extensive explanation of these two.

While some of these activities are applicable chiefly to someone with the political power and wealth of a monarch, we can engage in most of them according to our ability. The main point is to create merit, sustain the Dharma, and benefit sentient beings by making offerings to the Three Jewels and advancing projects that benefit the public to whatever extent we can.

> 231. In a respectful manner, make buddha images,
>   stupas, and vast monasteries,
>   providing extensive and excellent residences,
>   abundant riches, and so on.

> 232. From all kinds of precious substances,
>   please make well drawn,
>   beautifully proportioned images
>   of buddhas seated on lotus flowers.

Establish New Holy Objects

Nagarjuna exhorts his listeners to build large monasteries where the Sangha can reside and assemble. Use the most excellent building materials and construct them with a mind of respect. Inside the temples, place comfortable mats for the Sangha to sit on and provide them with whatever they need for their Dharma studies and practice. Make arrangements for abundant food and drink to be offered to the Sangha. By supporting them, the monastics will be able to properly fulfill their responsibility to learn, memorize, practice, and teach the Buddhadharma so that it will be purely maintained and accurately transmitted to future generations.

Make representations of the Buddha's body, speech, and mind—statues, paintings, texts, and stupas—from the best materials and precious substances and install them in the temples. Ensure that they are made by skilled artisans according to required measurements. Make them beautiful in appearance, so that whoever sees them will be inspired and filled with faith. Offer lotus seats for the statues, and decorate the stupas with jewel ornaments.

> 233. With every possible effort, take care of the holy Dharma
>   and the community of monks and nuns.
>   Adorn the stupas with gold
>   and with lattices made from gems.

Offer to Already Established Holy Objects

Maintain and restore temples and monasteries that have already been constructed and see to it that they are not damaged. Respect and care for Dharma texts—the holy Dharma—so that they do not get lost, dirty, or damaged. Since texts were written on palm leaves during Nagarjuna's time, this was especially important because books were extremely fragile. Protect the Sangha from harm caused by the four elements—earthquakes, floods, fire, and wind storms—as well as harm from animals and humans. Cherish them for the benefit of present and future generations.

> 234. Honor the reliquaries with offerings
>   of gold and silver flowers,
>   diamonds, coral, and pearls,
>   sapphires, lapis lazuli, and emeralds.

> 235. To honor those who teach the holy Dharma,
>   with goods and with services,

do what brings them joy
and respectfully devote yourself to the six dharmas.

236. Serve your gurus and listen respectfully;
     aid them and attend to them.
     Always respectfully honor
     [other] bodhisattvas as well.

Make Offerings to Holy Objects and Holy Beings

A *reliquary* could refer to either the bones or ashes of a holy being. It may also be the entire body of a holy being, as in the case of Yongzin Ling Rinpoche, whose body was preserved after his death. Make offerings to reliquaries, adorning the topmost parts of stupas with gold and jewels. Crown them with the sun and moon, and hang strands of precious jewels on them, similar to those depicted in drawings of mandalas. Offer flowers made of gold and silver, coral, pearls, sapphires, lapis lazuli, rubies, emeralds, and other jewels.

To your spiritual mentors, offer requisites such as food, beverages, clothing, shelter, and medicine. Offer your service to them by preparing their seats and blankets, or arranging for parasols, victory banners, ceremonial umbrellas, and canopies. Go to them and inquire if they have all they need, and respectfully ask about their health. In brief, offer whatever goods and services please them, and help them accomplish whatever virtuous projects they undertake to benefit sentient beings.

Listen to Dharma teachings attentively, with respect and veneration. Serve your Dharma teachers according to their needs. In addition, respectfully make offerings to those who are not your Dharma teachers but are still special beings, such as bodhisattvas.

237. You should not pay such respect, honor,
     or homage to others who are non-Buddhists.
     Through that [misplaced respect],
     the unknowing become attached to faulty [teachers].

Forgo Offering to the Unworthy

Do not pay respect, honor, or make offerings to the unworthy, those who teach or practice a wrong path. If the king were to show them great respect and make offerings to them, the citizens would think that they should follow suit. Since they lack discriminating wisdom, they could become enamored with these "teachers" and receive teachings from them. In that way, they would be led on a wrong path, which harms them in this life and for many lives to come.

Of course, the king should still be polite to these people, but honoring them simply because they wear special dress or have special titles is not wise.

Branches of the Collection of Wisdom

Nagarjuna now instructs us on specific activities to fulfill the collection of wisdom.

> 238. Offer manuscripts and volumes
> of the word of the King of Sages
> and the treatises that come from it,
> along with their prerequisites, pens and ink.

> 239. For the sake of increasing wisdom,
> provide for the livelihood of the schoolmasters
> in all the educational institutions of the land
> and formally grant estates to them.

Offer manuscripts and volumes of the Buddha's teachings and the reliable treatises that are derived from them. The sutras contain the Buddha's teachings that benefit beings by instructing the way to attain higher rebirth and highest good, and the treatises and commentaries help us unravel their meaning. Also provide the paper, ink, and pens required to copy these texts and to compose new ones.

Education is the source of great good, as educated citizens will contribute to the flourishing of society. If people are able to read and study the Buddha's words they will also help disseminate the Dharma, which will bring peace to individuals and to society as a whole. This being the case, find excellent teachers for all important subjects—mathematics, reading, writing, the arts and sciences. Provide them with housing, as well as whatever else they may need to teach without difficulty.

THE COLLECTION OF MERIT EXPANDED

What follows are more specific instructions to the king on how to enhance the collection of merit. First Nagarjuna teaches the king fourteen ways to use his wealth for the collective good. Just imagining a land where the wealthy and powerful care for others in the way Nagarjuna instructs brings joy to our hearts. While we may not have the great wealth or power of a king, we can adapt these instructions to our personal circumstances and employ them to create enormous merit. May we contribute what we can to this.

> 240. With [the proceeds from] your fields
> establish wages for doctors and barbers
> for the sake of the elderly, the young, and the ill
> so as to relieve the suffering of sentient beings.

> 241. You of good wisdom,
> establish rest houses and build parks and causeways,
> pools, pavilions, and cisterns;
> provide for bedding, grasses, and wood.

(1) Dispel the suffering of the elderly, children, the sick, and sentient beings tormented by great misery by providing people with doctors, dentists, health care professionals, and barbers who are always available. Give special assistance to those who need it.

(2) In towns and villages and at crossroads, construct hostels and guesthouses for travelers. This will protect travelers and enable them to have what they need—without such amenities life could be difficult for them. In the larger towns provide places where people can relax, such as gardens and parks where they can walk and converse. Flower gardens especially gladden the mind.

Make embankments around lakes and walkways along the shores that blend with the environment and offer people the pleasure of uplifting walks.

Build bridges over bodies of water that require them. Also install benches, pavilions, and the like where people can rest and enjoy themselves.

Leave water cisterns and other water vessels along the roadsides for travelers. Nearby those containers, provide beds and seats, food, and fodder for donkeys and horses. Leave firewood there too should travelers need to cook. Nagarjuna's reference here to *you of good wisdom* indicates the king, who should supply each of those rest areas with what an intelligent person considers useful for those who travel long distances.

> 242. Build pavilions in all towns,
>   at temples and in all cities.
>   Along any thoroughfare
>   where water is scarce, provide cisterns.

> 243. Out of your compassion, always care for the ill,
>   the homeless, those afflicted by suffering,
>   the downtrodden and unfortunate.
>   Respectfully apply yourself to aiding them.

(3) In villages and towns and nearby temples, make areas for people to relax and enjoy themselves.

(4) Along the roads where water is scarce, leave containers filled with water here and there so people can quench their thirst and care for their animals.

(5) With compassion, care for those who are sick so that they might quickly recover. Be a protector for the homeless who have no one to turn to and no place where they feel safe. Reach out to those stricken with suffering so that they may be free of their suffering. Pay special attention to the lower castes and those with low social standing who have particular problems. Attend to the problems of the poor, and tend to the suffering of all these people with compassion, respect, and joy. Do not be condescending when helping others, but help them as you would help yourself.

> 244. It is not proper for you to partake of seasonal foods
>   and beverages, produce, grains, and fruits
>   until you have offered them to monks and nuns
>   and those asking for alms.

245. At the sites of cisterns place shoes,
     parasols, and water filters,
     tweezers for removing thorns,
     needles, thread, and fans.

(6) Do not eat the food and drink procured from warmer climates in the winter and from cooler climates in the summer without first offering a portion to the Three Jewels, the monastic community, mendicants, and beggars. Always offer food to the Three Jewels and practice generosity to sentient beings.

(7) Provide shoes for people who lack them to prevent them from being bitten by snakes and pierced by thorns as they walk. Offer parasols and umbrellas for protection from the sun and rain. Make water strainers available so that insects in the water will not die, and provide tweezers for removing thorns, needles and thread to mend clothes, and fans for people to cool themselves. Put these near the cisterns where people can easily locate them.

246. At the cisterns also place the three kinds of fruit,
     the three kinds of salt, honey,
     eye medicine, and antidotes to poison.
     Also write formulas for medicinal treatments and spells.

247. At the cisterns also place ointments
     for the body, feet, and head,
     cradles, ladles and ewers,
     brass pots, axes, and so on.

(8) Eliminate the problems travelers face by making medicines and healing spells easily accessible. The three medicinal fruits are yellow myrobalan (*terminalia chebula*), beleric myrobalan (*terminalia belerica*), and emblic myrobalan (*emblica officinalis*). Butter and honey are medicines for certain nervous disorders due to imbalance of the internal winds. Medicine for the eyes and antidotes to poisons are also helpful to travelers. Make clear instructions on how to take the medicine for each particular illness, and write down mantras to recite that cure illnesses, and put these near the cisterns together with the medicinal substances.

(9) In the enclosures where the water cisterns are located, put oil and other ointments for travelers to use to protect their skin and to heal wounds. Leave cradles for infants and toddlers to sleep in. Also put out jugs to collect water, axes to cut firewood for cooking, and various pots, pans, pitchers, and utensils.

> 248. In cool, shady spots make small cisterns
> filled with potable water
> and provided with sesame, rice,
> grain, foods, and molasses.

> 249. At the openings of anthills
> have trustworthy persons
> constantly place food and water,
> molasses and piles of grain.

(10) Make shady areas near the cisterns, and nearby place sesame, rice, grains, molasses, oil, and various foods. Make sure the cisterns are filled with sufficient potable water.

(11) Instruct trustworthy people to keep ants supplied with food, by placing water, sugar, and oil from grains near the entrances to anthills without hurting the ants.

> 250. Both before and after each meal
> always offer in a pleasant manner
> food to hungry ghosts,
> dogs, ants, birds, and so on.

> 251. Always care extensively for [places] in the world
> that are oppressed or where crops have failed,
> that have suffered harm or where there is plague,
> or that have been conquered [in war].

> 252a. Provide seeds and food to farmers
> who have fallen on hard times.

(12) Before and after eating, give as much as you can to hungry ghosts, dogs, birds, and ants. One way of offering to hungry ghosts is by putting

rice or bread in your fist and reciting an offering mantra, as monastics do after the midday meal.

(13) Send aid to stricken areas whether they are located in your kingdom or elsewhere. Help those oppressed by another king and those whose crops failed. Send emergency aid to areas where the populace is struck by epidemics or where natural disasters have occurred. Help these people to rebuild their homes, plant their fields, and recover from illness. Take care of people in areas ravaged by war who desperately need help. Help all these people as extensively as you can.

(14) Distribute seeds and seedlings so farmers will have plentiful harvests and people will have enough to eat. Give them farming tools if needed. Some may not have the animals or farmhands needed to work their land—care for them by supplying them with what they need to sustain themselves, their families, and neighbors.

Wealthy countries nowadays don't have these kinds of visible problems; they are almost like pure lands. But in Nepal, Tibet, India, China, and Africa, many people are afflicted by such terrible hardships. We should help them as much as we can. Such generosity done with bodhichitta is the collection of merit.

> 252b. Eliminate excessive taxes
>   and reduce the portion [of products taxed].

> 253. Protect [citizens] from debt;
>   eliminate new tolls and reduce [excessive] tolls.
>   Eliminate the suffering of those
>   who wait at your door [with their petitions unanswered].

Giving Other Things and Governing Properly

These above fourteen are branches of collecting merit by giving what we own. In the following set of nine instructions Nagarjuna counsels leaders and officials on how to govern the land wisely.

(1) Eliminate high taxes levied by previous kings that burden people, and (2) reduce the amount of items that are taxed. (3) Protect those who are impoverished due to debt. (4) As a new king, eliminate tolls altogether or (5) reduce those that are burdensome. (6) When merchants come from

other places, do not be greedy for their possessions, imposing heavy taxes on them, confiscating or impounding their goods, or refusing to let them depart. If people wish to meet with you, do not keep them waiting with their petitions unanswered but try to see them soon.

> 254. Eliminate bandits from your own land
>   and in other lands as well.
>   Keep prices level
>   and place the proper value [on goods].

(7) Eliminate bandits in your land and in other lands too. If people in your land have been harmed or traumatized by robbers, alleviate their troubles and give them what they need. (8) Additionally, ensure that prices are fair and the proper value is placed on goods. During times of scarcity don't allow people to overcharge others, but keep prices at the level of what most people can afford.

> 255. Be thoroughly familiar
>   with all that your advisors say,
>   and always do whatever
>   is healthy for the world.

> 256. Just as you pay attention
>   to whatever you think will benefit you,
>   so too pay attention
>   to what you think will benefit others.

(9) Your ministers will want to discuss many things with you. Listen closely to their assessments and advice. Understand their attitudes and intentions, and use your own wisdom to discern if their advice is suitable and if it benefits your citizens. Do only what will benefit others, and do not let yourself be taken in by greedy or scheming advisors who do not care for you, the people in your land, or the environment.

In short, regard others' concerns as being as important as your own, and pay attention to what you think will benefit them. When others help you, you are happy. Similarly, when you help others, they will benefit and have a happy mind.

257. Like the earth, water, fire, and wind,
      wild herbs and the plants of the forest,
      make yourself [and your possessions]
      available for the general enjoyment [of all].

258. Even when taking their seventh step,
      bodhisattvas have the attitude of giving away all their
         possessions;
      this produces merit in them
      that is as limitless as the sky itself.

Give Everything Away

Sentient beings freely use the earth, water, fire, air, herbs, and other medicinal plants that grow in the forest. Similarly, as much as you can, put your possessions, body, and resources at the service of others so that sentient beings will derive maximum benefit.

If your mind will not let you give to others, then repeatedly make the aspiration, "May all I own—including my possessions and body—be used by others, and may others benefit from this." Thinking like this even for a short while will increase your capacity to give later. Try to give all you can according to your capability, and train in and enhance your wish to give. In brief, be generous whenever you can.

Just after bodhisattvas take birth in the lifetime in which they will attain full awakening, they take seven steps and declare that this will be their final life as a samsaric being. At that time, they haven't yet actualized their goal of full awakening, but they cultivate the intention to give everything to sentient beings. They protect this marvelous intention from deterioration by repeatedly thinking, "May I be able to give my body, wealth, and past, present, and future merit to sentient beings and may it manifest as whatever they want or need." Thinking like this creates merit as extensive as space.

This is similar to the taking-and-giving meditation, *tonglen*, where we imagine transforming our body, wealth, and virtue into whatever others want and need and then giving it to them. In fact, *Precious Garland* is the root source of this meditation, as we shall see later.

259. If you bestow well-adorned, beautiful maidens
     upon those who seek them,
     you will thereby attain the *dharanis*
     that hold the holy Dharma.

260. Previously the Victor bestowed
     eighty thousand maidens adorned
     with all kinds of ornaments
     accompanied by all kinds of goods.

Give According to What Others Want

Give beautiful maidens wearing fine clothing and adorned with jewels, along with everything needed to sustain them, to those who seek them. Doing so is a cause for attaining the full retention of the words and meaning of the Dharma without befuddlement.

We may wonder if it is suitable to give women—or any human being—to others as if they were possessions. In ancient Indian culture this was appropriate in situations where one had responsibility for maidens and authority over them—as would be the case with the great kings at that time. Nagarjuna cites as a precedent the act of the Buddha in a former life as King Anantakirti when he gave away eighty thousand maidens, together with jewelry, clothes, household items, and everything that they need.[30]

There is some similarity between this story and the Jataka tale about one of the Buddha's previous lives when he was a bodhisattva and gave his wife and children as gifts to a *raksha* (demon). Not all rakshas are evil—the one to whom the bodhisattva gave his wife and children treated them kindly. There is a world of difference between giving away one's wife and children callously, for money or other worldly gain, and giving them responsibly to someone who will take care of them, possibly better than oneself. Although giving in this way is contrary to our modern culture's emphasis on human

---

30. The commentary specifically says that the maidens took jewels and all the other items needed for their support with them, so it is reasonable to assume that the maidens were of marriageable age, and the king was providing dowries for them. In ancient India, and even in modern India, marriages are arranged and the bride and groom often have little choice in the matter.

rights, we cannot immediately claim that the bodhisattva, acting within the mores of an ancient culture, lacked compassion.

Once, some gods who revered the practice of virtue wanted to see whether the Buddha, who at the time was a bodhisattva king, was completely free of attachment and able to practice the perfection of generosity faultlessly. To do this, they emanated as mendicants who requested all of his possessions, which he happily gave them. To see if he still had subtler forms of attachment, they took the form of very pathetic and lonely people and begged the king for his wife, son, and daughter. Overwhelmed with compassion at their pitiful state, he gave them his family as well. To examine if he was free from the subtlest levels of attachment, they asked for his eye, hands, and other parts of his body. He gave these completely free of any self-centeredness and without fear, hesitation, or regret.

Bodhisattvas' practice of generosity, ethical conduct, and fortitude is beyond our comprehension; it is something we can only imagine and aspire to have one day. People say that they have great compassion for their children, but in fact their compassion is almost certainly mixed with attachment and is not very powerful. Giving rise to unadulterated compassion is difficult, and our compassion cannot even begin to compare with the depth and breadth of compassion bodhisattvas feel upon meeting someone in a pitiful state.

Enormous faith wells up in my mind when I contemplate these accounts of the Buddha's practice of giving on the bodhisattva path. I see that he was able to give without the slightest attachment to any person or possession, his reputation, or anything else. This is the kind of practice that people like us are not able to do at all. For example, if someone asked us for our spouse, there would be no way we could give that person away. Our attachment is so strong we would not even allow anyone to touch or even look at our spouse. At first glance, when we hear such stories about bodhisattvas' practice of generosity, they are so outside our experience that we have a hard time even considering them.[31]

---

31. In general, people in Asia traditionally approach these stories about bodhisattvas giving away their spouse and children from the viewpoint of the difficulty of separating from those we dearly love and treasure. Overcoming attachment to family is more than most people can imagine, and so they have great respect for bodhisattvas who do not have the slightest worldly attachment to people, possessions, or their bodies.

In Western cultures, we approach these stories from the perspective of human rights. To us the idea of owning people and then giving them away, especially a woman who has equal rights, is abominable. It connotes slavery, human trafficking, and sexual

To someday be able to give our body, possessions, and life as freely as bodhisattvas do, we start by repeatedly generating the bodhichitta motivation and proceed with the practices of the six perfections according to our ability.

> 261. To those who come begging,
>   lovingly give numerous and resplendent clothes,
>   ornaments, perfumes, and garlands,
>   and other objects of enjoyment.

Giving to the Needy

Give people whatever they need or want—jewelry, clothes, perfumes, garlands, food, drink, medicine, shelter, and more. Give them things that are in excellent condition, not faded, old, or torn. It is important to give without thinking that we will become well known for being rich and generous. Watch your motivation and make sure it is always compassionate.

> 262. There is no greater act of generosity
>   than to grant to the extremely unfortunate
>   who are bereft of some aspect of the Dharma
>   the happy chance [to receive teachings on it].

Give According to the Dharma

Giving according to the Dharma means to give what is appropriate and needed according to the time and situation. Helping those who want to listen to the Dharma but lack the material necessities to do so is especially good. A wonderful practice of generosity is providing for others' material needs so they can study and practice the Dharma. Due to your generosity, they now have the opportunity to listen, meditate, and gain realizations. Their practice benefits all beings, not only themselves.

---

abuse. As a Westerner, the editor recoils at human rights abuse of all kinds; as a student of anthropology, I separate the point of the story from its cultural overlays and can appreciate it.

If you have the necessary knowledge and skill to share the Dharma with others, it is a privilege to give talks, lead meditations and discussions, and give people Dharma advice to solve their problems. The sutras say that the gift of the Dharma is the highest gift.

263. You should even give poison
    to those for whom poison would be beneficial.
    But if even the best food will not help someone,
    do not give it to him.

264. It is said that if a snake has bitten one's finger,
    it is helpful to amputate it.
    Likewise, the Sage said that if it benefits others,
    one should even do something unpleasant.

Certain illnesses must be treated with poisonous substances, so give them to people who need them to recover from an illness. Be sensitive in each situation to see what is required and beneficial. Do not give someone the best things if that is not what will benefit her. For example, do not insist that a sick person eat rich food; give her the food that she needs to recover.

It may happen that to solve a problem we may have to do something that is unpleasant in the short term but efficacious in the long term. For example, a person may require surgery or another type of medical treatment that is unpleasant at present but will cure him. We should continually look for the best long-term solutions to difficulties, without regard to temporary pleasure.

THE COLLECTION OF WISDOM EXPANDED

The branches of the collection of wisdom are ways to approach the study and practice of emptiness. Adopting the twenty-five branches outlined below will facilitate our collection of wisdom, enabling it to increase easily and without many hindrances.

265. Have supreme respect for the holy Dharma
    and those who teach the Dharma.

Respectfully listen to the Dharma
and offer the Dharma to others.

(1) Offer to, honor, and respect the sutras, treatises, and commentaries that teach the path to liberation and awakening. To offer respect to Dharma books, buy cloth for covering them, construct clean and high places to store them, and embellish the external edges of the pages with yellow dye, a custom followed by Tibetans. Honor and serve those who teach the Dharma by offering them food, clothing, shelter, medicine, and the various things they need in order to teach and spread the Dharma.

(2) When attending discourses, be respectful and humble; leave all arrogance aside, as that will hinder learning the Dharma. Bow to the teachers to show respect and listen attentively, without chatting to others or standing up in the middle of teachings. Respectful behavior toward the Dharma and Dharma teachers will be a good example for the people in your land.

(3) Give texts to those who don't have books to study. Making a library with Buddhist texts and preserving ancient texts is an excellent offering to the Dharma and to all the people who will use the texts and benefit from studying them. In addition, answer questions and explain the Dharma to those who do not understand the meaning of the oral or written teachings.

266. Do not revel in worldly discourse;
    take delight in the transcendent.
    Just as you develop good qualities in yourself,
    develop them also in others.

(4) Do not enjoy listening to people criticize or gossip about others. Do not even take delight in conversation that is neither particularly harmful nor beneficial, such as meaningless stories that waste time and later manifest as distraction in meditation. Especially avoid discussions about topics that stir up the mind and inflame afflictions. (5) Instead, relish conversations about the Dharma, the determination to be free, bodhichitta, the six perfections, emptiness, liberation, awakening, and so forth. When you are together with others, try to turn the conversation to these topics and include other people in discussions on such matters.

(6) Just as you have the desire to generate the qualities of listening, thinking, and meditating, encourage others' interest in the Dharma and help those who already show an interest to follow up on it.

> 267. Do not be satisfied with the Dharma you have heard;
>   keep in mind its meaning and analyze it.
>   Always respectfully offer
>   a gift of thanksgiving to your gurus.

(7) Do not be satisfied with hearing only a little Dharma, thinking you already know a lot, or that you have heard that teaching before. Be an excellent disciple who is always thirsty for the Dharma and try to hear more teachings, read more books, and learn as much as possible. Be like the ocean, which is never satiated no matter how much water flows into it, but continues to take in more.

If you start to feel that you have listened to enough teachings, contemplate the benefits of listening to the Dharma as explained in the lamrim literature. This will inspire you to want to listen to Dharma discourses forever. In that way our mind will continuously improve because every time you hear a teaching you will understand it in a new and deeper way. Look at the example of many learned practitioners who attend teachings that they have already heard many times. We do not finish listening to teachings and studying until we become a buddha.

(8) In one day, you might have studied too many verses to remember all the words, but try to keep the meaning clear in your mind. Summarize what you have learned so that you will remember it, and continue to contemplate it later. After you have studied a great deal, you will have the capacity to explore many subjects extensively without getting them confused. The ability to contemplate topics broadly and deeply and still be able to express their essence concisely is a wonderful skill that will help you tremendously.

(9) Analyze the Dharma you have heard, so that the various divisions, definitions, and outlines of the material are clear in your mind. Think deeply about the teachings to ensure you understand them properly—this will improve your meditation.

(10) Respectfully offer your spiritual mentors the things they need. Do not offer things that you like but are unsuitable to offer to monastics.

268. Do not study profane [philosophical systems], such as that of the
       Charvakas.
     Give up debate that is for the sake of arrogance.
     Do not speak in praise of your own good qualities,
       but rather speak of even your enemies' good qualities.

(11) Do not listen to the teachings of the Charvakas and other non-Buddhist philosophers who assert that past or future lives do not exist and that our actions do not condition our later experiences. Reading their texts could harm your faith in the Buddha and cause you to have unnecessary doubts about karma and its results, which will in turn create obstacles to fulfilling the two collections.

(12) Study with a good motivation, free of arrogance and competition. When you discuss and debate the Dharma, give up the motivation to win the argument and defeat others. Abandon any desire to secure the reputation of being articulate and intelligent.

(13) Do not broadcast your own qualities, telling everyone all the good you have done, are doing, and will do. Be discreet about your own qualities and instead speak of others' qualities. If you have developed actual excellent qualities through your practice, other people may talk about them, but they are not for you to discuss. A sandalwood tree has a very pleasant fragrance, but the tree itself does not spread its own fragrance; it is the wind that carries it to other places.

(14) Do not criticize those you dislike but speak of their good qualities. Jealousy is often behind our dislike for someone, so turn your perspective so you can sincerely rejoice at others' opportunities, virtues, and good qualities. Speaking about these to others will eliminate the pain of jealousy.

269. Do not attack what is vital [to another],
       nor make statements with
       a negative attitude toward others.
     Instead, examine your own errors.

(15) When discussing the Dharma with others, do not speak in an offensive manner. When talking with people in general, avoid saying things that will hurt or offend them or touch a sensitive spot.

(16) Refrain from maliciously talking about the faults of others. There are occasions when it is appropriate to give somebody feedback regarding her faults with a good motivation. Do so when you know the person is open to hearing feedback, will take your words to heart, and give up that fault in the future. When you are tempted to shame or blame someone, it is better to look at your own faults and mistakes and eliminate those.

(17) Examine yourself to see if you have faults or not. It is easy to know the faults of others, just as it is easy to see the dirt on someone else's face. But to see the dirt on your own face, you have to look in a mirror. Similarly, you must look inside yourself to know your own faults. If you neglect to examine your own mind, you could easily think a fault is a good quality. This is disastrous for your Dharma practice as well as for your personal relationships.

> 270. You should eliminate in yourself
> those faults that the wise always decry in others.
> And to the best of your ability,
> eliminate them in others as well.

(18) Be conscientious about the traits that the buddhas and bodhisattvas renounce. Be familiar with these faults in yourself and counteract them. When it can benefit others, speak about your faults to others as a way of encouraging them to identify and counteract these faults in themselves.

In general, it is hard to find people who regularly speak of others' good qualities. To the contrary, when someone has a small fault, people are quick to jump on him and talk at length about it. You may become a great pundit due to study, contemplation, and meditation, but if you have a fault in another area, that fault will outshine all your qualities in the eyes of others. Be careful and don't become conceited; many people are on the lookout for faults, and those looking for good qualities are rare.

> 271. Do not be angry when others do harm,
> but realize that it is [the effect of] previous karma.
> Without causing any more suffering,
> eliminate your own faults.

(19) When others harm you, your body, or your possessions, avoid exploding in anger. Instead consider that this is a result of your own previous actions. Giving in to anger will result in more suffering in future lives. Speaking or acting out of anger usually exacerbates the present situation by making communication more contentious.

Train in four virtuous practices: (a) when insulted, do not retaliate by insulting the other person; (b) when hit, do not hit the other in return; (c) when others are angry with you, do not respond with anger; (d) when others observe your faults, do not react by commenting on theirs. These are four "austerities" that bodhisattvas practice. They are much more effective for transforming the mind than physical austerities that harm the body, and in many ways they are more difficult.

Though you may receive harm from all directions, recall the reasons to not retaliate. Remember that this situation is the result of your own destructive karma, and that if you want to avoid similar suffering in the future, you must stop creating its causes now. Also reflect that much suffering comes as a result of anger, whereas if you practice fortitude, many benefits will accrue.

Practicing fortitude does not mean capitulating to the other person or allowing him to continue his harmful behavior. Rather, after calming your mind, think clearly about a constructive way to communicate and then act to resolve the conflict.

> 272. Do what benefits others
>   without expecting anything in return.
>   Endure your suffering alone,
>   and share your pleasures with beggars.

(20) When you assist others, do not expect any repayment in the future, such as the other person praising you, telling others how kind you are, or giving you a gift. Help with compassion and care for others.

(21) When you experience suffering, bear it yourself without complaining to the people around you, "It's so unfair that I have to suffer," "No one helps me," or "I'm suffering so much because of the horrible things this other person did." Instead reflect that you are now able to see the result of the destructive karma you have created. Consider that this karma is now being exhausted and will no longer obscure your mind, and in this way, accept the situation.

Give to beggars or to anyone who asks for something. This not only makes them happy, but you will also experience continuous happiness in the future as a result of generosity.

> 273. Even if you have the excellent conditions
>   of a god, do not become inflated with conceit.
>   Do not be discouraged
>   even by poverty like that of a hungry ghost.

(22) Even though you may have many marvelous possessions, high social status, and a great following in this life, do not become puffed up with conceit. Dispel your arrogance by recalling that these possessions and circumstances are transient and perish in an instant. You have had hundreds of thousands of better possessions and situations in previous lives, but in a moment they were suddenly gone, and nothing remains of them now. Furthermore, everything you possess came from the kindness and efforts of others, so there is no reason to think you are better than others.

Conversely, you may find yourself absolutely impoverished, so lacking in normal human necessities such as money, food, drink, shelter, and clothing that you are just like a hungry ghost with nothing at all. Do not become despondent or let the situation adversely affect your mental peace. Understand that these conditions are due to karma you created in previous lives—stealing others' possessions, being stingy, or not allowing others to access what is rightfully theirs.

When life goes well, people often abandon their Dharma practice—and when things go badly, they also lose their practice. While it is much better for our practice to be somewhere in between, we cannot always control situations. We should learn to remain emotionally stable no matter the external situation.

> 274. For your own sake always speak the truth
>   even if it leads to your death
>   or the loss of your sovereignty.
>   Never speak in any other fashion.

> 275. Devote yourself always to the discipline
>   of acting in accord with your statements.

Glorious one, by that you will become
supremely authoritative for the sake of the world.

(23) Always be truthful and walk the path of truth. Speak and act truthfully, even if by doing so your life is endangered or you risk losing your power and wealth. Engage in work that is beneficial for sentient beings and never act just for your own sake. Even though lying and deception may give you an advantage in this life, do not give in to behavior that destroys your good character and makes others distrust you.

Though you may not gain in the short term by being truthful and honest, in the long term you will always profit. Maintaining your integrity will lead to excellent results in future lives. Ultimately, truth always wins, so forge ahead with confidence and engage in practices and actions that benefit others even though doing so may bring you difficulties in the present. While this point is directly relevant to someone in a position of power and leadership, it is meant for us as well. The newspapers are filled with stories of people who lie, cheat, and deceive others. You don't want to be one of them.

(24) Be sure to fully carry out everything you have undertaken for the sake of others. In addition, keep the discipline you have promised the Buddha, such as abandoning the ten paths of nonvirtue and maintaining the precepts you have taken. By doing so, you will be trusted by all—people will know you as someone who always means what he says and follows through with what he promises to do.

> 276. In all cases you should act
>   after first thoroughly examining [the situation].
>   By correctly seeing things as they are,
>   do not become dependent on others.

(25) Many of the above verses are part of the source material for the mind teachings (*lojong*). In brief, before you act, always examine your motivation to ensure you are not influenced by attachment, anger, arrogance, or jealousy. Examine the actions you are about to undertake to see if they are suitable and beneficial or not. Reflect on what to practice and abandon on the path, and act accordingly. Waiting until after you have acted to scrutinize the situation or to check your motivation is not a good idea; prevent mistakes and misdeeds before you do them!

The great Dharma masters encourage us to make decisions based on reason and our knowledge of the benefits and disadvantages of a particular course of action. Therefore, reflect on these and on the purpose before you act.

When you are able to assess your situation accurately and examine your own intentions honestly, you won't have to rely on other people telling you what is right and wrong. A fool must always depend on someone else to know what to do and not do. Cultivate your own wisdom.

9. The Fruits of Merit and Wisdom

Nagarjuna now explains the five common qualities and the twenty-five special qualities that will arise if we engage in amassing the two collections. Knowing these, we'll know how our practices fit into the overall scheme of the path and will practice with enthusiasm.

> 277. Through the Dharma your kingdom will be happy,
>   the vast canopy of your fame
>   will spread in all directions,
>   and ministers will bow to you.

Five Common Benefits of Amassing the Two Collections

(1) Respecting and practicing the Dharma causes the kingdom and world to be happier. Government leaders benefit the Dharma by ensuring that the country is run well, which in turn helps people to be able to practice well. When citizens practice well, the Dharma flourishes and famine, civil strife, and corruption decrease. It is evident that when things go wrong in a country, the Dharma cannot remain there.

Some young Tibetans say that we lost Tibet because we were too absorbed with the Dharma and did not form political relationships with other countries. They then conclude that Dharma practice is pointless. However, we cannot escape experiencing the results of our karma. For that reason, it is important to abstain from destructive actions, purify the ones already created, and engage in constructive actions.

(2) When your actions are aimed at the Dharma, you will receive endless benefits that come from listening to teachings, contemplating their meaning, and familiarizing yourself with what you have learned. You will be able to spread the Dharma far and wide, and one of many temporal

benefits from this is that your fame will spread everywhere, and happiness will reign in your kingdom. Many benefits will also ripen in future lives.

(3) By practicing well, you will naturally attract a following of good people, among them good ministers who will serve you and the kingdom well. Although this verse explicitly explains that practicing the Dharma well will benefit a ruler, it is also applicable to us. If we study and practice the Dharma well, we too will gradually attract a circle of disciples and be able to benefit them.

> 278. The causes of death are numerous;
>   those that sustain life are few,
>   and even they can cause death.
>   Therefore, always practice the Dharma.

> 279. If, in this way, you always practice Dharma,
>   the contentment that will arise
>   in you and in the world
>   will be abundant.

> 280. Through the practices you will sleep happily
>   and will awaken happily.
>   Because your inner nature will be without defect,
>   even your dreams will be happy.

(4) While you currently have a precious human life, extract the essence from the teachings and put it into practice immediately. Extensive study of the Dharma is the first step. Having studied broadly, you will see that the myriad teachings of the Buddha boil down to the three principal aspects of the path—the determination to be free, bodhichitta, and the correct view of reality.

Keeping death in mind spurs us to practice immediately. We have to work very hard to take care of this body and to stay alive, yet our death is inevitable. Sometimes the things we think extend life actually cause death—our house collapses, we choke on food, or we get in a car accident.

It is foolish to be complacent and think that we will not die because we are healthy and strong right now. We are constantly aging and approaching death; a small incident can cut our life short at any moment. Therefore, practice with joyous effort now. By practicing with sincerity, we will be free of fear and regret; we will sleep happily without worrying whether people will discover the truth behind our lies, and when we awaken, we will joyfully welcome a new day with appreciation for our opportunity to practice the Dharma and benefit sentient beings.

(5) We will certainly be happy and satisfied if we practice like this, and we will make others happy too. Earnestly practicing the Dharma ourselves increases the happiness of those around us, and living with happy people increases our own happiness.

Just as those who suffer from hunger and thirst are delighted when you give them food, people are happy when you take care of your kingdom and subjects with a loving, beneficial mind in accordance with the Dharma. On the other hand, acting harmfully, harboring resentment and ill will, seeking revenge, or punishing those who disagree with you prevent you from sleeping well at night. Even your dreams will be tormented, and you will awake in a bad mood. When you refrain from harming others and instead lovingly care for them, you will not suffer from fear of revenge or rebellion. Doing all actions with a happy mind will bring contentment in your heart now; your sleep will be peaceful, and you will awake refreshed. If you don't believe this, try it out for yourself.

While we do not have kingdoms to govern, each of us lives in an interdependent world where our actions affect others. If we cultivate genuine care and concern for others—no matter if they are our friends and relatives or strangers on the other side of the planet or even in another universe—we will naturally avoid harming them and will instead benefit them. This will result in both present and future happiness for others and ourselves.

> 281. Earnestly serve your parents,
> and respect the principals of your lineage;
> use your resources well, have fortitude, and be generous;
> speak gently without divisiveness,

> 282. and practice the discipline of truth.
> By doing these in this one life, you will become
> king of the celestial beings, and be a godly king even now.
> Therefore, devote yourself always to this kind of Dharma.

The Arising of Twenty-Five Special Qualities

Since all misery in the world comes from not having practiced the Dharma, now that we have a fortunate birth, the mental capacity, and the interest to learn the Buddha's teachings, we should enthusiastically do so. True appreciation of the Dharma depends on understanding that all of our experiences are due to our physical, verbal, and mental karma. For that reason, it's important to be able to discern virtue from nonvirtue. In this section, Nagarjuna describes twenty-five virtuous actions and their specific results in order to encourage us to fulfill the collections of merit and wisdom and thus attain buddhahood.

In speaking of the following sets of causes and their results, sometimes the cause is the principal cause of that specific result; for example, ethical conduct is the principal cause of higher rebirth. Other times, the cause is a cooperative condition for that result, not its principal cause. Love is the cooperative condition that assists our being able to accomplish our aims. Understanding this properly will prevent us from having unrealistic expectations regarding the results of our actions.

(1) The first practice to adopt is the *eightfold discipline*.

- *Earnestly serve your parents*—provide the food or other necessities your parents need when they are old. Help them with tasks such as cooking and washing clothes, take care of them when they are sick, comfort them when they are in pain. Speak kindly to them, and try to make them happy if they are troubled. In general, children should behave respectfully to their parents and make prayers for them to have long healthy lives and to create a great deal of merit. If you are not able to directly help your Dharma teachers, parents, the ill, and so forth, it is important at least to have a kind attitude toward them.
- *Respect the principals of your lineage.* This refers to offering service and respect above all to your principal guru as well as all your spiritual mentors and superiors in general. According to the Dharma, those who are younger should esteem and serve their elders. In particular, the Vinaya specifies that monastics must respect and offer service to those who are their seniors and more knowledgeable.

- *Use your resources well* by avoiding wrong livelihood and engaging in a wholesome livelihood. Do not use things obtained from wrong livelihood.
- *Cultivate fortitude* so you can remain even-tempered in all situations.
- *Be generous* to help others and create merit.
- *Speak gently* and avoid speaking harshly to others; rather, speak kindly.
- *Avoid divisiveness.* Do not make comments that divide people, telling one person what another person said about him, thus creating disharmony or aggravating disharmony that is already present.
- *Practice the discipline of truth.* Once again, Nagarjuna reminds us of the importance of speaking truthfully and acting with integrity.

Nagarjuna recommends we follow this eightfold discipline every day for the rest of our lives. As a result, we *will become king of the celestial beings*—that is, we will have a good rebirth as a human being or celestial being and on that basis will be able to continue to progress spiritually.

283. Giving the food of three hundred stew-pots
     every day, three times a day,
     cannot compare to even part of the merit
     of just a short moment of love.

284. Even if not liberated, you will attain
     these eight excellent qualities from practicing love:
     celestial and human beings will love you,
     and they will also protect you;

285. you will have peace of mind and much happiness
     and not be harmed by either poison or weapons;
     you will effortlessly attain your aims
     and be reborn in the realm of Brahma.

(2) Nagarjuna has frequently encouraged us to be *generous.* Those who have wealth should use it to accumulate merit, but there is no problem if you are

not wealthy. The main point is to cultivate bodhichitta and give with that motivation. We should also practice the three other types of generosity: the generosity of fearlessness that gives protection to those in danger, the generosity of love that comforts and encourages others, and the generosity of Dharma that leads them out of cyclic existence.

A fabulously wealthy person may give an abundance of food to hundreds of impoverished people many times a day. While she creates great merit through this generosity, this cannot compare to the merit generated from meditating on love for just a moment. Giving food, wonderful though it is, is limited because the amount of food and the number of beings receiving it are finite. But when we meditate on *love*, our mind expands to encompass all sentient beings, so the merit is immeasurable. Meditating on love not only leads to awakening, but eight benefits accrue in this life:

- Celestial and human beings will like you, and you will have good relationships with others.
- Non-humans will not harm you and will protect you.
- You will have happiness and peace of mind, free of inner turmoil.
- Your health will improve, and you will experience more physical pleasure.
- You will not be harmed by poisons.
- You will not be harmed by weapons.
- You will be able to accomplish your aims without great effort.
- In future lives you will take rebirth in the world of Brahma. The word *Brahma* doesn't always refer to the god Brahma. Here it refers to birth as a human or celestial being and experiencing the pleasures of that realm. One prayer says, "Please grant me the state of Brahma," meaning liberation.

286. If you lead others to develop bodhichitta
        and then make it firm,
        you will always have bodhichitta,
        as stable as the king of mountains itself.

(3) Another practice that generates incredible merit is *bodhichitta*, the aspiration to attain peerless awakening in order to benefit all sentient beings. Generating bodhichitta in our own mindstream, encouraging others to

generate it, helping to prevent it from degenerating in the minds of others, and helping to stabilize and increase it in their mindstreams—all these activities create vast merit. Even if we haven't realized bodhichitta, encouraging others to generate it and teaching them methods to do so—either the seven-point cause-and-effect instruction or the method of equalizing and exchanging self and others—will before long create a unique cause for you to gain bodhichitta that is as firm as Mount Everest.

> 287. Through faith you do not take rebirths that lack freedom.
> Through ethical conduct, you have fortunate rebirths.
> Through developing [your understanding] of emptiness,
> you attain non-attachment to all things.

(4) Through generating *faith* in the Buddha, Dharma, and Sangha and in the law of karma and its effects, you will not take rebirth in the eight unfree states described in the meditation on precious human life. Based on reasons, thinking "The Buddha's teachings on the four truths of aryas are true" or "the teaching on karma and its effect is true" also constitute faith. Of the three kinds of faith—lucid faith, aspiring faith, and the faith of convinced belief—these thoughts are the latter.

(5) The principal result of practicing the *ethical conduct* of abandoning the ten paths of nonvirtue is a fortunate rebirth as a human being or god. This is the essential practice to prevent rebirth in the lower realms.

(6) Through thinking about, realizing, and *familiarizing yourself with emptiness*, you will gradually be free of the discordant factors—the phenomena of the afflictive side, such as true duhkha and the true origins of duhkha. These will gradually be subdued until they totally vanish. Meditation on emptiness harms true-grasping. By destroying this noxious root, the flowers, branches, and fruit—the other afflictions—cannot survive.

> 288. By not being deceptive, you become mindful.
> Through reflection, you attain intelligence.
> Through reverence, you will realize the meaning [of the
>   Dharma].
> Through preserving the Dharma, you will become wise.

(7) The Sanskrit word *smriti* is translated as both "mindfulness" and "memory." Mindfulness is not simply observing what is happening, and memory isn't just recalling facts. This quality entails keeping precepts and virtue in mind, having stable focus on the object of meditation, and understanding things intelligently. *Abandoning deceit* in this life is a cause for having firm mindfulness/memory in future lives. Your mind will be clear and intelligent, and you will be able to understand teachings without great difficulty.

(8) Through *reflection* that analyzes the meaning of the Dharma, your wisdom will increase and you will gain new intelligence.

(9) *Reverence* for your Dharma teachers—expressed by serving them, appreciating them, speaking pleasantly to them, honoring them, having confidence in them, and aspiring to practice all that they teach—will help you to become an excellent Dharma teacher in the future. Listen with great respect, examine what you hear by using reasoning and through your own experience. In this way, you will realize the meaning of the Dharma.

(10) *Preserving the Dharma* begins with listening to many teachings. This gives you a lot to contemplate, and contemplation that correctly understands the meaning of what you have learned leads to meditation in which you will experience the Dharma yourself. In this way, you will be able to preserve the transmitted Dharma through hearing, reading, and studying, and you will preserve the realized Dharma through meditative experience.

> 289. Through eliminating obscurations
>   in listening to and imparting the Dharma,
>   you will gain the companionship of buddhas
>   and quickly fulfill your desires.

(11) One obscuration in *listening to and teaching the Dharma* is stinginess, which in this context means keeping your knowledge to yourself and not wanting to share it with others. Such behavior stems from a bad motivation. For example, one person is jealous of another's Dharma knowledge and so doesn't want to share her knowledge by answering questions; or a teacher is afraid that a student may come to understand the Dharma better than he does and will become a more well-known teacher, so he doesn't impart what he knows.

Of course, this doesn't mean you should teach new people everything you know about sutra and tantra, because that is neither appropriate nor beneficial. But when the students are intelligent and able to understand a topic, then no matter how deep you go, don't hold back but teach everything they need.

It is essential to listen to and teach the Dharma with a good motivation. As a result of doing this, you will meet with excellent spiritual mentors and good Dharma companions in future lives. The importance of having such people in our lives is reflected in the fact that we often dedicate our merit to never meet with bad companions on the path but only with excellent teachers and earnest Dharma friends who support us on the path and whom we support in return.

> 290. Through non-attachment, you accomplish your aims.
> Through lack of greed, your possessions increase.
> Through lack of arrogance, you will become prominent.
> Through fortitude for the Dharma, you attain the *dharani* [of not forgetting].

(12) *Subduing attachment* occurs gradually and is crucial in order to accomplish our Dharma wishes. A person of initial capacity reduces very gross attachment by contemplating that death is definite, that the time of death is unknown, and that at the time of death our body, possessions, friends, relatives, and reputation are left behind. The Dharma is our only friend, and our merit is the sustenance we take with us to the next life.

The middle capacity person lessens attachment to cyclic existence in general by reflecting on its disadvantages—its pleasures are impermanent and unsatisfactory in nature, and we lack true security and are subject to birth, aging, sickness, and death. Thinking like this does not immediately make us completely free of all attachment and desire for the pleasures of cyclic existence, but it definitely lessens it. In particular, we see that wherever we are born in cyclic existence there is no lasting happiness.

For the person of great capacity, "non-attachment" and "cutting attachment" mean freedom from the self-centered thought and practicing compassion for others. This freedom comes from meditation on the disadvantages of self-centeredness, the benefits of cherishing others, the kindness of others, love, and compassion. As we gradually diminish attachment, our respect for and commitment to the Dharma increases, as do our bodhichitta and wisdom.

(13) Through *not being greedy* or miserly your wealth increases. This doesn't mean that mere non-miserliness is the cause of an increase of wealth. Rather, practicing generosity without miserliness will bring wealth.

(14) Through *abandoning gross arrogance* and conceit, others will treat you with respect. Arrogance, haughtiness, pride, and conceit share the common characteristic of self-inflation. Such an attitude makes it difficult for your knowledge and good qualities to increase because you think you are already wonderful and thus have nothing to learn from others. Arrogance also repels people, as they don't like being around someone who considers herself superior. By abandoning gross arrogance and conceit and being humble, you will transform your mind. As a result your behavior will change for the better, and people will notice and seek you out due to your wisdom.

(15) *Fortitude for the Dharma* means having tolerance or forbearance with the Dharma of emptiness. When people with small minds hear that everything is empty of true existence, they are not able to bear it; they think it means everything is completely nonexistent. Being able to bear the meaning of emptiness means understanding that while phenomena are not truly existent, neither are they nonexistent. Emptiness is not nihilistic. Someone who can bear emptiness knows that the emptiness of true existence can be realized and that within being empty, actions and agents exist, and cause and effect function. This person can bear the presentation of the two truths. A result of having fortitude regarding emptiness is the retention of Dharma.

> 291. Through giving the five essences
> and fearlessness to those in danger,
> you will become impervious to all demons
> and the best of powerful beings.

(16) The five essences are molasses, the essence of sugarcane; butter, the essence of milk; honey, the essence of flowers (since bees make it through imbibing the nectar from flowers); salt, the essence of water; and sesame, the essence of grains. By *giving these five essences and helping beings in danger*, you will be free of fear, and spirits and bad friends will not be able to harm you. In addition, based on amassing merit and wisdom with a good motivation, giving the five essences and protecting those in danger will contribute to becoming powerful.

292. Through giving garlands of lamps to reliquaries,
     lights for those [hindered by] the dark,
     and oil for all these lamps,
     you will attain the divine eye.

(17) Verses 292–97 speak of causes for the six superknowledges (Skt. *abhijna*). While some hearers and solitary realizers cultivate these, not all do. Bodhisattvas use the superknowledges to identify sentient beings with whom they have a karmic connection and to know others' dispositions and how best to guide them on the path. The principal cause for gaining the first five superknowledges is single-pointed concentration of the first dhyana, the first meditative stabilization of the material realm. Making the following offerings is a cooperative condition.

Reliquaries include statues, texts, and paintings of buddhas and meditation deities. Make offerings to any or all of them with a sincere mind. *Offering lights*—electric lights, butter lamps, oil lamps, and so on, arranged like garlands or in any pleasing configuration—is also a cooperative condition for increased wisdom.

If you offer to reliquaries as well as install street lights in dark places where many people come and go, you will be born in an "enlightened eon"—a time when a wheel-turning buddha has appeared—as opposed to a dark eon that lacks Dharma teachings. It also results in attaining the *divine eye*—clairvoyance that enables one to see subtle and gross forms at a distance of up to a hundred *paktse*, or approximately eight hundred kilometers. Bodhisattvas can see beings in distant places and know whose mind is ripe to hear the Dharma and what teaching is appropriate for them at that time.

293. By offering cymbals and bells
     for the worship of reliquaries
     and also giving conch-horns and drums,
     you will attain the divine ear.

(18) The result of *offering music* made by cymbals, bells, conch shells, drums, and other instruments to reliquaries is to obtain the divine ear. This clairaudience enables you to hear Dharma teachings held in distant places as well as subtle and gross sounds and conversations within a radius

of a hundred *paktse*. The divine eye and divine ear are mental consciousnesses, not sense consciousnesses.

> 294. Do not speak of others' errors
>   or mention their physical handicaps.
>   By carefully protecting their minds,
>   you will attain the knowledge of others' minds.

(19) Avoid criticizing others or discussing their mistakes. If they are physically deformed in some way, do not talk about it—relate to them with
warmth as you would a dear friend. By refraining from harsh speech and
speaking in a way that spreads harmony, protect others' minds by *not provoking their afflictions* or offending them. As a result, you will attain the
superknowledge of being able to know others' minds. With that ability,
when you become a Dharma teacher, you will know who has attachment
and who is free from it, what topics the audience is receptive to hear and
what suits their dispositions and interests. You will know whether to speak
elaborately or briefly about different points, and in this way, you will be able
to fulfill their wishes by teaching what is just right for them.

> 295. By providing shoes and conveyances,
>   attending to those who are weak
>   and assisting your gurus with transportation,
>   the wise person attains supernormal powers.

(20) *Assist travelers* by giving boots, shoes, and appropriate footwear to
those who need them. If someone has difficulty traveling, provide animals
or vehicles to transport them. Help those who are weak, ill, or unable to
travel by themselves by carrying their load and assisting them in crossing
rivers. When your Dharma teachers go on a journey, serve them by arranging transport. Nowadays, this means you should drive your teachers or
book bus, train, and plane tickets for them and escort them to the station
or airport.

   Such actions are a cooperative cause for attaining supernormal powers.
These powers include the ability to pass through walls or mountains, dive
in and out of the earth as if it were water, walk on water, fly in space, make
your body appear and vanish, or project many emanations from your body

and then absorb them back into one body again. The purpose of this latter power is to appear in accordance with the needs and dispositions of sentient beings. Bodhisattvas, who use these powers discreetly and skillfully, inspire faith in others and arouse their interest in listening to teachings.

> 296. By making effort for the sake of the Dharma,
>   by keeping the Dharma treatises and their meaning in mind,
>   and by giving the Dharma immaculately,
>   you will come to remember your past lives.

(21) As much as possible, *keep the meaning of the teachings in mind* and contemplate them in meditation sessions and throughout your daily activities. Make your practice of giving the Dharma stainless by teaching solely with a wish to benefit others, free of expectations of receiving money, offerings, or service in return.

Through this you will attain the superknowledge of *remembering your past lives*. This superknowledge enables bodhisattvas to recall Dharma practices that they did before so they can continue doing them in this life. They also recall the destructive karma they have created and still need to purify.

> 297. Through correctly and truly understanding
>   that all things are essenceless,
>   you will attain the sixth superknowledge—
>   the supreme cessation of all defilements.

(22) By *understanding the meaning of emptiness* you will obtain the sixth superknowledge, the cessation of afflictive obscurations and/or cognitive obscurations. Make effort to correctly understand that all inner and outer phenomena are ultimately without any inherent essence. All phenomena have their own nature on the conventional level—for example, the nature of fire is hot and burning—but they do not exist by their own inherent nature. By realizing emptiness with an inferential reliable cognizer and continuing to meditate on it with the concentrated mind of serenity, in time you will realize emptiness directly. With this wisdom realizing emptiness, you will be able to gradually extinguish ignorance, afflictions, and polluted karma that cause rebirth in cyclic existence. Having attained the

extinction of defilements, you will know with confidence that you have attained liberation.

The six superknowledges are important aids to benefit others in an expansive way—for example, by understanding their karmic tendencies and way of thinking. They are also used to further your own practice, since you can swiftly travel great distances to hear teachings or listen to teachings given in distant places. When bodhisattvas employ the first five super-knowledges with compassion and skill, they can spread the Dharma to new places and help preserve and increase it where it already exists.

Four conditions are needed to work for sentient beings in a vast way—the six superknowledges, the five sublime eyes,[32] fortitude in dealing with problems and hardships for the sake of the Dharma,[33] and expertise in explaining Dharma.

> 298. In order to liberate all beings by meditating
>   on the uniform awareness of suchness
>   that has been moistened by compassion,
>   you will become a victor with supreme qualities.

(23) The *uniform awareness of suchness* refers to the wisdom realizing emptiness that sees all phenomena—afflicted and transcendental—as equally free of inherent existence. When this wisdom is supported by compassion, bodhichitta, and the method side of the path, it becomes the collection of wisdom that, together with the collection of merit, is capable of bringing forth the truth body and form bodies of a buddha.

Compassion moistens wisdom like water moistens a seed; it transforms wisdom from a cause for liberation into a cause of full awakening. That wisdom is now called the wisdom that possesses the supreme of all aspects, the wisdom that possesses the essence of compassion, and the wisdom

---

32. The five sublime eyes are: the physical eye is the ability to see faraway objects; the divine eye is the ability to see where sentient beings have taken rebirth after death; the wisdom eye is the realization of the emptiness of inherent existence; the Dharma eye is the ability to see whether someone's faculties are sharp or modest; the Buddha eye is omniscient wisdom.

33. For example, enduring with a happy mind whatever problems you might face when traveling to teachings, offering housing to Dharma teachers, hosting Dharma events, building places for statues, texts, and stupas, and so on.

with all supreme qualities, because it possesses all the excellent aspects of method.

> 299. Due to your unshakable resolve,
> your buddha land will be pure.
> By having offered precious gems to the King of Sages,
> you will shine with infinite light.

(24) *Unshakable resolve* refers to making millions of aspirations, determinations, resolutions, and prayers through which you will purify your buddha land and make it excellent. Each bodhisattva creates a pure and excellent buddha land in which she will awaken. When she awakens in the aspect of the enjoyment body, at the same time her buddha land will arise. (25) By *offering stainless sparkling jewels*, you will have a body that radiates light.

> 300. Thus realize that a karmic effect
> corresponds to its karmic cause.
> Therefore, you should always benefit beings—
> this will likewise benefit you.

In this section, Nagarjuna explained many ways for the king to improve the conditions of the country as a whole and to benefit the populace according to each person's disposition and prominent need. If he practices in the manner described by Nagarjuna, the king will directly benefit the citizens in the present and amass the collections of merit and wisdom that will result in attaining the two buddha bodies.

This completes the commentary on part III of the *Precious Garland*, "The Collections for Awakening."

IV. Royal Policy:
Instructions on the Practices of a Monarch

10. Practical Advice for Leaders

Nagarjuna begins this chapter by addressing the king in a heartfelt and straightforward way, telling him what he already knows but no one says— that most people will not give the king honest feedback or express their real thoughts to him. Instead, they will flatter him and say what they think he will like either because they are afraid of what the king will do if they say something he disagrees with or because they want to be on his good side to get something for themselves. Nagarjuna deferentially acknowledges that while he is a humble monk addressing a great monarch, out of affection for the king and care for the kingdom he will speak forthrightly. He then proceeds to give the king advice on royal policy.

LISTEN TO GOOD ADVICE

301. If the king acts in a way that contradicts the Dharma
    or does something that does not make sense,
    most of his subjects still praise him.
    Hence, it is hard for him to know what is appropriate and what
        is not.

Since it is difficult to know what feedback a king will or will not tolerate, to be safe most subjects only praise him. Even if the king acts contrary to the Dharma, his ministers, officials, attendants, and others who depend on him will say he did well. They are afraid that he will be offended and will punish them with imprisonment or execution if they are honest. Thus it is hard for a king to receive honest feedback and good advice.

302. If it is even difficult to say something
    beneficial but unpleasant to others,
    how can I, a monk, hope to do so to you,
    the monarch of a large realm?

303. But because of my affection for you,
    and also due to my compassion for beings,
    I myself will tell you what is quite helpful
    but not very pleasant.

Nagarjuna says to the king, "Since whatever you do all you hear is praise, you don't know which policies were useful and which were not. It is difficult to say anything unpleasant to anybody; how much more so is it to say such things to you, a king and lord of the earth? But I am now going to speak honestly and directly to benefit you, not out of jealousy, anger, or a wish to harm. As a monk, I want to give help that will be for your temporal and ultimate benefit, because by benefiting you I will also benefit others. So, without fearing your displeasure and without regard for my personal safety, I will tell you what is necessary for you to rule well, even though some of the advice may be unpleasant to hear at this moment."

In general, the Buddha said that we should not criticize others when motivated by an afflictive mental state. Motivated by compassion that wants only to benefit the king and those in his kingdom and beyond, Nagarjuna will take the risk to speak honestly. This is a good example of the courage it takes to act with compassion for the benefit of others.

304. The Blessed One said that at the right time
    one should say what is true, gentle, meaningful,
    and useful to one's disciples out of love.
    Hence, I tell you these things.

Nagarjuna now explains why he will speak to the king. "As teacher and student, you and I have a harmonious relationship; if this were not the case, I would not give you advice because you would not listen. The Buddha said that in such a situation, we should give wise advice motivated by compassion, speaking words that are true, kind, and meaningful. This is what I will now do."

305. If you remain steadfast while you listen
    to a true statement that is [spoken without] anger,
    then you will accept what you hear
    as if it were pure water that cleanses you.

306. Realizing that what I tell you
    is helpful in this context and others,
    implement it for your own sake
    and also for the sake of the world.

Nagarjuna recommends that the king be steadfast when he receives true advice and not become angry. Steadfastness is the mental stability derived from joyous effort, concentration, and wisdom. If someone says true words without anger, even if they sound harsh, it is suitable for you to listen closely and put the advice into practice.

"The advice I give you will enhance your qualities in this and future lives. It will help you in your Dharma practice as well as in ruling your kingdom. Understanding this, listen well. Through following this advice, you will benefit yourself and others, especially your subjects. You will also benefit your kingdom and the Dharma, making both of them stable and peaceful."

INCREASE YOUR GENEROSITY

307. If you do not give away to supplicants
    the wealth you gained through previous generosity,
    then due to your greed and lack of gratitude,
    you will not obtain that wealth again.

308. In this life, workers will not bear your provisions
    without [receiving] their wages.
    But a lowly beggar, though not paid wages,
    bears a hundredfold good qualities to your future life.

The result of our *generosity* to the poor and needy in previous lives has ripened in having wealth this life. To ensure we have such excellent conditions in the future, it is imperative to create the causes now by being generous. If we are stingy and do not share our wealth, in future lives we will not experience such prosperity again.

Workers will not carry our luggage without being paid wages. Yet beggars will carry a wealth of good qualities to our future lives without asking for any compensation. How does this work? When we give to beggars and the poor with a good motivation, we create enormous merit that will result in our having wealth in future lives. Since we cannot create this merit without the beggars, we are indebted to them for being the objects of our generosity. They "convey" to our future lives a hundred times the possessions we give them. Seen in this way, beggars benefit us more than porters whom we pay to carry our worldly possessions.

One reason the Buddha prescribed generosity as an initial practice is that it is quite easy. All religions teach generosity, and secular people, too, admire those who share their wealth. The Buddha made giving possessions and wealth an essential practice for lay followers. While monastics are also encouraged to share what they have, their principal practice is giving the Dharma.

Bodhisattvas continually think about how wonderful it would be to find somebody to give to. Just hearing the words "Please give me something" fills them with joy far greater than the joy that hearer and solitary realizer arhats experience abiding in the personal peace of nirvana for eons. The happiness bodhisattvas feel upon actually giving away their possessions and wealth is immeasurable.

Giving possessions and the roots of virtue of the three times is easier than giving our body. But arya bodhisattvas don't feel even the slightest suffering when they give their body away, even if it is dismembered. Ordinary bodhisattvas—those on the paths of accumulation and preparation—experience suffering when giving away their body, but they accept that voluntarily, thinking, "This suffering is nothing. It's child's play compared to the suffering of the hell beings and hungry ghosts."

If we practice generosity well but neglect ethical conduct, there is danger that the result of our generosity will ripen during a lower rebirth. For example, a person may generously share her possessions, but due to not keeping pure ethical conduct she is reborn as an animal—a wealthy and comfortable animal, such as a rich naga or a pampered pet. Later when she is born as a human being, she may be poor and have difficulty procuring the necessities for Dharma practice because the karmic seeds from generosity had already ripened when she was an animal.

If we regularly practice generosity, it is quite possible that some of the recipients of our offerings and gifts are aryas. Giving to them creates powerful merit because we establish a karmic link with them and they make prayers and dedications for us. Creating such a great root of virtue for liberation will help us in the future to cut the continuum of cyclic existence and attain nirvana.

Although at present we may not have an incredible amount of wealth with which to practice generosity, we can still enhance the mind of giving by repeatedly imagining giving away our body, possessions, and roots of virtue. Giving our time, energy, and expertise to those engaged in virtuous projects is also the practice of generosity.

> 309. Always keep your mind sublime
> and delight in sublime deeds.
> All sublime effects
> come from sublime actions.

Training in Vast Actions and Thoughts

Even if your present actions are modest, try to make a habit of thinking big. Vast thoughts lead to vast actions, which bring vast results. Making far-reaching aspirations to do extensive deeds for the benefit of sentient beings will broaden your perspective and enhance your motivation. This will enable you to act whenever you encounter more moderate situations in which you can be of service. As you gradually expand both your perspective and motivation, you will be able to undertake greater and greater projects as time goes on.

> 310. Establish glorious Dharma sites
> and famed centers of the Three Jewels
> that have not even been imagined
> by weaker kings.

Establish Magnificent Monasteries, Centers, and Educational Institutes

Nagarjuna advises the king to establish glorious monasteries, temples, educational institutes for Buddhist study, and centers for Dharma practice and meditation that cannot even be imagined by kings who lack the same wealth and power. Construct monasteries where the sangha can live, fill them with monastics, and provide all their material necessities so they can focus on Dharma study and practice. Build temples and fill them with statues, paintings, scriptures, and stupas. Statues and paintings represent the Buddha's body; texts symbolize the Buddha's speech, and stupas represent the Buddha's mind. Make elaborate offerings to them; doing this will inspire your citizens to make offerings too, and the merit this creates will benefit them and the entire kingdom.

Building Buddhist learning centers will bring your country great joy and happiness, and freedom from famine, drought, war, strife, and disease. There will be seasonal rain and crops will grow well. Centuries ago, an Indian scholar became a siddha—a realized practitioner—and through a combination of clairvoyance and reading the Buddha's scriptures, he examined what virtue would be most beneficial for his country. He found that the best was to build monasteries and enlarge the sangha. In his next life, he was born as a king and built Vikramashila Monastery, a great monastery on par with Nalanda.

Before Atisha went to Tibet, he worked to prevent many monasteries from deteriorating. Upon arriving in Tibet, he told Dromtonpa that the greatest of all virtues was building monasteries, and as a result Dromtonpa built Radreng Monastery. Je Tsongkhapa built Ganden Monastery and instructed his students to build as many monasteries as possible, which they did. Tsakho Ngawang Drakpa, the student who requested Je Tsongkhapa to teach the "Three Principal Aspects of the Path," built a hundred monasteries. He called the hundredth and last one "Now I have finished." Je Tsongkhapa's other disciples, Jamyang Choje Tashi Palden and Jamchen Choje, founded Drepung Monastery and Sera Monastery respectively. When we consider how many people have benefited directly and indirectly from these learning centers, we understand the usefulness and importance of building monasteries and will want to support those that already exist.

> 311. It is preferable not to create Dharma foundations
>   that do not inspire an opulent king,
>   because even after you die,
>   it will not be praised.

> 312. With all your resources you should make
>   those that, for being so exalted,
>   humble and encourage exalted [kings]
>   and overwhelm inferior ones.

As a result of establishing magnificent centers for the Buddhadharma, in this life you will become well known for creating so much virtue. People will speak well of you and you will become a great being, one who possesses significant merit and glory. However, if you are stingy or negligent and make Dharma centers that are uninspiring, you will lose a great opportunity to create merit, and others will criticize you.

If kings of equal or lower standing become famous through harmful actions, do not consider their deeds worthwhile or admirable, and do not act as they do. The disrepute that comes from such actions will remain after you have died. Instead, use your wealth to build vast foundations for the Three Jewels—monasteries and institutes that are so marvelous that less powerful kings will rejoice upon seeing them and be humbled, thinking they could not construct such things.

Do not become arrogant after constructing vast and magnificent monasteries, temples, and foundations of Dharma study and practice, thinking that it makes you superior to other kings. Instead think, "May my deeds inspire other kings to construct learning centers and benefit the Dharma." Likewise, when you see the virtuous actions of kings who are your equals, rejoice and think, "I must do like that."

313. Giving up all your possessions,
     powerless, you must go to the next life,
     but all that you used for the Dharma
     precedes you as constructive karma.

314. All of a previous king's possessions
     come under the control of his successor,
     so for that previous king
     what use will they be for Dharma, happiness, or fame?

315. You receive pleasure in this life from enjoying your wealth.
     Pleasure in the next life comes from giving it away.
     What you have wasted by neither enjoying nor giving
     will lead only to suffering—how could it bring happiness?

The Benefits of Generosity and the Disadvantages of Miserliness

Do not think that you can be generous later on—that you still have plenty of time before you die. That isn't true, for none of us know when we will die. Build monasteries, temples, and learning centers quickly, right now. You cannot take any of your wealth with you to the next life, so it's best to use it for the Dharma and for the benefit of sentient beings while you still have control over it.

When you die, all the wealth and possessions you leave behind will come under the control of the new king who will enjoy them. At that time they cannot help you in the least. Great wealth is the source of many problems, and by giving it away you will be free from those difficulties. You won't fear losing your possessions or worry about people stealing them. Nor will you fear fire destroying them or treacherous associates extorting them. If you are generous with your wealth and possessions, you will have the happiness and satisfaction of benefiting sentient beings and creating great merit.

In addition, generosity is the foundation of your happiness in future lives, whereas hoarding possessions will only lead to the pain of miserliness in this life and the lack of possessions in the future. If you don't use your wealth to create merit and support the Dharma, what is the use of having it? Your wealth is wasted sitting in the coffers, and you will not be happy now or in the future.

> 316. When dying, since you will lose your independence,
>   you will be unable to give away [your possessions]
>   through ministers who shamelessly cease to value you
>   and seek the affection of the new king.

> 317. Therefore, while healthy, quickly use all your resources
>   to build Dharma sites,
>   for you stand in the midst of death's causes
>   like a lamp in the midst of a storm.

You may think, "Now I am healthy, but when I am extremely ill and on the brink of death, I will give everything away." This is foolish thinking because when you are about to die you won't have any control over your wealth. Your ministers won't listen to you; they will be thinking about your successor and his interests. Even though you may have previously asked your attendants and officials to give your wealth and possessions away after you die, they will ignore your request in order to curry the favor of the new king. So now, while you are in good health and have control over your wealth, give it away to benefit others and to help the Dharma flourish. Do not procrastinate—act now because the conditions that bring about death are many and those that support life are few. Your life is fragile just like a candle in a storm. You will die soon.

If you don't use your wealth and possessions for Dharma projects, you will be tortured by clinging and fear at the time of death. When these emotions arise before the final dissolution of the coarse level of mind, they nourish karmic seeds, ripening them and propelling your mindstream into the next life. At this time it is especially important to have a virtuous mind so that seeds of virtuous karma will ripen. A mind filled with clinging and fear of separation from wealth, loved ones, and your body will make death painful and nourish the ripening of seeds of nonvirtuous karma. It is best to prepare your mind now by releasing attachment to possessions and wealth through practicing generosity.

318. You should also preserve,
    in the manner in which they have been established,
    any other Dharma centers, temples,
    and such initiated by previous kings.

Maintain Previously Established Dharma Sites

Maintain and support the centers and foundations for the Three Jewels that were established by previous kings. Continue any arrangement they had for making offerings, and do not let these sites deteriorate. If you are not able to do this, the efforts of the previous kings will be wasted.

319. They should be attended by those who practice nonviolence,
    who are virtuous in conduct and keep their precepts,
    who are kind to guests, truthful, and tolerant,
    who are not quarrelsome and are always energetic.

Appoint Suitable Managers

Once you have established monasteries, temples, and Dharma foundations, you must appoint managers who direct the work that needs to be done, decide the amount of food needed, the topics to be taught, and so on. They have to guide the community skillfully and estimate material needs accurately.

Choose qualified managers. Specifically, look for people with the following qualities: they are nonviolent and free of malevolence toward others; they respect virtue and are virtuous in conduct; they are a fully ordained or novice monastic who keeps the precepts well, or are at least a lay disciple with one precept; they are friendly to and take care of people who regularly stay at the temple as well as newcomers who visit occasionally; they are truthful, so that you can trust them; they are skilled, competent, and tolerant so that they can do what the job entails; they are agreeable and easy to get along with; and they are energetic and make a habit of putting effort into virtue.

320. The blind, sick, and downtrodden,
      the homeless, impoverished, and disabled
      should all, without trouble,
      equally obtain food and drink.

321. Support in an appropriate manner
      those Dharma practitioners who do not seek aid,
      and even support those who are
      living in the kingdoms of others.

Help Others Equally and Care for Those Who Aren't Seeking Anything

At these Dharma sites, ensure that people are treated equally. Everyone should receive the same amount of food, drink, and attention. It is contrary to the Dharma to be unfair or biased, helping the strong and ignoring the weak. The blind, sick, downtrodden, homeless, impoverished, disabled, and so on—in general anyone experiencing many difficulties or much suffering—should be welcomed and served in the same way as the healthy, rich, and powerful.

With compassion, provide for monastics and Dharma practitioners who do not expect anything from you. Make offerings to them of food, clothing, and so forth. Also care for those under the dominion of other kings who do not expect anything from you. Allow people who don't want to stay under your dominion to move to other kingdoms. Don't insist that they stay if it causes them suffering.

322. For every Dharma site,
    appoint Dharma teachers who are energetic,
    free of greed, knowledgeable, pious,
    and who will not hinder those [practicing there].

Appoint Kind and Wise Religious Leaders

After constructing magnificent Dharma institutions, you need to appoint excellent religious leaders to help the people who study and practice there. Look for people who are not lazy or easily distracted. People who attend the temple will continually ask the teachers many questions about the Dharma, so they must be knowledgeable concerning the Buddha's teachings and enjoy being with people and teaching them the Dharma. Since devotees will ask for help with personal problems, leaders must feel comfortable discussing such issues without getting emotionally involved. They should also not be disturbed by having to manage offerings made to the sangha.

Such leaders must be experts in acting in accord with the Dharma. For example, if the sangha is offered cattle or goats, this person knows how to skillfully care for the animals in accordance with the Dharma and should not harm them or treat them roughly.

323. Appoint as ministers
    policy experts who are pious, polite, and pure,
    devoted, courageous, of good family,
    ethically outstanding, and grateful.

Appointing Ministers

Government ministers must be familiar with the various customs of the world and know about the geography, climate, and history of other places.

They should be skillful in devising wise policies that suit the kingdom and be able to negotiate and enforce these policies. Other qualities to look for are the ability to cultivate cordial relationships with other kings and their own staff, and the ability to follow the king's instructions and enact his wishes. They must have good intentions, not carry grudges, and be able to interpret others' attitudes and actions toward the kingdom. Appoint Dharma practitioners as ministers, as they will act according to Buddhist principles and respect the king. If they are a little afraid of the king, that is fine—just as it is appropriate for children to not only love their parents but also be a little afraid of them.

Good ministers should be pure in that they do not act in ways that benefit only themselves, and they must have a good relationship with their subordinates. They should be of a good family—people who were raised properly and know how to act in various situations. They must have excellent behavior of body, speech, and mind, show a loving and friendly aspect toward living beings, but also be able to apply an angry aspect—motivated by compassion—when appropriate. Furthermore, they should care about the welfare of others so that they serve both the king and the citizens.

> 324. Appoint military advisors who are generous,
>   unattached, heroic, and polite,
>   who properly use [resources],
>   are steadfast, always vigilant, and pious.

Appointing Generals

Generals should be extremely generous and unattached to their body and possessions. It is difficult to find people who are completely free of attachment, but at least they must not have strong attachment to their body and possessions. They must do whatever they can to avoid violent confrontation, but they should be brave when the time comes to fight. They should be polite to others, and in particular feel fond of the king.

Generals must use material and human resources wisely and within reason, and not act recklessly. When there is need, they take what is necessary with moderation and know how to delegate authority. They should be steadfast, having a steady mind that can think clearly, make good decisions, and not fall under the sway of others. They should have firm intelligence and be wise in discerning what is right and wrong. They must be conscientious in body, speech, and mind and behave correctly. On the physical level, that means not taking intoxicants, for example. Somebody having these qualities is a good candidate for the king to appoint as a general.

> 325. Appoint as officials elders that behave
>   in accord with Dharma and are pure,
>   who are skillful and know what to do,
>   who are erudite, organized, impartial, and polite.

Appointing Treasurers and Other Officials

Treasurers and other officials must have a gentle nature, be friendly to people, and not easily irritated. They should not be rough, but by remembering the great kindness of others in this and previous lives, they should cherish living beings and be more concerned with the welfare of others than their own. Of course it is not easy to find such people, but as much as possible the king should appoint officials with these qualities.

Officials must have wisdom that discriminates between what is appropriate and inappropriate. When a new situation arises suddenly, they must be able to determine right away the best way to handle it. Being learned and having studied many treatises fosters this ability to think in a flexible way. They must be experts in their area of administration and be well organized, knowing how to set priorities wisely and how to implement policies skillfully.

It is also important that these officials are conscientious in body, speech, and mind—that they do not have many inappropriate thoughts, speak in unsuitable ways, or act foolishly. They should divide duties and possessions equally without being biased, be fond of the king, and not be reckless with his wealth and possessions. As polite individuals, they fulfill their responsibilities without turmoil or contention. In addition, they should be mature, neither too elderly nor young, inexperienced, and reckless. Of course, do not expect them to be perfect; being human, they will err at times.

> 326. Each month listen to their reports
>   of all income and expenses.

> Having listened, tell them all that should be done
> for the Dharma sites and so on.

Once you have appointed ministers, generals, treasurers, and other officials, you need to oversee them—don't just leave them be as if you had forgotten about them. Meet with them regularly and have them report to you about their duties. See how they are doing, determine if things are running smoothly or if they need assistance or more direct supervision. After you assess the situation, if needed give them further instructions to carry out their responsibilities. Look over the accounting books, checking on income and expenses to ensure that all is rectified.

> 327. If you rule for the sake of Dharma
>   and not for fame or out of desire,
>   then it will have a most meaningful result—
>   otherwise, your rule will be disastrous.

Nagarjuna says to the king, "I have given you these instructions so that you can rule according to the Dharma, not for the sake of fame or wealth. If you act accordingly, your rule will be fruitful for everyone, and the kingdom will run smoothly, Dharma will flourish, and the citizens will be well. However, running the kingdom for the sake of fame, wealth, power, or your own pleasure will be disastrous, not only now, but in the form of lower rebirths in future lives."

Govern Without Compromising Dharma Principles

> 328. King, hear how in this world,
>   where the one usually destroys the other,
>   you can still have both
>   the Dharma and a kingdom.

The king asks, "Many rulers behave in repugnant ways toward each other. They prey upon each other, conquer each other, vandalize each other's kingdoms, and in that way bring about the destruction of their own kingdom and sometimes lose their lives in the process. Many kings also exploit their populace, ignore their needs, and inflict suffering upon them. How can I govern without compromising my Dharma principles?" In response Nagarjuna tells him it is possible to maintain his rule and his Dharma practice in such a way that they do not conflict with each other—by being generous, kind, and fair.

The king then queries, "How should I deal with people who harm others by murdering or robbing them? The monarch institutes laws in the land, and usually such people are imprisoned or executed. However, punishing people seems contradictory to the Dharma, yet not doing anything is impractical and won't work."

Nagarjuna replies that nowadays many people deceive, cheat, and harm each other. To simply allow people who do evil actions to carry on will cause problems for law-abiding, virtuous subjects and make them unhappy and fearful. In addition, the people who harm others will continue to accrue great destructive karma that will lead them to take lower rebirths. So to help these people and to protect the public, it is necessary to enforce the law and punish, fine, imprison, or beat offenders. However, the purpose of this is to stop them from engaging in these actions in the future and to encourage them to change their behavior and engage in beneficial actions. The people who enforce the punishments must do so without malice or anger, but rather with compassion. You must think clearly how to run the kingdom without contradicting the Dharma.

329. May you always be accompanied by many [advisors]
    who are mature in knowledge, of good family,
    well versed in public policy, afraid of misdeeds,
    not contentious, and able to see what should be done.

Gather People of Unusual Qualities and Give Them Power

Don't empower just anyone to enforce the law. If administrators do not have certain qualities, they will punish innocent people but look the other way when friends and relatives commit crimes. Such capricious justice will harm the kingdom and turn people against you. People who are responsible for enforcing the law must be mature, knowledgeable, able to assess situations accurately, and understand when and how to punish someone so that it benefits the offender.

It is better if these officials are older—not so elderly that their memory is affected, but old enough so that they know life well, and are not brash, impulsive, or power hungry. They should also be from a good family so that they are educated, understand politics, and know what is good policy. They should be familiar with the customs of the world, cooperate with each other, refrain from negativity, and not be contentious. It is crucial that they understand the special purpose of retribution. The king will benefit from assembling many administrators with these qualities.

Deal Compassionately with Wrongdoers

330. Even if they rightly fine, imprison,
    or corporally punish [wrongdoers],
    you, being always moistened by compassion,
    should show kindness.

As long as they act with fairness, administrators with the above qualities may fine, incarcerate, beat, or scold offenders. They must assign these punishments judiciously, to the proper extent without being cruel. Although as the king you have given people the power to do this, you should never punish people yourself. Rather, out of compassion, listen to those who defend a lawbreaker, ask you to pardon him, and guarantee he will not repeat the misdeed. Even if the administrator has rightly and legally incarcerated the person or confiscated a portion of his property, have compassion—if you believe the person will not reoffend, lighten the punishment or pardon him.

331. King, out of compassion
    you should always make your mind focused upon benefiting all
        beings,
    even those that have committed
    the most serious misdeeds.

Some people do atrocious actions of intolerable evil, such as the five heinous crimes—killing their mother, their father, or an arhat, causing schism in the sangha, or wounding a buddha. Such actions will result in horrific suffering for that person in future lives. Knowing this, have compassion for this person and only wish to benefit him, even though he must be imprisoned in order to protect your subjects and to prevent him from creating more destructive karma.

> 332. You should particularly have compassion for
>   those that have committed the serious negativity of murder;
>   these ones who have ruined themselves are indeed
>   worthy of great persons' compassion.

Murderers and others who have done appalling, reprehensible actions are said to be the ultimate objects of compassion for bodhisattvas. With never-flagging love, bodhisattvas look upon them with special compassion because they have ruined their lives as well as the lives of others. Be like a bodhisattva and never abandon the attitude wishing to aid them. Never think that any person is too despicable to help or that anyone deserves to suffer. Such malevolent thoughts that wish to harm others will only lead to your having an unfortunate rebirth.

The reason to have great compassion for them is that they have brought about their own downfall. They have completely ruined their present life—which is the basis for attaining higher rebirth and the highest good—and have become their own worst enemy by creating the causes to experience so much pain and suffering in lower realms in future lives.

In the *Four Hundred Stanzas*, Aryadeva says that if a mother has many children, she feels more compassion and cares more for the child who is less intelligent. Those who are sharp and skillful will be able to manage in life, but the one who is less so will not. This is the way you should approach people who have committed the most despicable actions.

> 333. Either every day or every five days
>   release the weakest prisoners,
>   and see that it is not the case that the remaining ones
>   are never released, as is appropriate.

> 334. From thinking that some should never be released,
>   you develop [behaviors and attitudes] that contradict your
>   precepts.
>   From contradicting your precepts,
>   you continually accumulate more negativity.

Free Prisoners

Every day or every few days, observe the inmates to see who is physically weak or feeble and then free them. Though some of the remaining prisoners may be strong and healthy, do not use that as a reason to refuse to ever release them. Never think that you will keep even the worst offenders incarcerated for the rest of their lives with no chance of parole. However long they remain imprisoned, recognize that they can change.

If you vow with hatred never to release them, you will generate what is called an "anti-vow" in your mindstream due to having this strong negative intention. As long as you have this anti-vow, the ethical restraints you have—be it the five precepts of a lay Buddhist or monastic precepts—will not remain in your mindstream.

When you take ethical restraints, from that moment onward your virtue continually increases due to the power of keeping the precepts. Similarly, when you generate an anti-vow, from that moment onward you continually accumulate nonvirtue.

> 335. Until they are released,
>   those prisoners should be made content
>   by providing them with barbers, baths, food, drink,
>   clothing, and medical care.

> 336. As if you have the intention of making
>   unruly children behave properly,
>   you should discipline them out of compassion—
>   not out of anger or the desire for material gain.

Make the Prisons Pleasant

At Nagarjuna's time, prisons were especially horrible places where people were not only restricted in movement but also starved, tortured, and forced to live in filth. Nagarjuna instructs the king to do what hate-filled, revenge-seeking people shirk from doing—to supply the incarcerated with some of life's basic necessities and conveniences such as food, drink, clothing, medical care, baths, barbers—who doubled as dentists in ancient India—and so on.

Someone asks, "Isn't prison supposed to make them suffer? What's the sense of keeping them incarcerated if they are comfortable?" Nagarjuna responds by explaining that when parents discipline a child with obnoxious behavior, they don't do so for the sake of beating the child. Rather, knowing that objectionable behavior won't serve but will harm the child in this life, they want to help the child give up the bad behavior and punish him for that reason. Similarly, we should not imprison people for the purpose of harming them and making them miserable. Instead, discipline them out of compassion—as a means to help them examine their behavior, accept responsibility for their actions, and refrain from destructive deeds in the future. In this way, they will change and have a better life later. Imprisoning them due to anger or with the intention to confiscate their wealth is not correct.

337. Having properly examined
    and identified particularly hateful murderers,
    you should send them into exile
    without killing or harming them.

Send Those Who Cannot Be Reformed Elsewhere

People must be imprisoned if they are full of rage and viciously murder others or steal or destroy their property. After they have been incarcerated for some time, examine if they have changed. Do they regret their behavior? Have they learned to work with their anger and destructive impulses so that they no longer harm others? If so, release them, but monitor them to see that they don't offend again. If they are unable to adjust to society—if they repeat their bad behavior and there is no way to stop them—then banish them to another place. Since no one likes to be socially ostracized, hopefully he will examine his actions and change his behavior. Then he can start anew in another place.

REIGN SKILLFULLY

338. Independently survey all lands
    through the eyes of agents;
    always vigilant and mindful,
    do what should be done in accord with the Dharma.

Send Out Agents

In ancient India there were no systems of mass communication, so it was difficult for the king to know what was happening in distant parts of the land. To rule well and to act for the benefit of the people throughout the kingdom, he needed to know if there was fighting anywhere, if the harvest was sufficient, if an epidemic had broken out, and if people were happy or dissatisfied with government policies.

Unable to go everywhere himself, the king must send out agents who observe what is happening in different parts of the kingdom and report back to him. *Independently* may mean in this verse that only agents that agree to go should be sent; they shouldn't be forced to go. It may also mean that agents are sent to places that the king controls.

Here Nagarjuna indicates the qualities the king should look for when selecting agents: they should be conscientious, vigilant, and act correctly. They do not need to let others know that they are the king's agents, but rather they should observe with open eyes and return immediately to deliver an honest report to the king. When the king has accurate information concerning the goings-on throughout the kingdom, he will be able to govern well and in accordance with the Dharma.

339. Through extensive and suitable generosity,
　　　respect, and service, devote yourself always
　　　to those who are the foundation of good qualities.
　　　Do the same for the rest as is appropriate.

The sangha—meaning the monastics—is the foundation of good qualities, and it is appropriate to offer them requisites and to respect and serve them. As the leader of the country, encourage those who are close to you, as well as prominent families and common folks under your dominion, to make offerings to the sangha. In addition, help other people who are honorable as much as you can in whatever ways are suitable.

This topic follows the instruction to send out agents because agents will be able to see which sangha communities are in need. The agents will also be able to report on other sectors of the populace so the king may take care of them accordingly.

340. If the tree of kingship offers the shade of tolerance,
    the open flowers of respect,
    and the great fruit of generosity,
    then the birds, your subjects, will flock to it.

341. A munificent but majestic king
    will be beloved like a sugar candy
    with a hard crust made
    from cardamom and black pepper.

342. If you reign properly in this way,
    your kingdom will not be chaotic.
    It will not proceed improperly nor contradict the Dharma
    but will be in harmony with the Dharma.

The Relationship between the King and the Populace

The king is like a grand fruit tree. His tolerance is similar to the shade of a tree, where people can sit, enjoy, and be free from the heat. His respect for the honorable resembles beautiful flowers, and his vast generosity is likened to an abundance of fruit on the tree. In short, the king is both generous and tolerant, and his subjects will respond by respecting and trusting him.

Someone asks, "Must the king always be tolerant?" While he needs to be tolerant and generous in general, out of compassion he must sometimes look fierce. When he sees something that is extremely harmful, wrong, or destructive, for the benefit of the people he must forcefully show that it is not acceptable. When they see his power and strength in those situations, people know they can rely on his ability to protect and guide them with a strong hand when needed. The king has to be like a delicious candy that is soft and smooth on the inside, and hard and rough on the outside. He must be gentle inside but harsh on the outside when the situation calls for it. In this way, his rule will be meaningful and the kingdom will operate in accord with the Dharma.

343. You have not brought your kingdom with you from the previous
    life,
    nor will you bring it to the next.

You obtained it through Dharma,
so it is not right to violate Dharma for its sake.

344. King, through your efforts
see to it that you do not end up
perpetuating the stockpiling of suffering
through your kingship's stockpiles.

345. King, through your efforts
see to it that you manage
to perpetuate your stockpiling of kingship
through your kingship's stockpiles.

Cease Non-Dharma Activities

You didn't bring your marvelous kingdom with you from your past life, and you cannot take it with you to the future life. Since you have obtained this marvelous kingdom by practicing the Dharma in the past, do not engage in destructive, non-Dharma actions for its sake now.

At the moment you have the resources to procure what you need. If you use the kingdom's resources respectfully, wisely, and for good purposes, the kingdom will benefit now, and in future lives you will continually experience happiness. However, if you squander them or rule in a way that is not in accordance with the Dharma, affairs will proceed badly now, and these resources will become like a stockpile of suffering for you to experience in future lives. Don't use your resources to "buy" suffering for yourself and others.

This is similar to our currently having a precious human rebirth due to our having practiced the Dharma in previous lives. If we indulge in the ten nonvirtues and don't use our life in accordance with the Dharma, this wonderful life that we worked so hard to acquire will become meaningless. If we use it well, it will create a future life that is even better, and we will go from one life to the next continuously improving until we attain full awakening.

11. Spiritual Wisdom for Powerful People

THE EMPTINESS OF PAIN AND PLEASURE

While all sentient beings seek to have happiness and to avoid pain, very few recognize the illusory nature of these feelings. Thinking they exist inherently, we cling to pleasure and fear pain, this attachment and aversion adding a layer of mental suffering onto whatever physical suffering we may experience. In this chapter Nagarjuna examines samsaric happiness and pain closely and concludes that they are not trustworthy. He recommends that we put our energy into Dharma practice—specifically into realizing emptiness and dependent arising—in order to realize the illusory nature of happiness and pain. This way we free ourselves from the intense craving for pleasure and strong fear of pain that permeate so much of our lives. It is therefore crucial to realize the subtle emptiness of all persons and phenomena according to the Prasangika view. Hearers and solitary realizers—who practice the fundamental vehicle—realize the same emptiness as bodhisattvas, who practice the universal vehicle.

> 346. Even after a wheel-turning monarch attains
> [governance over] the whole world with its four continents,
> pleasure for him is still considered
> to be only twofold: physical and mental.

> 347. A pleasurable physical sensation
> is just comparatively less pain.
> Mental pleasure—by nature an attitude—
> is just conceptually created.

The Nature of Pleasure and Pain

In chapter 6, Nagarjuna analyzed lust and its object to help us overcome clinging and the sexual desire that distracts us from the path. Now that the king and we too are more mature in the Dharma, he goes deeper, analyzing the ultimate nature of pleasure and pain to demonstrate that they are both empty of inherent existence. He approaches this in several different ways.

In the following discussion, "happiness" and "pleasure" are varying translations of the Sanskrit word *sukha*; suffering, pain, and discomfort are all translations of the Sanskrit word *duhkha*, which in other contexts is translated as unsatisfactory. Happy, painful, and neutral feelings form the aggregate of feelings, which is one of the five aggregates that are the basis of designation of the person.

Even a wheel-turning monarch with control over the four continents definitely experiences only two kinds of pleasure: pleasant physical feelings and pleasant mental feelings. There is nothing more than these two, no grandiose states of happiness that are his privilege as a king.

Upon close examination we find that when physical pain and discomfort diminish, there is an appearance of happiness—this is what we call "pleasant physical feeling." This is a feeling of satisfaction or happiness that is derived from our sense consciousnesses, especially the tactile consciousness. It is not actual happiness; it is simply called happiness in dependence on the decrease of discomfort.

For example, when we are very cold and sit next to a heater, the suffering of cold diminishes and the appearance of happiness ensues. But if we continue to sit there, we will become too hot. If that original happiness was genuine happiness, the longer we sat there, the greater our pleasure should be. However, that is not the case. We can make many such examples in our life, from the happiness of a good meal to the happiness of a relationship or career satisfaction.

Thus all happiness in cyclic existence is not actual happiness because it is dependent on and designated in dependence on the decrease of pain. Pain, discomfort, and suffering, however, don't arise based on the decrease of happiness. Unpleasant feelings arise naturally; if we just leave our body alone and do nothing, we will become hungry, thirsty, or tired. Our muscles will begin to ache or an insect will bite us. Only when unpleasant feelings decrease does what we call "pleasure" arise. This is our situation because our body and mind are under the influence of afflictions and karma. For that reason, they are considered polluted and in the nature of duhkha; they are not something worth clinging to.

The feeling of mental happiness has the nature of an attitude and is merely created by conception. Conceptuality considers a feeling happiness and calls it happiness. *Mental pleasure—by nature an attitude* indicates that there is the appearance of pleasure arising in the mind that the mind then conceives to be actual happiness.

> 348. Since it is just comparatively less pain
>   or merely conceptually created,
>   all the pleasure in the world
>   is ultimately not really [pleasure].

All feelings of happiness and pleasure that we experience in cyclic existence—both physical and mental—are merely imputed by conception as happiness based on the decrease of painful or unpleasant feelings. Happy feelings in cyclic existence are not real happiness.

This does not mean that we are without conventional pleasure or happiness. We understand what people mean when they say, "I'm happy." However, this happiness isn't true happiness because it is actually just the diminishment of discomfort. In addition, it will not last. The object, person, or activity that appears to be the cause of that happiness cannot bring us happiness indefinitely. In fact, our contact with the person, situation, or thing will become uncomfortable at a certain point and we will long to do something else, be with someone else, or have something else. We can easily see this in our own experience. If those people were actually the cause of happiness and if the happiness were genuine happiness, this would not happen and our happiness would only increase.

> 349. The continents, countries, places, houses,
>   conveyances, seats, clothing, beds,
>   food, drink, elephants, horses, and women
>   are all enjoyed at distinct [points in time].

> 350. One has pleasure through
>   whichever of these the mind attends to,
>   but one does not attend to the rest.
>   Hence, they are not ultimately [causes of pleasure].

Refuting that Mental Pleasure Is Real

Someone says, "There is real mental pleasure because it has a cause that produces it. That cause is Ishvara." Those who state this believe Ishvara is the creator of the world as well as of all happiness and suffering. We reply that Ishvara doesn't produce happiness because Ishvara and happiness don't have a cause-and-effect relationship. We do not accept the existence of an independent creator.

These non-Buddhists believe that Ishvara is a permanent, functioning thing. However, if he were permanent he could not create experiences of happiness. A permanent cause cannot produce a result, because it is necessary for the cause to cease in order for the result to arise.

Thirteen sources of pleasure are listed here, including countries or different kingdoms; places, such as our birthplace; conveyances, which are various means of transport; seats, which could include other furniture; and people you're romantically or sexually attracted to. Contact with any of these brings pleasure. However, at the moment we experience pleasure from one of them, we do not derive pleasure from the rest because we are not experiencing them at that time. Since we can't experience all of them at once, when we are enjoying one of them the thought "pleasure" cannot arise with respect to the others. That shows that those things and people are not inherent sources of happiness. If they were, then even when we were not in contact with them the thought "happiness" would still arise.

Happiness depends on using or contacting an object, and thus does not arise independently. If it were inherently existent, happiness would exist independent of everything else—we wouldn't have to be in contact with that particular object in order to feel happiness from it. Furthermore, since inherently existent happiness would not depend on causes and conditions, it should continue forever without ceasing. Also, if an object brought inherently existent happiness, every time and in every situation we had contact with it we would experience happiness. However, we all know that an extra piece of pie when we are full brings misery, not happiness, and that a recent quarrel with a close friend makes being with her unpleasant. In short, those thirteen objects are causes for experiencing happiness, but they are not causes for experiencing either genuine happiness or inherently existent happiness.

351. When [all] five senses [or faculties]—the eye and so forth—
     [simultaneously] apprehend their objects,
     a thought [of pleasure] does not refer [to all of them];
     therefore, at that time they do not all give pleasure.

352. Whenever any of the [five] objects is known
     [as pleasurable] by one of the [five] senses,
     then the remaining [objects] are not so known by the remaining
         [senses],
     since they are not [ascertained as] objects at that time.

353. The mind apprehends an image of a past object,
     which has been apprehended by the senses
     and conceptualizes
     and believes it to be pleasurable.

Refuting the Collection of the Five Objects as Inherently Existent Physical Pleasure

Someone says, "Truly existent pleasure exists because its cause exists. That cause is the simultaneous experience of the five sense objects—sights, sounds, odors, tastes, and tactile sensations. Because we can experience the five objects simultaneously, we can experience truly existent physical pleasure from all of them simultaneously. In addition, when these five objects are known simultaneously by five conceptual consciousnesses, we experience five feelings of mental pleasure, one that accompanies each conceptual consciousness."

This person gives an example of experiencing all five sense objects at the same time, "At a dance performance, we can see the visual form of a dancer, smell the perfume on their body, hear the sound of the music, taste some honey, and also have the tactile sensation of soft clothing on our body. In this way the five senses can perceive the five objects at once, and due to this, the five sense consciousnesses can experience five truly existent pleasurable feelings at the same time."

To understand this argument, it is important to understand how sense and conceptual consciousnesses are generated. Nagarjuna explains that these five pleasurable feelings do not occur at once, because the five sense consciousnesses do not simultaneously ascertain the five sense objects. Without them simultaneously ascertaining the five objects, five conceptions that apprehend the five objects cannot subsequently arise simultaneously. Without a conception that apprehends the object, we cannot experience mental happiness from that object. Since five conceptions, each one apprehending a different sense object, cannot arise at the same time, there cannot be five pleasurable mental feelings simultaneously.

To explain Nagarjuna's argument more extensively: Only one sense consciousness can ascertain its object at any particular moment. At that time, the other sense consciousnesses are inattentive awarenesses. That is, their objects appear to them but they do not ascertain those objects. Because the other four sense consciousnesses don't ascertain their objects, they do not feel pleasure from them; instead a neutral feeling accompanies them.

For example, when you see a beautiful flower and are engrossed in looking at it, even though someone is playing music nearby, you aren't aware of it. The visual consciousness ascertains the beautiful flower while the auditory consciousness is inattentive and does not ascertain the music at that time. After a minute or so, you may become aware of the music because your attention shifts to the music and the auditory consciousness now ascertains it. At that time, your visual consciousness becomes inattentive regarding the beautiful flower. If there are two prominent objects—let's say a sight and a sound—the visual consciousness may ascertain its object for a few moments while the auditory consciousness is inattentive, and then the auditory consciousness may ascertain its object while the visual consciousness is inattentive. This may create the sensation that we're experiencing both at the same time when we aren't.

To examine the process of cognition further, when the visual consciousness apprehends blue, for example, that blue is the cause of the visual consciousness apprehending blue. The blue (the cause) has ceased at the time the visual consciousness (its result) is generated. In that case, does blue appear to the visual consciousness? Cause and result cannot exist simultaneously, so the blue that is the cause of the visual consciousness doesn't appear to the visual consciousness that is its result. Rather, the visual consciousness apprehends blue by means of generating an aspect of it. It is said that blue casts an aspect to the visual consciousness, and the visual consciousness is generated in the aspect of blue. Similarly, scientists say that the visual consciousness apprehends an object by means of an aspect of the object appearing on the retina.

After the visual consciousness ascertains a beautiful blue color and experiences pleasure, a conception of blue arises. Conception is thought and is a function of the mental consciousness. An image or conceptual appearance of blue appears to that conceptual consciousness, and that mind thinks "pleasure." At that time a feeling of mental pleasure accompanies that conceptual consciousness. It arises simply because the mind thinks "pleasure."

So while all the five objects can exist at the same time, a person's five sense consciousnesses cannot ascertain or realize all of them simultaneously. Only one sense consciousness at a time can realize its object. Therefore, there are not five simultaneous conceptual consciousnesses following five sense consciousnesses that realize those five objects. Thus, there are not five simultaneous feelings of mental pleasure accompanying five conceptual consciousnesses. Only one conceptual consciousness exists at a time. This refutes the assertion that we can experience five pleasurable feelings from the five sense objects simultaneously. These five cannot be experienced simultaneously by either the five sense consciousnesses or by five conceptual consciousnesses.

> 354. A single sense faculty knows a single [kind of] object.
> But without that [object], it is not really [a sense faculty],
> and without that sense [faculty],
> the object is not really an object.

The Actual Refutation

Each of the five sense faculties—eye, ear, nose, tongue, and body—is the dominant condition that causes its own respective sense consciousness— the visual consciousness and so forth—to know its respective object—visual forms, sounds, odors, tastes, and tactile objects. Regarding each sense, the sense faculty, object, and sense consciousness are posited in relation to each other. For example, we couldn't speak about sound if there were no ear faculty or auditory consciousness. Since the faculty, object, and consciousness are mutually dependent, they do not exist inherently. Because none of these three exist inherently, an inherently existent pleasurable feeling accompanying a sense consciousness cannot arise.

355. Just as a child comes into existence
    in dependence upon his or her parents,
    so too visual awareness is said to arise
    in dependence upon the eye and a visible form.

Refuting Inherently Existent Consciousness

Someone says, "The object and the sense faculty exist inherently because their result, the sense consciousness, arises."

The sense consciousness is indeed produced by the object and the sense faculty, in the same way that a child is produced by his or her father and mother. This shows that they do not exist inherently. Anything that exists dependent on other factors cannot exist independently. What this person says only strengthens our position, it doesn't harm it.

356. Past and future objects are unreal,
    and so are past and future faculties.
    [Present ones] are not distinct from these two [past and future
      ones].
    Hence, the present ones are also unreal.

357. The eye erroneously apprehends the circle
    formed by a torch whirling around.
    Likewise, the sense faculties apprehend objects
    as if they were in the present.

Refuting an Inherently Existent Object

We then say, "The present consciousness exists dependent on the past and future. Being dependent, it cannot exist inherently. Given that an object is not apprehended by an inherently existent past, present, or future consciousness, it, too, does not exist inherently. If it existed inherently, it would have to be posited without depending on anything else—not the past or the future, not the sense faculty or sense consciousness. In fact, the present color blue depends on all of these." In brief, the refutation is that consciousness does not inherently exist because it is a dependent arising.

He then says, "Yes, but doesn't the object of that present consciousness appear to it as inherently existent?" We reply, "Although it appears to be inherently existent, this is a mistaken appearance and the mind to which it appears is a mistaken consciousness. For example, when someone swirls a torch, it appears to the visual consciousness as a circle of fire, although it is not. Similarly, the object of the visual consciousness appears to it to be inherently existent, but it is not. Although the object appears to the visual consciousness as inherently existent, the visual consciousness does not apprehend it as inherently existent. Only erroneous mental conscious-nesses grasp objects as inherently existent."

> 358. The sense faculties and the sense objects
>   are thought to be composed of the five elements.
>   But since each of the elements is unreal,
>   they also are ultimately unreal.

Refuting the Inherent Existence of the Sense Faculties and Objects by Refuting Their Cause, the Elements

Someone says, "Sense objects and sense faculties exist inherently because their causes, the elements, exist inherently."

Sense objects and sense faculties are produced from the elements. They are literally called the "transformations of the elements," meaning that the elements are their cause. However, as we saw in chapter 4, whether the elements are considered individually or as a collection, they don't have any inherently existent reality. Taken one by one, none of the elements exists independent of all other factors, and the collection of the elements likewise is unreal—in other words, empty of inherent existence. This in turn means that the sense faculties and objects composed of the elements also lack inherent existence.

> 359. If the elements were distinct from each other, then fire could
>   occur without fuel.
>   But if they [form a single] composite,
>   then they have no [distinct] defining characteristics.
>   This analysis applies to the remaining [four elements].

Refuting Inherently Existent Elements

If the four elements were inherently existent, they would have to be either totally distinct from each other or identical to each other. If they were completely separate, each of them would exist independently, without relying on the others. In that case, it would absurdly follow that fire, which is caused by fuel, could exist even when there is no fuel. Fuel is composed of all four elements, especially earth, so fire is dependent on the other elements and cannot exist on its own.

If the elements formed a single composite, they couldn't be individually discerned. In that case, too, because they lost their individual identity and had no defining characteristics, they couldn't exist inherently. This analysis can be applied to the other elements as well.

> 360. In both these ways the elements are unreal,
>   so a composite formed from them is also unreal.
>   And since the composite is unreal,
>   form is also ultimately unreal.

Form Is Not Inherently Existent

In both ways—individually and as a composite—the elements do not exist inherently. Therefore, a collection of elements—such as form—cannot exist inherently. Since there are no inherently existent objects or sense faculties that cause physical pleasure, it too lacks inherent existence.

Earlier we noted that while hearers, solitary realizers, and bodhisattvas realize the same emptiness, bodhisattvas do so by means of many reasonings, which enable them to understand emptiness from many perspectives. Here we see an example of the extensive way in which inherent existence is refuted in Madhyamaka texts such as the *Precious Garland*. Spend some time reflecting on these various reasonings to expand your understanding of emptiness.

> 361. Consciousness, feeling, discrimination,
>   and volitional factors individually
>   in no way have any ultimate essence.
>   Therefore, they are ultimately unreal.

Refuting the Entity of Real Pleasure

Previously Nagarjuna refuted incorrect "proofs" of inherently existent pleasure. Now he refutes the entity or nature of feelings being inherently existent.

Someone says, "Pleasure inherently exists because consciousness, feeling, discrimination, and volitional factors arise simultaneously." Nagarjuna replies that feeling doesn't inherently exist because consciousness and the other aggregates do not inherently exist, neither individually nor as a collection. When each aggregate is examined individually, we see that it is made up of different components. In the case of feeling, for example, there are pleasurable, painful, and neutral physical feelings and mental feelings.

When the aggregates are examined as a group, it is again evident that the group depends on each aggregate. Furthermore, each aggregate is posited as an aggregate in dependence on the others. Therefore, the collection of aggregates doesn't inherently exist. In short, each aggregate consists of components, and each aggregate is posited in relation to the other aggregates. For both of these reasons, they lack inherent existence.

362. What one presumes is pleasure
     is actually a reduction in pain;
     likewise, the suppression of pleasure
     is what one presumes to be pain.

Refuting Inherently Existent Pain

We crave happiness and pleasure, and crave to be free of suffering and pain. The inherent existence of the nature of the happiness that we crave to have as well as the reasons proving it to be inherently existent have been refuted. Similarly, the inherent existence of suffering and the reasons supporting it have been disproved.

When suffering diminishes there is the appearance of pleasure, and we conceive "pleasure." We think "pleasure" because suffering has decreased. Similarly, when pleasure diminishes there is the appearance of discomfort and we think, "This is pain,"[34] and apprehend that pain as inherently

---

34. This does not contradict verses 347–48, where it says that while pleasure is the decrease

existent. The consciousness apprehending pain as inherently existent is a wrong consciousness; pain is not inherently existent, because if it were, it would arise independent of everything else. In fact, pain arises dependent on other factors. Pain is also posited in relation to pleasure—the two are mutually dependent. Thus, because pain is dependent, it is not real in the sense of not being inherently existent.

However, this does not mean that there is no real pain in cyclic existence, where *real* means "genuine." It's important not to confuse the two meanings of *real*: one is "inherently existent," the other is "genuine" or "actual." Happiness in cyclic existence is not real in either sense—it is not inherently existent, and it is not genuine happiness because it is simply the reduction of pain. In addition, continued contact with a pleasurable object will eventually turn into pain; it will never be continually pleasurable.

Suffering and pain are not real in the sense of being inherently existent. However, they are real in the sense of being genuine pain, in that continued contact with an object that causes pain will not turn into pleasure. We do not need to make special effort to experience pain—it comes to us automatically in cyclic existence—whereas we do need to make great effort to experience happiness and pleasure, though even then it's not certain we'll attain them.

363. Since they are essenceless,
> one eliminates the craving to obtain pleasure
> and the craving to avoid pain.
> Those who see thus attain liberation thereby.

Liberation Comes from Realizing Emptiness

This verse speaks of two types of craving, one that craves to meet with the object of pleasure, and one that craves to be separated from the object of pain. Both are forms of attachment and arise dependent on pleasurable or painful feelings, respectively. These feelings, in turn, arise dependent on

---

of suffering, pain is not the decrease of pleasure. Those verses clarified the nature of pleasure—it isn't actual pleasure because it is simply the decrease of suffering. Verse 362 indicates that because we mistakenly think a state of less suffering is inherently existent pleasure, we then think pain newly arises when that supposed pleasure decreases. In fact, there was first a small unpleasant feeling that we called pleasure, followed by a stronger unpleasant feeling that we called pain.

the object, sense faculty, sense consciousness, previous karma, attention, and so forth. None of these exist from their own side.

Realizing and meditating on the meaning of emptiness and dependent arising enables us to abandon these two cravings that arise in response to the two types of feeling. Those who see the emptiness of feelings and abandon the two types of craving for them will attain liberation. The wisdom realizing the meaning of emptiness and dependent arising will liberate us from cyclic existence.

Although ignorance is the fundamental root of cyclic existence, craving, clinging, and other forms of attachment are also powerful causes. Motivated by ignorance, polluted karma is created. Craving and clinging—the eighth and ninth of the twelve links of dependent arising—nourish that karma, so that it propels the next life. To overcome ignorance, craving, and clinging, we must exert ourselves to realize emptiness and dependent arising free of all conceptual elaborations, and to see them as mutually supportive.

364. "But who does this seeing?" Conventionally, the mind is said to
      do so.
But without mental factors, there is no mind.
Since [the mind] is unreal, we do not accept
that [two moments of mind] can be simultaneous.

Identifying the Subject, the Mind Cognizing Emptiness

Not only do external objects, the person, and even emptiness lack inherent existence, Nagarjuna now shows that the mind perceiving emptiness is also empty.

Someone queries, "Who sees this reality?" Conventionally, the mind sees this reality. While its object, emptiness, is an ultimate truth, the mind realizing emptiness is a conventional truth. The aryas' meditative equipoise on emptiness, to which all dualistic appearances have subsided, arises and disintegrates moment by moment. As a consciousness, it is an impermanent phenomenon. The wisdom realizing emptiness is a mental factor that accompanies the primary mental consciousness realizing emptiness. This primary mental consciousness and the wisdom accompanying it exist simultaneously and are mutually dependent. If one is missing, the other also isn't present. Both are empty of inherent existence, yet exist by being merely designated in dependence on their respective bases of designation.

The mind realizing emptiness does not see itself, just as the tip of a finger cannot touch itself and a knife cannot cut itself. Emptiness appears to this mind, but that mind itself—the aryas' meditative equipoise on emptiness—does not appear to the perspective of this mind realizing emptiness. Only emptiness appears to it. To observe itself, that wisdom would have to exist under its own power, independent of all other things. In that case, it would be inherently existent, and that doesn't make any sense at all! Therefore, two moments of mind, in which one realizes the other, can't occur simultaneously. They must be sequential.

Not Seeing Is the Highest Seeing

A sutra says that not seeing anything at all is seeing the meaning of emptiness. This means that when we examine how a phenomenon exists by looking for the designated object in the basis of designation, not finding anything truly existent is seeing emptiness. In other words, when we look for a truly existent object, we don't see anything that is truly existent.

Some people misinterpret this sutra passage to mean that not seeing anything at all is the meaning of seeing ultimate reality. They then wonder what is the use of seeing reality if you don't see anything.

A sutra also says that not seeing is the highest seeing; it is holy seeing. This means that when we search for the final mode of existence of phenomena and do not see true existence, then we see the actual mode of existence, suchness—the absence of true existence. To see this is holy; it is the highest seeing. Somebody then questions, "First you said 'not seeing anything' is the ultimate truth, and now you say 'seeing suchness' is the ultimate truth. That sounds contradictory."

We see no contradiction because "not seeing anything at all" means not seeing true existence. That is, true existence—the object of negation—is not seen by the arya's meditative equipoise on reality. "Seeing suchness" means seeing the actual mode of existence, seeing emptiness. So what is seen—emptiness—and what is not seen—true existence—are different.

However, some people mistakenly think that "not seeing anything at all" means not seeing any phenomenon in general—as opposed to our understanding that it refers to not seeing anything that is truly existent.

That leads them to say that when the arya's wisdom of meditative equipoise sees emptiness, it does not see any phenomena, and they conclude that nothing at all exists—neither conventional nor ultimate truths. In that case, the mind realizing reality itself would not exist. If the mind did not exist, when all obscurations are eliminated the mind itself would be eliminated. Such an assertion is the extreme of nihilism and is similar to the non-Buddhists' view. This fault follows from misunderstanding these sutra passages.

> 365. Having properly realized that in this way
>   beings are actually unreal, having no basis [for rebirth],
>   or any appropriation [of new aggregates],
>   one attains nirvana like a fire whose causes have ceased.

Attaining Nirvana Requires the Realization of Emptiness

When we have correctly realized that sentient beings are actually unreal—that they lack true existence—we realize that the conceived object of the true-grasping mind does not exist. We also understand that the mind grasping sentient beings as truly existent is an erroneous mind. Meditating on emptiness repeatedly over time brings about the gradual cessation of true-grasping, and as a result, the craving that leads to rebirth in cyclic existence ceases. Like a fire that is extinguished through lack of fuel, cyclic existence ceases through the lack of its cause, true-grasping ignorance, and the person attains liberation.

According to the Prasangikas, fundamental vehicle arhats have also realized the emptiness of true existence of persons and phenomena, because it is impossible to attain liberation without directly perceiving this emptiness. They cite many definitive sutras establishing that those practicing the hearer, solitary realizer, and bodhisattva vehicles all attain their own awakening by meditating on subtle emptiness. For example, in the perfection of wisdom sutras, the Buddha stated that somebody who wants to train in the stages of any of the three vehicles has to train in the perfection of wisdom.

This is a unique assertion of the Prasangika philosophers, who cite passages in the fundamental vehicle sutras in which the Buddha teaches subtle emptiness in order to show that hearers and solitary realizers do indeed meditate on it. *A Ball of Foam Sutta (Phenapindupama Sutta)* says:

Forms are like balls of foam,
Feelings like water bubbles;
Discriminations like a mirage,
Volitional factors like a plantain trunk,
and consciousnesses like illusions.
So explained the Kinsman of the Sun.

While the Svatantrikas and below have their own interpretations of this passage, Prasangikas say that through these analogies, the Buddha—the Kinsman of the Sun—explained that the aggregates also lack true existence.

Someone says, "This advice in the fundamental vehicle sutras was not to show the hearers and solitary realizers that they have to realize non-true existence to gain liberation, but to show that bodhisattvas have to realize non-true existence to gain awakening." Prasangikas respond that this not the case, since the Buddha gave advice separately to the bodhisattvas. In the same scripture, it says, "Just like that, in order for the bodhisattvas to attain liberation, they also have to realize emptiness." By saying, "also," the Buddha indicates that in addition to the hearers and solitary realizers needing to realize emptiness, the bodhisattvas do too.

366. Bodhisattvas, having also had this realization,
    become firmly intent upon awakening.
    It is due to just their compassion
    that they continue to take rebirth until awakening.

Somebody wonders, "Is there any difference between practitioners of the universal vehicle and those of the fundamental vehicle, since both have to realize emptiness to attain awakening?"

When they train in wisdom, bodhisattvas' meditation on emptiness has to be supported by the vast method side of compassion, bodhichitta, unshakable resolve, and dedication. The fundamental vehicle teachings do not say that the practice of hearers and solitary realizers must be supported in this way. Following the bodhisattva path requires not only gaining the realization of subtle emptiness but also the firm aspiration to attain full awakening for the benefit of all sentient beings and the collection of merit supported by bodhichitta.

Somebody says, "You say that bodhisattvas realize emptiness and through that eliminate the attachment, anger, and ignorance that cause rebirth in cyclic existence. If they no longer have the cause for rebirth in cyclic existence in their mindstreams, it is not correct to say that they stay in cyclic existence for a long time for the sake of others."

Lower-level bodhisattvas, who have not yet realized emptiness directly and nonconceptually, still take rebirth in cyclic existence under the influence of afflictions and karma. However, arya bodhisattvas continue to take births until awakening due to their compassion and wish to benefit sentient beings. They are not born in cyclic existence by the force of afflictions and polluted karma like ordinary beings are, but by the force of their compassion, unshakable resolve, and unpolluted karma.[35]

CORRECTLY UNDERSTANDING THE UNIVERSAL VEHICLE

While hearers, solitary realizers, and bodhisattvas all realize the same subtle emptiness, they differ in terms of the collections of merit and wisdom. Only bodhisattvas have the actual two collections, because the collections must be amassed with the motivation of bodhichitta. Not all creation of merit is the collection of merit.

In the following verses Nagarjuna speaks of the unique practice and benefits of the universal vehicle and confirms that there is one final vehicle. That is, although the Buddha taught the three vehicles of the hearers, solitary realizers, and bodhisattvas, everyone will eventually enter the bodhisattva vehicle and become fully awakened buddhas.

367. The Tathagata taught
      the bodhisattvas' collections in the universal vehicle.
      But it is derided by those
      who are confused and antagonistic.

---

35. While we use the expression "take birth in cyclic existence" for arya bodhisattvas, in fact many of them have mental bodies caused by the latencies of ignorance and unpolluted karma, and take rebirth due to their compassion and strong aspirations to benefit sentient beings. While they appear like ordinary beings who experience birth, aging, sickness, and death, they do not experience suffering, and their motivations are always altruistic.

The Universal Vehicle Is Disparaged by Those Who Are Confused

In the universal vehicle teachings, the Buddha extensively explained the necessity for bodhisattvas to train in the two vast collections of merit and wisdom in order to attain full awakening. Upon hearing those teachings some beings, due to their confusion and ignorance, became antagonistic and disparaged the universal vehicle.

Some people hold incorrect ideas concerning Mahayana, the universal vehicle. Because it was not practiced publicly at the time of Buddha, some people think it is not derived from the Buddha's words. Others are skittish about it because it necessitates practicing for three countless great eons to attain full awakening, and because bodhisattvas have to stay in cyclic existence in order to benefit sentient beings. In the ensuing verses Nagarjuna clears up misconceptions and encourages people to follow the universal vehicle, helping them recognize that it is the source of all happiness and benefit in the world.

> 368. Those who deride the universal vehicle
>   either cannot distinguish good qualities from faults,
>   or they mistake good qualities for faults,
>   or else they despise good qualities.

> 369. What harms others are faults;
>   what helps them are good qualities;
>   recognizing this, it is said that
>   those who deride the universal vehicle dislike good qualities.

The Reasons They Disparage It

Bodhisattvas practice giving up their own welfare and striving for the welfare of others. It is hard to see why people would not admire that. Nagarjuna presents three reasons why they wouldn't. First, they cannot distinguish good qualities from faults: they do not see working for the welfare of all sentient beings as a good quality and seeking only one's own liberation as a shortcoming. Second, they mistake good qualities for faults: they see relinquishing working for your own welfare and striving for others' benefit as a fault. Third, they have spontaneous dislike for the qualities of the universal vehicle. This could be because they lack imprints from previous lives that would make them appreciate the universal vehicle.

Some people know that harming others is a fault and helping them is a good quality, yet they still criticize the universal vehicle teachings. The universal vehicle scriptures contain the practice of the bodhisattva path in its entirety. While the fundamental vehicle scriptures contain the same points, they are only explained briefly. For example, love and compassion are discussed in the fundamental vehicle scriptures but are not explained fully. Other topics, such as the practice of unshakable resolve, which is essential for the bodhisattva path, is hard to find in the fundamental vehicle scriptures because they focus principally on the path to arhatship.

The Buddha taught the universal vehicle sutras during his lifetime, but they were not widely disseminated at that time. Although they were practiced quietly at certain monasteries or in private, many people did not know these teachings were the Buddha's word and thus criticized them.

370. By being unconcerned about one's own aims,
    one takes delight uniquely in the aims of others—
    this source of all good qualities is [the teaching of] the universal
        vehicle.
    Hence, one who disparages it is tormented.

371. Even a faithful person suffers due to misunderstanding it;
    someone else who is hostile suffers due to animosity.
    If it is said that even the faithful person is tormented,
    what about the one who is hostile?

The Faults of Disparaging the Universal Vehicle

Relinquishing working for our own welfare alone and striving one-pointedly to make others happy is the source of all peace and happiness in this and future lives. Disparaging this wondrous attitude and behavior is extremely destructive and propels someone into rebirth in the hell of unceasing torment after death.

Two kinds of people are hostile toward the universal vehicle. The first are those who have faith in emptiness and want to realize it, but don't know how to think about it properly. As a result they mistakenly think emptiness means that nothing whatsoever exists, and they dislike the universal vehicle for that reason. The second are actively hostile toward the universal vehicle because they bear enmity toward teachings on emptiness or they object to teachings that encourage us to give up working for our own benefit in favor of others.

If even those who have faith but think wrongly will be tormented in the hell realms, what need is there to speak about the result of bearing genuine animosity toward the universal vehicle? Since we wish to have happiness and attain nirvana, it's important to be careful not to deny emptiness or to denigrate altruism.

> 372. Physicians say that poison
>   may be eliminated with poison.
>   So how is it contradictory to say that
>   suffering may eliminate something unhelpful?

It's Appropriate to Experience a Little Suffering to Eliminate Great Duhkha

The second type of person above dislikes the universal vehicle because it encourages giving up self-concern and working for the benefit of others. The idea of giving away their body, eyes, head, arms, and legs frightens such people so much that they can't tolerate it and get angry.[36] They think that it's right to dislike the universal vehicle because it advocates giving away our body as well as our spouse, children, and possessions. From their perspective, that is asking too much.

When a doctor operates on the affected area of a person who is very ill, the purpose is to prevent the person from having to bear the greater suffering of dying. Experiencing a comparatively small amount of pain to save

---

36. Giving our body is a supreme act of generosity. We are usually faced with much easier practices; for example, forgoing a meal in order to share our food with others. The bodhisattva precepts stipulate that only arya bodhisattvas are allowed to give their bodies completely such that they give up their life. Bodhisattvas on the paths of accumulation and preparation are not permitted to do this, because continuing to practice with their present precious human lives is more beneficial for sentient beings in the long term. This is because ordinary bodhisattvas have not yet realized emptiness directly and so are not capable of controlling their next rebirth. Some may not yet be immune to lower rebirths. However, they can donate a kidney to someone who needs a transplant.

ourselves from greater pain is reasonable. Similarly, if someone who is to be executed has his sentence commuted to amputation of a limb, the person would be overjoyed and would gladly endure the loss of a limb in order to be able to continue living. While we don't go looking for suffering, when it comes our way—especially in the context of doing an action that will enable us to avoid great suffering in the lower realms or bring the great happiness of awakening—we should gladly endure it for that higher purpose.

373. [The scriptures] maintain: The mind is the prerequisite for all
     dharmas—
     the mind is the principal factor [in karma].
     So if one does something helpful with the intention to be helpful,
     how could it be unhelpful, even if suffering is involved?

374. If one does something unpleasant that will later be helpful,
     then what about doing something for oneself and for others
     that is both pleasant and helpful?
     This is an ancient principle.

Don't Be Angry at a Little Suffering That Can Eliminate All Our Duhkha

Even though the universal vehicle's practice of giving away the body and other things causes a small amount of suffering now, we shouldn't be upset about doing it or the pain that occurs. Being confident in the great benefit this will bring in the future for ourselves and others, tolerate this comparatively small suffering now. Although some bodhisattva practices may involve some discomfort or pain, they will act as a cause for the eradication of all our duhkha forever.

In general, when we have a virtuous motivation, our actions of body and speech become constructive. Even if this action produces a small amount of pain now, it remains virtuous and will bring happiness to ourselves and others in the future since our motivation is to benefit others.

Someone objects, "Sometimes people have a virtuous motivation but their physical and verbal actions cause problems." This is true. However, while the immediate result may be confusion or aggravation, acting with good intentions will still bring good results in future lives.

When bodhisattvas undergo the hardships of giving away their body or parts of their body they first generate a very strong virtuous motivation wishing to benefit others. Then, despite some temporary suffering, their action will bring an immensely salutary and vast result. This practice of bearing a smaller pain for a greater good is done by all the buddhas of the past, present, and future. Even ordinary people recognize that when great profit will accrue in the long term, it is worth pushing ahead despite a small problem in the short term.

> 375. If one will later attain great happiness
>   from forsaking some trivial pleasure now,
>   then sensible people, realizing that they will gain great happiness,
>   should abandon that trifling pleasure now.

> 376. If you cannot bear this,
>   then healers and such
>   who prescribe bitter medicine would disappear,
>   and that makes no sense.

Exert Yourselves for Great Happiness and Don't Be Attached to Small Happiness

When great happiness will be the ultimate result of an action, it is wise to give up small short-term happiness to attain it. All Dharma practitioners must do this, no matter whether they follow the hearer, solitary realizer, or bodhisattva path. To keep either the lay or monastic precepts we have to give up chasing every object of attachment we see, even though restraining ourselves may be unpleasant. If we aren't willing to do this, we won't take *bitter medicine* to save our lives, and that makes no sense at all. We put up with such things because they will bring a good outcome in the long term—otherwise we may hasten our own death.

Similarly, sometimes practicing the path to full awakening entails giving up some comparatively small and insignificant pleasures of this life to accomplish long-term joy for ourselves and others. It is only reasonable to do this.

In short, beings of less intelligence fear suffering and are thus incapable of doing certain bodhisattva deeds. Seeing the benefit of such compassionate deeds and courageously accepting whatever suffering doing them may entail, great bodhisattvas happily engage in such actions to benefit others and to swiftly fulfill the two collections.

377. The wise see that in some cases
  what is [usually] harmful can be helpful.
  All treatises propose
  both general rules and exceptions.

In general, everything in cyclic existence is duhkha in nature and thus to be abandoned. In that case, shouldn't we avoid giving away our body or parts of it on the bodhisattva path because it causes duhkha? While in general it is true that suffering is to be abandoned, there are exceptions when this is not the case. Treatises and commentaries always present a general situation as well as exceptions to it. For example, in general we want to relinquish rebirth in cyclic existence, but bodhisattvas, motivated by compassion, must take birth in order to benefit sentient beings and to collect the merit that will bring peerless awakening. Similarly, in general we need to take care of our bodies. But there is an exception in the case of bodhisattvas—when they see the time is right and that giving away their bodies will benefit others in a vast way, they do so without attachment. We must develop intelligence and skill in order to be able to discern what is generally the case and what is an exception.

378. The universal vehicle says
  that all activities should be motivated by compassion,
  and that wisdom will make them pure—
  what sensible person would deride this?

It Is Appropriate to Take Delight in the Universal Vehicle

The universal vehicle scriptures are based on compassion and wisdom, and everyone—even secular people who have no religion—appreciates compassion. These scriptures describe in full the way to cultivate great compassion and bodhichitta. They also give instructions on the bodhisattva practices of the six perfections and the methods to cultivate serenity and insight. Attaining serenity and insight enables us to generate the wisdom that understands emptiness, which purifies all the bodhisattva practices by contemplating that their agents, actions, and objects are mutually dependent and thus lack inherent existence.

Practicing the bodhisattva path leads to the fulfillment of the two collections of merit and wisdom by which practitioners attain a buddha's truth body and form body. Who can fault such a wonderful path and result? Since all of this is explained in detail in the universal vehicle scriptures, it is appropriate to appreciate them. Those who aspire for peerless awakening should be delighted to discover this explanation of how to attain their noble goal.

> 379. Discouraged by its vastness and profundity,
>   ignorant persons, due to their confusion,
>   today deride the universal vehicle
>   [and thus become] the foes of themselves and others.

When they merely listen to the explanation of the vast bodhisattva practices and the actual mode of existence, people of inferior intelligence become afraid and discouraged, and do not want to follow the bodhisattva path. Unable to bear even hearing about it, they criticize the universal vehicle. In this way, they become their own worst enemies and deprive themselves of the bliss of full awakening.

To be attracted to the universal vehicle in this life requires having latencies from studying and/or practicing it in previous lives. Those who lack such latencies misunderstand and criticize it. In doing so, they abandon the universal vehicle and the causes for peerless awakening, putting the chance to attain peerless awakening far away.

Showing the Universal Vehicle Scriptures
Are the Buddha's Word

Having explained the benefits of practicing the universal vehicle and the disadvantages of criticizing it, Nagarjuna now turns to allaying the doubts of those who wonder if the Buddha indeed taught the universal vehicle scriptures. He does this by first saying that since the bodhisattva vehicle includes such a wonderful practice that everyone appreciates, it must be taught by an awakened one. In addition, these scriptures contain all the essential points of the bodhisattva practice—the six perfections, the collection of merit and wisdom, and the methods to attain the form bodies and truth body of a buddha. If the Buddha didn't teach such a wonderful path and result, who else could have?

> 380. The nature of what the universal vehicle maintains
> is generosity, ethical conduct, fortitude, joyous effort,
> meditative stability, wisdom, and compassion—
> how could it contain a wrong statement?

The Universal Vehicle Scriptures Contain Not Even the Slightest Bad Explanation

The universal vehicle scriptures contain nothing harmful or incorrect that would bring the downfall of sentient beings. The six perfections—generosity, ethical conduct, fortitude, joyous effort, meditative stability, and wisdom—are noble qualities that everyone admires, even secular people. Furthermore, bodhichitta, which is the basis of these practices, and its cause, great compassion, as well as the steps in the two methods of generating bodhichitta are clearly explained in great detail by the Buddha in the universal vehicle scriptures. What could be faulty with this?

> 381. Others' aims are achieved through generosity and ethical
> conduct;
> one's own through fortitude and joyous effort;
> meditative stability and wisdom lead to liberation—
> this summarizes the universal vehicle teachings.

The Universal Vehicle Scriptures Contain All the Essential Points of the Bodhisattva Practice

The practice of the six perfections is the heart of the universal vehicle, and they are fully explained in its scriptures. *Generosity* is the principal cause that enables us to have the material things we need in life, and *ethical conduct* is the principal cause for attaining a higher rebirth. Temporarily these two practices benefit others, in that our generosity benefits the recipients of our gifts and offerings, and our ethical conduct benefits those we otherwise may have harmed through lack of restraint. Of course generosity and ethical conduct benefit us too, but here they are said to benefit others from the viewpoint of who receives the immediate benefit.

From the temporal and immediate viewpoint, *fortitude* and *joyous effort* accomplish our own benefit. Fortitude prevents us from destroying our virtue through anger, and it helps us avoid creating new nonvirtue by getting angry. When we delight in virtue, joyous effort spurs us to create virtue we didn't have before and makes us happy to increase the virtue we already have.

The practices of *meditative stability* and *wisdom* encompass serenity and insight, which are the main causes of attaining *liberation.* Serenity is the ability to stay on the meditation object one-pointedly for as long as we wish, free of excitement and laxity. Wisdom gained by insight knows the ultimate nature of reality. At the moment, we may intellectually understand emptiness—we may know the reasons phenomena lack inherent existence or be able to explain emptiness to others. However, this does not mean we have realized emptiness. One reason for this is poor concentration that prevents us from entering meditative equipoise on emptiness. Our concentration is interrupted by excitement and laxity that move our mindfulness off the object. Once we are able to concentrate properly, this will help us to realize emptiness directly, which in turn will bring about liberation. In this way, meditative stability and wisdom lead to liberation.

All the bodhisattva practices can be subsumed into these six. Thus they are said to summarize the universal vehicle teachings. Meditation on these six is practicing and meditating on the meaning of the universal vehicle scriptures. Reciting the words that explain them is maintaining the words of the universal vehicle scriptures.

> 382. In brief, the teachings of the Buddha include
> what benefits oneself and others, and [the way to attain]
>   liberation.
> These topics are contained in the six perfections.
> Therefore, they are also the Buddha's words.

The Universal Vehicle Scriptures Were Taught by the Buddha

The fundamental vehicle scriptures teach the causes for higher rebirth and highest good, and in this way, they enable us to attain our own aim—

liberation from cyclic existence. These are also taught in the universal vehicle scriptures, which additionally teach the practices that benefit others. While some bodhisattva practices are taught in the fundamental vehicle scriptures, they are not described in the detail or to the extent that they are in the universal vehicle scriptures. Nevertheless, since the main practices of these two vehicles are similar and both are based on the four truths of aryas, the teachings of both vehicles must be the word of the Buddha. No one else could have delineated such a magnificent and correct path.

383. Those blinded by ignorance cannot tolerate the universal vehicle,
in which the Buddha taught the great path
consisting of merit and wisdom
that leads to awakening.

The Need to Learn the Complete Bodhisattva Path from the Universal Vehicle Scriptures

Like a highway that is broad enough for many people to travel on, the universal vehicle is a great path that will benefit all sentient beings in the universe. It is the path followed by all the buddhas and bodhisattvas of the three times and ten directions.

Some Buddhists reject the Buddha's teachings on the emptiness of inherent existence, saying that liberation is attained by realizing the four truths of the aryas. They assert that realizing the lack of a self-sufficient, substantially existent person is the selflessness of person, and some of these schools—the Vaibhashika and Sautrantika—do not assert a selflessness of phenomena. Those that do—the Chittamatra and Svatantrika—do not assert the lack of inherent existence as the selflessness of both persons and phenomena.

The Madhyamikas differ, saying, "If realizing only the four truths were necessary to attain liberation, why would the Buddha have taught the emptiness of inherent existence in so many sutras? If there were no selflessness of phenomena, why did the Buddha teach it?"

The followers of the lower tenets systems do not understand that full awakening arises from the vast collections of merit and wisdom, and that the collection of wisdom is accumulated by meditating on the emptiness of inherent existence of persons and phenomena. All this and more is explained in the universal vehicle scriptures.

384. Since [a Victor comes from] merit that is as inconceivable as
     space,
     a Victor is said to have inconceivable good qualities.
     Hence one should accept the greatness of buddhas,
     as [explained] in the universal vehicle.

385. Even just the ethical conduct [of the Buddha]
     was beyond Shariputra's ken.
     Why then wouldn't one accept that
     the greatness of the buddhas is inconceivable?

Universal Vehicle Scriptures Show the Limitless Causes for Attaining the Form Body

As limited beings, we are unable to understand the Buddha's limitless and inconceivable qualities. One time the Buddha asked the arhat Shariputra if he could understand one quality of the Buddha—his ethical conduct. Shariputra replied that he couldn't fathom it at all! Because the Buddha's qualities are so subtle and difficult to understand, they are not visible to sentient beings. We cannot know or understand even one of the Buddha's qualities, let alone all of them.

Because the causes of the Buddha's form body and truth body are incomparable, the qualities of these two resultant bodies are also inconceivable. From inconceivable and limitless causes—the collections of merit and wisdom—come inconceivable and limitless results. For that reason, we should accept the magnificent qualities of the Buddha that are explained in the universal vehicle scriptures and also accept that these scriptures were taught by the Buddha. It doesn't make sense to be irritated by teachings that instruct us how to be like our Teacher.

386. The non-arising taught in the universal vehicle
     and the extinction [taught] for other [Buddhists] are [both]
     emptiness.

Therefore, one should accept that
extinction and non-arising are ultimately the same.

387. Emptiness is the majesty of the awakened one;
    reflecting thus with reasoning,
    how could the wise not maintain
    that what is said in the universal vehicle and the other are equal?

The Knowledge of Extinction and the Knowledge of Non-Arising Are the Same

The fundamental vehicle's explanation of the knowledge of extinction and the universal vehicle teachings on the knowledge of non-arising are the same in indicating the meaning of emptiness. Nagarjuna bases this explanation on a fundamental vehicle scripture in which the term *extinction* refers to the primordial extinction of duhkha and the aggregates—that is, the emptiness of inherent existence that is the ultimate nature of duhkha and the aggregates. In universal vehicle scriptures *non-arising* refers to phenomena not arising by their own nature, that is, they do not arise inherently. Afflictions, karma, and duhkha are not inherently produced; they do not arise under their own power. Thus the *knowledge of extinction* spoken of in the fundamental vehicle means knowing that self-grasping, afflictions, polluted karma, and so forth are naturally empty of inherent existence, and the *knowledge of non-arising* spoken of in the universal vehicle means knowing that none of these arise inherently and thus do not exist inherently; they are naturally empty of inherent existence.

One reason some hearers do not like the universal vehicle scriptures is because they think that the principal cause for attaining liberation as explained in the fundamental vehicle scriptures isn't explained in the universal vehicle scriptures. However, as explained above, the fundamental vehicle scriptures' explanation of the knowledge of extinction is the same as the universal vehicle scriptures' explanation of the knowledge of non-arising. They both refer to the realization of emptiness, which is the essential cause of liberation. For that reason hearers should accept the subtle emptiness that is taught in their own scriptures and accept that the universal vehicle scriptures are the word of the Buddha.

In short, it is appropriate for fundamental vehicle practitioners to accept the universal vehicle teachings for two reasons. First, the principal cause for attaining liberation is indicated in the universal vehicle scriptures because its explanation of non-arising (non-inherently existent arising) and the fundamental vehicle explanation of extinction are the same in indicating emptiness. Second, as shown in the explanation of verse 365, the emptiness explained in the universal vehicle scriptures is also explained in the fundamental vehicle scriptures, and no one can attain liberation without realizing emptiness. For both of these reasons, the universal vehicle scriptures can be accepted as the Buddha's word.

If you can't accept the emptiness of inherent existence, you can't accept the cause of the truth body. Emptiness is the focal object of aryas' meditative equipoise, and as such, it is the "cause" of the truth body. Those who are able to analyze with reasoning will find that the explanations in the universal vehicle scriptures of no inherent arising and in the fundamental vehicle scriptures of extinction are equal in indicating emptiness. This being the case, the universal vehicle scriptures should be accepted as the Buddha's word.

388. What the Tathagata stated with a [hidden] intention
    is not easy to understand.
    For this reason, there is said to be one vehicle, and also three.
    Therefore, protect yourself by being equanimous.

389. By being equanimous, you do nothing wrong;
    but negativity comes from anger—how could virtue?
    Hence, those who seek what is good for themselves
    should not despise the universal vehicle.

If You Don't Understand the Universal Vehicle, Maintain a Neutral Attitude Toward It

A skillful teacher, the Buddha taught according to the dispositions and interests of his disciples. Depending on whom he was addressing, to one audience he spoke of three final vehicles, while to another he said there was one final vehicle. *Three final vehicles* means that once those following the hearer, solitary realizer, and bodhisattva paths reach the culmination of their respective paths, they will abide in the nirvana that is the final goal of that path. In the case of hearers and solitary realizers, that is to become an arhat and attain a nirvana in which all afflictive obscurations have been extinguished and rebirth in cyclic existence has ceased. As long as those arhats are alive there is the remainder of the polluted aggregates they were born with. When they die, they shed those remaining aggregates and enter nirvana. This is the termination or extinction of the continuity of the aggregates; what is left is called the sphere of nirvana. There is no talk of the personal existence of an arhat. Thus at the time of nirvana with remainder, the person exists, as does the polluted body. At the time of nirvana without remainder, there is merely the sphere of nirvana—there is no person.

The Vaibhashikas, Sautrantikas, and Chittamatrins Following Scripture assert three final vehicles, while the Chittamatrins Following Reasoning, Svatantrikas, and Prasangikas assert that there is one final vehicle and that eventually all sentient beings will attain full awakening. Arhatship is not the final end point because although arhats have abandoned afflictive obscurations, they still have cognitive obscurations. This means they have not abandoned every obscuration possible, nor have they cultivated all the good qualities that our minds are capable of cultivating.

Furthermore, Prasangikas say that at the time hearer or solitary realizer arhats pass away, they abandon the polluted body, but the continuity of consciousness remains. They abide in meditative equipoise on emptiness until the Buddha "wakes them up" and prompts them to enter the bodhisattva path. At that time, they engage in fulfilling the collections of merit and wisdom by practicing the six perfections, and eventually attain buddhahood. A buddha's nirvana is called "non-abiding nirvana" because the person abides in neither cyclic existence nor in the personal peace of a hearer or solitary realizer arhat.

In brief, while the Buddha knew that everyone will eventually attain full awakening and thus accepted one final vehicle, he did not teach this to everyone. For the purpose of taking care of people whose interests and dispositions rendered them suitable for entering into and practicing the hearer or solitary realizer vehicle, the Buddha taught that there are three final vehicles. Those disciples were intent on gaining liberation from cyclic existence and were not interested in training in the universal vehicle with its emphasis on bodhichitta and the six perfections. After they trained in the hearer and solitary realizer paths and attained arhatship, the Buddha knew that they would later enter the universal vehicle.

Sometimes there was a difference between the Buddha's own thought and what he taught to specific disciples. This does not mean that he contradicted himself or spoke falsely; rather he was an extremely skillful teacher whose sole intention was to lead all sentient beings to the bliss of peerless awakening. To meet the needs of his varied disciples, the Buddha gave both definitive and provisional teachings. According to the Prasangikas, definitive teachings are those that explicitly teach the emptiness of inherent existence. Provisional teachings do not accord with the literal meaning of the words and need to be interpreted differently to discover the Buddha's final intention. When it comes to the teachings on emptiness, there is a great deal of discussion among the philosophical systems about which teachings are definitive and which are provisional. This must ultimately be decided by employing reasoning.

Some people criticize the universal vehicle teachings because they do not understand the difference between definitive and provisional teachings or they reject the thought that everyone will eventually follow the bodhisattva path to buddhahood. Nagarjuna cautions those people: Rather than get upset and create destructive karma from anger, remain equanimous and impartial, and in this way protect yourselves from creating nonvirtue. Anger is never virtuous, so it's better to put the issue on the back burner for the time being rather than to disparage teachings you do not understand or find useful at that moment.

> 390. The bodhisattvas' aspirational prayers
>   are not taught in the hearer vehicle,
>   nor are their practices, nor the dedication.
>   How could one become a bodhisattva through that [vehicle]?

> 391. [In the other vehicles] the buddhas did not state
>   the foundation for the bodhisattva's awakening.
>   What source is better than the Victors
>   for attaining reliable knowledge on this topic?

Not All Bodhisattva Practices Are Explained Completely in Fundamental Vehicle Scriptures

Someone asks, "The fundamental vehicle scriptures teach the practice of all three vehicles, so what do you mean when you say the practice of the universal vehicle isn't explained in them?" In the fundamental vehicle scriptures, the Buddha didn't explain in a complete way all of the vast practices of the bodhisattvas. For example, bodhisattvas' aspirational prayers, the details of their practice of the six perfections, and their dedication of merit are not described there. The bodhisattvas' aspirational prayers are the wide array of powerful aspirations bodhisattvas make, especially once they have attained the first bodhisattva ground—the bodhisattva path of seeing. These are strong aspirations and resolute determinations that grow in number, strength, and expanse as bodhisattvas ascend through the ten bodhisattva grounds.

Similarly, bodhisattvas' practice of the six perfections becomes more and more profound as they ascend the grounds. In addition, bodhisattvas dedicate merit in extraordinarily vast ways—the "King of Prayers" is a good example of this. Some verses in this prayer from the *Flower Ornament Sutra* (*Avatamsaka Sutra*) ask us to imagine on each atom a buddha teaching the Dharma to a huge assembly of bodhisattvas. We also visualize a vast assembly of bodhisattvas on each atom making oceans of offerings to an enormous assembly of buddhas. While aspirational prayers, generosity, dedication of merit, and so forth are taught in the fundamental vehicle, they are not taught as extensively or completely. Bodhichitta is mentioned, but the detailed methods to cultivate it are not taught. The fundamental vehicle also does not teach how to engage in the vast practices of the two collections that lead to the two buddha bodies. Thus, while it is possible to become a bodhisattva and attain buddhahood following only the fundamental vehicle scriptures, it is more difficult.

392. The path that is shared with the hearers includes the foundations
  [for the arhat],
  the meanings of the aryas' truths, and the aids to awakening.
  If buddhahood were the result of that path,
  how could buddhahood be superior [to arhatship]?

Practicing the Four Truths and the Thirty-Seven Aids Is Not Sufficient to Attain Full Awakening

Someone inquires, "Why is there the need to explain so many other practices when just meditating on the four truths and the thirty-seven aids to awakening for three countless great eons will bring buddhahood?"

The sixteen aspects of the four truths of the aryas and the thirty-seven aids to awakening are practices that hearers, solitary realizers, and bodhisattvas share in common. However, meditation on those alone won't lead to the unique result of buddhahood. The state of a buddha is superior to that of an arhat; buddhas have eradicated all obscurations and developed all excellent qualities limitlessly, whereas arhats have eliminated only the afflictive obscurations, not the cognitive obscurations. The causes of buddhahood include those of the hearers' practice—with the exception of the motivation to attain one's own personal nirvana. In addition, those aspiring for buddhahood generate bodhichitta and engage in all the bodhisattva practices on the method side of the path. Thus, unlike the hearer and the solitary realizer practitioners who can attain their goal through practicing only the teachings in the fundamental vehicle scriptures, bodhisattvas must also practice the bodhisattva deeds as taught in the universal vehicle scriptures in order to become buddhas.

393. The subject matter of engaging in practices for awakening
　　　is not discussed in the [fundamental vehicle] sutras,
　　　but it is discussed in the universal vehicle.
　　　Hence, judicious persons should accept [the universal vehicle].

Wise People Accept the Universal Vehicle Scriptures as the Buddha's Word

The Buddha did not teach the essential points of the bodhisattva practices in the fundamental vehicle sutras, which contain the essential practices for hearers and solitary realizers. But these points were taught in the universal vehicle scriptures.

While hearers and solitary realizers understand the same emptiness of inherent existence as bodhisattvas, they do so by using one reasoning, whereas bodhisattvas employ many reasonings to realize emptiness. In this way, bodhisattvas' understanding of emptiness is more well-rounded, and they are better able to explain emptiness to others because of their knowledge and experience meditating on diverse reasonings. Therefore, the wise should accept the universal vehicle teachings as taught by the Buddha.

394. A language teacher will make [some students]
        read from a diagram of the alphabet.
        Likewise, the Buddha taught the Dharma
        in accord with his disciples' abilities.

395. The Dharma he taught to some
        is for the purpose of stopping negativity.
        To some, it is aimed at the practice of virtue.
        And to some, he taught one that is based on duality.

396. He taught to some a Dharma not based on duality.
        And to some, he taught a profound Dharma that terrifies the
            timid;
        its essence is wisdom and compassion,
        and it is the means to attain full awakening.

The Purpose of Teaching Three Vehicles

A skillful teacher instructs children according to their capabilities. A child may want to be a doctor, but she cannot begin her education with medical studies that are way above her head; she must first learn the alphabet as a means to be able to study complex subjects later. Similarly, the Buddha taught the three vehicles and the four philosophical tenet systems as skillful ways to lead trainees gradually, according to their present capabilities, to the final state of awakening.

To some people the Buddha taught the practice of stopping the negativity of the ten paths of nonvirtuous actions. In this way, they stop creating causes for lower rebirths. To some he emphasized the practice of virtue by engaging in the ten paths of virtuous actions, so that they create the causes for higher rebirths in future lives. In the lamrim literature, both of these pertain to initial capacity practitioners. He did not teach these disciples the methods to free themselves from cyclic existence because they were not sufficiently prepared to do so at that time.

To those who were more capable—the middle capacity beings—the Buddha taught practices based on duality so that they could abandon cyclic existence and attain liberation. The Buddha taught these people— principally Vaibhashikas and Sautrantikas—that even higher rebirths should be abandoned because they are within cyclic existence. To free themselves from all birth in cyclic existence and attain liberation, these practitioners were instructed to meditate on the sixteen aspects of the four truths and the thirty-seven aids to awakening. Since it was appropriate for their disposition, he taught them to meditate on the selflessness of persons—that is, the absence of a self-sufficient, substantially existent person—as the means to attain liberation. Neither the Vaibhashikas nor the Sautrantikas were ready to hear that grasping the inherent existence of persons and phenomena is the root of cyclic existence or that both persons and phenomena are selfless. Thus the Buddha taught them a view based on duality, saying there are external objects that are unrelated to the mind.

Showing a Dharma not based on duality, the Buddha taught disciples who aspired for awakening the selflessness of phenomena according to the Chittamatra view. Here the selflessness of phenomena means that an object and the consciousness apprehending it do not exist as separate entities. To these disciples, the Buddha said there were no external objects—that is, things are of the nature of the mind in the sense that they arise from the same substantial cause as the mind apprehending them. However, in order not to push them beyond their capacity, he also taught them that the apprehending mind is truly existent. While the Chittamatra view is subtler than those of the Vaibhashikas and Sautrantikas in that it asserts a selflessness of phenomena, that selflessness of phenomena is still coarse compared to that of the Madhyamikas.

To those with a Prasangika disposition, the Buddha taught a profound Dharma that terrifies the timid. Its essence is wisdom and compassion because it is supported by the methods of bodhichitta and the six perfections. This view asserts a subtler selflessness of both persons and phenomena than taught to others. To Madhyamikas in general, he taught the emptiness of true existence as that was suitable for those with both Svatantrika and Prasangika dispositions. However, to Prasangikas he taught the subtlest view, the emptiness of inherent existence.

Again we see the Buddha's magnificent skill as a spiritual guide. He gave more superficial explanations to suit the mentality of initial capacity practitioners, and as they progressed he gradually taught subtler views. In this way, he helped trainees steadily expand their capacity and intelligence.

397. Hence, the wise should cease
      to despise the universal vehicle,
      and they should generate special faith
      so as to attain true, complete awakening.

398. Through faith in the universal vehicle
      and by the practices stated therein,
      one will attain unexcelled awakening
      and all kinds of joy along the way.

When they reflect on the above explanation of the universal vehicle, its teachings, and its results, the wise respect these teachings of the Buddha. If we wish to attain the complete awakening of a buddha, we should cultivate special faith in the universal vehicle and the bodhisattva path. That will inspire us to generate bodhichitta, enter the bodhisattva path, and follow it until we reach buddhahood. Even though we do not make specific effort to attain worldly happiness, we will nevertheless experience much worldly happiness along the way.

399. A Dharma—in essence compassion—
      consisting of generosity, ethical conduct, and fortitude
      was taught especially for householders.
      You should resolutely internalize it.

While the three practices of generosity, ethical conduct, and fortitude are also practiced by monastics, the Buddha taught them especially to householders because they are easier for householders to practice. The king can easily put these teachings into practice while ruling his kingdom. Here ethical conduct refers to the five precepts of male and female lay practitioners, as well as the eight precepts that householders can take for just a day. Nagarjuna encourages the king to become familiar with these practices and make sure they are supported by love, compassion, and bodhichitta so they will become the collection of merit. In addition, when doing these bodhisattva practices, reflect on the emptiness of the agent, object, and action, so that you also collect wisdom. Of course, this advice is meant for us as well as for the king.

400. However, if you are unable to rule in accord with Dharma,
    because the world is opposed to Dharma,
    then for the sake of Dharma and glory,
    it makes sense for you to become a monastic.

Advice to Ordain if You Are Unable to Engage in These Practices as a Lay Follower

As a king, if you find it is impossible to rule your kingdom according to Dharma, then you should become a monastic. Because sentient beings are unruly and have such harsh, rough minds overwhelmed with a multitude of afflictions, it can be difficult to govern them. If the only way to rule is by killing, beating, and punishing them, you will create a great deal of destructive karma and your Dharma practice will drastically degenerate. In this case, it is better for you to go forth from the householder life and become a monastic. This way you will create great virtue and be a good example for your subjects. They will respect you for that.

The reason Nagarjuna encourages the king to ordain is not because the king is weak-minded. Nor is he directing the king to neglect his duties or escape from his responsibilities. Rather, sentient beings' minds are filled with afflictions and to prevent them from harming each other, the king would have to inflict harm on them, thus creating a lot of nonvirtuous karma. Instead of being entangled in that samsaric web, it would be better for the king to become a monastic. That way he would create less destructive karma and it would send a strong message to his subjects that living according to the Dharma is more important than the power, glory, and wealth of kingship.

This completes the commentary on part IV of the *Precious Garland*, "Royal Policy: Instructions on the Practices of a Monarch."

V. Practices of a Bodhisattva

12. Abandoning Afflictions and Cultivating Goodness

To be fit to engage in the bodhisattva practices, we need to reduce our afflictions and misguided behavior as much as possible. This is easier to do when we have the support of precepts and live with others who are diligently practicing the path to awakening. For these reasons, it is helpful to become a monastic. Monastics have more time and freedom to study and practice the Dharma, and their simple lifestyle is conducive to maintaining ethical conduct.

ELIMINATING FAULTS

401. Thereupon, as a monastic you should first become serious about
      your training,
      focusing on the pratimoksha along with the Vinaya,
      and also on becoming learned
      and determining the meaning [of what you study].

402. Then you should eliminate those faults
      that are cited in the *Kshudravastuka*.
      Assiduously learn to recognize them,
      widely known to be fifty-seven in number.

After becoming a monastic, you should be serious about your training, paying special attention to ethical conduct. Vinaya, the monastic code, delineates the prohibitive precepts—the actions monastics are to abandon—and the prescriptive precepts—the activities they are to do. The *Pratimoksha Sutra*, which fully ordained monastics recite every fortnight during a ceremony to purify and restore their precepts, contains the list of prohibitive precepts. The Skandhaka section of the Vinaya describes the prescriptive precepts. You should learn these, reflect on them deeply, and put them into practice. Doing this will establish a sound basis for your Dharma practice.

For lay followers, taking the five lay precepts brings similar benefit. Whether we are monastics or lay followers, involvement in destructive physical and verbal actions impedes our cultivation of bodhichitta, engagement in the bodhisattva deeds, and fulfillment of the two collections. To stop physical and verbal negativities, we must tame our mind, for without the impetus of the mind's motivation, the body and speech do not act.

For this reason, Nagarjuna now points out fifty-seven defects in attitude and behavior that we need to diminish as much as possible and eventually forsake altogether. While you read about these fifty-seven faults in the ensuing verses, examine your mind and behavior and make many examples of when and how these faults manifest in you. Then contemplate the various antidotes to them so that when they arise, you can apply them and thus prevent these faults from taking control of your mind.

Abhidharma texts such as the *Treasury of Knowledge* by Vasubandhu and the *Compendium of Knowledge* by Asanga present the afflictive mental states in different ways. The *Precious Garland* was composed before either of these, and Nagarjuna relied on the enumeration of auxiliary afflictions (Skt. *upaklesa*) in the *Kshudravastuka*, an Abhidharma text that preceded Vasubandhu's and Asanga's treatises. In some cases, the names of the afflictions and their definitions are the same in all these texts, in other cases they are not. Do not get confused by different presentations. Rather, apply what these texts teach to your mind. With mindfulness, maintain awareness of your precepts and values; with introspective awareness, monitor which of these mental states arise in your mind. Swiftly apply Dharma antidotes when needed with a conscientiousness that cherishes ethical conduct.

> 403. Wrath is severe mental agitation;
> rancor comes from constantly having it.
> Concealment is hiding one's negativity.
> Hostility is an addiction to negativity.

1. *Wrath,* which arises from anger, is a strong animosity toward someone coupled with the desire to inflict harm on him. We become angry at someone or something, and when that anger builds up and becomes more intense, it becomes wrath.

2. *Rancor* is a strong sense of resentment due to habituating your-self to wrath over time. Similar to holding a strong grudge, it torments the mind.

3. *Concealment* hides our faults and negativities from others so that they won't think we've done the destructive actions we have done. When others point out our misdeeds, we deny them.

4. *Hostility* is a stubborn liking for bad behavior such that we are not willing to give it up, even if it harms us or the people we care about.

> 404. Dissimulation is deceptiveness;
>   pretension, crookedness of mind.
>   Jealousy is irritation at others' good qualities.
>   Miserliness is fear of giving.

5. *Dissimulation* refers to a way of deceiving others that uses decep-tion to make others think that we want to benefit them when we don't.

6. *Pretension* is pretending to have good qualities we don't have so that others will think well of us.

7. *Jealousy* is the inability to bear others' good qualities or opportu-nities due to our attachment to receiving gifts, service, or respect.

8. *Miserliness* is stinginess, holding tightly onto our possessions or Dharma knowledge out of fear of giving or sharing them.

> 405. Non-integrity is not to be ashamed of yourself;
>   inconsideration of others is not being embarrassed with regard
>   to others.
>   Haughtiness is the incapacity of honoring others.
>   Fury is a mental disturbance caused by anger.

9. *Non-integrity* means to not refrain from bad behavior due to a lack of self-respect. An example is to knowingly transgress our precepts when no one else is around without caring about it or having a sense of self-respect. The great masters remind us that since the buddhas' knowledge encompasses all phenomena, they are aware of our actions. This prevents us from recklessly

thinking we can do whatever we like as long as no one else knows.

10. *Inconsideration of others* refers to not refraining from bad behavior because we do not care about the impact it has on others. An example is behaving in a careless, unbecoming, or harmful way in front of others—friends, colleagues, or even our spiritual mentors—and not caring about the effect it has on them or how they view our conduct.

11. *Haughtiness* is an inflated sense of self that makes us unable to honor or respect those worthy of respect. Based on some small good quality we may have, we get puffed up and don't want to show respect to those who have genuine good qualities.

12. *Fury* is an angry mood that wishes to engage in bad behavior. It shows on our face in the form of furrowed brows, flushed complexion, and glaring eyes.

> 406. Being arrogant is being conceited.
>   To be heedless is to not apply oneself to virtue.
>   Pride is of seven kinds;
>   I will [now] explain each of them.

13. *Arrogance* is conceit or an inflated sense of self based on our possessions, good health, wealth, youth, social standing, learning, and so forth. It is a source of heedlessness.

14. *Heedlessness* is negligence and the lack of conscientiousness that wants to act in an unrestrained way without creating virtue or guarding the mind from bad activities.

15. The seven types of *pride* that follow are counted as one of the fifty-seven auxiliary afflictions.

> 407. Concerning these, the [first] is called "pride";
>   it is where one thinks of oneself
>   as even inferior to the inferior, equal to the equal,
>   or greater than or equal to the inferior.

(1) The first of the seven types of *pride* itself has three branches. The first is thinking we are *inferior to the inferior*, "I am the worst of the worst." This

is actually an exaggerated sense of self and a perverse pride, because we think we are somehow special because we are the worst. We're proud of how degenerate and depraved we are. The second branch of pride concerns thinking that *we are equal to the equal*—this pride enjoys competing with others. The third thinks *we are greater than or equal to the inferior*. Like the others, this form of pride is based on comparing ourselves to others, but the conclusion is that we are better than or equal to those we consider degenerate, lowly, or inferior people.

> 408. It is presumptive pride for one to presume
>   that one is equal to someone who is better.
>   If one presumes oneself to be
>   even better than one's betters,

> 409. this is pride beyond pridefulness,
>   thinking oneself to be even loftier than the lofty.
>   It is excessively bad,
>   like developing sores on top of one's boils.

(2) *Presumptive pride* refers to thinking we are equal to someone who is in fact better than us. For example, someone has a good trait, and we think we're just as good as she is when in fact we aren't.

(3) *Pride beyond pridefulness* is being particularly presumptuous, thinking that we are more excellent than the people who are superior to us. This type of pride is over the top, and for that reason it's compared to developing sores on top of boils. Having a boil is bad enough but to have sores on top of a boil means we think we're the best of the best. Nothing good is going to come from this, for it leads to rebirth in an unfortunate realm. Even when someone with pride beyond pridefulness is born as a human being, the person is ugly, stupid, and humiliated by others.

> 410. The five empty aggregates
>   are called "the appropriated."
>   When one apprehends them as I,
>   this is called the conceit of thinking "I am."

(4) *The conceit of thinking "I am"* is based on grasping the I as truly existent. It misapprehends the five aggregates, believing they truly exist, and then grasps a truly existent person in dependence on them. Based on this misapprehension of the aggregates that are the basis of designation of the person, this conceit proudly thinks, "I am." In fact, both the aggregates and the person are empty of true existence.

> 411. To presume that one has attained a result
>   that one has not attained is to have conceited pride.
>   The wise know that boasting
>   about one's negative deeds is erroneous pride.

(5) *Conceited pride* leads us to believe we have attained a result on the path that we haven't. For example, we think, "I've realized emptiness," when we've just had an unusual experience in meditation, or we think, "I am a bodhisattva" because one day our meditation on compassion went better than usual.

(6) *Erroneous pride* refers to boasting about our misdeeds. For example, we succeed in taking revenge on someone who harmed us in the past and feel especially proud of ourselves for accomplishing this. We relish our defiance and are proud of our harmful actions.

> 412. Deriding oneself, thinking,
>   "I cannot manage,"
>   is the pride of inferiority.
>   Such are the seven forms of pride, in brief.

(7) The *pride of inferiority* makes us feel overwhelmed and leads us to think, "I'm unable to cope with this." It also arouses depression, which thinks we are useless and no one cares about us. Holding such a wrong view of ourselves makes us demoralized, causes self-pity, and discourages us from engaging in virtue.

In brief in this verse could mean that this is a summary of what is explained in the *Abhidharma Sutra* or that it's the summary of many other different types of pride.

413. Hypocrisy is to restrain the senses
   for the sake of acquisition and respect.
   Flattery is to utter primarily pleasant phrases
   for the sake of acquisition and respect.

16. Nagarjuna now returns to the remaining fifty-seven afflictions, where the next five consist of the five wrong livelihoods. *Hypocrisy* refers to restraining our senses so that we look like an excellent Dharma practitioner in order to receive offerings, service, or respect from others.

17. *Flattery* is saying nice things to people with the intention that they will give us offerings or respect. This is very different from the virtuous practice of praising others' good qualities.

414. Hinting is praising others' possessions
   so that one might obtain them.
   Harassment is openly deriding others
   in order to acquire something from them.

415. The desire to acquire things through what has been acquired
   is to praise what has already been acquired.
   Carping is constantly remarking
   on the mistakes that others have made.

18. *Hinting* is praising others' possessions in the hopes of obtaining them.

19. *Harassment* is criticizing others—for example, accusing someone of being stingy or playing favorite in order to get something for ourselves. It is a form of coercion that puts someone in such an uncomfortable position that he will give us what we want.

20. *Insinuation* is the desire to acquire things by praising what we have received before with the hope that the person will give it to us again. This is the last of the five wrong livelihoods, which apply especially to monastics.

21. *Carping* or nagging is constantly talking about others' mistakes, reminding them of their errors, and discussing them with others as well.

416. Stupefaction is the state of being overwhelmed
     that comes from not thinking clearly or from illness.
     Boredom is the attachment of the lazy
     when they are deprived of what they need to support themselves.

417. Discrimination of differences is an attitude
     obscured by attachment, aversion, and confusion.
     The failure to examine one's mind
     is what is called inattention.

22. *Stupefaction* refers to being irritated, unable to think clearly, and feeling overwhelmed. It may come from illness or dissatisfaction.

23. *Boredom* is another kind of stupefaction. It arises due to dissatisfaction, laziness, and not having what you need. It can be caused by a lazy person's attachment to his inferior possessions.

24. *Discrimination of differences* is, for example, discriminating between self and others, between what I want and don't want, or between friend and enemy. Such discriminations are caused by attachment, aversion, and confusion.

25. *Inattention* is the opposite of introspective awareness. It does not monitor what is going on in our mind and is unaware if the mind is virtuous or nonvirtuous, or if it is under the influence of attachment, anger, or ignorance.

418. Not treating spiritual mentors in the manner of the Blessed One
     is the loss of respect that occurs
     due to being lazy about concordant activities.
     It is agreed that this makes one a negative person.

419. Longing is a lesser mental obscuration
     that comes from desirous attachment.
     Obsession comes from lusting for something;
     it is an extreme mental obscuration.

26. *Loss of respect* occurs when, out of *laziness*, we don't show respect for those who are worthy of respect—such as our spiritual mentors. This behavior is contradictory to what the Buddha prescribed.

27. *Becoming a negative person* refers to a spiritual teacher who is supposed to be teaching the Dharma but instead teaches an incorrect doctrine. Such a person is to be avoided.

28. Desirous attachment may be great, middling, or small. *Longing* arises from the smaller kind of desirous attachment. For example, when we think something is beautiful, longing for it will ensnarl us in sense objects and thus cause us to be entangled in cyclic existence. As we'll see in the next several auxiliary afflictions, there are many different kinds of attachment that differ in terms of strength or in terms of the object they desire.

29. *Obsession* stems from great desirous attachment. It craves and is obsessed with the objects of the five senses—sights, sounds, odors, tastes, and tactile objects—and is a great entanglement that forcefully keeps us trapped in cyclic existence.

420. Avarice is a mental state of attachment
    brought about by being attached to one's possessions.
    The attachment to others' possessions
    is called unsuitable greed.

421. Lusting in opposition to Dharma
    is to approve of attachment to women, who should be avoided.
    Fraud is when one who does not have good qualities
    pretends to have good qualities.

30. *Avarice* is having strong desire for and attachment to our own possessions such that we can't bear to part with them.

31. *Unsuitable greed* is also a form of attachment, but here the object is others' possessions. This covetousness thinks how nice it would be to have a beautiful thing that is owned by another person. This state of mind easily arises in us, especially in a shopping center.

32. *Lusting* is yet another form of attachment, but here the object is a person we are sexually attracted to. Motivated by lust, people glorify sexual relations, praise the qualities of someone they're attached to, and being distracted, they act in ways opposite to the Dharma.

33. *Fraud* is also a form of attachment. Desiring to make a good
      impression on others, we give them the impression we have good
      qualities we don't have.

   422. Great desire is an extreme yearning
        that leaves behind the good fortune of contentment.
        Craving approval means thinking,
        "I will be known as having good qualities, no matter what."

   423. Non-fortitude means that one is unable to bear it
        due to harm or when one suffers.
        Impropriety is the failure to respect what should be done
        with regard to preceptors and gurus.

34. *Great desire* is extreme greed. Lacking the fortune of being
      content with what we have, we constantly search for more and
      better.

35. *Craving approval,* we try to make others think we are rich, well
      connected, or whatever quality we believe will impress others.
      Extremely attached to what other people think of us, we try to
      create a good appearance or project a good reputation in order
      to gain praise, approval, and reputation from others.

36. *Non-fortitude* is not being able to tolerate any harm from oth-
      ers or even a small suffering that comes our way. We easily
      get upset when criticized and become anxious over a minor
      illness or injury.

37. *Impropriety* means not acting in the correct manner, specifi-
      cally a student not having respect for his or her preceptor—the
      one who gives them precepts and ordination—or their gurus—
      spiritual mentors. It also includes failing to show respect or to
      do what is proper in relation to our parents.

   424. Not heeding instructions means
        that one does not take seriously statements that accord with
            Dharma.
        Conceptuality concerning one's relatives
        is an attachment that [arises through] fondness for one's relatives.

425. Likewise to be attached to one's country
 is to overstate its good qualities.
 The notion that one will not die means that
 one is not concerned with death due to fearing it.

38. *Not heeding instructions* is disregarding and rejecting teachings, advice, or statements that are in accord with the Dharma. For example, if we act in a mistaken way and a friend comments on it with the wish to help us, we not only reject their advice but also retort, "Don't comment on my behavior, and I won't comment on yours."

39. Rampant *conceptuality concerning our relatives* is attachment mixed in with fondness and affection. Based on this we worry about our families, miss them, and long to see them.

40. *Attachment to our country* is to overstate its good qualities.

41. *The notion that we won't die* means that we refuse to think about death because we find it unnerving. While this isn't an affliction per se, it interferes with our practice of virtue and should be abandoned. Our mindfulness of death and impermanence will spur us to practice the Dharma now, without putting it off until later or thinking that we have to first create the perfect circumstances for Dharma practice before doing it.

426. Conceptuality in connection with recognition
 is thinking, "Somehow [I must make] people
 take me as their guru
 by virtue of my excellent qualities."

427. Conceptuality in connection with infatuation
 is to dwell on how
 one might help or hurt others,
 due to being affected by attachment or malice for them.

42. *Conceptuality in connection with recognition* involves telling others about our excellent qualities or acting in a way such that they will recognize us as a special person with the motivation

that they will take us as their guru, give us offerings, and benefit us in other ways as well. While similar to craving approval mentioned in verse 422, this is more specific, because here we seek perks from their viewing us as their spiritual mentor.

43. *Conceptuality in connection with infatuation* is the thought wanting to help others because we are attached to them. While in general helping others is good, here it is polluted by the motivation of attachment.

44. *Conceptuality in connection with malice* involves thinking how to harm someone because we bear ill will toward her. While this and the preceding one want to either help someone we're attached to or harm someone we don't like, the actions we do motivated by these are not definite to help or harm. Sometimes what we do with attachment to help someone harms her and what we do with malice to harm someone winds up benefiting her.

> 428. Erratic displeasure is an unsteady mind.
> Desiring union is a mind that is stained.
> Lassitude is the laziness of one who lacks energy—
> it comes from being physically listless.

45. *Erratic displeasure* means that sometimes we dislike somebody or something and sometimes we like that same one. It is an impulsive and fickle mind.

46. *Desiring union* does not necessarily refer to sexual union, but more generally wants to meet whatever object, person, or situation we find attractive. The mind is sullied by that attachment.

47. *Lassitude* is a type of laziness that arises from being physically inactive or exhausted. We become indifferent, lack enthusiasm for creating virtue, and procrastinate.

> 429. Affect is the transformation of body and face
> that occurs through negative mental states.
> Physical discomfort from eating too much food
> is physical sluggishness.

430. It is taught that the state of extreme mental dejection
    is mental depression.
    Longing for the desirable
    is yearning for the five sensory objects.

48. *Affect* is the transformation of our body and speech due to attachment. When we're attached to someone or something, our physical appearance and behavior as well as the tone of our voice and what we say changes from what it normally is.

49. *Physical discomfort* that comes from eating too much food is a form of lethargy and torpidity that doesn't want to eat more at that moment.

50. *Mental dejection* is a mind that is fainthearted, despondent, and discouraged. It may arise in relation to Dharma practice, feeling we just can't do it, or in relation to work.

51. Longing *for the desirable* means having sensual desire—attachment to our experience of the five sense objects. This and the next six can be grouped together to form the five hindrances to attaining serenity.

431. Harmful intent comes from nine causes—
    it is the intent to harm others on the part of one who is
        concerned
    about some misfortune in the three times
    with regard to oneself, one's friends, or one's enemies.

432. Dullness is a state of inactivity
    due to physical and mental heaviness.
    Drowsiness is sleep;
    excitement is a lack of physical and mental tranquility.

52. *Harmful intent* is ill will and malice; it arises from nine causes. With respect to ourselves, we think, "He harmed me, is harming me, or will harm me." With respect to our friends and relatives, we think, "She harmed my dear ones, is harming my dear ones, or will harm my dear ones." In relation to our enemies or the people we don't like, we think, "He helped my enemy, is helping

my enemy, or will help my enemy." When we think any one of these nine thoughts, our minds become deeply disturbed and we want to harm the other person.

53. *Dullness* refers to heaviness of the mind and body, which make one unsuitable for doing anything.

54. *Drowsiness* refers to sleepiness, a state when the five sense consciousnesses gather inside. The list of five hindrances counts dullness and drowsiness together as one, because in both the body and mind are listless and can't function properly.

55. *Excitement* is restlessness, when the mind is not peaceful and is distracted to objects of attachment. This differs from scattering when the mind cannot stay on the meditation object and may go to a diversity of objects—including objects of aversion or fear. In contrast, with excitement the mind is distracted specifically to an object of attachment.

> 433. Remorse is to lament one's negative activities;
>   it arises from agonizing about them later.
>   Doubt is to be of two minds about
>   the [four] truths, the Three Jewels, and so on.

56. *Remorse* is regret concerning an action that we feel wretched about having done. Excitement and remorse are counted as one in the list of the five hindrances because in both cases the mind is in turmoil and not peaceful. Remorse in this case does not refer to reasonable regret for our nonvirtue and misdeeds, which is virtuous, but to feelings of guilt and self-blame, when we agonize over a destructive action we did years ago in an unforgiving way that torments us. Such drastic self-recrimination is unrealistic and obscures the mind. Here remorse may also involve regret for our virtuous actions and kind deeds; this is nonvirtuous.

Regret is called a changeable mental factor, because depending on what we regret, it can be either virtuous or nonvirtuous. Sleep, investigation, and analysis are also changeable mental factors, depending on the situation. If we generate bodhichitta or think about the Dharma before falling asleep, the sleeping mind becomes virtuous. Going to sleep with desire or anger will make our sleep nonvirtuous. We create virtuous karma when we either superficially investigate or precisely analyze a virtuous object with a positive intention, whereas to do so with a nonvirtuous object and a harmful intention become nonvirtuous.

57. *Doubt* is being of two minds regarding important topics such as the four truths of the aryas, the Three Jewels, two truths, and karma and its effects. Doubt is uncertain about their existence and prevents us from going forward on the path. If left unremedied, doubt may increase and become a wrong view.

These fifty-seven faults are subdivisions of objects to be abandoned and are posited in different ways. Some are mental factors with their meanings; some are the causes of a given mental factor, revealing the way we think; and some are the bad behaviors that result from a particular mental factor. Although the mental state isn't always explicitly mentioned, we can get an idea of its causes or its resultant behavior. Because these fifty-seven make it difficult to generate bodhichitta and create obstacles to practicing the six perfections, they are to be abandoned by everyone who wants to be a bodhisattva—householder bodhisattvas and especially monastic bodhisattvas.

THE SIX PERFECTIONS AND COMPASSION

Once we have subdued the fifty-seven defects, we have fewer interfering obstacles and are in a better position to cultivate good qualities. Now Nagarjuna will explain the temporal good qualities—the six perfections and compassion, which are cultivated by all bodhisattvas. He follows this by describing the excellent qualities of the ten grounds, which pertain to the arya bodhisattvas, and the ultimate excellent qualities possessed only by buddhas.

434. A bodhisattva should forsake these [faults];
one with [monastic] precepts must forsake even more—
since when one is freed of these faults,
one can easily develop positive qualities.

435. In short, the good qualities that a bodhisattva should develop
are generosity, ethical conduct, fortitude,

joyous effort, meditative stability,
wisdom, compassion, and so on.

The more we free ourselves from the fifty-seven defects, the easier it will be to cultivate good qualities, specifically the six perfections: generosity, ethical conduct, fortitude, joyous effort, meditative stability, and wisdom. These and other good qualities are accomplished with compassion. *And so on* indicates that the bodhisattvas' practices are limitless but are subsumed in the six perfections.

The six practices of generosity and so forth are done by hearers and solitary realizers, and some of them are done by non-Buddhists as well. However, for them to become bodhisattvas' qualities and perfections, three unique factors are necessary. First, these activities must be motivated by uncontrived bodhichitta. Second, they must be supported by an understanding of emptiness—specifically, thinking that the agent doing the action, the object, and the action itself are empty of inherent existence and exist dependent on each other. Third, at the conclusion of the action, the merit must be dedicated to the attainment of full awakening. When cultivated as perfections in this way, these practices transcend people's usual generosity and so forth.

436. Generosity is to give up one's wealth;
        ethical conduct is to endeavor to help others;
        fortitude is the abandonment of anger;
        joyous effort is enthusiasm for virtue.

437. Meditative stability is unafflictive one-pointedness;
        wisdom is definitively determining the truths' meaning.
        Compassion is a state of mind that savors
        only loving-kindness for all sentient beings.

Individually Identifying the Meaning of Good Qualities

Generosity is the intention to give that is free from attachment, and motivated by this intention, it is the physical and verbal actions of giving. There are different types of generosity: the giving of possessions, love, protection, and the Dharma. Here Nagarjuna emphasizes the generosity of possessions—the wish to give away our wealth. There is discussion whether the karma of giving is the intention to give, the act of giving, or both. Sautrantikas and Chittamatrins believe that karma is the mental factor of intention—in this case the intention to give. For Vaibhashikas and Prasangikas the physical and verbal actions motivated by that intention are also karma.

Ethical conduct is usually defined as non-harmfulness and restraint from destructive behavior. In terms of the bodhisattva practices, however, it refers to giving up striving solely for our own purpose and instead endeavoring to benefit others and to accomplish their aims. This includes relinquishing the thought seeking our own liberation and instead striving for full awakening for the benefit of all sentient beings.

The act of giving up our own aims and working for others' aims helps to counteract the ten destructive paths of action. For example, when we engage in the three destructive physical actions of killing, stealing, and unwise or unkind sexual behavior, we do so to benefit ourselves, and our actions harm others. Now we refrain from those actions in order to benefit others. Similarly, we harm others when we engage directly or indirectly in the four verbal and three mental paths of nonvirtuous action, so we abandon them and act in an opposite manner in order to benefit others. The same way of thinking can be applied to the bodhisattva and tantric ethical restraints: transgressing them is motivated by self-centeredness. Instead we endeavor to keep them for the benefit of others.

To protect us from nonvirtue—the essence of ethical conduct—the Buddha recommended "binding the senses," which involves monitoring how we interact with the world around us. Instead of letting our eyes wander here and there, looking at any attractive object or person we happen to see, we keep our gaze focused on what we are doing. We are careful what music we listen to and how others' words can easily spark afflictions in us. Similarly, we are aware of what we allow our nose, tongue, and body sense faculties to come in contact with. Being mindful of our precepts and using introspective awareness to monitor the state of our mind increase our ability to bind the senses.

Those who follow the Prasangika system say that in addition to being the mental factor of intention, ethical conduct is also a type of form that is an object of mental consciousness. For example, when someone takes the pratimoksha precepts—monastic precepts and the five lay precepts— she receives a subtle imperceptible form that is said to act like a dam that prevents those actions. Ethical conduct is also form in that those who keep perfect ethical conduct have a brilliance or luster to their complexion that may be seen by ordinary people. Chandrakirti speaks about this in the *Supplement*, and perhaps you have also seen this with certain people.

Fortitude is also of three types: abandoning anger when others harm us, tolerating suffering such as sickness, and bearing hardships and difficulties when practicing the Dharma. "Tolerate" does not mean that we grit our teeth and bear it; such a mental state is not happy, relaxed, and peaceful. Here it means the ability to accept pain or difficulty without getting upset.

Joyous effort is taking delight in virtue. This enthusiastic attitude makes us eager to practice and enables us to complete all the other perfections as well as the two collections. *Meditative stability* is one-pointed concentration that is free of afflictive thoughts such as laxity and excitement.

Wisdom ascertains the meaning of the four truths and the two truths, which involves analyzing their different classifications and meanings. This wisdom is integrated with the aims of others, so that wisdom and method are combined. *Compassion* is the mind that views all sentient beings equally, with one taste, and wishes them to be free from duhkha and its causes. When supported by wisdom, compassion can be used skillfully to benefit others.

Each of these perfections is to be practiced with the others. We'll use the example of generosity to demonstrate this as follows. The *generosity of generosity* refers to giving the roots of virtue we've accumulated from being generous to all sentient beings. The *ethical conduct of generosity* means to abandon wrong attitudes such as wishing for our own liberation when practicing generosity. The *fortitude of generosity* involves not retaliating if the recipient of our generosity is ungrateful or harms us; it also means having the ability to endure any suffering that may arise while being generous, such as being cold or getting sick. The *joyous effort of generosity* is maintaining enthusiasm and taking delight in being generous. The *meditative stability of generosity* refers to maintaining our focus and concentration while giving, especially maintaining our motivation of bodhichitta. The *wisdom of generosity* sees the agent, object, and action of generosity as empty of true existence yet arising dependent on one another.

438. From generosity comes wealth; happiness from ethical conduct.
From fortitude comes beauty; splendor from joyous effort.

Through meditation, one is peaceful; through wisdom comes
liberation.
Compassion accomplishes all aims.

The Temporal Effects of Each Good Quality

These temporal results of each good quality occur while we are practicing the path, before we attain awakening. Generosity leads to great wealth, which we can then use to benefit others and create more merit. The result of ethical conduct is the happiness of a higher rebirth as a human being or god. While stainless prayers and our general practice of the six perfections also lead to higher rebirth, ethical conduct is principal.

The practice of fortitude leads us to having a body with a pleasing appearance. Due to this, others will be attracted to us, which gives us the opportunity to share the Dharma and benefit them. From joyous effort comes brilliance. A peaceful mind is a result of meditative stability, and wisdom is the principal cause of liberation from cyclic existence. Compassion enables us to accomplish all aims of ourselves and others. Knowing these results inspires us to create their causes as much as we can by practicing the six perfections.

This brings us to an interesting point. As discussed earlier, there are three kinds of phenomena: evident, slightly obscure, and very obscure. Each one is known through a different reliable cognizer: evident phenomena through our senses, slightly obscure phenomena through inference, and very obscure phenomena through scriptural authority or the authoritative testimony of a highly realized being.

When we look at the statements above—for example, that generosity in our present life leads to wealth in future lives—which of the three kinds of phenomena is at play? It definitely isn't an evident phenomenon, because we can't know this through our five senses—we can't see it or hear it. Since it must be understood by the mental consciousness, it must be either a slightly obscure or very obscure phenomenon.

For sure, the specific details of generosity leading to wealth is very obscure. Let's say Pat makes an offering to a charity today. Knowing exactly when this karma will produce its result, what kind of wealth Pat will receive, and what rebirth this karmic seed will produce can only be known by the authoritative testimony of a fully awakened being who can clearly see everything in the past, present, and future. Only a buddha has the omni-science necessary to know these specific details.

But we know there must be a reason that supports the general prin-ciple that wealth comes from generosity. But what is that reason? Is it the authoritative testimony of the Buddha—that he stated this and since only he has the full ability to know this and has no reason to deceive us, we can accept it? On the other hand, it makes sense that generosity leads to wealth—but how can we explain this using a syllogism such as "generosity leads to wealth because…"?

We don't need to rely on the authoritative testimony of the Buddha to understand, for example, that a table is impermanent. Although he did state this, we know it is true because we use various reasons such as "the table is impermanent because it is changing moment by moment." But the reason that proves happiness comes from virtue and suffering comes from nonvirtue is not as clear. We can take it further and ask, "Is the fact that suffering arises from afflictions and karma slightly obscure or very obscure? Is the fact that we attain liberation through practicing the true path slightly obscure or very obscure?"

As mentioned in chapter 1, highest good is realized first, then higher rebirth, because we ascertain the highest good by inference and higher rebirth by referring to a valid scripture. Thus the former is easier to ascertain.

Liberation and full awakening are slightly obscure phenomena that can be realized through inference by the power of the fact. With respect to the four truths, liberation—or true cessation—attained through meditating on the wisdom that understands emptiness—true path—is a slightly obscure phenomenon. True duhkha coming from afflictions and karma—true origin—is also a slightly obscure phenomenon. These can all be known through inference by the power of the fact, as explained by Nagarjuna in chapter 24 of *Treatise on the Middle Way*. Similarly, that happiness comes from virtue and suffering comes from nonvirtue is also slightly obscure. This would make it seem that wealth arising from generosity and the happiness of higher rebirths resulting from ethical conduct are also slightly obscure.

Citing scriptures that say these are actually very obscure phenomena, some people make the syllogism, "The scriptural passage 'from generos-ity arises wealth' is nondeceptive with respect to its indicated meaning, because it is a scripture that passes the three analyses." The three analyses are the criteria that demonstrate a scripture is valid. If we conclude that "from generosity arises wealth" is very obscure, it would seem that virtue yielding happiness and nonvirtue yielding unhappiness would also be very obscure. In that case, are the four truths very obscure? We can't say that.

Other people say that knowing the specifics of when a certain act of generosity will ripen into wealth and other such details are very obscure, but the general principle that wealth arises from generosity and suffering arises from nonvirtue are slightly obscure phenomena. However, giving the reason to prove this with a syllogism is very difficult. On the other hand, it seems reasonable and makes sense, so it's hard to say that it's very obscure. This is a controversial topic and there is much to think about here.

> 439. Through the simultaneous
> perfection of all seven,
> one attains the sphere of inconceivable wisdom—
> lordship over the world.

The General Result of the Six Perfections and Compassion

All seven refers to the six perfections and compassion. By becoming familiar with these on the learner paths—the bodhisattva paths of accumulation, preparation, seeing, and meditation—and continually enhancing them, we will finally attain the sphere of inconceivable wisdom, the wisdom of a completely perfect buddha. *Lordship over the world* indicates that we will also become the protector of the three worlds of sentient beings[37] by attaining the state of peerless awakening. Ordinary beings cannot know the state of full awakening as it is—it is beyond our thoughts. Only other buddhas can actually see it directly.

---

37. *The three worlds of sentient beings* refers to the desire, material, and immaterial realms, or alternatively to the world under, on, and above the ground.

13. Excellent Qualities of the Ten Bodhisattva Grounds

Having encouraged us by explaining the temporal results of the excellent qualities that arise from practicing the six perfections and compassion, Nagarjuna now turns to the special excellent qualities of the arya bodhisattvas on the ten grounds. These qualities are difficult to fathom, but if we practice well, we will definitely attain them because causes bring their results.

INTRODUCTION

In this section we will discuss the entity of the bodhisattva grounds and the way that each ground attains its various qualities. But first, an introduction to the bodhisattva grounds will prepare us to delve more deeply into the subject.

A bodhisattva's unpolluted wisdom that directly realizes emptiness and is supported by the special method of compassion, bodhichitta, and so forth is called an ultimate ground and ultimate bodhichitta. A person who has this ultimate bodhichitta is an ultimate bodhisattva, a bodhisattva on any of the ten bodhisattva grounds. The first bodhisattva ground begins at the time a bodhisattva becomes an arya and actualizes the bodhisattva path of seeing.

This wisdom realizing emptiness is called a "ground" because it is the ground or basis for attaining higher qualities, just as the earth is the basis for harvests. It is called an "arya ground" because it is the basis or foundation for attaining the higher qualities of aryas.

On the arya path, bodhisattvas have periods of meditative equipoise on emptiness and times when they do other activities, the latter being called "subsequent attainment." The wisdom of meditative equipoise is of three types: (1) uninterrupted paths that eliminate certain levels of afflictions,

(2) liberated paths that occur when a certain level of afflictions has been forever abandoned and can never arise again, (3) meditative equipoise which is neither of those two—for example, the meditative equipoise that occurs after a liberated path and before the next uninterrupted path. All three of these are unpolluted by either the appearance of true existence or true-grasping. Aside from that, all other consciousnesses—including those of an arya in the time of subsequent attainment—are polluted by ignorance or its latencies. Ignorance here is the true-grasping ignorance, which is not completely abandoned until the eighth ground. The latencies of ignorance are the stains of ignorance that remain even after ignorance itself has been eradicated. They are completely eliminated just before attaining buddhahood.

We can compare ignorance to onions in a pot and the latencies of ignorance to the smell of onions that remains after the onions have been removed. Ignorance and other afflictions are afflictive obscurations that are eradicated upon attaining arhatship if someone is a hearer or solitary realizer, or upon attaining the eighth bodhisattva ground if one follows the bodhisattva path. The latencies of ignorance as well as the appearance of true existence that they cause are both cognitive obscurations. Bodhisattvas eliminate them during the eighth, ninth, and tenth grounds, which are called "pure grounds" because they are no longer polluted by ignorance and other afflictive obscurations, even during subsequent attainment. Full awakening is attained after the tenth ground, upon the eradication of the cognitive obscurations. Hearer and solitary realizer arhats are also no longer polluted by ignorance, although their mindstreams are still polluted by the latencies of ignorance when they are not in meditative equipoise on emptiness. The only type of mind in the continua of sentient beings—beings who are not buddhas—that is unpolluted and free from the influence of ignorance and its latencies is an arya's meditative equipoise on emptiness.

The wisdom of subsequent attainment functions after bodhisattvas arise from meditative equipoise on emptiness. This wisdom is of two types: the wisdom that engages in the method aspect of the path—it practices generosity, ethical conduct, and fortitude, teaches the Dharma, and so forth—and the wisdom that pertains to the wisdom aspect of the path—it sees all phenomena as like illusions. After aryas arise from meditative equipoise on emptiness, phenomena still appear truly existent to them due to their cognitive obscurations. However, they know that such appearances are false and like illusions.

Although ultimate bodhichitta—the wisdom realizing emptiness—is not manifest during arya bodhisattvas' subsequent attainment, the mind at this time is still referred to as a ground. Bodhisattvas progress sequentially through the ten grounds by the force of their collection of merit and the gradual eradication of defilements. Each ground abandons its own portion of defilements. Ignorance and afflictions are not abandoned all at once but gradually throughout the first seven grounds. The latencies of ignorance and the subtle dualistic appearance are eliminated gradually during the last three grounds, which are called "pure grounds" because they are free from afflictive obscurations.

The division of ultimate bodhichitta into ten grounds is done on the basis of the increase of four types of good qualities that occur from one ground to the next:

1. *A set of twelve qualities that increases from one ground to the next.*
   On the first ground, in one instant, these arya bodhisattvas are able to: directly see the faces of a hundred buddhas, receive the blessings of those hundred buddhas, go to a hundred buddha realms, see a hundred buddha fields, vibrate a hundred worldly realms, live for a hundred eons, see a hundred eons into the past and a hundred eons in the future, enter into and arise from a hundred different concentrations due to their great mental agility, open a hundred different doors of doctrine, mature a hundred sentient beings, emanate a hundred bodies, and surround each of those bodies with a retinue of a hundred arya bodhisattvas.

   On the first ground, arya bodhisattvas can to do all twelve amazing activities, listed above, in an instant. On the second ground, bodhisattvas receive the blessings of one thousand buddhas, go to one thousand buddha realms, see one thousand buddha fields, and so on. On the third ground, the number is one hundred thousand; on the fourth, one billion; on the fifth, ten billion; on the sixth, one trillion; on the seventh, one quadrillion; on the eighth ground, the number of all the atoms of one hundred quadrillion worlds; on the ninth, the number of atoms in one quintillion worlds; on the tenth, the number of atoms in an inexpressible number of buddha lands. In addition, these bodhisattvas have the incredible qualities of spontaneous, uncontrived bodhichitta and the wisdom realizing emptiness nondually.

2. *The ability of each ground to purify different levels of defilements and to progress to a higher path.* Each ground has the power to purify a specific portion of defilements, thus making the mind progressively purer. This is compared to the waxing moon, where more and more of the moon appears while the shadow decreases.

3. *The perfection that is brought to a superior level of excellence.* On the first ground the practice of the perfection of generosity reaches a superior level of excellence; on the second, ethical conduct; the third through the tenth respectively are fortitude, joyous effort, meditative stability, wisdom, skillful means, unshakable resolve, power, and exalted wisdom.

   The six perfections exist in a complete form only at the Buddha's ground. However, the practice of the six perfections exists from the bodhisattva path of accumulation through the end of the continuum of a sentient being. On each of the ten grounds the practice of one of the perfections reaches a superior level of excellence.

4. *The ripening rebirth that the bodhisattvas are able to take by choice through the power of their aspiration and roots of virtue in order to benefit others.* Just as the power of bodhisattvas' prayers and virtuous roots increase as they progress through the ten grounds, so does their ability to intentionally take different ripening rebirths to benefit sentient beings.

Bodhisattvas on the first ground are able to take rebirth as a wheel-turning monarch with control over the southern continent, Jambudvipa; on the second ground, as a wheel-turning monarch with control over all four continents; on the third ground, with control over the Heaven of the Thirty-Three; on the fourth, with control over the Heaven Free of Combat; on the fifth, with control over Tushita; on the sixth, with control over the Heaven Delighting in Emanations; on the seventh, with control over the Heaven Controlling Others' Emanations. The two wheel-turning monarchs are human rebirths, whereas the next five are lords of the five levels of the desire realm gods. Bodhisattvas are born as the chief among those gods and work for their benefit.

On the eighth ground, bodhisattvas can be born as a wheel-turning monarch with power over the three thousand worlds. One world consists of the sun, moon, Mount Meru, and everything from Brahma's world downward. A thousand of these is called "one thousand worlds." Two thousand worlds is one thousand worlds squared—that is, a million. Three thousand worlds is one thousand worlds to the third power—that is, a billion. This is called the worldly realm of the great thousand of the three thousand worlds. Sometimes it is simply referred to as the "three thousand worlds."

On the ninth ground, bodhisattvas' ripening rebirth is as a great Brahma, lord of a million worlds; on the tenth ground, it is as Maheshvara, king of the gods in the Highest Land.

The purpose of being born as a monarch with control over Jambudvipa or any of the other places is that you have the power to do a lot of good. Even on our planet, the leaders of countries have tremendous power to affect the citizens for the better or for the worse. One reason Nagarjuna taught the *Precious Garland* to a king is that if arya bodhisattvas are in governing positions, they will serve the people well and improve conditions on the planet. Of course, as long as we are in cyclic existence, suffering will still exist; but for bodhisattvas who want to benefit sentient beings in a temporal way and ultimately lead them to the highest good, worldly power is an asset. When a wheel-turning buddha appears in the world, the power of the wheel-turning monarchs and of all leaders diminishes and their magnificence is outshone. All beings who have created good karma, including celestial beings, humans, demigods, and gandharvas (heavenly musicians who dwell in the wilderness), bow down to the Buddha.

THE TEN GROUNDS

440. Just as the eight grounds of the hearer
are discussed in the hearer vehicle,
so too the ten grounds of the bodhisattva
are taught in the universal vehicle.

The Ten Bodhisattva Grounds: Their Entities and Qualities

The hearer vehicle explains eight grounds, each with its individual name and qualities: stream-enterer, once-returner, and so on. Similarly, the ten grounds of arya bodhisattvas are explained in the universal vehicle. These grounds surpass the practice and attainments of ordinary bodhisattvas on the paths of accumulation and preparation.

> 441. The first of these is called the Joyous
>   because the bodhisattvas experience great joy,
>   since the three fetters have been eliminated
>   and they have been born into the tathagata family.

> 442. Through the maturation of that [ground],
>   the perfection of generosity becomes supreme,
>   they are able to make a hundred worlds quake,
>   and they become the Great Lord of Jambudvipa.

In these and the upcoming series of verses, Nagarjuna bases his explanation on the *Sutra of the Ten Grounds*. The first ground is called the *Joyous* because it is free of the portion of afflictions that are objects to be abandoned by the path of seeing. This uninterrupted path eliminates those afflictions by applying the actual antidote: the wisdom directly and nonconceptually realizing emptiness. In the liberated path that immediately follows the uninterrupted path, these afflictions have been abandoned in such a way that they have been eradicated from that person's mindstream. In the period of subsequent attainment, this bodhisattva then experiences a unique joy from being free of that portion of the afflictions.

To put this in the form of a syllogism: there is a reason to call the first ground the Joyous, because it generates a unique joy from being free of the objects to be abandoned by the path of seeing. The objects to be abandoned by a first ground bodhisattva are the three fetters: the acquired forms of the view of a personal identity, doubt, and the view of rules and practices (also called the view that holds bad ethics and modes of conduct as supreme). A stream-enterer in the hearer vehicle also abandons these three fetters. While they are explicitly mentioned as objects of abandonment of a first grounder, this bodhisattva also abandons the acquired forms of all afflictions, including the acquired forms of all five afflictive views.

When bodhisattvas attain the first ground, they are born into the tathagata family or tathagata lineage. Being born into the tathagata lineage and having the tathagata lineage are not the same. All sentient beings have the tathagata lineage—or buddha nature—the potential to become a fully awakened buddha. However, in the short term it is not sure if we will enter the hearer, solitary realizer, or bodhisattva vehicle. When a bodhisattva is born into the tathagata lineage, this means he or she has gone beyond the hearers and solitary realizers and cannot fall back to become one of them, let alone be born as a hell being, hungry ghost, or animal. This bodhisattva is definitely progressing toward full awakening.

First grounders develop a particular ability to shake a hundred worldly realms, one of the twelve qualities mentioned above. The ripening result is that they can choose to take rebirth as a wheel-turning monarch with control over our world, traditionally known as Jambudvipa.

On the first ground, bodhisattvas' practice of generosity becomes superior, greatly exceeding the practice of generosity done by the ordinary bodhisattvas on the paths of accumulation and preparation. First grounders' practice of generosity is such that if somebody asked them to give away their arms, legs, fingers, eyes, or the like, they would be able to do so happily, without any suffering or sense of loss, and without creating any nonvirtue. This is impossible for a bodhisattva on the small, medium, or great levels of the path of accumulation or on any of the four levels of the path of preparation—heat, peak, fortitude, or highest mundane dharma. While these lower bodhisattvas will happily and without hesitation give away their wealth and possessions, they are not able to give away parts of their body in the same way. They have some apprehension about doing this because they will experience physical pain and mental suffering. Knowing that they will eliminate great suffering by experiencing this comparatively small suffering, they put effort into practicing generosity of parts of their body. However, they do not feel the same joy while doing this that first grounders do.

443. The second ground is called the Stainless
    because [bodhisattvas'] tenfold activities
    of body, speech, and mind are stainless,
    and they naturally adhere to those [ethical activities].

444. Through maturation of that [ground] the perfection of ethical
    conduct becomes supreme;
they become glorious rulers with the seven treasures, wheel-
    turning monarchs, beneficent to beings.
Through its maturation they become monarchs that rule all four
    continents,
and they gain expertise in turning beings away from unethical
    behavior.

The second ground is called *Stainless* because the ten nonvirtuous paths
of actions do not stain the body, speech, and mind of these bodhisattvas,
neither when awake nor asleep. They do not even dream about creating
destructive actions, but rather they spontaneously abide in pure ethical
conduct without the need to exert a lot of effort. First ground bodhisattvas
are not able to practice ethical conduct in quite the same way; their ethical
conduct is not unstained in their dreams.

As a ripening result of second grounders' supreme practice of ethical
conduct, they are able to take birth as a glorious wheel-turning monarch
with control over the four continents and in possession of the seven precious possessions—the precious wheel, jewel, queen, minister, elephant,
horse, and general—which are symbolic of worldly power. These bodhisattvas have a thousand sets of twelve qualities in the time of subsequent
attainment.

According to the Chittamatrins and below, a cause of a ripening result
must be either polluted nonvirtue or polluted virtue. However, Madhyamikas also accept unpolluted ripening causes. For example, Madhyamikas
posit the signs and marks of the Buddha as ripening results of the unpolluted, uninterrupted paths of the ten grounds. This is the same as saying
that they are the ripening results of the practice of the ten perfections.
In addition, each of the grounds has ripening results of practice, such as
being able to take birth as a wheel-turning monarch with control over
four continents. These unpolluted ripening results experienced by arya
bodhisattvas are produced by concordant causes: unpolluted virtue created
on the bodhisattva path.

Due to having such perfect ethical conduct, second grounders attain
a peaceful radiance—a physical characteristic that sets them apart from
lower bodhisattvas. In general, people with pure ethical conduct tend to

have such radiance, and it is even more pronounced with second grounders. For example, many people who see His Holiness the Dalai Lama think
that he appears differently than other people.

> 445. The third ground is [called] the Luminous
>   because the light of peaceful wisdom arises,
>   the concentrations and superknowledges have arisen,
>   and attachment and anger have completely ceased.

> 446. Through the maturation of that [ground],
>   they practice supreme fortitude and joyous effort;
>   they become the celestials' skilled,
>   great lord who averts all sensual desire.

The third ground is called the *Luminous* because while these bodhisattvas
one-pointedly meditate on emptiness, a sign that is like a light appears.
Called the "light indicating the end of all obstacles is approaching," it sig-
nals the impending end of cognitive obscurations. These bodhisattvas must
attain only a few more grounds before buddhahood. The light does not
appear to the mind of meditative equipoise, nor does that mind attend
to the light, because only emptiness appears to this mind of meditative
equipoise—no conventional phenomena appear to it. However, while these
bodhisattvas sit in meditation, there is the appearance of a light shining
on them, as if they were sitting in the sun with the sunlight striking them.
This is a sign that the end of all obstacles is approaching.

When those bodhisattvas arise from meditation, a light resembling the
red light at dawn appears to their wisdom of subsequent attainment. It is
like an appearance of the radiance of a light. For example, an electric light
has a white radiance that exudes from it but does not appear to it. In the
same way, the light comes from that wisdom of meditative equipoise but
does not appear to it and is not realized by it.

Third ground bodhisattvas attain the four concentrations of the material realm, four immaterial absorptions, five superknowledges, and four
immeasurables in a way superior to before.

When Nagarjuna says *attachment and anger have completely ceased*,
this does not mean that these bodhisattvas have completely eradicated all
attachment, anger, and ignorance. Further degrees of these afflictions will

be eliminated later on; only the attachment and anger that are the portion of the objects to be abandoned by the third ground have been extinguished.

Some forms of attachment and anger arise due to grasping the person as self-sufficient substantially existent. On the first seven grounds, different portions of this *innate* grasping and its seeds are ceased; the *acquired* form was abandoned previously at the first ground. When a portion of this grasping is abandoned, so is the corresponding portion of attachment and anger that arises due to it.

Similarly, on each of the first seven grounds a portion of the innate true-grasping and its seeds is ceased. When that portion on each ground is abandoned, the attachment and anger that arise due to it are also extinguished. All true-grasping, its seeds, attachment, and anger are extinguished by the eighth ground.

On the third ground, bodhisattvas excel in the practice of the perfection of fortitude. Not only do they not get upset in the slightest if somebody harms their possessions, but they do not get upset even if someone were to cut up their body in small pieces. Undisturbed, they have special empathy and compassion for the person cutting them. Their fortitude and compassion increase as a result of the harm they receive.

When we hear that each ground excels in the practice of a particular perfection, it doesn't mean that the other perfections don't also improve on that ground—they do. For example, although bodhisattvas' practices of the perfections of generosity and ethical conduct became supreme on the first and second grounds respectively, these practices continue to improve on the third and fourth grounds, and so on. The practice of the perfection of joyous effort, which will become supreme on the fourth ground, also increases on the third ground because bodhisattvas exert great effort with a joyful mind when practicing fortitude.

The ripening result of third grounders is to be reborn as a lord of the Heaven of the Thirty-Three. They are also able to be born as Indra, lord of gods, or as other powerful gods. Bodhisattvas deliberately take these kinds of births for the sake of others, in order to accomplish others' aims.

> 447. The fourth is called the Radiant
>   because the radiance of true wisdom arises,
>   and [bodhisattvas] distinctively develop
>   all the aids to awakening.

448. Through the maturation of that [ground]
    they become the celestial ruler in the abode of the Suyana
      [deities].
    They become skilled,
    destroying the source of the view of a personal identity.

The fourth ground is called the *Radiant*. On this ground, bodhisattvas excel in the practice of the perfection of joyous effort, and through that they radiate the light of pacifying *wisdom*, a light that is far superior to that of the third ground. During meditative equipoise, third grounders have a light that resembles the sunlight at dawn, but the light of the fourth grounder is far more radiant during both meditative equipoise and subsequent attainment. This is due to having a superior practice of wisdom that is adept in the subtle points of the *thirty-seven aids to awakening*. The ripening result of the fourth ground is birth as a monarch in the Heaven Free of Combat, the third of the desire god realms.

Regarding these bodhisattvas being skilled and destroying the source of the view of a personal identity, we can understand that bodhisattvas destroy the ignorance that supports the view of a personal identity grasping the person as self-sufficient substantially existent or that they destroy the ignorance that accompanies the view of a personal identity grasping the person as inherently existent. In either case, it is that portion of ignorance and of the view of a personal identity that is abandoned by the fourth ground.

449. The fifth is the Indomitable,
    since one cannot be subdued by any demons,
    and one gains expertise in knowing
    the subtle meaning of the aryas' truths and such.

450. Through the maturation of that [ground]
    they become the celestial ruler of Tushita
    and refute all the tirthikas' beliefs
    concerning the efficacy of austerities.

Fifth ground bodhisattvas are called the *Indomitable* because the maras—worldly demon gods—and their retinue are not able to overcome or defeat them. These bodhisattvas excel in the practice of the perfection of meditative

stability and gain expert wisdom in being able to distinguish and comprehend the subtle points of the four truths of the aryas.

Fifth grounders' ability to stay one-pointedly on their object of meditation is remarkable. They can enter into and emerge from various levels
of meditative absorptions of the material and immaterial realms. Their
meditative stability is much superior to that of the fourth grounders due
to their incredible qualities—they have abandoned more defilements and
the method that sustains their meditation is much stronger. While ordinary
beings who haven't entered a path and non-Buddhists can attain serenity,
their concentration is nowhere near that of the fifth ground bodhisattvas.

The ripening result for fifth ground bodhisattvas is the ability to take
birth in the desire god realm called Tushita. This is different from the
Tushita where the future Buddha, Maitreya, resides.

Motivated by wrong views and other afflictions, non-Buddhists—
tirthikas—may try to debate with these bodhisattvas. However, the tirthikas
are unable to defeat them; the qualities of the fifth ground bodhisattva are
beyond our conception.

> 451. The sixth is called the Approaching
>   because they approach the qualities of a buddha
>   and are enhanced by the attainment of cessation
>   through uniting insight and serenity.

> 452. Through the maturation of that [ground],
>   they become lord of the Celestials Who Delight in Emanations.
>   Unsurpassable by the hearers,
>   they eliminate arrogant pride.

Fourth, fifth, and sixth ground bodhisattvas each attain a particular wisdom
practice. On the fourth ground it is the wisdom that is expert in understanding the subtle points of the thirty-seven aids to awakening; on the fifth a
wisdom of the subtle points of the four truths of the aryas; and on the sixth a
wisdom that is expert in the subtle points of the forward and reverse order of
the twelve links. The sixth ground is also when bodhisattvas attain a superior
practice of the perfection of wisdom. For these reasons, this ground is called
the *Approaching* because these bodhisattvas are approaching awakening and
are much closer to it than bodhisattvas on the lower grounds.

Bodhisattvas on the fifth ground excel in the practice of the perfection of meditative stability, and bodhisattvas on the sixth ground excel in the practice of the perfection of wisdom. Combining these together, sixth grounders unite serenity and insight—serenity being the refinement of concentration and insight the cultivation of wisdom. In this way, they attain a very powerful mind that meditates on emptiness. Just as a group of blind people can quickly go where they want to go when accompanied by someone who can see, the practices of generosity, ethical conduct, and so on can quickly bring their results in full awakening due to this powerful wisdom that sees the ultimate nature.

While the union of serenity and insight can be developed even before entering the path as well as on the path of accumulation, its object is not emptiness. Rather, it focuses on the disadvantages of the lower levels of meditative concentration and the benefits of the higher levels, in this way invigorating practitioners to attain higher levels of concentration. It may also focus on subtle impermanence and so forth.

Practitioners who have gained serenity and realized emptiness before entering the path have the wisdom arising from contemplation focused on emptiness, but not the wisdom arising from meditation focused on emptiness. Thus at that level they do not have a union of serenity and insight focused on emptiness. The wisdom that arises from meditation focused on emptiness comes only on the heat level of the path of preparation; it is not present on the path of accumulation. One simultaneously attains the insight viewing emptiness, the wisdom arising from meditation on emptiness, the union of serenity and insight on emptiness, and the heat stage of the path of preparation of the universal vehicle.

The union of serenity and insight of the sixth ground bodhisattvas is unique and far superior to that of lower-level bodhisattvas because now their union of serenity and insight is supported by qualities of the method aspect of the path that were previously not present.

Bodhisattvas from the sixth ground onward also attain the equipoise of cessation, as uniquely described by the Prasangikas. Here *cessation* means emptiness. On the sixth ground, bodhisattvas attain the ability to absorb their mind directly into emptiness for long periods of time. Of course, on the fourth and fifth grounds bodhisattvas are able to meditate on emptiness, but not in the same way as the sixth-level bodhisattva.

The reason for calling emptiness "cessation" is that space is the pure emptiness of all physical obstruction; it is a void that is the absence of its object of negation—physical obstruction. Similarly, emptiness is the absence of its object of negation—true existence, inherent existence, and so on. Since it is a pure emptiness in which all those objects of negation have been ceased, it is called cessation. Bodhisattvas enter into meditative equipoise on that cessation or emptiness.[38]

There are ordinary and unique ways of entering into meditative absorption, and there are also different levels of emptiness because there are different assertions of selflessness. The selflessness Vaibhashikas and Sautrantikas assert is superficial, while that asserted by members of the upper systems is subtler. The selflessness asserted by the Prasangikas is the subtlest. The same applies to cessation—some are subtler and others grosser. Similarly, there are corresponding differences in the subtlety of the mind that absorbs into those cessations.

The *attainment of cessation* refers to the absorption into cessation, a meditation in which cessation is the object. From the sixth ground onward bodhisattvas attain a unique absorption into cessation that does not occur on or before the fifth ground. This is because their way of absorbing into cessation is held by the superior practice of the perfection of wisdom.[39] For this reason, sixth grounders are said to have an intelligence that is advanced in the union of serenity and insight.

The ripening result is being born as the lord of the Heaven of Delighting in Emanations.

---

38. Although inherent existence has never existed, it is said to have ceased when one directly realizes the emptiness of inherent existence because the appearance of inherent existence and grasping at inherent existence are not present at that time. That wisdom realizes only emptiness.

39. Prasangika proponents say that absorption in cessation is an exalted wisdom of single-pointed meditative equipoise on emptiness that depends on the supramundane path that attains it and the mind of the peak of existence. There are two ways of talking about the common and unique absorptions in cessation: (1) The unique is qualified by a superior practice of the perfection of wisdom on the sixth ground and above, while the common one is shared with the first through the tenth grounds; (2) The absorption into emptiness as asserted by the Prasangika system is unique, and that which is explained in Vasubandhu's *Treasury of Knowledge* and Asanga's *Compendium of Knowledge* (*Abhidharmasamucchaya*) is common. According to some schools, the absorption in cessation is a state in which the coarse mind and mental factors have been temporarily stopped. This type of absorption in cessation does not realize emptiness.

Sixth ground bodhisattvas are *unsurpassable by the hearers* and solitary realizers in terms of their intelligence. From the seventh ground onward, bodhisattvas outshine fundamental vehicle arhats through the power of their wisdom. Because sixth grounders are close to the seventh ground, hearers cannot surpass these bodhisattvas or outshine their wisdom.

Because they have a unique absorption in cessation, excel in the practice of the perfection of wisdom, are unsurpassable by hearer arhats, and are close to the seventh ground where they overcome hearer and solitary realizer arhats by the power of their mind, sixth ground bodhisattvas overcome those with the pride of superiority—the pride of fundamental vehicle arhats. Of course, their "pride" is not afflictive pride because as arhats, they have eliminated all afflictions.

453. The seventh is the Far Advanced
    because the number [of excellent qualities] has advanced far,
    since on this [ground] they enter moment by moment
    into the equipoise of cessation.

454. Through the maturation of that [ground],
    they become the powerful ruler of the celestials.
    They become a great leader of Jnanacharyas,
    knowing the realizations of the aryas' [four] truths.

Seventh ground bodhisattvas have advanced much further than sixth grounders. In one very short instant, they are able to enter into and arise from the unique absorption in cessation—emptiness—that was attained on the sixth ground. Because they excel in the practice of the perfection of skillful means, their way of entering into and arising from absorption in cessation is more adept: they can do it very quickly, and their intelligence is sharper, more proficient, and agile. Their agility in meditation resembles that of a skilled cyclist who does not wobble or become unsteady however fast he may go.

Arya bodhisattvas outshine hearers and solitary realizers in two ways— once on the first ground and again on the seventh ground. On the first ground, they outshine them through their lineage, because in addition to having the wisdom directly perceiving emptiness, they have the practices of special method supported by bodhichitta. This is similar to a monarch's child; from the moment she is born, she is served and honored even by the monarch's senior ministers. This is due to her royal lineage, which surpasses the lineage of the ministers. Similarly, first ground bodhisattvas are of the tathagata lineage and are on their way to awakening. Just as the ministers are initially more knowledgeable than the royal child, hearer arhats have eliminated all afflictive obscurations whereas first grounders have not. However, just as the royal child will one day become the monarch while the ministers will not, arya bodhisattvas will one day become buddhas. This is the meaning of first ground bodhisattvas outshining hearer and solitary realizer arhats through their lineage.

On the seventh ground, bodhisattvas outshine fundamental vehicle arhats through the power of their wisdom, because they can enter into and arise from meditation on emptiness in each brief instant. This is extremely difficult to do because in meditative equipoise on emptiness the mind and emptiness are one taste, but these bodhisattvas can go back and forth between cognizing ultimate truth and conventional truth very quickly. Seventh ground bodhisattvas are like the monarch's child as an educated and intelligent youth. Because she is close to being a monarch herself, she outshines the ministers, just as seventh grounders outshine hearer arhats by the power of their wisdom.

The ripening result is being able to take birth as a king of gods in the Heaven of Controlling Others' Emanations.

These bodhisattvas have wisdom understanding the four truths, the thirty-seven aids to awakening, and the forward and reverse orders of the twelve links superior to that which they had previously attained. They also possess an excelling practice of the perfection of method that supports that wisdom. As a result of these qualities and attainments, they have powerful intelligence, and they become great leaders among the knowledgeable teachers.

455. The eighth is the youth's ground, the Immovable,
  because, free of conceptions, they are unshakable.
  The range of their physical, verbal,
  and mental activities is inconceivable.

456. Through the maturation of this [ground],
  they become a Brahma who rules a thousand worlds;
  they are unsurpassed by the hearers and solitary realizers
  in determining the meaning of the Dharma.

Bodhisattvas on the eighth ground cannot be moved by the apprehension of signs or by the conception apprehending a self—both refer to true-grasping—or by the stains of the afflictive obscurations. Ordinary bodhisattvas and other ordinary beings who have not abandoned true-grasping are not able to understand the range of the physical, verbal, and mental activities of these bodhisattvas just as they are. That is, the way in which those bodhisattvas engage in virtuous activities of body, speech, and mind and the vastness of their virtuous activities is inconceivable for others.

The ripening result of the eighth ground is the ability to become a great Brahma king of the thousand worlds and thereby perform actions that are vastly beneficial for others. Hearer and solitary realizer arhats cannot surpass these bodhisattvas in analyzing, understanding, and explaining the meaning of the Dharma.

Eighth ground bodhisattvas and fundamental vehicle arhats have both eradicated the afflictive obscurations, and there is no difference between them from this point of view. However, they differ from the viewpoint of method because fundamental vehicle arhats do not have the exceptional factors of the method side of the path that bodhisattvas have. In order to gain these factors, those arhats have to follow the guidance of a spiritual mentor of the universal vehicle and generate bodhichitta by training in the seven-point cause-and-effect instruction or in equalizing and exchanging self and others. Upon gaining uncontrived bodhichitta, they then enter the bodhisattva path of accumulation, and from there up to the eighth ground they do not have any further objects to be abandoned since they have already abandoned afflictive obscurations. Upon reaching the eighth ground, they have to begin to abandon cognitive obscurations. From the path of accumulation through the end of the tenth ground, they must create great merit by training in the vast bodhisattva practices and then fulfill the collections of merit and wisdom in order to become a buddha.

> 457. The ninth, like a regency,
>   is called Excellent Intelligence,
>   since by attaining true awareness,
>   [these bodhisattvas] have excellent understanding on this
>   [ground].

458. Through the maturation of this [ground],
   they become the lord of a million worlds;
   they are unsurpassed by arhats and such
   regarding qualms in the minds of beings.

As they are close to buddhahood, ninth ground bodhisattvas are like royal heirs who will soon be enthroned as monarchs. They excel in the four specific perfect understandings—the Dharma, its actual words, its meaning, and confidence or eloquence in expounding the Dharma—that, while not the same as the buddhas' understandings, are concordant with them. This ground is called *Excellent Intelligence* because these bodhisattvas have attained an exceptional practice of those four. The ripening result is being able to take rebirth as a Brahma lord over a million worlds.

When people ask these bodhisattvas questions, they are able to reply correctly without mistakes or contradictions between the explicit and implicit meanings or between earlier and later statements. Of course these bodhisattvas are not able to answer in the totally unmistaken and perfect way that buddhas do, but because they are so close to the buddhas' ground, they are extremely capable of accomplishing the aims of sentient beings by resolving their qualms and teaching them in accordance with their dispositions, thoughts, and interests. In this respect these bodhisattvas cannot be surpassed by arhats.

459. The tenth is the Cloud of Dharma
   because [bodhisattvas] rain down the holy Dharma,
   and these bodhisattvas are anointed
   with rays of light by the buddhas.

460. Through the maturation of that [ground],
   they become the celestial ruler of the Pure Abode,
   master of inconceivable objects of wisdom,
   supreme among great lords.

Rain falls from a cloud and causes crops to grow. Similarly, through a vast rain of teachings, tenth ground bodhisattvas cause the growth of "crops" of excellent virtue in the mental continua of trainees.

During meditative equipoise, tenth grounders enter into innumerable millions of concentrations, and at the conclusion of the vajra-like concentration all the buddhas radiate light from the hair curl on their foreheads and bestow the empowerment of great rays of light on these bodhisattvas, blessing them so they obtain omniscient mind. At this time, all their cognitive obscurations are completely extinguished and these bodhisattvas become fully enlightened buddhas.

The ripening result is birth in the pure abode of Akanishta. Literally, *Akanishta* means "not below," indicating that it is above all other realms. This Akanishta is above the Akanishta of the seventeen levels of the form realm, which is a place within cyclic existence. At the end of their continua as sentient beings all bodhisattvas take birth and attain awakening in the pure abode of Akanishta according to the sutra system and the Madhyamaka tenet system. Bodhisattvas of the final continuum are bestowed the empowerment of great light rays, and when they become buddhas the signs and marks that they possess become the actual signs and marks of the enjoyment body. According to the sutra system, it is not possible to attain awakening in the desire realm, although this is possible according to the tantric system.

Through the uninterrupted path that is the actual antidote to the objects to be abandoned on the tenth ground, bodhisattvas eradicate all remaining stains. This abandonment becomes the true cessation of a buddha—a buddha's nature truth body, the emptiness of that buddha's mind. The bodhisattva's exalted wisdom realizing emptiness becomes the wisdom truth body—the omniscient mind—of that buddha. All exalted wisdoms in the continuum of a buddha are omniscient mind.

In general, the emanation bodies arise from the enjoyment body, which is their dominant condition. A supreme emanation body comes into the world and performs the twelve deeds of a buddha, including turning the Dharma wheel. When tenth ground bodhisattvas become buddhas, they attain the four bodies simultaneously, although the supreme emanation body comes later. A buddha can also emanate as many other things, such as water, earth, fire, and various objects that benefit beings. All of them accomplish the aims of sentient beings. The supreme emanation body is the only emanation that comes into the world and performs the twelve deeds—from entering the mother's womb to passing into parinirvana.

Tenth ground bodhisattvas become supreme among great lords, meaning that they become buddhas. Bodhisattvas on all ten grounds are called "great lord" but only buddhas are called "supreme great lord." They are masters of inconceivable objects of wisdom, meaning they have the omniscient wisdom of all the buddhas.

14. The Magnificent Qualities of a Buddha

ULTIMATE EXCELLENT QUALITIES

Having explained the temporal excellent qualities and the excellent qualities of the bodhisattvas on the ten grounds, Nagarjuna now turns to the culmination of the path, the resultant excellent qualities of a buddha, which can be subsumed in the ten powers of a buddha. In addition, he teaches us a daily recitation practice that will contribute to amassing the incalculable merit necessary to attain buddhahood. Regularly reciting and contemplating these twenty verses will open our heart to the compassion, wisdom, and power that will enable us to be of greatest benefit to all sentient beings.

> 461. These ten are renowned
> as the ten bodhisattva grounds.
> The buddhas' ground is different—
> in all ways immeasurably vast.

> 462. It is merely called
> "Possessing Ten Powers."
> Each of those powers is as limitless
> as the countless number of beings.

The Boundless Qualities of a Buddha Summarized in Ten Powers

The first half of verse 461 summarizes the ten bodhisattva grounds as explained by the Buddha in the sutras. Since bodhisattvas become buddhas, Nagarjuna proceeds to describe the buddhas' ground, which is superior to the ten grounds of bodhisattvas in all aspects. It is inconceivably vast and its qualities limitless; it is merely said to possess the ten powers, which comprise all the buddhas' qualities.

Even one instant of consciousness of an awakened being is able to see all phenomena extremely clearly, just as we see things in the palm of our hand. While buddhas are in meditative equipoise they can engage in all the activities of subsequent attainment. For them, the actions of meditative equipoise and the actions of subsequent attainment are non-contradictory. This attribute is unique to buddhas; even very high bodhisattvas cannot do both simultaneously.

Generally speaking, we say that any consciousness in the continuum of a buddha is omniscient mind, a final exalted wisdom that realizes all phenomena directly. The wisdom of meditative equipoise of a buddha is omniscient mind; it is able to directly see all phenomena of the subsequent attainment and at the same time has nondual perception of emptiness. Similarly, a buddha's wisdom of subsequent attainment that sees the wide diversity of conventional phenomena can simultaneously realize their emptiness nondually.

Buddha's ground is vast in its reach and replete with the ten powers, each of which possesses inconceivable qualities. Just as sentient beings are immeasurable, the qualities of a buddha's powers are immeasurable. Just as space is limitless, stretching out in the ten directions, so too are a buddha's qualities. The objects known by each of the ten powers are immeasurable, so the powers that know them are also limitless. The ten powers are explained in the *Greater Sutta on the Lion's Roar* (*Mahasihanada Sutta*) in the Pali canon and in the *Sutra of the Ten Grounds* in the Sanskrit tradition, as follows:

1. *Power of knowing sources and non-sources.* A source is the cause of something; for example, virtue is the source of happiness and nonvirtue is the source of pain. Countless sentient beings of the three times have their own innumerable, different kinds of great, middling, and small suffering, and each of these arise from innumerable causes—the countless afflictions and nonvirtuous karmas in the continua of those beings. Sentient beings also experience countless different kinds of happiness and pleasant feelings that arise from innumerable virtuous causes. A non-source is the non-arising of something; for example, happiness never arises from nonvirtue and suffering never comes from virtue. Knowing all this in detail in the briefest moment is the

power of the exalted wisdom that understands sources and non-sources.

Some discussion arises regarding this power. Since it realizes sources and non-sources, both sources and non-sources should exist. But happiness resulting from nonvirtue is a non-source and doesn't exist; the same is the case for virtue producing suffering. Because these are nonexistent and cannot be realized by a reliable cognizer, are they non-sources or not? If you say that there are no non-sources, then non-sources cannot be realized, in which case the power realizing non-sources must also not exist. That power is omniscient mind, and saying this is nonexistent doesn't work! While we cannot realize that suffering comes from virtue since that does not exist, we can realize its nonexistence. We can realize that virtue is not the source of suffering and nonvirtue is not the source of happiness.

2. *Power of knowing the ripening of karma.* The innumerable sentient beings of the past, present, and future experience innumerable ripening results. The specific karmic causes for each of those rebirths is understood in detail with this power.

3. *Power of knowing the various interests.* This power knows all the various interests and thoughts of each sentient being—what they appreciate and how to best communicate with them—all in an instant.

4. *Power to know sentient beings' different dispositions.* The term translated as "disposition" can also be translated as "element." This power knows the disposition of each sentient being as well as the divisions and characteristics of the elements, such as the eighteen elements and the sixty-four elements.

5. *Power of knowing sentient beings' various faculties.* This knows the superior and inferior faculties of sentient beings. Superior faculties are aryas' unpolluted five faculties of faith, effort, mindfulness, concentration, and wisdom. Inferior faculties are the three poisons in the minds of the sentient beings. This power knows which faculties are very strong and which are not.

6. *Power of knowing the paths that lead to various destinations.* In an instant, this power knows that some people are following the bodhisattva path and will traverse the ten grounds to awakening,

while others will progress on the five paths of the hearer or solitary realizer and attain arhatship. It also knows that some people's path will lead to rebirth in the lower realms due to having created the ten paths of nonvirtuous karma.

7. *Power of knowing the afflictions and purifications.* By knowing the disadvantages of the more afflictive states and the benefits of the less afflictive ones, this power knows exactly how to engage in the various concentrations, such as the four meditative stabilizations and the four immaterial absorptions, and is extremely skilled in entering and leaving them in an instant.

8. *Power of remembering previous lives.* This power knows each rebirth that the Tathagata has taken as a sentient being, even those in the distant past. In an instant, it knows where each rebirth occurred and the events that took place during that lifetime.

9. *Power of knowing the births and deaths of all sentient beings.* Without any confusion, this power knows all the past, present, and future deaths and rebirths of each sentient being—where, when, and in which realm they occur—in a single instant.

10. *Power knowing the cessation of pollution.* Here *pollution* means ignorance, afflictions, and their latencies. This power knows that by meditating on the wisdom directly realizing selflessness, the afflictions are extinguished and true cessation—the state of extinction of those afflictions—is actualized. It also knows the level of cessation of pollutions of all sentient beings.

The ten powers are posited from the viewpoint of ten objects of a buddha's omniscient mind. In fact, each power is omniscient mind. Although the bodhisattvas of the three pure grounds—the eighth, ninth, and tenth grounds—have amazing realizations and superknowledges, they do not have these ten powers, which exist exclusively in the continua of buddhas.

463. The limitlessness of a buddha's [excellent qualities]
     is said to be like
     the limitlessness of space, earth, water,
     fire, and wind in all directions.

464. If the causes are [reduced] to a mere [measure]
    and not seen to be limitless,
    then one will not be confident
    that the [good qualities of] the buddhas are inestimable.

Just as the five elements in the universe are limitless, so too are a buddha's excellent qualities. This is a result of the immeasurable causes that give rise to the buddhas' marvelous qualities—prostrating; making offerings; hearing, thinking, and meditating on the teachings; practicing the six perfections, and so on. Bodhisattvas diligently and joyfully create these causes with bodhichitta. Their compassion and desire to benefit sentient beings are inestimable, beyond the capacity of anyone to apprehend.

The inconceivability and immeasurability of the buddhas' qualities is due to an *inestimable* collection of merit. Without understanding the limitless causes of the various qualities of the buddhas, we will not be able to comprehend or appreciate the ten powers or their inconceivability. Knowing that the causes of even one of a buddha's qualities is beyond our imagination and ability to know inspires confidence in the excellence of the buddhas and their ability to guide us to awakening.

The Way to Amass Limitless Merit

465. Therefore, each day, three times a day,
    before a statue, stupa, or elsewhere,
    you should perform the recitation
    of the following twenty verses.

A good way to accumulate the great amount of merit necessary to attain the bodhisattva grounds and the buddhas' ten powers is to recite and contemplate the following twenty verses in the presence of the Three Jewels—here symbolized by a stupa, statue, or painting of the buddhas and bodhisattvas—or in the presence of an assembly of the arya sangha or your spiritual mentor. By accumulating immeasurable merit in this way, we will be able to attain the state of a buddha that possesses innumerable excellent qualities.

466. Honoring in all ways the Buddha, Dharma, Sangha,
    and also the bodhisattvas,
    I take refuge in them and pay homage
    to those worthy of homage.

467. I turn away from all negativity
    and embrace all merit.
    I rejoice in all the merit
    [amassed by] all sentient beings.

468. With bowed head and palms together
    I beseech all perfect buddhas
    to turn the wheel of Dharma,
    and remain as long as beings remain.

These three verses are a brief presentation of the seven branches of practice for purifying and creating of merit. First we *pay homage*, *prostrate*, and *take refuge* in the Three Jewels by respectfully bowing with our body, speech, and mind. The buddhas are those who possess the four buddha bodies; the Dharma is the true paths and true cessations in the continua of aryas; the sangha consists of all the aryas, as well as the bodhisattvas who are not yet aryas. We physically bow by joining our palms and bowing down to touch the five points—two knees, two hands, and forehead—to the floor. We verbally bow by reciting this verse, and we mentally bow by visualizing the Three Jewels in front of us and having a mind of faith.

Verse 467 expresses the branches of *confession* and *rejoicing*. Taking responsibility for our destructive behavior, we reveal the negativities we have done and make a determination to restrain ourselves from doing these in the future. We do this by way of the four powers: having regret (not guilt!) for our behavior, taking refuge and generating bodhichitta, making a determination to avoid the action in the future, and engaging in a remedial activity.

To accumulate as much merit as possible through the practices of generosity, ethical conduct, fortitude, and so on, we rejoice at any and all virtuous actions of body, speech, and mind that we and all others have done, are doing, and will do. Rejoicing in the virtue of others with admiration free of jealousy has a profound effect on our minds.

Verse 468 articulates the two branches of *requesting the buddhas to teach* and *imploring them to remain until cyclic existence ends*. Putting our palms together at our heart, we request spiritual mentors who are not turning the Dharma wheel to teach without delay after they have attained awakening. We then request the buddhas and bodhisattvas who are contemplating passing into parinirvana not to do so, but to stay for a very long time—as long as sentient beings wander in cyclic existence—in order to teach and guide us.

> 469. Through the merit of doing this
> and the merit I have done and will do,
> may all sentient beings be endowed
> with unsurpassed bodhichitta.

This begins the many verses that detail the last branch, the dedication of merit. May all the *merit*, virtue, and goodness that we and all others have done, are doing, and will do ripen in the peerless awakening of all beings.

> 470. May all sentient beings have immaculate faculties
> and transcend the unfree [states].
> May they control their own actions
> and live by right livelihood.

> 471. May all embodied beings have jewels in their hands,
> and may a limitless [amount] of all kinds of necessities
> remain inexhaustible
> for as long as cyclic existence endures.

Here we dedicate so that all the sentient beings may generate stainless faculties in their mindstreams. In addition, may all who currently live in the eight unfree states be free of those situations so that they can practice the Dharma without hindrances. *May they control their own actions* so that they have physical, verbal, and mental freedom—freedom in what they think, say, and do, freedom to come and go—and not be tormented, oppressed, and controlled by others. This can include not being controlled by ignorance and afflictions so that they can make wise decisions and act according to their virtuous aspirations. May they earn their *livelihood* by good means, never by the five wrong livelihoods. May they never engage in occupations that involve harming sentient beings.

From the moment of their birth, may all sentient being have everything they need to accomplish all their virtuous aspirations, as if they were born with jewels in their hands. May these excellent conditions never be exhausted as long as cyclic existence remains.

> 472. At all times may all women
>   become supreme persons.
>   May all beings be endowed
>   with intelligence and legs.

> 473. May all beings have a good complexion
>   and also a good physique.
>   May they be radiant and pleasant to behold.
>   Free of illness, may they be strong and live long.

May those who prefer not to take a female rebirth be reborn as a male. This line can also express the fervent wish that all women become buddhas or other supreme persons. One interpretation of *intelligence and legs* is the higher training in wisdom and ethical conduct. "Legs" means ethical conduct, because keeping pure ethical conduct is the method that leads to wisdom. Another interpretation is that "intelligence" means right view and "legs" refers to the remaining aspects of the path. There are more interpretations as well.

May all beings have a color and body of great splendor. This splendor refers to the magnificence certain people have even if they are not good looking. May they be radiant, have a pleasant appearance, and be free from illness. May they have a strong constitution and live long. These are seven qualities of higher rebirth.

> 474. May they all gain expertise in skillful means
>   and become free of all duhkha.
>   May they be devoted to the Three Jewels
>   and have the great treasure of Buddhadharma.

Skillful means refers to skill in the means of pacifying and eliminating true duhkha and true origin. May beings be free of the duhkha of all three

realms, and to accomplish this, may they take heartfelt refuge in the causal
and resultant three refuges. The causal refuges are the external Buddha,
Dharma, and Sangha that we rely on to learn and practice the path. The
resultant three refuges are the Buddha, Dharma, and Sangha that we will
become by practicing the path. May all beings possess the great wealth of
Buddha's doctrine, the ten powers.

> 475. May they be adorned with love, compassion,
>   joy, [the ability to] remain equanimous in the face of hardship,
>   generosity, ethical conduct, fortitude,
>   joyous effort, meditative stability, and wisdom.

> 476. Thus adorned, may they complete all the collections,
>   and [obtaining] brilliant signs and marks,
>   may they traverse without hindrance
>   the ten grounds to the inconceivable.

May all beings be imbued with the four immeasurables when they relate
to other sentient beings, and may they receive love, compassion, joy, and
equanimity from others. May they remain equanimous and calm in the face
of pain, hardship, outbursts of afflictions, and negative mental states. May
they complete the two collections of wisdom and merit by being adorned
with the practices of the six perfections. Most meditational deities are beautified with jeweled ornaments that represent the six perfections and other
good qualities developed on the path. While external ornaments may be
lovely, internal qualities are the best ornaments.

While they train in the path, may all beings have clear signs and marks
that are a similitude of those of the buddhas. May they be able to traverse
the ten grounds without obstacles or interruptions.

> 477. May I also be adorned with these good qualities
>   and all others as well.
>   May I become free from all faults,
>   and may I attain supreme love for all beings.

> 478. May I perfect the virtues
>   to which all beings aspire,

and may I always dispel
the duhkha of all embodied beings.

Above, we dedicated all the virtue that we accumulated by paying homage, bowing, taking refuge, confessing, rejoicing, requesting teachings,
and requesting the buddhas not to pass away, together with all the virtue
accumulated by ourselves and others in the three times. All this virtue was
dedicated for the benefit of all sentient beings, and can be summarized by
dedicating for them to be free of all faults and adorned with all qualities—
that is, to become an omniscient buddha who is the sole friend and protector of all wandering in cyclic existence.

Having dedicated like this for others, we now dedicate in the same way for
ourselves. *May I also* indicates that we steer our merit so that it will also ripen
in our being adorned with those as well as the other marvelous qualities that
are explained in the sutras. May we have supreme love for all sentient beings; no
matter who they are or how they treat us, may we always view them with affection and wish them well. May we perfect all virtues, and in any way possible
may we eliminate the duhkha of all embodied beings and inspire them with
hope and confidence. Without being impeded by internal or external obstacles,
may we be able to fulfill both the temporal and ultimate aims of others.

479. In all worlds may all beings
   who are feeling anxious due to fear
   become completely fearless
   merely by hearing my name.

May we always be able to eliminate the fears, dangers, and anxiety of all
sentient beings in all worlds in the ten directions. Each sentient being experiences different fearful situations—illness, injury, war, death, loss of loved
ones, depression, rejection, abandonment, poverty, loneliness, and so forth.
May merely hearing my name eliminate all of that fear and any dangers
and threats that lie behind it. By thinking of me, may their minds turn to
the Dharma, and by putting the Dharma into practice, may their fears be
allayed and their anxiety vanish.

480. From seeing and thinking of me
   and from merely hearing my name,

may beings become clear-minded,
undisturbed, and at ease.

481. May it be definite that they will awaken,
and in all their future lives, may they attain the five
superknowledges.
In all ways may I always do
what brings benefit and happiness to all beings.

May all beings who see me, think of me, or hear my name abide in joy. May their minds be lucid and free of confusion and distress. May they be comfortable, free of afflictions and misdeeds, thereby abiding naturally, free of all adventitious faults.

May they progress without regression on the path to awakening. May they be definite in the bodhisattva path and never fall to the paths of the hearers and solitary realizers. May they never be reborn in the lower realms.

Throughout all their lives may they attain the five superknowledges, which are a supreme method for benefiting others. May I continually be able to *benefit* them and bring them happiness and fulfillment according to their individual dispositions, interests, and faculties.

482. May I always dissuade all at once
all those beings of any world
who intend to engage in negativity
without doing them any harm.

In the various worlds, many beings have committed destructive actions, many are currently involved in destructive actions, and many are planning to engage in destructive actions. May I be able to stop them from engaging in negativity without harming them. By skillful and non-threatening means and with compassion and courage, may I be able to intercede and prevent all harmful actions such that neither the potential victim nor the potential perpetrator is harmed. It's helpful for us to imagine various situations in which one being is about to harm another physically, verbally, or mentally, and think of how we might intercede to change the direction of the situation.

483. Like the earth, water, wind, and fire,
    medicinal herbs, and the trees in the wilderness,
    may I always freely be an object of enjoyment
    by all beings as they wish.

Just as the four natural elements, flowers, trees, medicinal herbs, and so forth in unowned, isolated places are used by everyone according to their wish, may my physical, verbal, and mental abilities be similarly useful for sentient beings to accomplish their well-being. Whoever they are, may I bring them happiness.

484. May I be beloved of beings,
    and may they be more beloved to me than myself.
    May I bear the results of their negativity,
    and may they have the results of all my virtue.

When I am able to be a spiritual guide and protector for destitute sentient beings and help them out of their distressing state, may they cherish me and hold me as dear as their own lives. In the same way, may I always hold them dear and care more for their welfare than my own. By exchanging myself with others, may I happily experience the results of their negative actions, and may they experience the results of all my virtue.

The aspiration *may I bear the results of their negativity, and may they have the results of all my virtue* is the heart of the practice of equalizing and exchanging self and others. It summarizes the essential points of this profound practice that are contained in the sutras and is the source of the thought-training practice of taking and giving, called *tonglen* in Tibetan.

There is a story behind these lines that dates back hundreds of years. Geshe Chekawa was a highly accomplished Nyingma tantric practitioner from a respected family in Tibet. After hearing the "Eight Verses of Thought Training" composed by Langri Tangpa, and finding it beneficial for his mind, he left behind his family and estate and went in search of someone who held this lineage. Finally, he found Geshe Sharawa and attended one of his teachings, but Geshe Sharawa taught the practice of the hearer vehicle, and nothing about the vast and profound universal vehicle teachings.

Later, when Geshe Sharawa was circumambulating a stupa, Geshe Chekawa approached him and inquired if he could ask some Dharma questions.

Geshe Sharawa responded, "I already told everything you could possibly want to know and cleared up all doubts in the teaching you attended. What else do you have to ask?"

Geshe Chekawa then asked Geshe Sharawa if he had the lineage for the "Eight Verses of Thought Training." Geshe Sharawa responded that he would give him teachings on this, but Geshe Chekawa would need to stay there for some months to receive the explanation and meditate on it. Agreeing to this, Geshe Chekawa asked what the source of the teaching was, and Geshe Sharawa told him that it was Nagarjuna's *Precious Garland*. All thought-training teachings, and in particular the taking-and-giving meditation, have this verse as their source.

The previous verse asked us to selflessly give our body, speech, and mind so that we may be useful for sentient beings, becoming whatever they need. This teaches the importance of cherishing others even more than ourselves. In the present verse, we consider our own happiness insignificant and practice exchanging self and others by taking all sentient beings' duhkha and its causes and giving our happiness and virtue to them in return.

May I bear the results of their negativity expresses the practice of taking in the taking-and-giving meditation. To meditate on this, recite this line three times. The first time, think of all the various forms of suffering included in the truth of duhkha, such as the three types of duhkha, the eight kinds of suffering, and the six disadvantages of cyclic existence. Imagine these leaving sentient beings through their right nostrils and inhale them through your left nostril. Their suffering then dissolves into the lump of self-centeredness at your heart, causing it to vanish.

The second time, imagine taking all the causes that give rise to this duhkha—the root afflictions, auxiliary afflictions, and actions motivated by these disturbing states of mind—the ten paths of nonvirtuous karma, the five heinous crimes, and so forth. Inhaling the source of all others' duhkha, imagine this dissolving into the lump of self-centeredness at your heart and dismantling it. In this way, take all others' afflictive obscurations and use them to annihilate your own self-centeredness.

The third time, imagine taking the cognitive obscurations—the imprints of true-grasping ignorance and the appearance of true existence that prevent the simultaneous cognition of all phenomena. These, too, dissolve into and destroy the lump of self-centeredness at your heart. Focus on the feeling of being completely free from self-preoccupation. How wonderful that would be!

May they have the results of all my virtue is the practice of giving. This line is also recited three times. The first time, imagine that your body becomes like a wish-fulfilling jewel that is able to accomplish all the wishes of sentient beings. This wish-fulfilling jewel radiates white light, which leaves your right nostril and enters sentient beings' left nostrils. The light gives others whatever they need to pacify the pain of burning in the hot hells, freezing in the cold hells, the misery of thirst and hunger of the hungry ghosts, animals' suffering of being hunted and eaten, as well as the respective sufferings of the humans and gods. In short, imagine your body becomes whatever any being needs in order to dispel the suffering others experience.

The second time, imagine that your possessions become like a wish-fulfilling jewel that radiates out whatever is necessary to dispel the various gross and subtle duhkha that sentient beings experience and to bring them peace, comfort, and security. Imagine that sentient beings become completely tranquil.

The third time, imagine that your three roots of virtue become a wish-fulfilling jewel. Again imagine giving to various sentient beings whatever they need for temporal and ultimate happiness. Think that their misery is pacified and all their needs are fulfilled. Imagine that they are interested in the Dharma, have faith in the Three Jewels, listen to and practice teachings, and ascend the bodhisattva grounds to become buddhas.

Alternatively, when you give your body, imagine sentient beings receive an excellent body—a precious human rebirth with all eighteen qualities, which is a very special basis for practicing the path. When you give your possessions, imagine they receive all the various things they need to practice the Dharma. When you give your virtue, imagine they cultivate all the roots of virtue and gain all the realizations from relying on a spiritual mentor up through the bodhisattva grounds and paths, culminating in their attaining full awakening.[40]

We may wonder how we can take on others' destructive karma and give them our virtue when everyone has to experience the results of his or her own karma. While we cannot actually experience their misery and give them our happiness, the point of this meditation is to train our mind in the attitude that wants to be able to do this. This meditation increases our

---

40. A more detailed explanation of the taking-and-giving practice can be found in chapter 11 of Geshe Jampa Tegchok's *Transforming Adversity into Joy and Courage*.

love and compassion and accumulates a tremendous amount of merit. It familiarizes our mind with the experience of cherishing others more than ourselves and being delighted to alleviate their pain and give them joy. When we eventually become a high-level bodhisattva, we will be able to give our body away without any hesitation or sense of regret—for example, giving our flesh to those in need of fresh meat like the Buddha did when he gave his body to a starving tigress so she could feed her cubs. Needless to say, at that stage we will be able to give away our possessions easily and will have an astonishing ability to act for the welfare of others without experiencing any hardship.

At present our taking-and-giving meditation is done in our imagination—we do not actually give happiness to sentient beings or take their suffering. If we do not engage in this powerful method to train our minds, later on we will not be able to actually practice exchanging self and others or engage in the vast deeds of bodhisattvas.

> 485. As long as there is even one sentient being
> somewhere who is not yet free,
> may I remain [in the world] for that being's sake,
> even if I have attained peerless awakening.

May I stay in the world and work for the welfare of others not just for a day, a week, or a month, but for as long as there are sentient beings who have not yet been liberated from cyclic existence. May I stay in cyclic existence performing the vast actions of bodhisattvas for the sake of others, even if there is only one sentient being left in cyclic existence.

This powerful dedication concludes the twenty verses that Nagarjuna recommended the king recite and contemplate daily. In short, the excellent qualities of awakening are immeasurable, and thus the merit needed to produce these is also immeasurable. One way to do this is to recite these twenty stanzas and contemplate their meaning often, three times a day if possible, if not twice or at least once.

> 486. If the merit of making such statements
> were to be material,
> it would not fit into worlds
> as numerous as the grains of sand of the Ganges.

487. This is what the Blessed One said,
     and the reason is here to be seen—
     the worlds of beings are immeasurable,
     and the intention to aid them is likewise.

Immeasurability of the Merit of Those Excellent Qualities

Reciting and contemplating the meaning of these twenty verses produces merit and virtue so enormous that if it could be transformed into matter, it would not be able to fit into the number of worlds equal to the number of grains of sand in the River Ganges. *Grains of sand* refers to the particles of sand under and along the banks of the Ganges as well as the particles of water flowing in the river.

Just as the objects for whom we accumulate this merit—sentient beings—are innumerable, so too the merit that is accumulated is immeasurable. If you help one sentient being you create one excellent virtue, so if you help innumerable sentient beings, you accumulate virtue that is also innumerable. If you generate a mind that wishes to benefit the immeasurable number of sentient beings, the result will also be immeasurable. This merit is certain to result in the incalculable qualities of awakening. The source of this explanation is found in the *King of Concentration Sutra* (*Samadhiraja Sutra*) and the *Akshayamati Sutra*, where the Buddha stated that the result is limitless because the cause is limitless.

Similarly, if our intention is immeasurable love, compassion, and bodhichitta, the result will also be immeasurable. We must expand our way of thinking when we contemplate the causes to become bodhisattvas and buddhas and to actualize their magnificent deeds and qualities. The narrow mind of ordinary beings won't do.

15. Closing Words of Advice

To conclude this vast and profound teaching contained in the *Precious Garland*, Nagarjuna encourages us to take joy in the practice and gives us final advice to observe four practices, rely on a qualified spiritual mentor, and be mindful in order to conduct ourselves in the best way in all situations. He makes clear that this teaching is not just for the king but for all of us, and he encourages us to contemplate its meaning and to train in and integrate excellent qualities in our mind and life.

JOYFULLY PRACTICE THE DHARMA

488. Thus concludes my brief explanation
    of the Dharma to you.
    Always consider this Dharma to be beloved to you,
    just as you are beloved to yourself.

489. Those who consider the Dharma to be beloved
    are truly holding themselves as beloved.
    For if one wants to benefit those whom one loves,
    one can do so by means of the Dharma.

Nagarjuna says here that he has explained these jewel-like practices to the king. They contain in summarized form all the essential points that are like jewels extracted from the ocean of sutras. Cherish these teachings dearly just like you cherish your life.

Some people think that it is reasonable to hold their life dear because its destruction is a great loss, but they do not think that the destruction of Dharma practice is such a great loss. Nagarjuna disagrees, saying that if we hold our body and life dear, then we should cherish these practices all the more. If we consider the loss of our body devastating, we should consider the loss of these practices as even worse. In other words, if we cherish our life and want to have a series of fortunate rebirths, we must cherish their causes. The value of such a life is to be able to practice the Dharma and create these causes. If we don't cherish and practice the Buddha's teachings, having a fortunate birth and a long life are useless.

> 490. Therefore, be devoted to the Dharma, just as you are devoted to
>   yourself.
>   Be devoted to correct practice, just as you are devoted to
>   Dharma.
>   Be devoted to wisdom, just as you are devoted to correct
>   practice.
>   Be devoted to the wise, just as you are devoted to wisdom.

Observing the Four Practices

This verse explains four important practices or attitudes to cultivate. *Therefore* indicates that for the reason explained in the previous verse, first we must cherish the practice of the Dharma like our body or life. If we cherish ourselves, we should be devoted to the Dharma, because the Dharma will bring us the happiness we seek.

Second, to be devoted to the Dharma requires practicing it correctly, so we should put energy into doing that and gaining realizations. To practice it correctly and attain realizations, developing wisdom is crucial, since correct practice depends on knowing the difference between what to practice and what to abandon. To gain wisdom, we must rely on a wise spiritual mentor to teach and guide us.

In short, if we cherish ourselves, we cherish the Dharma, practice it correctly to attain realizations, cultivate wisdom, and correctly rely on a spiritual mentor.

RELY ON A SPIRITUAL MENTOR

> 491. One who, due to his own failings, has doubts about a pure,
>   loving, and intelligent teacher
>   who speaks with restraint about what is helpful ruins his chances
>   of attaining his aims.

Thinking, "I am under the care of one who is pure, loving, and
　　wise,
and who states with restraint what is helpful," vow to spiritually
　　discipline yourself, King.

The Disadvantages of Not Relying on a Spiritual Mentor

To progress on the path, it is essential to rely on a spiritual mentor who teaches us the Dharma and guides us on the path. Before forming a mentor-disciple relationship, we must examine potential mentors to see if they have the qualities necessary to lead us on the path. Once we have formed this relationship with someone, it is important to rely on him or her correctly so that we can benefit from the teachings and advice. Relying on him incorrectly—for example, getting angry at him—not only impedes us from progressing on the path but also has many deleterious effects. The time to look for a potential teacher's faults is before we take him as our spiritual mentor. After forming the relationship, we need to focus on his good qualities.

These mentors are *pure* in that they are not concerned with receiving respect and offerings; they also restrain themselves from engaging in destructive actions with their body, speech, and mind. *Loving*, they are fond of their students. *Intelligent*, they accurately distinguish what to practice and what to abandon. They *speak appropriately* and are able to give many types of teachings, instructions, and explanations. They are not restricted to knowing just a few Dharma points or a few texts, but rather they can teach in an expansive way with a beneficial motivation that sincerely cares for the temporal and ultimate welfare of the disciples. They speak about what is beneficial and teach what is helpful to earnest disciples seeking correction and guidance.

Disciples whose minds are clouded and do not appreciate the qualities of their spiritual mentors or the important role their spiritual mentors play in their lives put roadblocks in their own spiritual progress. Their minds become critical and increasingly disturbed, which creates many doubts and immobilizes them in their studies and practices. To avoid this, we should appreciate being under the care of a wise and compassionate teacher and take advantage of this opportunity by taking the instructions we receive to heart and disciplining ourselves spiritually. If not, we waste an amazing opportunity that is difficult to come by.

Both students and teachers in a spiritual mentor-disciple relationship must be careful. If the students do not rely on their teachers properly, they create destructive karma that leads them to rebirth in the lower realms. Disciples should think, "I must rely on my spiritual mentors by making offerings, assisting them with their projects and needs, and offering my practice—I need to practice according to the instructions and guidance I receive. If I don't do that, I harm myself by ruining my opportunity to achieve my spiritual aims and creating dreadful karma that will result in my own misery." Understanding that if such a thing occurred it would destroy the chance of attaining liberation and awakening, disciples must decide to be very careful so as not to diminish their own virtue.

Spiritual mentors who do not teach the Dharma correctly or take advantage of their disciples' trust create the causes for rebirth in the lower realms. When both spiritual mentor and disciple appreciate the importance of their relationship and mindfully guard against negative motivation and poor conduct, the disciple will blossom.

> 492. Know, in brief, the qualifications of spiritual friends.
> You should receive teachings from
> those who are content, compassionate, and ethical,
> and possess the wisdom that dispels negative mental states.

> 493. Having understood [what they teach],
> you should respectfully put it into practice.
> Through this excellent system,
> you will attain the supreme achievement.

The Qualifications of a Spiritual Mentor

To give a brief description of the qualifications of suitable spiritual mentors: they should be content, free of desire to receive veneration and offerings. They should abide with good ethical conduct and have a compassionate motivation toward their disciples, not seeking fame, respect, and offerings. They must be wise regarding the methods to eliminate the disciples' afflictions and be skilled in explaining what to practice and abandon. These four qualities—contentment, compassion, ethical conduct, and wisdom—subsume many other qualities. Thus disciples should seek spiritual mentors with these qualities, and spiritual mentors must do their best to cultivate and embody these qualities.

If you receive instructions from a spiritual mentor who possesses these four qualities, listen with great reverence and respect. When such a spiritual mentor gives you advice, take it to heart with an understanding of the goodness of such a mentor. While sometimes spiritual mentors may need to speak strongly to disciples, the disciples should recognize the compassion behind this and appreciate their teachers' care. If we understand these excellent instructions and follow them with respect and appreciation, we will attain buddhahood.

Conduct Yourself in the Best Way in All Situations

494. Speak the truth, and speak gently to beings.
    Be pleasant, unassailable, and skilled in public policy;
    do not wish to humiliate others;
    be independent, and always speak well.

495. With enmity well subdued,
    be generous, dignified, and mentally peaceful.
    Do not procrastinate, and do not be rash;
    do not be dishonest, and be courteous.

Speak the truth, but speak it gently to all to help them feel at ease—never speak harshly with the intention to harm. We should speak in such a way that just hearing our voice is a cause for others to collect merit. You may have noticed that Nagarjuna has commented on the importance of truthful speech repeatedly in the *Precious Garland*. This is the basis of trust; without it, the good deeds we do will always be suspect.

Be pleasant, not demanding and intrusive; say things that cause people to feel happy when they hear you. Be unassailable by explaining the Dharma that is difficult to find—the Dharma that is profound, vast, and magnificent—to the circle of people around you who live with good ethical conduct. If people in your circle have poor ethical conduct, teach them according to their level and their faculties. Don't simply throw up your hands and say, "There's no point in explaining the Dharma to you. You will never understand, and even if you did, you won't practice. So just forget it!" Don't seek to make others feel bad about themselves by *humiliating* them.

Gain the information you need, ask for others' input, but make your own decisions based on your own wisdom, without succumbing to pressure or threats from others. Speak well, with self-control; do not speak with a mind that is under the control of afflictions.

Subdue all enmity and dysfunctional tendencies, which are latent potentials of negative mental states. Be generous and dignified; do not be resentful or seek revenge. Explain instructions without mental scattering or laziness, and do not allow your mind to become reckless. Be conscientious and mentally peaceful; act without laziness, deceit, or guile. Treasure other sentient beings and be courteous to them.

> 496. Be auspicious like the full moon,
>   and radiant like the autumn sun.
>   Be profound like the ocean,
>   and steadfast like Mount Meru.

Be like the full moon—calming, disciplined, and beautiful. Be magnificent and joyful like the *autumn sun*, rich with the scent of harvests. Be profound like the ocean by sharing teachings and advice that are deep. Be as stable as *Mount Meru*, not happy one day and unhappy the next. Learn how to make your own mind peaceful so that people know what to expect when they see you. Those who are moody—elated one day and dejected the next—are hard to be with.

> 497. Freed from all negativities
>   and adorned with all good qualities,
>   be the sustenance of all beings
>   and become omniscient.

Free yourself from all afflictions and destructive karma; adorn yourself not with jewels but with excellent qualities. Be the sustenance of all sentient beings by being of ultimate benefit to them. Be the method that provides them with benefit, happiness, and everything they need, especially the Dharma. Try to be like the Buddha who possesses all these qualities. By your sincere practice, one day you will become a buddha.

498. This Dharma is not explained only for a king. It is also taught,
    as is appropriate, to other beings out of the desire to benefit
    them.

Nagarjuna now clarifies that he gave these teachings not just for the king
but for others to learn and practice as well. His overarching intention is for
all beings to attain awakening. Thus, everybody should respect and practice
these teachings that are given with the desire to benefit. Thinking that these
practices are just for the king and that we don't need to take them to heart
or put them into practice would be a huge error on our part.

Take This Advice to Heart

499. King, it would be good for you
        to contemplate this discourse every day,
        so that you and other beings
        will attain true, complete awakening.

Nagarjuna says here, "Your majesty, this is an explanation of how all beings
can attain higher rebirth and highest goodness. It is appropriate for you
to reflect each day on this teaching that will bring higher rebirth, liberation, and full awakening to all when they practice it." This advice is for us
as well—we should not just read this book or jot down a few notes on the
text, but contemplate it daily. To do so will benefit us and, by extension,
all sentient beings.

500. Be ethical and have the highest respect for spiritual mentors; be
        patient, devoid of jealousy and greed.
    [Enjoy] the wealth of aiding others without expectations of
        return and be helpful to those who are deprived.
    Be devoted to the supreme, avoid those who are not, and
        embrace the Dharma.
    For the sake of awakening, this is what those who seek it should
        always do.

Nagarjuna now gives us his final heartfelt advice. All of you who are interested in the Dharma, want to be of service to all sentient beings, and seek

peerless awakening, guard well your ethical conduct. Understanding your spiritual mentors to be the foundation of the path, have great respect for them. Be patient with everyone at all times and in all situations. Do not be jealous of your companions when they engage in virtuous activities and develop virtuous qualities, but instead rejoice, thinking how wonderful it is. When beggars come to you hoping to receive some of your possessions, do the best you can to satisfy their needs, provided that doing so is useful. Whether you help them by giving the Dharma or your possessions, give out of love, compassion, and a wish to benefit. Don't hope to receive fame, appreciation, or even a good rebirth in return.

Benefit those who are destitute. Happily serve people whose knowledge and other good qualities render them special, even if they are not your own spiritual mentors. Take care of them, keep them as your companions, and follow their good example. Do not keep company with people who are reckless, unethical, and deceitful. Remember your purpose is to attain awakening for yourself and others and engage in the practices described in this text as much as possible.

This concludes part V of Nagarjuna's *Precious Garland*, "Practices of a Bodhisattva," which explains the methods for monastic and lay disciples to attain higher rebirth and the highest good.

SARVAM MANGALAM BHAVATU!

Glossary

Absolutism: believing that phenomena inherently exist.

Affirming negative: a negation that implies something else.

Afflictions: mental factors that disturb the tranquility of the mind. These include disturbing emotions and wrong views.

Afflictive obscurations: obscurations that mainly prevent liberation; afflictions, their seeds, and polluted karma.

Aggregates: the four or five components that make up a living being: form (except for beings born in the immaterial realm), feelings, discriminations, volitional factors, and consciousnesses.

Appearing object (Tib. *snang yul*): the object that actually appears to a consciousness. The appearing object of a conceptual consciousness is a conceptual appearance of something.

Apprehended object (Tib. *'dzin btangs kyi yul*): the main object with which the mind is concerned; i.e., the object that the mind is getting at or understands. Synonymous with engaged object.

Arhat: someone who is liberated from cyclic existence.

Arya buddha: a person who is fully awakened, such as an enjoyment body or emanation body.

Arya: someone who has directly and nonconceptually realized the emptiness of inherent existence.

Basis of designation: the collection of parts or factors in dependence on which an object is designated.

Bodhichitta: a main mental consciousness induced by an aspiration to bring about others' welfare and accompanied by an aspiration to attain full awakening oneself.

Bodhisattva ground: a consciousness in the continuum of an arya bodhisattva characterized by wisdom and compassion. It is the basis for the development of good qualities and the basis for the eradication of ignorance and mistaken appearances.

Bodhisattva: someone who has spontaneous bodhichitta.

Buddha: all aspects of a buddha. It includes the four buddha bodies.

Cognitive obscurations: obscurations that mainly prevent full awakening; the latencies of ignorance and the subtle dualistic view that they give rise to.

Collection of merit: a bodhisattva's practice of the method aspect of the path that accumulates merit.

Collection of wisdom: a bodhisattva's practice of the wisdom aspect of the path that develops the wisdom realizing emptiness.

Conceived object (Tib. *zhen yul*): the object conceived by a conceptual consciousness; synonymous with the apprehended or engaged object of a conceptual consciousness.

Conceptual appearance: a mental image of an object that appears to a conceptual consciousness.

Conventional existence: existence.

Conventional truths: that which is a truth in the perspective of true-grasping.

Cyclic existence (Skt. *samsara*): the cycle of rebirth that occurs under the control of afflictions and karma.

Definitive: teachings that speak about the ultimate nature of reality and can be accepted literally (according to the Prasangikas).

Dependent arising: this is of three types (1) causal dependence—things arising due to causes and conditions, (2) mutual dependence—phenomena existing in relation to other phenomena, and (3) dependent designation—phenomena existing by being merely designated by terms and concepts.

Desire realm: one of the realms of cyclic existence; the realm where sentient beings are overwhelmed by attraction to and desire for sense objects.

Duhkha: unsatisfactory experiences of cyclic existence.

Emanation body: the buddha body that appears as an ordinary sentient being to benefit others.

Emptiness: the lack of inherent existence, lack of independent existence.

Enjoyment body: the buddha body that appears in the pure lands to teach arya bodhisattvas.

Environmental result: the result of karma that influences what environment we live in.

Evident phenomena: phenomena we can perceive with our five senses.

Form body: the buddha body in which a buddha appears to sentient beings; it includes the emanation and enjoyment bodies.

Four truths of the aryas: the truth of duhkha, its origin, its cessation, and the path to that cessation.

Full awakening: buddhahood; the state where all obscurations have been abandoned and all good qualities developed limitlessly.

Fundamental vehicle: the path leading to the liberation of hearers and solitary realizers.

God: a being born as a heavenly being in the desire realm or in one of the meditative absorptions of the material or immaterial realms.

Hearer: someone practicing the fundamental vehicle path leading to arhatship who emphasizes meditation on the four truths of the aryas.

Hungry ghost (Skt. *preta*): someone born in a realm where the denizens suffer from extreme hunger and thirst that can never be satisfied.

Ignorance: a mental factor that is obscured and grasps the opposite of what exists. There are two types: ignorance regarding reality and ignorance regarding karma and its effects.

I-grasping: grasping oneself to exist inherently.

Immaterial realm: the samsaric realm in which sentient beings do not have a material body.

Inattentive awareness: a consciousness that doesn't ascertain its object, even though that object is appearing to it.

Inference: a mind that ascertains its object by means of a correct syllogism.

Inherent existence: existence without depending on any other factors; independent existence.

Karma: volitional action.

Latencies: predispositions, imprints, or tendencies.

Liberation: the state of freedom from cyclic existence.

Lower realms: unfortunate states of rebirth as a hell being, hungry ghost, or animal.

Material realm: a realm in cyclic existence in which the beings have subtle bodies; they are born there due to having attained various states of concentration.

Meditative equipoise on emptiness: an arya's mind focused single-pointedly on the emptiness of inherent existence.

Mind: the clear and aware part of living beings that cognizes, experiences, thinks, feels, and so on.

Mindstream: the continuity of mind.

Monastic: someone who received monastic ordination; a monk or nun.

Nature truth body: the buddha body that is the emptiness of a buddha's mind and that buddha's true cessations.

Nihilism: believing that our actions have no ethical dimension; believing that nothing exists.

Nirvana with remainder: (1) the state of liberation when an arhat is still alive and has the remainder of the polluted aggregates, (2) the time of subsequent attainment of an arya where true existence still appears to the mind.

Nirvana without remainder: (1) the state of liberation when an arhat has passed away and no longer has the remainder of the polluted aggregates, (2) an arya's meditative equipoise on emptiness when there is no appearance of true existence.

Nirvana: liberation.

Non-abiding nirvana: a buddha's awakening that does not abide in either cyclic existence or personal liberation.

Non-affirming negative: a negation that does not imply something else.

Nonduality: the non-appearance of subject and object, inherent existence, conventional truths, and conceptual appearances in an arya's meditative equipoise on emptiness.

Non-thing: (1) a permanent or unconditioned phenomenon, (2) a nonexistent.

Object of negation: what is negated or refuted.

Permanent: unchanging, static. It does not mean eternal.

Permanent, unitary, independent self: a soul or self (Skt. *atman*) asserted by non-Buddhists.

Person: a living being designated in dependence on the four or five aggregates.

Polluted: something under the influence of ignorance or the latencies of ignorance.

Pratimoksha: the different sets of ethical precepts that assist in attaining liberation.

Provisional: teachings that speak about the variety of phenomena and/or cannot be taken literally.

Reliable cognizer: a nondeceptive mind that enables us to accomplish our purpose.

Result similar to the cause: the karmic result that corresponds to its cause. It is of two types: the result similar to the cause in terms of our experience and the result similar to the cause in terms of our habitual behavior.

Ripening result: the karmic result that is a rebirth; the five aggregates a being takes.

Scriptural authority: relying on a scripture that has met three criteria that deem it reliable.

Self: this has two meanings, depending on the context: a person, or inherent existence.

Self-grasping: grasping inherent existence.

Self-sufficient substantially existent person: a self that is the controller of the body and mind. Such a self does not exist.

Sense faculties: subtle material inside the eye, ear, nose, tongue, and body that, together with a sense object, produce a sense consciousness perceiving that object.

Sentient being: any being with a mind, except for a buddha.

Six perfections: the practices of generosity, ethical conduct, fortitude, joyous effort, meditative stability, and wisdom that are motivated by bodhichitta and sealed with the wisdom seeing them as both empty and dependent.

Slightly obscure phenomena: phenomena that can initially be known only by inference.

Solitary realizer: a person following the fundamental vehicle who seeks liberation, who emphasizes understanding the twelve links of dependent arising.

Superknowledge: special powers gained through having deep states of concentration.

Tathagata: a buddha.

True cessation: the cessation of a portion of afflictions or a portion of cognitive obscurations.

True existence: inherent existence.

True-grasping: grasping persons and phenomena to exist truly or inherently.

Truth body (Skt: *dharmakaya*): the buddha body that includes the nature truth body and the wisdom truth body.

Twelve links: a system of twelve factors that explains how we take rebirth in samsara and how we can be liberated from it.

Ultimate existence: existence that is findable by ultimate analysis; inherent existence.

Ultimate bodhichitta: synonymous with ultimate ground.

Ultimate ground: a bodhisattva's unpolluted wisdom that directly realizes emptiness and is supported by the special method of compassion, bodhichitta, and so forth.

Ultimate nature: the ultimate or deepest mode of existence of a person or phenomena.

Ultimate truth: the ultimate mode of existence of all persons and phenomena; emptiness.

Universal vehicle (Skt: Mahayana): the path to buddhahood.

Very obscure phenomena: phenomena that can be known only by relying on the testimony of a reliable person or a valid scripture.

View of a personal identity: grasping an inherently existent I or mine (according to the Prasangika system).

Vinaya: monastic discipline.

Wisdom truth body: the buddha body that is a buddha's omniscient mind.

Further Reading

Ārya Nāgārjuna. *A Strand of Dharma Jewels.* Seattle: Kalavinka Press, 2008.

Cozort, Daniel. *Unique Tenets of the Middle Way Consequence School.* Ithaca, NY: Snow Lion Publications, 1998.

Dunne, John, and Sara McClintock, trans. *The Precious Garland: An Epistle to a King.* Boston: Wisdom Publications, 1997.

Hopkins, Jeffrey. *Meditation on Emptiness.* Boston: Wisdom Publications, 1983.

Hopkins, Jeffrey, trans. *Nāgārjuna's Precious Garland: Buddhist Advice for Living and Liberation.* Ithaca, NY: Snow Lion Publications, 2007.

Ngawang Samten, ed. *Ratnāvalī of Ācārya Nāgārjuna with the Commentary of Ajitamitra.* Sarnath: Central Institute of Higher Tibetan Studies, 1990.

Padmakara Translation Group. *The Precious Necklace*, chapter 3. Nantes, France, 2008.

Tsong Khapa, rJe. *Ocean of Reasoning: A Great Commentary on Nāgārjuna's Mūlamadhyamakakārikā.* Translated by Geshe Ngawang Samten and Jay Garfield. New York: Oxford University Press, 2006.

van der Kuijp, Leonard. "Notes on the Transmission of Nāgārjuna's *Ratnāvalī* in Tibet." *The Tibet Journal* 10.2 (Summer 1985): 3–19.

Several of Nagarjuna's other texts have been translated into English and are available at http://www.tibetanclassics.org.

Index

A

Abhidharma, 9, 125–26, 330

Abhidharma Sutra, 334

Abhidharmakosha. See *Treasury of Knowledge* (Vasubandhu)

Abhidharmasamucchaya. See *Compendium of Knowledge* (Asanga)

Abhisamayalamkara. See *Ornament of Clear Realization* (Maitreya)

absolutism, 69, 77, 80–81, 86–87, 140, 154

accumulation, path of, 188, 270, 349, 354, 356, 357, 363, 367

adultery, 28, 34–35

adventitious stains, 73–74, 143

affirming negatives, 73

afflictions
  cessation of, 68, 74
  eliminating, 218–19
  I-grasping and, 52
  at nirvana, views on, 71–72
  nonvirtue as, 28
  rebirth and, 223
  of sentient beings, 103
  in twelve links, 63–64

afflictive obscurations, 14, 19–20, 57, 76, 109, 367

agent and action, 5, 92–93, 126, 127

aggregates, mental and physical, 102–3
  arising of, 51–52
  bondage to, 109
  conceit of apprehending as I, 333–34
  conventional existence of, 108
  duhkha of, 64–65
  emptiness of, 52
  fear of emptiness and, 46
  I as dependent on, 58–60
  investigating, 47–48, 54, 55–56, 134
  lack of inherent existence of, 82, 83
  at nirvana, views on, 71–72

  refuting inherent existence of, 91, 92, 298–99
  self and, 111
  self-grasping of, 61–62
  selflessness of, 114–19
  views on, 70

Akanishta, 221, 369

Akshayamati Sutra, 386

analogies and examples
  for aggregates, 304
  for birth in cyclic existence, 21–22
  bitter medicine, 310
  cow leading herd, 33, 94
  cows wandering in jungle, 33, 34
  eczema, 181
  fire and fuel, 118, 123, 132, 298
  fireflies and sunlight, 200
  grand fruit tree, 287
  handling snakes, 154
  illusory elephant, 145–47
  lamp's flame, 78, 79
  mirages, 81–83, 86
  monarch's child, 365–66
  pig chased by dog, 65
  plantain tree, 137–38
  rabbit's horn, 111
  reflection in mirror, 53, 56, 58–59
  sandalwood tree, 242
  sight obscured by floaters, 131
  snake as rope, 111–12
  snake grasped incorrectly, 47
  sprout and seed, 94–95, 97n17
  sugarcane bark, 186–87
  sunlight and darkness, 132
  turtle's mustache, 111, 141

analysis, 24
  of attachment to body, 182–83
  as changeable mental factor, 342–43
  mistaken understandings of, 83–84
  of phenomena, 82, 85, 120–23, 127–28

of pleasure and pain, 290–300
of scripture, 318, 348–49
sevenfold, 119
ultimate, 80, 112, 132, 134, 138–40
using tetralemma, 141–42
wisdom and, 241, 256, 346
See also reasoning
Ananda, 60
anger, 37, 39, 41–42, 218, 243–44, 330,
    359–60
animal realm, 38, 42, 222, 223, 270, 357
animal sacrifice, 24, 40, 158
anti-vows, 284
appearance
    conventional view of, 53
    false, 45, 50, 56–57, 146–47
    illusory, 147, 148
    pacifying dualistic, 132
appearing objects, 57, 82, 153
apprehended objects, 57, 61n8, 82, 89, 115,
    153
arhats, 188
    Ananda as, 60
    and bodhisattvas, distinguished, 365, 367
    and buddhas, distinguished, 14, 215,
        321–22
    happiness of, 182
    liberation of, 6, 69–70, 71
arrogance, 37, 152, 242, 245, 258, 273, 332
arya bodhisattvas, 15, 103, 211–12, 219–20,
    270, 305, 308n36, 343. *See also* grounds,
    bodhisattva
arya buddhas, 206–7
Aryadeva, 7. See also *Four Hundred Stanzas
    on the Middle Way* (Aryadeva)
Asanga, 38, 330, 364n39
asceticism, 27, 31–32, 33–34
aspirations, 235, 271, 321
Atisha, 272
attachment
    arising of, 155
    benefits of taming, 169
    to bodies of others, 173–78
    capacity for subduing, 257
    consequences of, 175
    due to pleasure and pain, 300–301
    to family, 237n31
    faults of, 337–39, 340, 341
    freedom from, 65, 182–83

karma of, 39
to one's own body, 179–83
reflection on, 41–42
on third ground, 359–60
types of, 218–19
awakening
    attaining, 214–15
    conditions for attaining, 143–44
    four immeasurable factors for, 216–17,
        221–22
    full, 3, 20, 25, 45, 46
    generosity and, 163
    principal causes of, 185, 186–89, 203, 250
    three types, 17
    understanding, 19–20
awareness
    erroneous, 49
    introspective, 330, 345
    nondual, 203
    probing, 112
    of suchness, 262
    of the ultimate, 128–30

B
Ball of Foam Sutta, 303–4
basis of designation, 111, 138, 302
    aggregates as, 46–47, 59, 61, 72, 91, 102,
        115–17, 134, 290, 334
    elements as, 120–21
    six constituents as, 112–14
Bhavaviveka, 110
blameworthy activities, 29–30, 32
bodhichitta, 3, 19, 66, 190
    actual engaging, 214
    aspiring, 214
    in fasting practices, 32
    generating, 36, 185, 186, 188, 254–55
    increasing merit with, 215
    limitations of, 23
    as mistaken not erroneous, 153
    need for, 224
    in six perfections, 344
    in two collections, 208–9, 211–12, 233
    two types, 186–87
    ultimate, 189, 351, 353
    uncontrived, 367
    in universal vehicle, 304, 311, 321
    wisdom and, 17, 25
bodhisattva vehicle/path, 6n2, 349, 381

discouragement on, 215–17, 312
emptiness on, 17, 303
entering, 189, 214, 304–5, 319, 325
scriptures as source of, 307, 315–16
two collections and, 312
wisdom and method on, 192
See also grounds, bodhisattva; perfections, six; universal vehicle
bodhisattvas
  arising of, 52
  aspiration of, 66
  buddhahood of, 190
  and buddhas, compared, 374, 375
  causes of, 186–87, 189, 203
  compassion of, 213, 220–21, 283
  faculties of, 187–88
  four "austerities" of, 244
  generosity of, 235, 270
  generosity toward, 162–63
  homages to, 9
  levels of understanding of, 110
  liberation of, 304
  offering to, 227
  pleasing, 159
  signs of, 191
  superknowledges of, 259, 359
  See also arya bodhisattvas
body
  cause of, 198
  constituents of, 113
  impurity of, 149, 150, 173–83
  investigating, 54, 55
  offering, 235, 237, 238, 270, 308, 310, 311, 357, 384, 385
  refuting inherent existence of, 92
  selflessness of, 116–17
Brahma kings, 355, 366, 367
Buddha, 207
  as basis of offering, 192
  compassion of, 34
  on final vehicle, 318–20
  generosity of, 236–37
  homage to, 13–14
  mind, four qualities of, 198
  parinirvana of, views on, 70
  past lives of, 220, 236–37
  scriptural authority of, 23
  silence of, 100, 102–3, 141, 145, 149
  teaching method of, 3, 4, 58, 138–39

buddha bodies
  four, 70, 106, 190–91, 206, 369, 376
  two, 209–10, 211, 263, 321
  See also individual buddha body
buddha lands. *See* pure lands
Buddha Maitreya, 362
buddha nature, 143, 190, 357
buddha qualities, 197–98, 374–75. *See also* ten powers of buddhas
buddhahood
  and arhatship, differences in, 14, 215, 321–22
  causes of, 144, 216
  cognitive obscuration and, 57, 352
  as highest good, 16, 17
  Prasangika view of, 319
  reasons for aspiring to, 215, 221
  on tenth ground, 190, 368–70
  three essential factors for, 7
  two collection and, 208–9, 212–13, 220, 252
  in universal vehicle, 3, 6n2, 320–21, 325
Buddhapalita, 7
buddhas
  appearance of, 144–45
  arising of, 52
  and arya buddhas, differences between, 206–7
  generosity toward, 162–63
  homages to, 9
  meditative equipoise of, 372
  pleasing, 159
  principal cause of, 187
  respecting images, 225–26
  and sentient beings, relationship of, 142–43, 214–15
  ten powers of, 371–74
  twelve deeds of, 369
  See also thirty-two signs of buddhas

C
capacity, three levels of, 323–24
causal dependence, 67, 78–79, 209
cause and effect
  dependent arising of, 78–79, 106, 124–25
  function of based on emptiness, 5
  of higher rebirth and highest good, 16–17
  lack of inherent existence of, 77–78
  in Prasangika system, 80–81

in reasoning, 116
of rebirth, 20
refuting inherent existence of, 92
as related factors, 127
causes
   concordant, 198, 358
   discordant, 141
   principle, 24, 185–87, 190–91, 207–8,
      224, 252, 259, 313, 317–18, 347
celestial realm
   bodhisattva's ripening result in, 359,
      360, 361, 362, 365, 368
   collection of merit and, 222–23, 251,
      253–54
   contemplating, 41–42
   as higher rebirth, 16, 17, 20–21, 155
   karma and, 169, 204
cessation, 72–73
   of all defilements, 261
   equipoise of, 363–64, 365
   true, 22, 74, 76–77, 190, 348, 369, 374,
      376
   two methods of, 100–101
Chandrakirti, 7, 111–14. See also *Supple-*
   ment to the Middle Way (Chandrakirti)
Charvaka School, 148, 242
Chekawa, Geshe, 382–83
Chittamatra system, 6
   capability in, 324
   erroneous understanding of emptiness
      in, 110
   inherent existence in, 48
   karma in, 345
   ripening results in, 358
   selflessness in, 315
   vehicles in, 319
clairvoyance, 259, 260
clear light, actual and example, 221
Clear Words (Chandrakirti), 7
cognitive obscurations, 3
   of arhats, 215
   Buddha's freedom from, 14
   eliminating, 188
   inherent existence as, 57
   in taking-and-giving practice, 383
   on tenth ground, 369
cognizer, reliable
   apprehending I, 115

of cause and effect, 80
compassion as, 153
of dependent arising and emptiness,
   209, 210
of emptiness, 109
during meditative equipoise, 48
and objects, mutual dependence of, 79
of ordinary beings, 82
in Prasangika method, 76
of three types of phenomena, 347–49
as valid mind, 51
Collected Topics, 120n23
Collection of Advice, 4
collection of merit
   of bodhisattvas, 189
   of buddhas, 185n26, 375
   characteristics of, 204–7
   contemplating, 198
   differences in, 105
   form bodies and, 191, 208
   immeasurability of, 386
   physical suffering and, 217–18
   specific deeds for, 225–28, 229–39
   See also two collections
Collection of Middle Way Reasoning,
   4–5, 7, 8
collection of wisdom, 189, 190–91, 207–8,
   218–19, 228–29, 239–46
companions, 155, 164, 165–67
compassion, 19
   of Buddha, 15
   buddhahood and, 7
   contemplating, 66
   of friends, 166
   general result of, 349
   generating, 185, 186
   immeasurable, 31
   limitations of, 23
   as mistaken not erroneous, 153
   mixed with attachment, 237
   of spiritual mentors, 390–91
   temporal effects of, 347
   in two collections, 220–21
   in universal vehicle, 311–12
   wisdom and, 262–63
   for wrongdoers, 282–85
Compendium of Knowledge (Asanga),
   330, 364n39
Compendium of Sutras, 4, 7

conceived object, 53, 61–62, 104, 109, 115, 149

concentrations, four of material realm, 21, 42, 259, 359, 362, 374

conceptions, four distorted, 150, 180

conceptuality
  contextual meanings of, 108n19
  faults of, 339–40
  mere designation of, 110–11
  mistaken views on, 58

conditions
  cooperative, 252, 259
  dominant, 295, 369

consciousness
  mental aggregates of, 113
  mistaken, 19, 50, 53, 56–57, 152–53, 177, 297, 300
  objects of, 140
  refuting inherent existence of, 99–100

constituents, six, 108, 112–14, 133–34, 137–38

convention, mere, 106–7, 109–11

conventional existence
  and inherent, differentiation, 78–79
  of persons, 48
  of phenomena, 100, 108–9
  Prasangika view of, 80
  realistic view of, 75
  of samsara, 101
  three criteria for, 111–12
  as ultimately false, 50–52

creators, 141, 292

crown protuberance, 195–96, 205

cyclic existence
  analogies for, 33, 34
  applying tetralemma to, 141–42, 148
  attachment in, 301
  beginningless and cessation of, 142–43
  bodhisattvas in, 220
  cause and effect of, 21–22
  cause of, 52, 59–60, 155
  contemplating defects of, 65, 66
  dependent existence of, 67, 101
  determination to be free from, 63, 64, 65, 224
  emptiness of, 66
  I-grasping and, 50
  Nagarjuna's understanding of, 6
  reflecting on, 257

refuting inherent existence of, 93–94

root of, 3, 61–62

D

Dashabhumika Sutra. See Sutra of the Ten Grounds

death, 169
  generosity and, 274–75
  Prasangika view of, 73
  without regret, 42
  remembering, 155, 167–68, 250–51, 257, 339
  twelve links and, 63

debate, 97n17, 98–99, 123, 242, 362

Dechö Sangpo, 8

dedication, 321, 344, 377–82, 385

definitive meaning, 58, 107–8, 139, 303, 320

dependent arising
  causal dependence, 67, 78–79, 209
  emptiness and, 106, 108, 109, 210–11, 301
  of persons and aggregates as subject, 209–10
  purpose of understanding, 68
  reasoning of, 78–80, 119, 123–26, 127–28, 209
  Svatantrika view of, 81

designation, mere, 106–7, 109–11, 114, 133, 134

desire, two kinds, 42–43

desire realm, 21n4, 39n5, 41, 349n37, 355, 369

Dharma, 184–85, 227
  acting in accordance with, 157
  benefits of studying, 17
  cherishing, 387–88
  as completely virtuous, 16–17
  conduct conducive to, 391–94
  difficulty of realizing, 149–50
  diligence in, 167–68
  four important practices, 388
  four perfect understandings of, 368
  four ways of attracting others to, 155, 160
  gift of, 239, 254, 270
  lacking respect for, 32–33
  listening to, 256–57
  misunderstanding, 151–54
  preserving, 255, 256

profundity of, 104, 145
reflecting on, 255, 256
respect for, 226–27, 239–40, 249
suitability for, 17, 102–3, 151
sustaining, 160
unique aspects of, 88–89
Dharma eye, 60, 262n32
Dharma-conch, 205–6
dharmakaya. *See* truth body
dispositions
Buddha's skillful method with, 15, 58, 103, 139
knowing others', 259, 260–61, 373
receptivity and, 215
of three vehicles, 6n2, 318–19, 324
divine eye and ear, 259–60
Drepung Monastery, 272
Dromtonpa, 272
duhkha
cessation of, 68
of change, 170
four aspects of, 180
freedom from, 4, 17, 52–53
Prasangika view of, 76
protection from, 15
purpose of understanding, 63
of sentient beings, 213
in taking-and-giving practice, 383
three types, 64–65
true, 112
in twelve links, 63, 64
See also suffering

E
"Eight Verses of Thought Training" (Langri Tangpa), 382, 383
eighteen unshared qualities, 14
eightfold discipline, 252–53
eighty marks, 198–99, 204, 205
elemental derivatives, 120, 122, 125–26
elements
five, 297–98
four, 119, 120–26, 128–29
emanation body, 14, 15, 70, 190, 206–7, 369
emptiness
appearing as object, 46
arhats realization of, 52–53
and awakening, importance of to, 3–4, 6

benefits of realizing, 68
buddhas' nondual perception of, 372
as cessation, 364
conceptual realization f, 146
conventional existence of, 69
conventional truth and, 210
correct understanding of, 48
differences in perception of, 130–31
direct perception of, 109–10
emptiness of, 51
fortitude regarding, 258
as foundationless, 104
as free from extremes, 140
importance of correct understanding of, 18–19, 105–6, 150
inferential, 188
misperception of, 47–48
misunderstanding, 154, 302–3
and nirvana, inseparability of, 72
primordial existence of, 131
qualities of, 151
realized by reliable cognizer, 77
refuting non-true existence of, 132
refuting true existence of, 100
refuting wrong views of, 138–39
result of familiarization with, 255, 261–62
in six perfections, 344
subtle, 303–4, 317
suitable vessels for understanding, 18–19, 23, 151–52
in three vehicles, 104, 317–18
topics preparing for understanding, 18
wrong views of, 87
See also suchness; wisdom realizing emptiness
Engaging in the Bodhisattvas' Deeds (Shantideva), 173
enjoyment body, 14, 15, 70, 152, 190, 206–7, 263, 369
environment, caring for, 183
environmental results, 34, 36–37, 38, 158–59, 170
equanimity, 21, 31, 42, 152, 379
essentialists, 4–6, 6n1, 84, 85–87
externalism, 80. *See also* absolutism
ethical conduct, 27, 32, 43, 378, 393–94
in accumulating merit, 189, 237
aspiration for others', 379

blameworthy activities, abandoning,
29–30, 32
concentration and, 68
faith and, 23
generosity and, 270
for householders, 325, 330
karma and, 105
for monastics, 329–30
nonharming as essential to, 32
perfection of, 345–46
result of, 255
on second ground, 358–59
of spiritual mentors, 390–91
textual source for, 9
training in, 156
evident phenomena, 19–20, 347
existence, contextual meanings of, 100n18
extremes, four, 141–42, 148–49
extremes, two, 45, 69, 76–77, 80–81,
83–84, 88–89, 104, 140, 154

F
faith
of bodhisattvas, 188
as cause of higher rebirth, 22
limitations of, 23
from pondering Buddha qualities,
197–98
praise and, 13
qualities of, 24
three kinds, 255
as virtuous, 40
faults, 243–44, 306–7, 329–43
fear, 218
causing in others, 183–84
eliminating, 380
of emptiness, 46–47, 48–50, 68, 69,
104–5, 107–8
of losing wealth, 274
fearlessness, 14, 31, 160, 254, 258
feelings, aggregate of, 290, 299, 301
fetters, three, 356
Finely Woven (Nagarjuna), 4, 5
five essences, 258
five heinous crimes, 282
five paths, 6n2, 374. See also individual
paths
five sublime eyes, 262
Flower Ornament Sutra (Avatamsaka

Sutra), 321
form body
attaining, 15, 203, 312, 313
collection of merit and, 207, 208–11,
224, 262
limitless causes of, 316
qualities of, 197
two types, 14, 190–91
fortitude, 43
in accumulating merit, 189, 237
in accumulating wisdom, 244
aspiration for others', 379
cultivating, 253
for Dharma, 257, 258, 262
householders practice of, 325
on third ground, 359, 360
three kinds, 32, 346
training in, 156
four arya truths, 15, 22, 89, 180, 315,
321–22, 348–49, 362, 365, 366
Four Hundred Stanzas on the Middle Way
(Aryadeva), 7, 110, 111, 112, 283
four opponent powers, 36
Friendly Letter, 8
fundamental vehicle, 3, 307
afflictive obscurations in, 367
emptiness in, 289
extinction in, 316–18
liberation in, 303–4, 314–15
limitations of, 305, 320–22, 365, 366
Prasangika view of, 303–4
See also hearer vehicle; solitary realizer
vehicle

G
gambling, 172
Ganden Monastery, 272
Geluk school, 6n1
gender identity, 172n25
generosity, 32, 43, 394
in accumulating merit, 189, 233, 235–39,
253
in accumulating wisdom, 244–45
aspiration for others', 379
benefits of, 269–71, 274–75
on first ground, 356, 357
four kinds, 31, 253–54
householders practice of, 325
results of, 258

in sustaining Dharma, 160
training in, 155, 156, 162–63, 165
governance, proper, 233–35, 277–82, 286,
    326
grasping
    innate and acquired, 50n6, 360
    types and meanings of, 49–50
    See also I-grasping; self-grasping; true-
        grasping
Great Treatise on the Stages of the Path
    (Tsongkhapa), 7, 28
Greater Sutta on the Lion's Roar, 372
grounds, bodhisattva, 351, 355, 371
    eighth, 366–67
    fifth, 361–62
    first, 356–57
    fourth, 360–61
    mental bodies on, 190
    ninth, 367–68
    second, 357–59
    sequential progress through, 353–55
    seventh, 365–66
    sixth, 362–65
    tenth, 368–70
    third, 359–60
Gyaltsap Je, 8, 209

H
happiness
    attachment and, 181–82
    bringing to others, 184
    cause of, 41
    as characteristic of higher rebirth, 20, 21
    as decrease of pain, 290–91, 299
    from Dharma practice, 251, 252
    generosity and, 162
    illusory nature of, 289
    reflection on, 41–42
    short- and long-term, 310–11
    true, 170
    worldly, 325
harm, abandoning, 29, 30
hearer vehicle, 6n2, 17, 203
    aspiration in, 187, 188
    eight grounds of, 356
    emptiness in, 289, 317
    liberation in, 52–53, 60, 66
    merit and wisdom in, 208
    Prasangika view on, 75, 87–88

six practices in, 344
two obscurations in, 352
Hedonists. See Charvaka School
hell realm, 21n4, 151–52, 183
    disparaging universal vehicle and,
        307–8
    freedom from, 42, 143, 357
    as ripening result, 36, 38
    three poisons and, 222, 223
higher rebirth, 42
    ascertaining, 19–20
    causes and effects of, 154–68, 223–24
    causes of, 24, 27–41, 38
    desire for, 42–43
    ethical conduct and, 23
    faith and, 22–23
    karma and, 20
    meaning of, 16, 17
    order of teaching, 18–19
    as ripening result, 41
    seven qualities of, 378
highest good, 16, 17, 108
    ascertaining, 19–20
    causes and effects of, 137–54
    higher rebirth and, 154–55
    order of teaching, 18, 19
    superior vessels for, 24
highest yoga tantra, 212
householders, 29–30, 325, 329–30
human birth, precious, 182, 213, 250–51,
    252, 255, 288, 384
human realm, 21n4, 42–43, 180, 222–23.
    See also higher rebirth
human rights, 236–37
hungry ghosts, 21n4, 38, 42, 222–23,
    232–33, 245, 270, 357, 384
hunting, 183, 184

I
ignorance, 39–40
    beginningless and cessation of, 142
    as causal motivation, 43
    dependent arising of, 126, 127
    falsity of, 52
    latencies of, 352
    of ordinary beings, 147
    reflection on, 41–42
    self-grasping, 3, 19, 21, 40, 45, 48, 63, 66,
        109, 145

true-grasping, 112, 132, 218–19, 352

I-grasping, 48–50, 51–57, 56–57, 59, 61–62, 67, 155–56

Illumination of the Middle Way Thought (Tsongkhapa), 7

immaterial realm, 21n4, 39n5, 41, 42, 349n37, 362. *See also* meditative absorptions, four immaterial

immeasurables, four, 31, 42, 359, 379, 380, 386

impermanence, 18
  of body, 92
  of person, 96–97, 101–2
  of phenomena, 120
  remembering, 155, 167–68, 339
  subtle, 149–50, 363
  three attributes of, 94–95

imprints, 105, 163, 187, 188, 215, 307, 383

inference, 19, 20, 58, 60, 347, 348

insight, 311–12, 314, 362, 363

intelligence, 37, 40, 365, 366, 378

intoxicants, 29, 35–36, 171–72, 181–82

Ishvara, 292

J

Jains, 88–89, 148–49

Jamyang Choje Tashi Palden, 272

Jataka Tales, 220, 236–37

jealousy, 37, 242, 331, 394

Jnanagarbha, 9

joy
  of bodhisattvas, 219, 220, 270, 356–57
  in Dharma practice, 156, 227, 325, 387–88
  immeasurable, 31, 379
  of others, 184, 230, 385
  in three realms, 21n4
  in understanding emptiness, 48

joyous effort, 313–14, 344, 346–47
  aspiration for others', 379
  on bodhisattva grounds, 354, 359, 360, 361
  in Dharma practice, 251
  steadfastness from, 269
  two collections and, 208

K

karma, 18
  afflictions and, 52

of body and mind, 290
cessation of, 68
complete, three criteria for, 28
in continuum of person, 101–2
control of sentient beings, 103
dependent arising of, 127
of erroneous paths, 27
faith in, 22, 23, 24, 25
four principal aspects of, 22–23
in giving-and-taking practice, 384–85
going beyond, 108
ignorance and, 112
importance of understanding, 252
misunderstanding, 152
momentariness of, 96–97
of nihilists and essentialists, 84, 105
pacifying, 76
polluted, 21–22, 109
propelling, 40, 41, 43
purifying, 168
rebirth and, 155, 169–70
results, self experiencing, 115, 116
ripening result of, 223
from self-grasping of person, 60
of sexual desire, 179
in tenet systems, 149
twelve links and, 62–65
understanding, 19, 20, 263
understanding others', 262
views on, 87–88
virtuous and nonvirtuous, 39

killing, 24, 28, 34–35, 36, 170, 183, 283

kindness
  of all beings, remembering, 173, 186, 245, 257, 279
  benefits of, 156
  as motivation, 160, 172, 184
  toward wrongdoers, 282–83
  See also loving-kindness

King of Concentration Sutra, 386

"King of Prayers," 321

kings, qualities of, 164–65, 287–88

Kshudravastuka, 329, 330

L

Langri Tangpa, 382, 383

lay practitioners. *See* householders

laziness, 212, 336, 340, 392

leadership

appointing and overseeing others,
277–80
attracting followers, 250
beneficial actions of, 184
of bodhisattvas, 355
caring for animals and environment,
183
companions for, 165–67
Dharma principles in, 157, 185, 249,
280–82
power of, 170
truth in, 161, 246
See also governance, proper
Levels of Yogic Practice (Asanga), 38
liberation
of arhats, 52–53
aspiration for, 65, 66
as emptiness, 74
emptiness of, 66
as freedom from extremes, 83–84
as highest good, 20
understanding, 19–20
views on, 60, 69–70
wisdom as necessary for, 45, 46
See also three doors of liberation
lineage, respecting, 252
Ling Rinpoche, Yongzin, 227
livelihood, 29, 37, 253, 335, 377–78
Lokayatas. *See* Charvaka School
love, 19, 325
as cooperative condition, 252
cultivating, 169
eighty marks and, 198–99
generosity of, 160, 253, 254, 344, 394
immeasurable, 31, 213, 379, 380, 386
as mistaken not erroneous, 153
non-attachment and, 257
as root of virtue, 222
for sentient beings, 186, 197, 283, 385
loving-kindness, 40, 344
Lui Gyaltsen, Lotsawa, 9
lust, 169, 179, 218, 289, 337. *See also* sexual
attraction
lying, 28, 35, 36, 161

M
Madhyamaka system, 6n1, 73–74, 109,
315, 358. *See also* Prasangika system;
Svatantrika Madhyamaka system

*Mahasihanada Sutta. See Greater Sutta
on the Lion's Roar*
Maheshvara, 355
Maitreya, 191, 206–7. *See also* Buddha
Maitreya
Manjushri, 9
material realm, 21n4, 39n5, 41, 349n37. *See
also* concentrations, four of material
realm
medicinal substances, 231
meditation
on compassion, 189
on dependent arising, 68
on emptiness, 19, 23, 113, 119, 255
examining I and aggregates, 53–56
on love, 254
Nagarjuna's understanding of, 6
taking-and-giving (*tonglen*), 235, 382–85
on twelve links, 64–66
using refutation in, 101
wisdom, role of in, 76
meditation, path of, 6, 60, 349
meditative absorptions, four immaterial,
42, 359, 362, 364–65, 374
meditative equipoise on emptiness
appearance in, 82
momentariness of, 301–2
order of, 59–60
perception of phenomena in, 128–32,
146, 147
of persons, 47–48, 60
Prasangika view of, 75
purity of, 352
purpose of, 108
three types of wisdom of, 351–52
meditative stability, perfection of, 313–14,
344, 346–47, 354, 362, 363, 379
mental bodies, 190, 305
mental factors, 43, 101, 301–2, 342–43,
345–46, 364n39
merit
accumulating, 66, 156
from composing treatises, 13–14
daily recitation for, 375–82, 385
dedicating, 156
for hearing Buddha's teachings, 7–8
for realizing emptiness, 45, 46, 47
transcending, 75, 107–8
See also collection of merit

method, 19, 58, 189, 190–91, 208, 209, 211,
    262–63
Milarepa, 163
mind
  apprehending body, 180
  cognizing emptiness, 301–2, 303
  empty nature of, 73–74
  I and, 54
  investigating, 101
  in lower realms, 38
  object emptiness in, 129
  refuting inherent existence of, 91–92
  taming, results of, 42
  tranquility in, 164
  true-grasping, 104
  valid, 51, 57
mind teachings (*lojong*), 246
mindfulness, 255, 256, 330
mindfulness, four establishments of, 174,
    180
miserliness, 274–75, 331
momentariness, 95, 97–98, 116
monasteries, establishing and maintain-
    ing, 225–26, 271–73, 275–77
monasticism, 30, 230–31, 286, 326, 329,
    335, 343
mother tantra, 173
motivation
  to be free from cyclic existence, 65
  to benefit others, 162, 184
  examining, 246–47
  in giving advice, 268–69
  role in results, 38
  for taming negativities, 330
  in teaching Dharma, 256–57
  vastness of, 271
  virtuous, 156–57, 159–60, 309–10

N
Nagarjuna, 4–7, 107. See also *Precious
    Garland of Advice to a King*
Naiyayikas, 88–89
name, mere, 106–7, 109–11, 133, 137–38,
    148
nature truth body, 190, 206–7, 369
negativity, 75, 107–8, 169, 218, 381, 392
nihilism, 69, 84
  abandoning, 154
  advice for avoiding, 151, 152

Buddha's refutation of, 140
fear and, 46
freedom from, 80–81
karma and, 105
as nonvirtuous action, 27, 29
in tenet systems, 48
as wrong view, 74
Nirgranthas. *See* Jains
nirvana, 6, 89, 100–101
  ascertaining through reasoning, 19–20
  Dharma as, 104
  emptiness and, 74, 303–5
  non-abiding, 66, 319
  refuting inherent existence of, 93–94
  with remainder, 69, 75–76, 319
  without remainder, 69–70, 72, 75–76,
    319
  views on, 71–73
no more learning, path of, 6, 60
non-affirming negative, 73, 133
non-anger, 39, 40, 42, 43, 222, 224
non-arising, 316–18, 372–73
non-attachment, 39, 40, 42, 43, 175,
    222–23, 224, 255, 257
non-confusion, 39, 40, 42, 43, 222, 224
nonexistence, contextual meanings of,
    100n18
nonviolence, 159, 193, 275–76
nonvirtuous actions, 27–29, 42, 158–59,
    217–18
Nyungné, 32

O
object of negation, 54, 56–57, 58–60,
    112–13, 364
obscurations, two, 199, 319, 352, 353. *See
    also* afflictive obscurations; cognitive
    obscurations
*Ocean of Reasoning: The Great Commen-
    tary on the "Middle Way"* (Tsong-
    khapa), 7, 62
offerings, 31, 221–22, 226–27, 228, 259, 277.
    See also under body
omniscience, 14, 102, 103, 190, 207, 348,
    369–70, 372–74
Ornament of Clear Realization (Mai-
    treya), 191, 206–7

P

pain, 289–90, 299–301. *See also* suffering
past lives, recalling, 261, 374
paths
  of action, 23, 36
  five, 6n2, 374 (*See also* individual paths)
  imperfect, 31–34, 38
  three principal aspects of, 250
  true, 76–77, 89
  uninterrupted, 369
  unmistaken, 33–34
  virtuous, 39
perfection of wisdom sutras, 3, 303
perfection vehicle, 3, 212, 220
perfections, six, 66, 168
  bodhisattva factors in, 344
  developing, 343–46
  division by two collections, 208
  as ornaments, 379
  relationship between, 346
  temporal effects from, 347–49
  on ten grounds, deepening of, 321, 360
  two aims in, 313–15
  and wisdom, relationship of, 363
  See also individual perfection
persons
  as conceptual designations, 111
  conventional existence of, 48
  emptiness of, 47–48
  investigating, 113
  momentariness of, 101–2
  provisional and definitive teachings on,
    137–39
  selflessness of, 108–9, 115–19, 134
  two ways of cognizing, 49
  views on, 70
pervasion, ascertaining, 54–55
Phenapindupama Sutta. See *Ball of Foam
  Sutta*
phenomena
  conditioned, 92, 132
  correct view of, 79, 85, 106–7
  dependent existence of, 137–38
  as illusory, 110, 137–38, 147
  innate and acquired, 62
  as made of parts, 98–99
  momentariness of, 97–98
  seeing clearly, 82
  self-grasping of, 59, 61

  selflessness of, 108–9
  in tenet systems, 70
  two types of reasoning on, 4
  types of, 19–20, 23, 120, 212, 347–49
  ultimate nature of, 51, 129
  unconditioned, 133
pleasure, 289, 290, 291, 292, 293–99,
    294–95, 300–301
post-meditation, 146–47. *See also* subse-
    quent attainment
Prasangika system
  buddhahood, view of, 319
  cause and effect in, 80–81
  cessation in, 363–64
  death, view of in, 73
  definitive teachings in, 320
  dependent arising in, 124–25
  disposition for, 324
  distinctions in view of, 74–75, 88–89
  ethical conduct in, 345–46
  final vehicle in, 319
  as free from extremes, 76–77, 80–81
  inherent existence in, 6
  mistaken consciousness in, 57, 153
  Nagarjuna's role in, 7
  negation in, 134
  nirvana in, 71–73, 75
  object of negation in, 59, 70, 112–13
  refutation of contradicting conven-
    tional knowledge, 78–79
  refutation of hearers view of karma, 87–88
  refutation of nihilism, 86–88
  self-grasping and true grasping in, 49
  stains, view of in, 74
  subtle emptiness in, 289, 303–4
pratimoksha, 345–46
Pratimoksha Sutra, 329
precepts, 36, 68, 283–84, 310, 345–46
Precious Garland of Advice to a King
  classification of, 3, 4
  composition of, 330
  emphasis of, 6, 7
  purpose of, 13, 16–17
  title, meaning of, 8
  tonglen in, 235, 383
  translator's homage, 9
  use of dialogue in, 87
preparation, path of, 110, 270, 349, 356,
    357, 363

pride, 332–34, 362, 365
prostrations, 217–18
provisional teachings, 4, 58, 139, 320
punishments and prisons, 281–85
pure lands, 15, 190, 221, 263, 353
purity, two kinds, 73–74

Q

questions, four ways to reply, 103
Questions of Rashtrapala Sutra, 3

R

Radreng Monastery, 272
Rashtrapala-paripriccha Sutra. See *Questions of Rashtrapala Sutra*
Ratnavali. See *Precious Garland of Advice to a King*
realms, six, 222–23. *See also* individual realm
realms, three, 21n4, 39n5, 349. *See also* desire realm; immaterial realm; material realm
reasoning
  of being not identical or separate, 114
  of bodhisattvas, 298, 367
  from cause and effect, 77–78
  as correct path, 34
  of dependent arising, 78–80, 119, 123–26, 127–28, 209
  in determining definitive teachings, 320
  diamond slivers, 67, 119
  emptiness and, 19, 151
  five principle types, 119, 120
  Nagarjuna's use of, 107
  obscure phenomena and, 348
  of one and many, 99–102
  potential for awakening in, 212
  in proving lack of inherent existence, 56
  scripture for, 85
  syllogisms in, 150, 209
  textual sources on, 4–7
  things as parts, 98–99
  three criteria for, 149–50
  in three vehicles, 322
  See also analysis
rebirth
  awakening and, 143
  of bodhisattvas, 305, 311, 354–55 (*See also* grounds, bodhisattva)

cessation of, 52
contemplating, 66
end of, 188
karma and, 61, 62–63, 169–70, 223
liberation from, 75, 76
in lower realms, 18, 33, 36, 38, 41, 42, 105, 155, 169–85
of nihilists and essentialists, 84
reflection on, 41–42
value of fortunate, 388
See also higher rebirth
refuge, 17, 36, 197–98, 215, 379
Refutation of Objections (Nagarjuna), 4, 5
remedial activities, 36
results
  environmental, 36–37, 38, 158–59, 170
  similar to the cause, 34–35, 41
  three types, 36–37, 38, 39
ripening results, 34, 38, 41, 223, 373
  on bodhisattva grounds, 357, 358, 360, 361, 362, 364, 366, 367, 368, 369
  of meditation on emptiness, 197, 206
  from motivation, 37
  nonvirtuous, 36, 41, 158–59, 169, 183
  of two collections, 207
rupakaya. *See* form body

S

Samadhiraja Sutra. See *King of Concentration Sutra*
Samdhinirmochana Sutra. See *Sutra Unraveling the Thought*
Samkhyas, 88–89, 148
Sammitiya, 138–39
samsara. *See* cyclic existence
Sautrantika system, 6n1
  Buddha's teachings in, 138–39
  capability in, 323–24
  cessation in, 364
  erroneous understanding of emptiness in, 110
  inherent existence in, 48
  karma in, 345
  liberation, views in, 69–70
  nirvana, views in, 73, 74–75
  selflessness in, 315
  vehicles in, 319
schoolmasters, providing for, 228–29
scriptures

authority of, 19, 20, 23, 99
definitive and provisional, distinctions
    between, 4
of fundamental vehicle, 307, 315
Nagarjuna's use of, 107
perfection of wisdom, 3, 303
reassurance of, 212
three analyses of, 348–49
seeing, path of, 6, 60, 62, 110, 349, 351, 356
self, two types, 115
self-grasping
    ascertaining, 57
    ignorance, 3, 19, 21, 40, 45, 48, 63, 66,
        109, 145
    at nirvana, two types, 72, 73
    order of generation of two types, 59–60,
        61–62
    of person, 128
    two types, 49, 71
selflessness, 155
    as lacking inherent existence, 138–40
    misunderstanding, 103
    order for realizing two types, 59–60,
        61–62
    of persons, 114–19
    of phenomena, 120–33
    profundity of, 46
    two types, 49
    of unconditioned space, 133
    views on, 52–53, 315, 364
senses
    binding doors of, 163, 345
    consciousnesses of, 293–95, 296
    dependent arising of, 126, 127, 293–97
    faculties of, 295, 297–98
    objects of, 293–95, 296–97, 297–98, 337,
        341
sentient beings
    appearance to ordinary, 82
    Buddha as friend to, 15
    conditions for benefiting, 262
    as countless, meaning of, 142, 213,
        216–17
    definition of, 57n7
    faculties of, 373, 377
    potential for liberation of, 143–44
Sera Monastery, 272
serenity, 311–12, 314, 341–43, 362, 363
seven branches of practice, 376–77

seven precious possessions, 358
Seventy Stanzas on Emptiness (Nagar-
    juna), 4, 5
sexual attraction, 172, 174, 175–78, 181–82,
    337
sexual orientation, 172n25
Shakyamuni Buddha, 145, 207, 220. See
    also Buddha
Shantideva, 7, 173
Sharawa, Geshe, 382–83
Shariputra, 316
signlessness, 3–4, 81
Sixty Stanzas of Reasoning (Nagarjuna),
    4, 6, 108, 112, 208–9
skillful means, 365, 366, 378–79
slightly obscure phenomena, 19–20, 23,
    347, 348, 349
solitary realizer vehicle, 6n2, 17, 203
    aspiration in, 187, 188
    emptiness in, 289
    liberation in, 52–53, 66
    merit and wisdom in, 208
    Prasangika view on, 75
    signs in, 191, 199
    six practices in, 344
    two obscurations in, 352
space, refuting inherent existence of,
    133
speech, 253
    in accumulating wisdom, 240–43,
        245–46
    of Buddha, 187, 206
    nonvirtuous, 28, 35, 163–64
    result from proper, 260
    truthful, 161–62
spiritual mentors
    and disciples, relationship of, 389–90,
        391
    need for, 34
    not meeting, 37
    offering to and honoring, 31, 227, 241
    qualifications of, 390–91
    relying on, 388–90
    respecting, 252, 256, 336, 394
stages of the path (lamrim), 14
stealing, 28, 34–35
stinginess, 37, 256
stream-enterers, 356
stupas (caitya), 191–92, 225–26, 227

subsequent attainment, 75, 110, 351–53, 356, 358, 359, 372

subtle body, 173

suchness, 81–82, 262, 302

suffering
  bearing, 244, 308–11
  bodhicitta and, 211–12
  generosity in eliminating, 162
  karma and, 169–70
  of lower realms, 38
  from nonvirtue, 159
  reflection on, 41–42
  two collections and, 217–18

superknowledges, 259–62, 359, 381

Supplement to the Middle Way (Chandra-kirti), 7, 49, 56, 119, 126, 162, 186, 187, 203, 346

Sutra of the Ten Grounds, 38, 356, 372

Sutra Pitaka, 9

Sutra Unraveling the Thought, 85

Svatantrika Madhyamaka system, 6, 46
  dependent arising in, 81, 124–25
  disposition for, 324
  erroneous views of emptiness in, 79–80, 108, 110
  final vehicle in, 319
  inherent existence in, 48
  karma in, 88
  liberation in, 60
  selflessness in, 315
  two extremes in, 86–87

T

tantra vehicle, 3, 212, 220–21

tathagata essence, 190

tathagata lineage, 356, 357, 366

teachers, harmful, 15

ten powers of buddhas, 14, 371–74

tenet systems
  Buddha bodies in, 70
  cause and effect in, 79–80
  erroneous views of emptiness in, 108
  four main, 6n1
  inherent existence in, 48
  nirvana in, 75
  objects of negation in, 54
  profane, 242
  purpose of, 323–24
  selflessness in, 52–53, 315, 364

two extremes in, 86–88

vehicles, views of in, 319

views of person in, 148–49

Tenzin Gyatso, Fourteenth Dalai Lama, 359

thirty-seven aids to awakening, 321–22, 361, 362, 366

thirty-two signs of buddhas, 206
  distinctions in, 199–200
  merit needed for, 205–6
  principal causes of, 185, 186–89
  purpose of, 189, 191, 197
  reflecting on, 198
  specific causes of each, 191–97

thousand-spoked wheel, 192

three doors of liberation, 3–4, 155

three higher trainings, 68, 182

Three Jewels, 13, 207, 376

Three Pitakas, 9

three poisons, 40, 42, 222–23, 224

Tibet, politics in, 249

times, three, 67, 68, 91–93, 127

tranquility, 155, 163–64, 165

transmigration, 63–67

Treasury of Knowledge (Vasubandhu), 28, 330, 364n39

Treatise on the Middle Way (Nagarjuna), 4–7, 91
  agent and action in, 92–93
  aggregates in, 118
  cause and effect reasoning in, 77
  dependent arising and emptiness in, 211
  diamond slivers reasoning in, 67
  inference in, 348
  on misperception of emptiness, 47

treatises, 7–8, 13

true-grasping, 48–50, 69–70
  on bodhisattva grounds, 360, 367
  of body, 177
  cessation of, 303
  extinguishing, 75–76
  of false appearance, 82
  as foundationless, 104–5
  ignorance, 112, 132, 218–19, 352
  wisdom eliminating, 188

trust, 161, 391

truth (honesty), 155, 160–62, 165, 245–46, 253, 268–69, 391

truth body

attaining, 203
attributes of, 14–15
buddhas as, 144–45
causes of, 106, 316, 318
collection of wisdom and, 207, 208–11
and form body, union of, 208
misunderstanding, 152
truths, two
bearing, 258
in cognizing emptiness, 301–2, 303
as complementary, 106
integrated understanding of, 211
interdependence of, 69, 85
practice of, 189
sense objects and, 140
on seventh ground, 366
two collections and, 209–10
Tsakho Ngawang Drakpa, 272
Tsongkhapa, Je, 7, 28, 62, 65, 272
Tushita, 354, 361–62
twelve links of dependent origination,
62–63
attachment in, 301
meditation on, 64–66
reversal of, 68
samsara and, 101
seventh ground understanding of, 366
sixth ground understanding of, 362
three phases of, 63–64
See also dependent arising
two aims, 13–14, 15, 16, 313–15, 380
two collections
aspirations for, 379
buddha bodies and, 312
common benefits of, 249–51
entities of, 222–24
feeling discouraged about, 211–12,
216–20, 221–22
immeasurable results of, 207–11
in tenet systems, 315–16
in universal vehicle, 306
See also collection of merit; collection
of wisdom

U
universal monarchs, 191, 192, 199–200
universal vehicle
Buddha's awakening, view of in, 70
as Buddha's word, 307, 312–18, 322–23

collection of merit in, 203, 204
compassion and wisdom, role of in,
311–12
disparaging, 307–10, 312
equanimity toward, 318–20
and fundamental vehicle, differences
between, 304–5, 307
misconceptions about, 306–7
special faith in, 325
two divisions of, 3
See also bodhisattva vehicle/path

V
Vaibhashika system, 6n1
capability in, 323–24
cessation in, 364
erroneous understanding of emptiness
in, 110
inherent existence in, 48
karma in, 345
liberation, views on, 69–70
nirvana, views on, 71–73, 74–75
selflessness in, 315
vehicles in, 319
See also Sammitiya
Vaisheshikas, 88–89, 95–96
Vaishnavas, 95, 96–97
vajra vehicle. See tantra vehicle
vajra-like concentration, 369
Vasubandhu, 28, 330, 364n39
Vatsiputriyas, 149
vehicles, three, 6n2, 17, 104, 318–19,
323–24
very obscure phenomena, 19–20, 23, 212,
347, 348–49
views
correct and incorrect, distinctions
between, 74–75
of personal identity, 33, 49–50, 59–60,
155, 156, 361
worldly, 74, 75, 84
wrong, 33–34, 35–36, 105–6 (See also
extremes, two)
See also tenet systems
Vikramashila Monastery, 272
Vinaya, 9, 24, 173, 252, 329–30
virtue
aspiration for, 379, 380
benefits of, 156–57, 171

as cause of awakening, 144
creating, 42, 155
desire as, 43
faith and, 24
four practices of, 244
happiness and, 184
immeasurable, 216
polluted, 223
three roots of, 222–23, 224
wisdom and, 25
See also collection of merit
virtuous activities, 214–15, 251–63, 273, 367, 394

W
wealth, 229–33, 253–54, 258, 269–71, 274–75, 347–49
wheel of Dharma, 151, 187, 189, 192, 376–77
wheel-turning monarchs, 289, 290, 354–55, 357, 358
wisdom
    accumulating, 156, 188
    of aryas, 82
    as cause of highest good, 22
    cultivating, 224
    in cutting root of cyclic existence, 66
    free from two extremes, 185, 186, 187–88
    householders accumulation of, 325
    importance of, 388
    nondual, 188

perceiving ultimate reality, 50–51
    qualities of, 25
    as root of virtue, 222
    of spiritual mentors, 390–91
    with supreme of all aspects, 262–63
    training in, 155, 164–65
    in universal vehicle, 311–12
    See also collection of wisdom
wisdom, perfection of, 344, 346, 347, 362–63, 364–65, 379
wisdom realizing emptiness
    in Collection of Middle Way Reasoning texts, 4, 6
    in cutting samsara, 101
    development of, 45
    faith and, 22–24
    higher rebirths and, 38
    ignorance and, 68
    pacifying extreme views, 76
    purpose of, 52
    results from, 261–62
    three vehicles and, 17
wisdom truth body, 190, 369
wish-fulfilling jewel, 384
wishlessness, 3–4
women, views on, 157, 172–73, 236–37

Y
Yogacharabhumi. See *Levels of Yogic Practice* (Asanga)

About the Author

Born in 1930, Khensur Jampa Teg-chok became a monk at the age of eight. He studied major Buddhist treatises at Sera Monastic University in Tibet for fourteen years before fleeing his homeland in 1959. The former abbot of the Jé College of Sera Monastic University in India, he was also a beloved teacher at several FPMT centers including Istituto Lama Tzong Khapa in Italy, Land of Medicine Buddha in California, and Nalanda Monastery in France. He is the author of *Transforming Adversity into Joy and Courage: An Explanation of the Thirty-Seven Practices of the Bodhisattvas*, *Insight into Emptiness*, and *Commentary on Seven-Point Mind Training*. Khensur Tegchok passed away in October of 2014.

About the Editor

Bhikshuni Thubten Chodron is an American Buddhist nun in the Tibetan tradition. Ordained in 1977, she is a student of H. H. the Dalai Lama and other Tibetan masters. She teaches Buddhism internationally, is the author of many Dharma books, including *Buddhism for Beginners*, and is the founder and abbess of Sravasti Abbey, a Buddhist monastic community in Washington State, USA, where she lives. See thubtenchodron.org and sravasti.org.

ALSO BY KHENSUR JAMPA TEGCHOK RINPOCHE

Insight into Emptiness

The Kindness of Others: A Commentary on the Seven-Point Mind Training

Transforming Adversity into Joy and Courage

ALSO BY THUBTEN CHODRON

An Open-Hearted Life: Transformative Methods for Compassionate Living from a Clinical Psychologist and a Buddhist Nun

Buddhism for Beginners

Buddhism: One Teacher, Many Traditions (with H. H. the Dalai Lama)

Cultivating a Compassionate Heart: The Yoga Method of Chenrezig

Don't Believe Everything You Think

Good Karma: How to Create the Causes of Happiness and Avoid the Causes of Suffering

Guided Meditations on the Stages of the Path

How to Free Your Mind: Tara the Liberator

Living with an Open Heart: How to Cultivate Compassion in Daily Life (with Russell Kolts)

Open Heart, Clear Mind

Taming the Mind

Working with Anger

www.thubtenchodron.org

What to Read Next from Wisdom Publications

Insight into Emptiness
Khensur Jampa Tegchok and Thubten Chodron

"One of the best introductions to the philosophy of emptiness I have ever read."—José Ignacio Cabezón, professor of Religious Studies, University of California, Santa Barbara

Buddhism
One Teacher, Many Traditions
His Holiness the Dalai Lama and Thubten Chodron
Foreword by Bhante Gunaratana

"This book will reward those who study it carefully with a deep and wide understanding of the way these traditions have mapped their respective visions of the path to enlightenment."—Bhikkhu Bodhi, translator of *In the Buddha's Words*

Nāgārjuna's Middle Way
Mūlamadhyamakakārikā
Mark Siderits and Shōryū Katsura

"Authoritative, vivid, and illuminating."—Graham Priest, author of *Logic: A Very Short Introduction*

The Middle Way
Faith Grounded in Reason
His Holiness the Dalai Lama and Thupten Jinpa

"How fortunate we are to have access to these brilliant teachings given by the Dalai Lama. A truly inspiring book."—*Mandala*

About Wisdom Publications

Wisdom Publications is the leading publisher of classic and contemporary Buddhist books and practical works on mindfulness. To learn more about us or to explore our other books, please visit our website at wisdompubs.org or contact us at the address below.

Wisdom Publications
199 Elm Street
Somerville, MA 02144 USA

We are a 501(c)(3) organization, and donations in support of our mission are tax deductible.

Wisdom Publications is affiliated with the Foundation for the Preservation of the Mahayana Tradition (FPMT).